ELEMENTS OF FORECASTING

SECOND EDITION

FRANCIS X. DIEBOLD
UNIVERSITY OF PENNSYLVANIA

SOUTH-WESTERN
™
THOMSON LEARNING

Australia · Canada · Mexico · Singapore · Spain · United Kingdom · United States

Elements of Forecasting, Second Edition by Francis X. Diebold

Publisher: Jack Calhoun
Senior Developmental Editor: Dennis Hanseman
Senior Marketing Manager: Lisa Lysne
Production Editor: Tamborah E. Moore
Manufacturing Coordinator: Charlene Taylor

Cover Design: Jennifer Lambert
Internal Design: Barbara Libby
Production House: Professional Book Center
Compositor: Professional Book Center
Printer: RR Donnelley, Crawfordsville

Printed in the United States of America
2 3 4 5 03 02 01

For more information contact South-Western, 5101 Madison Road, Cincinnati, Ohio, 45227 or find us on the Internet at http://www.swcollege.com

For permission to use material from this text or product, contact us by
- **telephone: 1-800-730-2214**
- **fax: 1-800-730-2215**
- **web: http://www.thomsonrights.com**

Library of Congress Cataloging-in-Publication Data

Diebold, Francis X.,
    Elements of forecasting / Francis X. Diebold.—2nd ed.
        p. cm.
    Includes bibliographical references and index.
    ISBN 0-324-02393-6
        1. Forecasting—Statistical methods. 2. Forecasting—Problems, exercises, etc. I. Title

H61.4.D54 2000
003'.2—dc21

00-056305

This book is printed on acid-free paper.

To Lawrence Klein, Marc Nerlove, and Peter Pauly,
who taught me forecasting

PREFACE

Most good texts arise from the desire to leave one's stamp on a discipline by training future generations of students, coupled with the recognition that existing texts are inadequate in various respects. My motivation is no different, and there is a real need for a concise and modern introductory forecasting text.

A number of features distinguish this book. First, although it uses only elementary mathematics, it tries to convey a feel for the important advances made since the work of Box and Jenkins some thirty years ago. In addition to standard models of trend, seasonality, and cycles, it touches upon topics such as:

- data mining and in-sample overfitting
- statistical graphics and exploratory data analysis
- model selection criteria
- recursive techniques for diagnosing structural change
- ARMA models as approximations to the Wold representation
- nonlinear models, including neural networks and regime-switching
- volatility models
- unit roots and stochastic trends
- smoothing techniques in their relation to stochastic-trend unobserved-components models

- vector autoregressions
- cointegration and error correction
- predictive causality
- forecast evaluation and combination
- simulation and related methods such as bootstrapping

Much such material appears in the "Problems and Complements" following each chapter, which form an integral part of the book. The Problems and Complements are organized so that instructors and students can pick and choose, according to their backgrounds and interests.

Second, the book does not attempt to be exhaustive in coverage. In fact, the coverage is intentionally selective, focusing on the core techniques with the widest applicability. The book is designed so that it can be covered realistically in a one-semester course. Core material appears in the main text, and additional material that expands on the depth and breadth of coverage is provided in the Problems and Complements, as well as the Bibliographical and Computational Notes, at the end of each chapter.

Third, the book is applications-oriented. It illustrates all methods with detailed real-world applications, many of them international in flavor, designed to mimic typical forecasting situations. In many chapters, the application is the centerpiece of the presentation. In various places, it uses applications not simply to illustrate the methods but also to drive home an important lesson, the limitations of forecasting, by presenting truly realistic examples in which not everything works perfectly!

Fourth, the book is in touch with modern modeling and forecasting software. It uses Eviews—a good modern computing environment for forecasting—throughout. I am not a software salesman, however, so the discussion is not wed to any particular software. Students and instructors can use whatever computing environment they like best. Many of the data and Eviews programs used in the book are provided on the Web site.

The book should be useful to students in a variety of fields, including business, finance, economics, public policy, statistics, and even engineering. The book will be directly accessible at the undergraduate and master's levels; the only prerequisite is an introductory statistics course that includes linear regression. To help refresh students' memories, chapter 1 includes an appendix that reviews linear regression from a forecasting perspective. The book should also be of interest to those with more advanced preparation because of its hard-to-find direct focus on forecasting (as opposed to general statistics, econometrics, time series analysis, or anything else). I have used the material for this book successfully for several years as the primary text in my undergraduate forecasting course, as a background text for various other undergraduate and graduate courses, and as the primary text for master's-level forecasting seminars given to professionals in industry, finance and government.

This second edition maintains the emphasis of the first edition on providing an intuitive building-block approach to the development of modern and practical methods for producing, evaluating, and combining forecasts. Within that framework, several improvements have been implemented, including:

- Reworked and rearranged material to maximize clarity and pedagogical effectiveness
- Greater attention to possible pitfalls associated with numerical optimization and strategies for avoiding them
- Attention to differences across software packages in choice, implementation, and accuracy of numerical algorithms
- New Problems and Complements that emphasize practical hands-on implementation of the methods developed in the text

Throughout, my intent has been to apply polish where needed, while avoiding the temptation to fix parts that "ain't broke." I hope I have succeeded.

Many people have contributed to the development of this book—some explicitly, some without knowing it. One way or another, all of the following deserve thanks:

Scott Armstrong	University of Pennsylvania
Alan Auerbach	University of California, Berkeley
David Bivin	Indiana University – Purdue University at Indianapolis
Chris Chatfield	University of Bath
Jen-Chi Cheng	Wichita State University
Siddhartha Chib	Washington University
Peter Christoffersen	McGill University
Joerg Clostermann	University of Applied Sciences, Fachhochschule Ingolstadt
Dean Croushore	Federal Reserve Bank of Philadelphia
Michael Donihue	Colby College
Robert F. Engle	University of California, San Diego
Robert Fildes	University of Lancaster
Antonio Garcia-Ferrer	Universidad Autonoma de Madrid
Patrick A. Gaughan	Farleigh Dickinson University
Clive Granger	University of California, San Diego
Craig Hakkio	Federal Reserve Bank of Kansas City
Eric C. Howe	University of Saskatchewan
Der-An Hsu	University of Wisconsin, Milwaukee
Lawrence R. Klein	University of Pennsylvania
Tae-Hwy Lee	University of California, Riverside

David Lilien	University of California, Irvine
Jose Lopez	Federal Reserve Bank of New York
Ron Michener	University of Virginia
Ray Nelson	Brigham Young University
Llad Phillips	University of California, Santa Barbara
Russell Robins	Tulane University
Philip Rothman	East Carolina University
Glenn D. Rudebusch	Federal Reserve Bank of San Francisco
Robert Rycroft	Mary Washington College
John H. Shannon	Royal Melbourne Institute of Technology
Robert Stine	University of Pennsylvania
James H. Stock	Harvard University
Mark Strazicich	University of Central Florida
Norman Swanson	Texas A&M University
Hiroki Tsurumi	Rutgers University
William Veloce	Brock University
Mark W. Watson	Princeton University
Barry Weller	The Pennsylvania State University, Erie
Kenneth D. West	University of Wisconsin
Tao Zha	Federal Reserve Bank of Atlanta

I am especially grateful to my developmental editor, Dennis Hanseman, and the rest of the team at South-Western, especially Jack Calhoun, without whose encouragement this book would not have been written. I am similarly grateful to Morris Davis, Atsushi Inoue, John Schindler, and Anthony Tay, four energetic and enthusiastic graduate students who read and improved the entire manuscript.

Finally, I apologize and accept full responsibility any errors and short-comings that may remain—minor and major—in spite of ongoing efforts to eliminate them.

ABOUT THE AUTHOR

FRANCIS X. DIEBOLD is Lawrence R. Klein Professor of Economics and Statistics and Director of the Institute for Economic Research at the University of Pennsylvania, and a Research Associate at the National Bureau of Economic Research in Cambridge, Massachusetts. Diebold works in forecasting, econometrics, economics and finance. He has published widely and has served on the boards of leading journals, including *Econometrica* and *Review of Economics and Statistics*. He is a fellow of the Econometric Society and the winner of several awards for outstanding teaching. Diebold has held visiting appointments at Princeton University, the Graduate School of Business at the University of Chicago, and the Stern School of Business at New York University. He received his B.S. from the Wharton School in 1981 and his Ph.D. in 1986, and from 1986–1989 he served as an economist under Paul Volker and Alan Greenspan at the Board of Governors of the Federal Reserve System in Washington, D.C. You can reach him on the World Wide Web at http://www.ssc.upenn.edu/ ~ diebold.

CONTENTS

3   **Statistical Graphics for Forecasting   49**

4   **Modeling and Forecasting Trend   72**

5   **Modeling and Forecasting Seasonality   103**

6   Characterizing Cycles   116

7   Modeling Cycles: MA, AR, and ARMA Models   143

8   Forecasting Cycles   183

12   Unit Roots, Stochastic Trends, ARIMA Forecasting Models, and Smoothing   323

INTRODUCTION TO FORECASTING: APPLICATIONS, METHODS, BOOKS, JOURNALS, AND SOFTWARE

Forecasting is important—forecasts are constantly made in business, finance, economics, government, and many other fields, and much depends upon them. As with anything else, there are good and bad ways to forecast. This book is about the good ways—modern, quantitative, statistical/econometric methods of producing and evaluating forecasts.

1. FORECASTING IN ACTION

Forecasts are made to guide decisions in a variety of fields. To develop a feel for the tremendous diversity of forecasting applications, let us sketch some of the areas where forecasts are used and the corresponding diversity of decisions aided by forecasts.

1. Operations planning and control. Firms routinely forecast sales to help guide decisions in inventory management, sales force management, and production planning, as well as strategic planning regarding product lines, new market entry, and so on. Firms use forecasts to decide what to produce (what product, or what mix of products, should be produced), when to produce (whether we should build up inventories now in antici-

1

pation of high future demand, or how many shifts should be run), and where to produce (whether we should have one plant or many, and if many, where we should locate them). Firms also use forecasts of future prices and availability of inputs to guide production decisions.

2. Marketing. Forecasting plays a key role in many marketing decisions. Pricing decisions, distribution path decisions, and advertising expenditure decisions all rely heavily on forecasts of responses of sales to different marketing schemes.

3. Economics. Governments, policy organizations, and private forecasting firms around the world routinely forecast the major economic variables, such as gross domestic product (GDP), unemployment, consumption, investment, the price level, and interest rates. Governments use such forecasts to guide monetary and fiscal policy, and private firms use them for strategic planning, because economy-wide economic fluctuations typically have industry-level and firm-level effects. In addition to forecasting "standard" variables such as GDP, economists sometimes make more exotic forecasts, such as the stage of the business cycle that we'll be in six months from now (expansion or contraction), the state of future stock market activity (bull or bear), or the state of future foreign exchange market activity (appreciation or depreciation). Again, such forecasts are of obvious use to governments as well as firms—if they are accurate!

4. Financial speculation. Speculators in asset markets have an interest in forecasting asset returns (stock returns, interest rates, exchange rates, and commodity prices), and such forecasts are made routinely. There is endless debate about the success of forecasts of asset returns. On the one hand, asset returns should be very difficult to forecast; if they were easy to forecast, you could make a fortune easily, and any such "get rich quick" opportunities should already have been exploited. On the other hand, those who exploited them along the way may well have gotten rich! Thus, we expect that simple, widely available methods for forecasting should have little success in financial markets, but there may well be profits to be made from using new and sophisticated techniques to uncover and exploit previously unnoticed patterns in financial data (at least for a short time, until other market participants catch on, or until your own trading moves the market).

5. Financial risk management. The forecasting of asset return volatility is related to the forecasting of asset returns. In the last ten years, practical methods for volatility forecasting have been developed and widely applied. Volatility forecasts are crucial for evaluating and insuring risks associated with asset portfolios. Volatility forecasts are also crucial for firms and investors who need to price assets such as options and other derivatives.

6. Capacity planning. Decisions on whether to expand or contract capacity are crucial for any business. Firms want enough capacity to meet demand, but don't want a large amount of excess capacity on average. Capacity planning decisions rely heavily on a variety of forecasts related both to product demand and supply. Typical questions include: What are the trends in market size and market share? Are there cyclical or seasonal effects? How quickly and with what pattern will a newly built plant or a newly installed technology depreciate?

7. Business and government budgeting. Businesses and governments of all sorts must constantly plan and justify their expenditures. A major component of the budgeting process is the revenue forecast. Large parts of firms' revenues typically come from sales, and large parts of governments' revenues typically come from tax receipts; both of these revenues exhibit cyclical and long-term variation.

8. Demography. Demographers routinely forecast the populations of countries and regions all over the world, often in disaggregated form, such as by age, sex, and race. Population forecasts are crucial for planning government expenditure on health care, infrastructure, social insurance, antipoverty programs, and so forth. Many private-sector decisions, such as strategic product line decisions by businesses, are guided by demographic forecasts of particular targeted population subgroups. Population, in turn, depends on births, deaths, immigration, and emigration, which are also forecast routinely.

9. Crisis management. A variety of events corresponding to crises of various sorts are frequently forecast. Such forecasts are routinely issued as probabilities. For example, in both consumer and commercial lending, banks generate default probability forecasts and refuse loans if the probability is deemed too high. Similarly, various international investors are concerned with probabilities of default, currency devaluations, military coups, and so forth, and use forecasts of such events to inform their portfolio allocation decisions.

The variety of forecasting tasks that we have just sketched was selected to help you begin to get a feel for the depth and breadth of the field. Surely you can think of many more situations in which forecasts are made and used to guide decisions.

With so many different forecasting applications, you might think that a huge variety of forecasting techniques exists, and that you have to master all of them. Fortunately, that is not the case. Instead, a relatively small number of tools form the common core of almost all forecasting methods. Needless to say, the details differ if one is forecasting the Netscape stock price one day and the population of Scotland the next, but the principles underlying the forecasts are identical. Thus we focus on the underlying core principles, which drive all applications.

2. FORECASTING METHODS: AN OVERVIEW OF THE BOOK

Now let us sketch what follows in the chapters ahead, to give you a broad overview of the forecasting landscape. If some of the terms and concepts seem unfamiliar, rest assured that we will study them in depth in later chapters.

Forecasting is inextricably linked to building **statistical models.** Before we can forecast a variable of interest, we must build a model for it and estimate the model's parameters using observed historical data. Typically, the estimated model summarizes dynamic patterns in the data; that is, the estimated model provides a statistical characterization of the links between the present and the past. More formally, an estimated forecasting model provides a characterization of what we expect in the *present,* conditional upon the *past,* from which we infer what to expect in the *future,* conditional upon the present and past. Quite simply, we use the estimated forecasting model to extrapolate the observed historical data.

In this book we focus on core modeling and forecasting methods that are very widely applicable; variations on them can be applied in almost any forecasting situation. The book is divided into two parts. The first provides background and introduces various fundamental issues relevant to any forecasting exercise. The second treats the construction, use, and evaluation of modern **forecasting models.** We give special attention to basic methods of forecasting trend, seasonality, and cycles, in both **univariate** and **multivariate** contexts.[1] We also discuss special topics in forecasting with regression models, as well as forecast evaluation and combination.

Along the way, we introduce a number of modern developments, sometimes in the text and sometimes in the Problems and Complements that follow each chapter. These include model selection criteria, recursive estimation and analysis, ARMA and ARIMA models, unit roots and cointegration, volatility models, simulation, vector autoregressions, and nonlinear forecasting models. Every chapter contains a detailed application; examples include forecasting retail sales, housing starts, employment, liquor sales, exchange rates, and shipping volume.

In this chapter, we provide a broad overview of the forecasting landscape, and we include an appendix that reviews linear regression from a forecasting perspective.

---

1. See the Problems and Complements at the end of this chapter for a discussion of the meanings of "univariate" and "multivariate."

In chapter 2, we highlight six considerations relevant to all forecasting tasks: the decision-making environment, the nature of the object to be forecast, the way the forecast will be stated, the forecast horizon, the information on which the forecast will be based, and the choice of forecasting method.

In chapter 3, we introduce certain aspects of statistical graphics relevant to forecasting. Graphing the data is a useful first step in any forecasting project, as it can often reveal features of the data relevant for modeling and forecasting. We discuss a variety of graphical techniques of use in modeling and forecasting, and we conclude with a discussion of the elements of graphical style— what makes good graphics good and bad graphics bad.

Subsequent to chapter 3, the chapters proceed differently—each treats a specific set of tools applicable in a specific and important forecasting situation. We exploit the fact that a useful approach to forecasting consists of separate modeling of the unobserved components underlying an observed **time series,** such as trend components, seasonal components, and cyclical components.[2] Trend is that part of a series' movement that corresponds to long-term, slow evolution. Seasonality is that part of a series' movement that repeats each year. Cycle is a catch-all phrase for various forms of dynamic behavior that link the present to the past and hence the future to the present.

In chapter 4 we discuss trend—what it is, where it comes from, why it is important, how to model it, and how to forecast it. In Chapter 5 we do the same for seasonality. In chapters 6 and 7 we discuss cycles; we introduce the important idea of a covariance stationary time series, as well as the notions of autoregressive (AR), moving average (MA), and mixed (ARMA) processes. The forecasting of cycles is tremendously important and somewhat involved, so we devote the entirety of chapter 8 to it. In chapter 9, we assemble all that we learned in earlier chapters; we model and forecast a series with trend, seasonality, and cycles present simultaneously.

In chapter 10 we consider regression models in detail. In particular, we make the distinction between "conditional" forecasting models—useful for answering "what if" questions (e.g., What will happen to my sales if I lower my price by 10 percent?) but not directly useful for forecasting—and "unconditional" forecasting models, which are directly useful for forecasting. We also treat issues concerning the proper dynamic specification of such models, including distributed lags, lagged dependent variables, and serially correlated errors, and we study and apply vector autoregressive models in detail.

In chapter 11, in contrast to our earlier development of methods for constructing and using various forecasting models, we consider the *evaluation*

---

2. We define the idea of a time series more precisely in subsequent chapters, but for now just think of a time series as a variable of interest that has been recorded over time. For example, the annual rainfall in Brazil from 1950 to 1996, a string of 47 numbers—is a time series. On the basis of that historical data, you might want to forecast Brazilian rainfall for the years 1997 through 2000.

of forecasting performance once a track record of forecasts and realizations has been established. That is, we show how to assess the accuracy of forecasts and how to determine whether a forecast can be improved. We also show how to combine a set of forecasts to produce a potentially superior composite forecast.

Chapters 1 through 11 form a coherent whole, and some instructors may want to stop there, depending on time constraints and course emphasis. For those so inclined to proceed to more advanced material, in chapter 12 we introduce the idea of "stochastic trend," meaning that the trend can be affected by random disturbances.[3] We show how to forecast in models with stochastic trends and highlight the important differences between forecasts from **stochastic**-trend and **deterministic**-trend models. Finally, we discuss "smoothing" methods for producing forecasts, which turn out to be optimal for forecasting series with a certain type of stochastic trend.

3. USEFUL BOOKS, JOURNALS, SOFTWARE, AND ONLINE INFORMATION

As you begin your study of forecasting, it is important that you begin to develop an awareness of a variety of useful and well-known forecasting textbooks, professional forecasting journals where original forecasting research is published, forecasting software, and online information sources.

Books

A number of good books exist that complement this one; some are broader, some are more advanced, and some are more specialized. Here we discuss a few that are broader or more advanced to give you a feel for the relevant literature. More specialized books are discussed in subsequent chapters when appropriate.

Wonnacott and Wonnacott (1990) is a well-written and popular statistics book, which you may wish to consult to refresh your memory on statistical distributions, estimation, and hypothesis testing. It also contains a thorough and very accessible discussion of linear regression, which we use extensively throughout this book.[4]

Pindyck and Rubinfeld (1997) is a well-written general statistics and econometrics text, and a very useful refresher for basic statistical topics, as

---

3. The word "stochastic" simply means "involving randomness." A process is called "deterministic" if it is not stochastic.

4. You may also want to explore this chapter's appendix, which provides a concise review of the linear regression model.

well as a good introduction to more advanced econometric models. Similarly useful books include Maddala (in press) and Kennedy (1998).

As a student of forecasting, you'll want to familiarize yourself with the broader time series analysis literature.[5] Chatfield (1996) is a good introductory book, and is useful as a background reference. More advanced books, which you may want to consult later, include Granger and Newbold (1986) and Harvey (1993). Granger and Newbold, in particular, is explicitly oriented toward those areas of time series analysis that are relevant for forecasting, and it is packed with fine insights and ideas. Hamilton (1994) is a more advanced book suitable for doctorate-level study.

A number of specialized books are also of interest. Makridakis and Wheelwright (1997) and Bails and Peppers (1997) display good business sense, with interesting discussions of, for example, the different forecasting needs of the subunits of a typical business firm and communicating forecasts to higher management. Modeling and forecasting techniques of particular relevance in finance are discussed in Taylor (1996).

Finally, Makridakis and Wheelwright (1987) is an informative and well-written collection of articles, written by different experts in various subfields of forecasting, dealing with both forecasting applications and methods. It provides a nice complement to this text, with detailed descriptions of forecasting in action in various business, economic, financial, and governmental settings.

Journals

A number of journals cater to the forecasting community. The leading academic forecasting journals, which contain a mixture of newly proposed methods, evaluation of existing methods, practical applications, and book and software reviews, are the *Journal of Forecasting* and the *International Journal of Forecasting*. In addition, the *Journal of Business Forecasting Methods and Systems* is a good source for case studies of forecasting in various corporate and government environments.

Although a number of journals are devoted to forecasting, the interdisciplinary nature of forecasting results in a rather ironic outcome: a substantial fraction of the best research is published not in the forecasting journals but

---

5. Most forecasting methods are concerned with forecasting time series. The modeling and forecasting of time series are so important that an entire field called **"time series analysis"** has arisen. Although the origins of the field go back hundreds of years, major advances have occurred in the last 50 years. Time series analysis is intimately related to forecasting because quantitative time series forecasting techniques require that quantitative time series models first be fit to the series of interest. Thus, forecasting requires knowledge of time series modeling techniques. A substantial portion of this book is therefore devoted to time series modeling.

rather in the broader applied econometrics and statistics journals such as *Journal of Business and Economic Statistics, Review of Economics and Statistics,* and *Journal of Applied Econometrics,* among many others. Several recent journal symposia have focused on forecasting; see, for example, Diebold and Watson (1996); Diebold and West (1998); and Diebold, Stock, and West (1999).

Software

Just as some journals specialize exclusively in forecasting, so too do some software packages. Likewise, forecasting tools can also be found scattered throughout econometric/statistical software packages with capabilities much broader than forecasting alone.[6]

One of the best such packages is Eviews, a modern Windows environment with extensive time series, modeling, and forecasting capabilities.[7] Eviews can implement almost all of the methods described in this book (and many more). Most of the examples in this book are done in Eviews, which reflects a balance of generality and specialization that makes it ideal for the sorts of tasks that will concern us.[8] If you feel more comfortable with another package, however, that's fine—our discussion is not wed to Eviews in any way, and most of our techniques can be implemented in a variety of packages, including Minitab, SAS, and many others.[9]

If you go on to more advanced modeling and forecasting, you'll probably want to have available an open-ended high-level computing environment in which you can quickly program, evaluate, and apply new tools and techniques. Matlab is one very good such environment.[10] Matlab is particularly well suited for time series modeling and forecasting.[11]

Although most forecasting is done in time series environments, some is done in "cross sections," which refers to examination of a population at one point in time. Stata is an outstanding package for cross-section modeling,

---

6. Rycroft (1993) provides a thorough comparative discussion of a variety of forecasting software.

7. The Eviews web page is at http://www.eviews.com.

8. A number of other good software packages are reviewed by Kim and Trivedi (1995).

9. S+ also deserves mention as a fine computing environment with special strengths in graphical data analysis and modern statistical methods. See Hallman (1993) for a review of S+.

10. Matlab maintains a web page that contains material on product availability, user-written add-ons, and so on, at http://www.mathworks.com.

11. Rust (1993) provides a comparative review of Matlab and one of its competitors, Gauss.

with strengths in areas such as qualitative response modeling, Poisson regression, quantile regression, and survival analysis.[12]

Online Information

A variety of information of interest to forecasters is available on the World Wide Web. The best way to learn about what's out there in cyberspace is to spend a few hours searching for whatever interests you, using one of the powerful browsers available, such as Netscape or Microsoft's Internet Explorer.

Any list of good web sites for forecasters is likely to be outdated shortly after its compilation; hence, we mention just one, which is constantly updated and tremendously authoritative: Resources for Economists, at http://econwpa.wustl.edu/EconFAQ/EconFAQ.html. It contains hundreds of links to data sources, journals, professional organizations, and so on. Frankly, the Resources for Economists page is all that is needed to launch you on your way.

4. LOOKING AHEAD

A forecast is little more than a guess about the future. Because forecasts guide decisions, good forecasts help to produce good decisions. In the remainder of this book, we motivate, describe, and compare modern forecasting methods. You will learn how to build and evaluate forecasts and forecasting models, and you will be able to use these tools to improve your decisions. Enjoy!

PROBLEMS AND COMPLEMENTS

1. (Forecasting in daily life) We are all forecasting, all the time.

    (a) Sketch in detail three forecasts that you make routinely, and probably informally, in your daily life.
    (b) What decisions are aided by your three forecasts?
    (c) How might you measure the "goodness" of your three forecasts?
    (d) For each of your forecasts, what is the value to you of a "good" as opposed to a "bad" forecast?

---

12. For a review of Stata, see Ferrall (1994). The Stata web page is at http://www.stata.com. The page has product information, user-supplied routines, course information, and so on, as well as links to other statistical software products, many of which are useful for forecasting.

2. (Forecasting in business, finance, economics, and government) What sorts of forecasts would be useful in the following decision-making situations? Why? What sorts of data might you need to produce such forecasts?

   (a) Shop-All-The-Time Network (SATTN) needs to schedule operators to receive incoming calls. The volume of calls varies depending on the time of day, the quality of the television advertisement, and the price of the good being sold. SATTN must schedule staff to minimize the loss of sales (too few operators leads to long hold times, and people hang up if put on hold) while also considering the loss associated with hiring excess employees.

   (b) You are a U.S. investor holding a portfolio of Japanese, British, French, and German stocks and government bonds. You are considering broadening your portfolio to include corporate stocks of Tambia, a developing economy with a risky emerging stock market. You are willing to do so only if the Tambian stocks produce higher portfolio returns sufficient to compensate you for the higher risk. There are rumors of an impending military coup, in which case your Tambian stocks would likely become worthless. There is also the chance of a major Tambian currency depreciation, in which case the dollar value of your Tambian stock returns would be greatly reduced.

   (c) You are an executive with Grainworld, a huge corporate farming conglomerate with grain sales both domestically and abroad. You have no control over the price of your grain, which is determined in the competitive market, but you must decide what to plant, and how much to plant, over the next two years. You are paid in foreign currency for all grain sold abroad, which you subsequently convert to dollars. Until now the government has bought all unsold grain so as to keep the price you receive stable, but the agricultural lobby is weakening, and you are concerned that the government subsidy may be reduced or eliminated in the next decade. Meanwhile, the price of fertilizer has risen because the government has restricted production of ammonium nitrate, a key ingredient in both fertilizer and terrorist bombs.

   (d) You run BUCO, a British utility supplying electricity to the London metropolitan area. You need to decide how much capacity to have on line, and two conflicting goals must be resolved in order to make an appropriate decision. You obviously want to have enough capacity to meet average demand, but that won't be enough, because demand is uneven throughout the year. In particular, demand skyrockets during summer heat waves—which occur randomly—as more and more people run their air conditioners constantly. If you don't have sufficient capacity to meet the peak demand, you get bad press. On the other hand, if you have a large amount of excess capacity over most of the year, you also get bad press.

3. (Data on the web) A huge amount of data of all sorts is available from the World Wide Web. Frumkin (1994) provides a useful and concise introduction to the construction, accuracy, and interpretation of a variety of economic and financial indicators, many of which are available on the web. Search the web for information on U.S. retail sales, U.K. stock prices, German GDP, and Japanese federal government expenditures. Summarize and graph your findings. The Resources for Economists home page at http://econwpa.wustl.edu/EconFAQ/EconFAQ.html is a fine place to start.

4. (Univariate and multivariate forecasting models) In this book we consider both "univariate" and "multivariate" forecasting models. In a univariate model, a single variable is modeled and forecast solely on the basis of its own past. Univariate approaches to forecasting may seem simplistic, and in some situations they are, but they are tremendously important and worth studying for at least two reasons. First, although they are simple, they are not necessarily simplistic, and a large amount of accumulated experience suggests that they often perform admirably. Second, it is necessary to understand univariate forecasting models before tackling more complicated multivariate models.

In a multivariate model, each of a set of variables is modeled on the basis of its own past, as well as the pasts of the other variables, thereby accounting for and exploiting cross-variable interactions. Multivariate models have the *potential* to produce forecast improvements relative to univariate models, because they exploit more information to produce forecasts.

Keeping in mind the distinction between univariate and multivariate models, consider a wine merchant seeking to forecast the price per case at which 1990 Chateau Latour, one of the greatest Bordeaux wines ever produced, will sell in the year 2010, at which time it will be fully mature.

(a) What sorts of univariate forecasting approaches can you imagine that might be relevant?

(b) What sorts of multivariate forecasting approaches can you imagine that might be relevant?

(c) What are the comparative costs and benefits of the univariate and multivariate approaches to forecasting the Latour price?

(d) Would you adopt a univariate or multivariate approach to forecasting the Latour price? Why?

CONCEPTS FOR REVIEW

Deterministic	Stochastic
Forecasting	Time series
Forecasting model	Time series analysis
Multivariate	Univariate
Statistical model	

REFERENCES AND ADDITIONAL READINGS

Bails, D. G., and Peppers, L. C. (1997), *Business Fluctuations,* second edition. Englewood Cliffs, N.J.: Prentice Hall.

Chatfield, C. (1996), *The Analysis of Time Series: An Introduction,* fifth edition. London: Chapman and Hall.

Diebold, F. X., Stock, J. H., and West, K. D., eds. (1999), Forecasting and Empirical Methods in Macroeconomics and Finance, II, special issue of *Review of Economics and Statistics,* 81.

Diebold, F. X., and Watson, M. W., eds. (1996), New Developments in Economic Forecasting, special issue of *Journal of Applied Econometrics,* 11, 453–594.

Diebold, F. X., and West, K. D., eds. (1998), Forecasting and Empirical Methods in Macroeconomics and Finance, special issue of *International Economic Review,* 39, 811–1144.

Granger, C. W. J., and Newbold, P. (1986), *Forecasting Economic Time Series,* second edition. Orlando, Fla.: Academic Press.

Ferrall, C. (1994), "A Review of Stata 3.1," *Journal of Applied Econometrics,* 9, 469–478.

Frumkin, N. (1994), *Guide to Economic Indicators,* second edition. Armonk, N.Y.: M. E. Sharpe.

Hallman, J. (1993), "Review of S+," *Journal of Applied Econometrics,* 8, 213–220.

Hamilton, J. D. (1994), *Time Series Analysis.* Princeton, N.J.: Princeton University Press.

Harvey, A. C. (1993), *Time Series Models,* second edition. Cambridge, Mass.: MIT Press.

Kennedy, P. (1998), *A Guide to Econometrics,* fourth edition. Cambridge, Mass.: MIT Press.

Kim, J., and Trivedi, P. (1995), "Econometric Time Series Analysis Software: A Review," *American Statistician,* 48, 336–346.

Maddala, G. S. (in press), *Introduction to Econometrics,* third edition. New York: Macmillan.

Makridakis, S., and Wheelwright S. (1987), *The Handbook of Forecasting: A Manager's Guide,* second edition. New York: Wiley.

Makridakis, S., and Wheelwright, S. C. (1997), *Forecasting: Methods and Applications,* third edition. New York: Wiley.

Pindyck, R. S., and Rubinfeld, D. L. (1997), *Econometric Models and Economic Forecasts,* fourth edition. New York: McGraw-Hill.

Rust, J. (1993), "Gauss and Matlab: A Comparison," *Journal of Applied Econometrics,* 8, 307–324.

Rycroft, R. S. (1993), "Microcomputer Software of Interest to Forecasters in Comparative Review: An Update," *International Journal of Forecasting,* 9, 531–575.

Taylor, S. (1996), *Modeling Financial Time Series,* second edition. New York: Wiley.

Wonnacott, T. H., and Wonnacott, R. J. (1990), *Introductory Statistics,* fifth edition. New York: Wiley.

APPENDIX: THE LINEAR REGRESSION MODEL

Ideas that fall under the general heading of **linear regression analysis** are crucial for building forecasting models, using them to produce forecasts, and evaluating those forecasts. Here we provide a brief review of linear regression to refresh your memory and to provide motivation from a forecasting perspective.

Suppose that we have data on two variables, y and x, as in Figure A.1, and suppose that we want to find the linear function of x that gives the best forecast of y, where "best forecast" means that the sum of squared forecast errors, for the sample of data at hand, is as small as possible. This amounts to finding the line that best fits the data points, in the sense that the sum of squared vertical distances of the data points from the fitted line is minimized. When we "run a regression," or "fit a regression line," that is what we do. The estimation strategy is called **ordinary least squares.**

The adjective "ordinary" distinguishes the ordinary least squares estimator from fancier versions. The ordinary least squares estimator, you may recall, has a well-known mathematical formula. We won't reproduce it here; suffice it to say that we simply use the computer to evaluate the formula. This contrasts with another important type of least squares estimator, the nonlinear least squares estimator. When we estimate by nonlinear least squares, we use a computer to find the minimum of the sum of squared residual function directly, using numerical methods. For the simple regression model at hand, the two approaches produce the same result, and ordinary least squares is simpler, so we prefer ordinary least squares. Many useful forecasting models, however, involve nonlinear restrictions across parameters, which cannot be imposed using ordinary least squares but can be imposed using nonlinear least squares. In such cases we use nonlinear least squares.

FIGURE A.1   Scatterplot of y vs. x

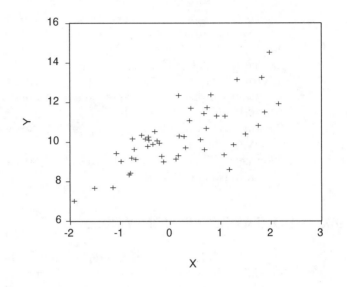

In Figure A.2, we illustrate graphically the results of regressing y on x. The best-fitting line slopes upward, reflecting the positive correlation between y and x. Note that the data points don't satisfy the fitted linear relationship exactly; rather; they satisfy it on average. To forecast y for any given value of x, we use the fitted line to find the value of y that corresponds to the given value of x.

Thus far we haven't postulated a probabilistic model that relates y and x; instead, we simply ran a mechanical regression of y on x to find the best forecast of y formed as a linear function of x. It is easy, however, to construct a probabilistic framework that lets us make statistical assessments about the properties of the fitted line and the corresponding forecasts. We assume that y is linearly related to an exogenously determined variable x, and we add an independent and identically distributed (iid) **disturbance** with zero mean and constant variance:

$$y_t = \beta_0 + \beta_1 x_t + \varepsilon_t$$

$$\varepsilon_t \overset{\text{iid}}{\sim} (0, \sigma^2)$$

$t = 1, \ldots, T$. The intercept of the line is β_0, the slope is β_1, and the variance of the disturbance is σ^2.[13] Collectively, β_0, β_1, and σ^2 are called the model's

---

13. We speak of the **regression intercept** and the **regression slope**.

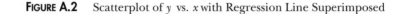

FIGURE A.2   Scatterplot of y vs. x with Regression Line Superimposed

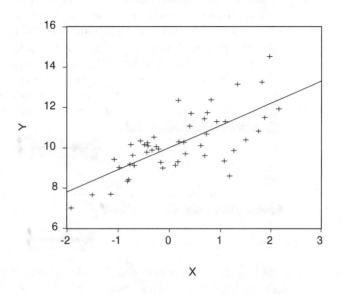

parameters. The index t keeps track of time; the data sample begins at some time called "1" and ends at some time called "T."

If the regression model postulated above holds true, then the expected value of y conditional upon x taking a particular value, say x^*, is

$$E(y \mid x^*) = \beta_0 + \beta_1 x^*$$

That is, the **regression function** is the *conditional expectation* of y. As we shall see in detail later, the expectation of future y conditional upon available information is a particularly good forecast. In fact, under fairly general conditions it is the best possible forecast. The intimate connection between regression and optimal forecasts makes regression an important tool for forecasting.

We assume that the model sketched above is the true model, or **population model.** If we knew β_1 and β_2 we could make a forecast; the variance of the corresponding forecast error would be σ^2. The problem, of course, is that we don't *know* the values of the model's parameters. When we run the regression, or "estimate the regression model," we use a computer to *estimate* the unknown parameters by solving the problem

$$\min_{\beta} \sum_{t=1}^{T} \left[y_t - \beta_0 - \beta_1 x_t \right]^2$$

where β is shorthand notation for the set of two parameters, β_0 and β_1.[14] We denote the set of estimated parameters by $\hat{\beta}$, and its elements by $\hat{\beta}_0$ and $\hat{\beta}_1$. Each estimated coefficient gives the weight put on the corresponding variable in forming the best linear forecast of y. We can think of β_0 as the coefficient on a "constant" variable that is always equal to 1. The estimated coefficient on the constant variable is the best forecast in the event that x is zero. In that sense it is a baseline forecast. We use the set of estimated parameters, $\hat{\beta}_0$ and $\hat{\beta}_1$, to make forecasts that improve on the baseline. The **fitted values, or in-sample forecasts,** are

$$\hat{y}_t = \hat{\beta}_0 + \hat{\beta}_1 x_t$$

$t = 1, \ldots, T$.

Forecasts are rarely perfect; instead, we make errors. The **residuals, or in-sample forecast errors,** are

$$e_t = y_t - \hat{y}_t$$

$t = 1, \ldots, T$. Forecasters are keenly interested in studying the properties of their forecast errors. Systematic patterns in forecast errors indicate that the forecasting model is inadequate; forecast errors from a good forecasting model must be unforecastable!

Now suppose we have a second exogenous variable, z, which we could also use to forecast y. In Figure A.3 we show a scatterplot of y against z, with the regression line superimposed. This time the slope of the fitted line is negative. The regressions of y on x and y on z are called **simple linear regressions;** they are potentially useful, but ultimately we would like to regress y on *both* x and z. Fortunately, the idea of linear regression generalizes readily to accommodate more than one right-hand-side variable. We write

$$y_t = \beta_0 + \beta_1 x_t + \beta_2 z_t + \varepsilon_t$$

$$\varepsilon_t \overset{iid}{\sim} (0, \sigma^2)$$

$t = 1, \ldots, T$. This is called a **multiple linear regression model.** Again, we use the computer to find the values of β_0, β_1, and β_2 that produce the best forecast of y; that is, we find the β values that solve the problem

$$\min_{\beta} \sum_{t=1}^{T} \left[y_t - \beta_0 - \beta_1 x_t - \beta_2 z_t \right]^2$$

---

14. Shortly we will show how to estimate σ^2 as well.

FIGURE A.3   Scatterplot of y vs. z with Regression Line Superimposed

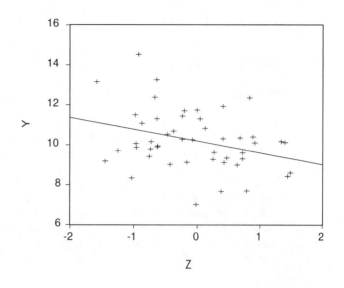

where β denotes the set of three model parameters. We denote the set of estimated parameters by $\hat{\beta}$, with elements $\hat{\beta}_0$, $\hat{\beta}_1$, and $\hat{\beta}_2$. The fitted values are

$$\hat{y}_t = \hat{\beta}_0 + \hat{\beta}_1 x_t + \hat{\beta}_2 z_t$$

and the residuals are

$$e_t = y_t - \hat{y}_t$$

$t = 1, \ldots, T$. Extension to the general multiple linear regression model, with an arbitrary number of right-hand-side variables (k, including the constant), is immediate.

This time, let us do more than a simple graphical analysis of the regression fit. Instead, let us look in detail at the computer output, which we show in Table A.1. We do so dozens of times in this book, and the output format and interpretation are always the same, so it's important to get comfortable with it quickly. The output is in Eviews format. Other software will produce more or less the same information, which is fundamental and standard.

The printout begins by reminding us that we're running a least squares (LS) regression, and that the left-hand-side variable (the "dependent variable"—see the Additional Problems and Complements at the end of this appendix) is y. It then shows us the sample range of the historical data, which happens to be 1950 to 1997, for a total of 48 observations.

TABLE A.1   Regression of y on x and z

LS // Dependent Variable is Y

Sample: 1950-1997
Included observations: 48

Variable	Coefficient	Std. Error	t-Statistic	Prob.
C	9.996089	0.145257	68.81667	0.0000
X	1.060485	0.148238	7.153958	0.0000
Z	-0.447736	0.181358	-2.468798	0.0174

R-squared	0.578590	Mean dependent var	10.22772
Adjusted R-squared	0.559861	S.D. dependent var	1.485344
S.E. of regression	0.985422	Akaike info criterion	0.031090
Sum squared resid	43.69752	Schwarz criterion	0.148040
Log likelihood	-65.85521	F-statistic	30.89217
Durbin-Watson stat	1.965915	Prob(F-statistic)	0.000000

Next comes a table listing each right-hand-side variable together with four statistics. The right-hand-side variables x and z need no explanation, but the variable C does. C is notation for the constant variable mentioned earlier. The C variable always equals 1, so the estimated coefficient on C is the estimated intercept of the regression line.[15]

The four statistics associated with each right-hand-side variable are the estimated coefficient ("Coefficient"), its standard error ("Std. Error"), a t-Statistic, and a corresponding probability value ("Prob."). The **standard errors** of the estimated coefficients indicate their likely sampling variability, and hence their reliability. The estimated coefficient plus or minus one standard error is approximately a 68% confidence interval for the true but unknown population parameter, and the estimated coefficient plus or minus two standard errors is approximately a 95% confidence interval, assuming that the estimated coefficient is approximately normally distributed.[16] Thus large coefficient standard errors translate into wide confidence intervals.

Each **t-statistic** provides a test of the hypothesis of variable irrelevance: that the true but unknown population parameter is zero, so that the corre-

---

15. Sometimes the population coefficient on C is called the **constant term,** and the regression estimate is called the estimated constant term.

16. The coefficient will be normally distributed if the regression disturbance is normally distributed or if the sample size is large.

sponding variable contributes nothing to the forecasting regression and can therefore can be dropped. One way to test variable irrelevance, with, say, a 5% probability of incorrect rejection, is to check whether zero is outside the 95% confidence interval for the parameter. If so, we reject irrelevance. The t-statistic is just the ratio of the estimated coefficient to its standard error, so if zero is outside the 95% confidence interval, then the t-statistic must be bigger than 2 in absolute value. Thus we can quickly test irrelevance at the 5% level by checking whether the t-statistic is greater than 2 in absolute value.[17]

Finally, associated with each t-statistic is a **probability value,** which is the probability of getting a value of the t-statistic at least as large in absolute value as the one actually obtained, assuming that the irrelevance hypothesis is true. Thus, if a t-statistic were 2, the corresponding probability value would be approximately 0.05. The smaller the probability value, the stronger the evidence against irrelevance. There is no magic cutoff, but typically probability values less than 0.1 are viewed as strong evidence against irrelevance, and probability values below 0.05 are viewed as very strong evidence against irrelevance. Probability values are useful because they eliminate the need for consulting tables of the t distribution. Effectively the computer does it for us and tells us the significance level at which the irrelevance hypothesis is just rejected.

Now let us interpret the actual estimated coefficients, standard errors, t-statistics, and probability values. The estimated intercept is approximately 10, so that, conditional on x and z both being zero, our best forecast of y would be 10. Moreover, the intercept is very precisely estimated, as evidenced by the small standard error of 0.15 relative to the estimated coefficient. An approximate 95% confidence interval for the true but unknown population intercept is $10 \pm 2(.15)$, or [9.70, 10.30]. Zero is far outside that interval, so the corresponding t-statistic is huge, with a probability value that is zero to four decimal places.

The estimated coefficient on x is 1.06, and the standard error is again small in relation to the size of the estimated coefficient, so the t-statistic is large and its probability value is small. The coefficient is positive, so that y tends to rise when x rises. In fact, the interpretation of the estimated coefficient of 1.06 is that, holding everything else constant, we forecast that a one-unit increase in x will produce a 1.06-unit increase in y.

The estimated coefficient on z is –0.45. Its standard error is larger relative to the estimated parameter, and its t-statistic smaller, than those of the other coefficients. The standard error is nevertheless small, and the absolute value of the t-statistic is still well above 2, with a small probability value of 2%.

---

17.   If the sample size is small, or if we want a significance level other than 5%, we must refer to a table of critical values of the t distribution. It should also be pointed out that use of the t distribution in small samples also requires an assumption of normally distributed disturbances.

Hence, at conventional levels we reject the hypothesis that z contributes nothing to the forecasting regression. The estimated coefficient is negative, so y tends to fall when z rises. We forecast that a one-unit increase in z will produce a 0.45-unit *decrease* in y.

A variety of diagnostic statistics follow; they help us to evaluate the adequacy of the regression. We discuss many of them elsewhere in detail. Presently, we introduce them very briefly.

Mean Dependent Var 10.23

The **sample mean of the dependent variable** is

$$\bar{y} = \frac{1}{T} \sum_{t=1}^{T} y_t$$

The statistic measures the **central tendency,** or **location,** of y.

S.D. Dependent Var 1.49

The **sample standard deviation (SD) of the dependent variable** is

$$SD = \sqrt{\frac{\sum_{t=1}^{T} (y_t - \bar{y})^2}{T-1}}$$

This statistic measures the **dispersion,** or **scale,** of y.

Sum Squared Resid 43.70

Minimizing the **sum of squared residuals** is the objective of least squares estimation. It is natural, then, to record the minimized value of the sum of squared residuals. In isolation it is not of much value, but it serves as an input to other diagnostics that we will discuss shortly, and it is useful for comparing models and testing hypotheses. The formula is

$$SSR = \sum_{t=1}^{T} e_t^2$$

Log Likelihood −65.86

The **likelihood function** is the joint density function of the data, viewed as a function of the model parameters. Hence, a natural estimation strategy, called **maximum likelihood estimation,** is to find (and use as estimates) the parameter values that maximize the likelihood function. After all, by construction, those parameter values maximize the likelihood of obtaining the data that were actually obtained. In the leading case of normally distributed regression disturbances, maximizing the likelihood function turns out to be equivalent to minimizing the sum of squared residuals; thus, the maximum-likelihood parameter estimates are identical to the least-squares parameter estimates. The number reported is the maximized value of the log of the likelihood function.[18] Like the sum of squared residuals, this value is not of direct use, but it is useful for comparing models and testing hypotheses. We won't use the likelihood function directly; instead, we will focus on the sum of squared residuals.

F-statistic 30.89

We use the **F-statistic** to test the hypothesis that the coefficients of all variables in the regression except the intercept are jointly zero.[19] That is, we test whether, taken jointly as a set, the variables included in the forecasting model have any predictive value. This contrasts with the t-statistic, which we use to examine the predictive worth of the variables one at a time.[20] If no variable has predictive value, the F-statistic follows an F distribution with $k-1$ and $T-k$ degrees of freedom.

$$F = \frac{(SSR_{res} - SSR)/(k-1)}{SSR/(T-k)}$$

where SSR_{res} is the sum of squared residuals from a *restricted* regression that contains only an intercept. Thus the test proceeds by examining how much the SSR increases when all the variables except the constant are dropped. If it increases by a great deal, there is evidence that at least one of the variables has predictive content.

---

18. Throughout this book, "ln" refers to a natural (base e) logarithm.

19. We don't want to restrict the intercept to be zero, because under the hypothesis that all the other coefficients are zero, the intercept would equal the mean of y, which in general is not zero.

20. In the degenerate case of only one right-hand-side variable, the t and F statistics contain exactly the same information, and $F = t^2$. When there are two or more right-hand-side variables, however, the hypotheses tested differ, and $F \neq t^2$.

Prob (*F*-statistic) 0.000000

The **probability value of the *F*-statistic** gives the significance level at which we can just reject the hypothesis that the set of right-hand-side variables has no predictive value. Here, the value is indistinguishable from zero, so we reject the hypothesis overwhelmingly.

S.E. of Regression 0.99

If we knew the elements of β, then our forecast errors would be the ε_t values, with variance σ^2. We would like an estimate of σ^2 because it tells us whether our forecast errors are likely to be large or small. The observed residuals, the e_t values, are effectively estimates of the unobserved population disturbances, the ε_t values. Thus the sample variance of the e's, which we denote s^2 (read **"s-squared"**), is a natural estimator of σ^2:

$$s^2 = \frac{\displaystyle\sum_{t=1}^{T} e_t^2}{T-k}$$

s^2 is an estimate of the dispersion of the regression disturbance and hence is used to assess goodness of fit of the model as well as the magnitude of forecast errors that we are likely to make. The larger the s^2, the worse the model's fit, and the larger the forecast errors we are likely to make. s^2 involves a degrees-of-freedom correction (division by $T-k$ rather than by T or $T-1$), which is an attempt to get a good estimate of the out-of-sample forecast error variance on the basis of the in-sample residuals.

The **standard error of the regression,** or *SER*, conveys the same information; because it is an estimator of σ rather than σ^2, we simply use s rather than s^2. The formula is

$$SER = \sqrt{s^2} = \sqrt{\frac{\displaystyle\sum_{t=1}^{T} e_t^2}{T-k}}$$

The standard error of the regression is easier to interpret than s^2, because its units are the same as those of the e's, whereas the units of s^2 are not. If the e's are in dollars, then the squared e's are in dollars squared, so s^2 is in dollars squared. By taking the square root at the end of it all, *SER* converts the units back to dollars.

It is often informative to compare the standard error of the regression to the mean of the dependent variable. As a rough rule of thumb, the *SER* of a good forecasting model shouldn't be more than 10 or 15 percent of the mean of the dependent variable. For the present model, the *SER* is about 10 percent of the mean of the dependent variable, so it just squeaks by.

Sometimes it is informative to compare the standard error of the regression (or a close relative) to the standard deviation of the dependent variable (or a close relative). The standard error of the regression is an estimate of the standard deviation of forecast errors from the regression model, and the standard deviation of the dependent variable is an estimate of the standard deviation of the forecast errors from a simpler forecasting model, in which the forecast each period is simply $\bar{y}$. If the ratio is small, the variables in the model appear very helpful in forecasting y. *R*-squared measures, to which we now turn, are based on precisely that idea.

R-squared 0.58

If an intercept is included in the regression, as is almost always the case, *R*-squared must be between zero and one. In that case, **R-squared,** usually written $\boldsymbol{R^2}$, is the percent of the variance of y explained by the variables included in the regression. R^2 measures the in-sample success of the regression equation in forecasting y; thus, it is widely used as a quick check of **goodness of fit,** or forecastability of y based on the variables included in the regression. Here the R^2 is about 58 percent—good but not great. The formula is

$$R^2 = 1 - \frac{\displaystyle\sum_{t=1}^{T} e_t^2}{\displaystyle\sum_{t=1}^{T} (y_t - \bar{y})^2}$$

We can write R^2 in a more roundabout way as

$$R^2 = 1 - \frac{\dfrac{1}{T}\displaystyle\sum_{t=1}^{T} e_t^2}{\dfrac{1}{T}\displaystyle\sum_{t=1}^{T} (y_t - \bar{y})^2}$$

which makes clear that the numerator in the large fraction is very close to s^2, and the denominator is very close to the sample variance of y.

Adjusted *R*-squared 0.56

The interpretation of the **adjusted R^2** is the same as that of R^2, but the formula is a bit different. Adjusted R^2 incorporates adjustments for degrees of freedom used in fitting the model, in an attempt to offset the inflated appearance of good fit, or high forecastability of y, if a variety of right-hand-side variables is tried and the "best model" selected. Hence, adjusted R^2 is a more trustworthy goodness-of-fit measure than R^2. As long as there is more than one right-hand-side variable in the model fitted, adjusted R^2 is smaller than R^2; here, however, the two are quite close (56% vs. 58%). Adjusted R^2 is often denoted $\overline{R}^2$; the formula is

$$\overline{R}^2 = 1 - \frac{\dfrac{1}{T-k}\sum\limits_{t=1}^{T} e_t^2}{\dfrac{1}{T-1}\sum\limits_{t=1}^{T} (y_t - \overline{y})^2}$$

where k is the number of right-hand-side variables, including the constant term. Here the numerator in the large fraction is precisely s^2, and the denominator is precisely the sample variance of y.

Akaike Info Criterion 0.03

The **Akaike information criterion,** or *AIC*, is effectively an estimate of the out-of-sample forecast error variance, as is s^2, but it penalizes degrees of freedom more harshly. It is used to select among competing forecasting models. The formula is

$$AIC = \exp\left(\frac{2k}{T}\right)\frac{\sum\limits_{t=1}^{T} e_t^2}{T}$$

Schwarz Criterion 0.15

The **Schwarz information criterion,** or *SIC*, is an alternative to the *AIC* with the same interpretation, but a still harsher degrees-of-freedom penalty. The formula is

$$SIC = T^{\left(\frac{k}{T}\right)}\frac{\sum\limits_{t=1}^{T} e_t^2}{T}$$

As they arise in the course of our discussion, we will discuss in detail the sum of squared residuals, the standard error of the regression, R^2, adjusted R^2, *AIC*, and *SIC*, the relationships among them, and their roles in selecting forecasting models. Thus we will say no more here. It is worth noting, however, that other formulas, slightly different from the ones given here, are sometimes used for *AIC* and *SIC*, as discussed in greater detail in chapter 4.

Durbin-Watson Stat 1.97

We mentioned earlier that we're interested in examining whether there are patterns in our forecast errors, because errors from a good forecasting model should be unforecastable. The **Durbin-Watson statistic** tests for correlation over time, called **serial correlation,** in regression disturbances. If the errors made by a forecasting model serially are correlated, then they are forecastable, and we could improve the forecasts by forecasting the forecast errors. The Durbin-Watson test works within the context of the model

$$y_t = \beta_0 + \beta_1 x_t + \varepsilon_t$$

$$\varepsilon_t = \varphi \varepsilon_{t-1} + v_t$$

$$v_t \overset{iid}{\sim} N(0, \sigma^2)$$

The regression disturbance is serially correlated when $\varphi \neq 0$. The hypothesis of interest is that $\varphi = 0$. When $\varphi = 0$, the ideal conditions hold, but when $\varphi \neq 0$, the disturbance is serially correlated. More specifically, when $\varphi \neq 0$, we say that ε_t follows an autoregressive process of order one, or AR(1) for short.[21] If $\varphi > 0$ the disturbance is positively serially correlated, and if $\varphi < 0$ the disturbance is negatively serially correlated. **Positive serial correlation** is typically the relevant alternative in the applications that will concern us. The formula for the Durbin-Watson statistic (*DW*) is

$$DW = \frac{\sum_{t=2}^{T} (e_t - e_{t-1})^2}{\sum_{t=1}^{T} e_t^2}$$

---

21. The Durbin-Watson test is designed to be very good at detecting serial correlation of the AR(1) type. Many other types of serial correlation are possible; we discuss them extensively in chapter 7.

FIGURE A.4　　Residual Plot for the Regression of y on x and z

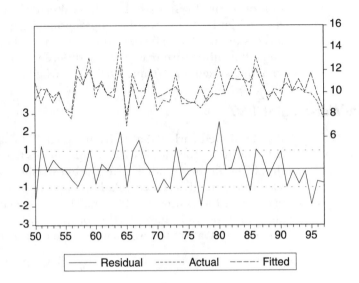

DW takes values in the interval $[0, 4]$, and if all is well, DW should be around 2. If DW is substantially less than 2, there is evidence of positive serial correlation. As a rough rule of thumb, if DW is less than 1.5, there may be cause for alarm, and we should consult the tables of the DW statistic, available in many statistics and econometrics texts. Here the Durbin-Watson statistic is very close to 2, so there is no evidence of residual serial correlation.

After running a regression, it is usually a good idea to assess the adequacy of the model by plotting and examining the actual data (y_t's), the fitted values ($\hat{y}_t$'s), and the residuals (e_t's). Often we refer to such a plot, shown together in a single graph, as a **residual plot.**[22] In Figure A.4, we show the residual plot for the regression of y on x and z. The actual (short dash) and fitted (long dash) values appear at the top of the graph; their scale is on the right. The fitted values track the actual values fairly well. The residuals appear at the bottom of the graph (solid line); their scale is on the left. It's important to note that the scales differ; the e_t values are in fact substantially smaller and less variable than either the y_t or the $\hat{y}_t$ values. We draw the zero line through the residuals for visual comparison. There are no obvious patterns in the residuals.

---

22. Sometimes, however, we use "residual plot" to refer to a plot of the residuals alone. The intended meaning will be clear from the context.

ADDITIONAL PROBLEMS AND COMPLEMENTS

1. (Mechanics of fitting a linear regression) On the data disk you will find a set of data on y, x, and z. The data are different from, but similar to, those underlying the graphing and regression fitting that we performed in this appendix. Using these data, produce and interpret graphs and regressions analogous to those reported in this appendix.

2. (Regression semantics) Regression analysis is so important, and is used so often by so many people, that a variety of terms have evolved over the years, all of which are the same for our purposes. You may encounter them in your reading, so it is important to be aware of them. Some examples include:

   (a) Ordinary least squares, OLS, least squares, LS (sometimes LS is used to refer to nonlinear least squares as well)
   (b) y, left-hand-side variable, regressand, dependent variable, endogenous variable
   (c) x's, right-hand-side variables, regressors, independent variables, exogenous variables, predictors
   (d) probability value, prob-value, p-value, marginal significance level
   (e) Schwarz criterion, Schwarz information criterion, SIC, Bayes information criterion, BIC

3. (Regression with and without a constant term) Consider again Figure A.2, in which we showed a scatterplot of y vs. x, with the fitted regression line superimposed.

   (a) In fitting that regression line, we included a constant term. How can you tell?
   (b) Suppose that we had not included a constant term. How would the figure look?
   (c) We almost always include a constant term when estimating regressions. Why?
   (d) When, if ever, might you explicitly want to exclude the constant term?

4. (Desired values of diagnostic statistics) For each of the diagnostic statistics listed below, indicate whether, other things being the same, "bigger is better," "smaller is better," or neither. Explain your reasoning. (*Hint:* Be careful, think before you answer, and be sure to qualify your answers as appropriate.)

   (a) Coefficient
   (b) Standard error
   (c) t-statistic
   (d) Probability value of the t-statistic

(e) *R*-squared
(f) Adjusted *R*-squared
(g) Standard error of the regression
(h) Sum of squared residuals
(i) Log likelihood
(j) Durbin-Watson statistic
(k) Mean of the dependent variable
(l) Standard deviation of the dependent variable
(m) Akaike information criterion
(n) Schwarz criterion
(o) *F*-statistic
(p) Probability value of the *F*-statistic

5. (Regression disturbances: skewness, kurtosis, and normality)

(a) **Skewness** measures the amount of asymmetry in a distribution. If a distribution is symmetric, skewness equals zero; the larger the absolute size of the skewness statistic, the more asymmetric is the distribution. A large positive value indicates a long right tail, and a large negative value indicates a long left tail. Skewness is defined in population as

$$S = \frac{E(y-\mu)^3}{\sigma^3}$$

where $\sigma = \sqrt{E(y-\mu)^2}$ and $\mu = E(y)$. We estimate skewness from a sample of data by replacing mathematical expectations with sample averages, which yields

$$\hat{S} = \frac{\frac{1}{T}\sum_{t=1}^{T}(y_t - \bar{y})^3}{\hat{\sigma}^3}$$

where

$$\hat{\sigma} = \sqrt{\frac{1}{T}\sum_{t=1}^{T}(y_t - \bar{y})^2} \text{ and } \bar{y} = \frac{1}{T}\sum_{t=1}^{T} y_t$$

(b) The **kurtosis** of a random variable is a measure of the thickness of the tails of its distribution relative to those of a normal distribution. A normal random variable has a kurtosis of 3; a kurtosis above 3 indicates "fat tails" or **leptokurtosis;** that is, the distribution has more probability mass in the tails than the normal distribution. Kurtosis is defined in population as

$$K = \frac{E(y - \mu)^4}{\sigma^4}$$

We estimate kurtosis from a sample of data by replacing mathematical expectations with sample averages,

$$\hat{K} = \frac{\frac{1}{T} \sum_{t=1}^{T} (y_t - \bar{y})^4}{\hat{\sigma}^4}$$

(c) The **Jarque-Bera test** statistic (JB) effectively aggregates the information in the data about both skewness and kurtosis to produce an overall test for normality. The statistic is

$$JB = \frac{T}{6} \left(\hat{S}^2 + \frac{1}{4} (\hat{K} - 3)^2 \right)$$

where T is the number of observations.[23] Under the null hypothesis of independent normally distributed observations, the Jarque-Bera statistic is distributed as a chi-squared random variable with 2 degrees of freedom in large samples.

(d) Other tests of conformity to the normal distribution exist, such as the Kolmogorov-Smirnov test, and may, of course, be used. We use the Jarque-Bera test in this book because of its simplicity and its convenient and intuitive decomposition into skewness and leptokurtosis components.

ADDITIONAL BIBLIOGRAPHICAL AND COMPUTATIONAL NOTES

See any good introductory statistics or econometrics book for a more complete discussion of regression theory and for tables of significance points of the normal, t, F, and Durbin-Watson distributions.

Dozens of software packages—including spreadsheets—implement linear regression. Most include an intercept automatically, unless explicitly instructed otherwise. That is, they automatically create and include a C variable.

---

23. The formula given is for an observed time series. If the series being tested for normality is the residual from a model, then T should be replaced with $T - k$, where k is the number of parameters estimated.

ADDITIONAL CONCEPTS FOR REVIEW

Adjusted R-squared

Akaike information criterion

Central tendency, or location

Conditional expectation

Constant term

Dispersion, or scale

Disturbance

Durbin-Watson statistic

Fitted values, or in-sample forecasts

F-statistic

Goodness of fit

Jarque-Bera test

Kurtosis

Leptokurtosis

Likelihood function

Linear regression analysis

Maximum likelihood estimation

Multiple linear regression model

Ordinary least squares

Parameters

Population model

Positive serial correlation

Probability value

Probability value of the F-statistic

R-squared

Regression function

Regression intercept

Regression slope

Residual plot

Residuals, or in-sample forecast errors

s^2

Sample mean of the dependent variable

Sample standard deviation of the dependent variable

Schwarz information criterion

Serial correlation

Simple linear regression

Skewness

Standard error

Standard error of the regression

Sum of squared residuals

t-statistic

SIX CONSIDERATIONS BASIC
TO SUCCESSFUL FORECASTING

In chapter 1 we sketched a variety of areas where forecasts are used routinely, and we took a brief tour of the basic forecasting tools that you will master as you progress through this book. Now let us back up and consider six types of questions that are relevant for *any* forecasting task.[1]

1. (**Decision Environment** and **Loss Function**) What decision will the forecast guide, and what are the implications for the design, use, and evaluation of the forecasting model? Related to these issues, how do we quantify what we mean by a "good" forecast, and in particular, the cost or loss associated with forecast errors of various signs and sizes? How should we define optimality of a forecast in a particular situation? How do we compute optimal forecasts?

2. (**Forecast Object**) What is the object that we need to forecast? Is it a time series, such as sales of a firm recorded over time, or is it an event, such as devaluation of a currency? What is the quantity and quality of the data? How long is the sample of available data? Are we forecasting one object or many (e.g., sales of each of 350 products)? Are there missing observations? Unusual observations?

3. (**Forecast Statement**) How do we wish to state our forecasts? If, for example, the object to be forecast is a time series, are we interested in a single

---

1. There are, of course, many possible variations, combinations, and extensions of the questions; you should try to think of some as you read through them.

"best guess" forecast? Or a "reasonable range" of possible future values that reflects the underlying uncertainty associated with the forecasting problem? Or a probability distribution of possible future values? What are the associated costs and benefits?

4. (**Forecast Horizon**) What is the forecast horizon of interest, and what determines it? Are we interested, for example, in forecasting one month ahead, one year ahead, or ten years ahead? The best modeling and forecasting strategy will likely vary with the horizon.

5. (**Information Set**) On what information will the forecast be based? Are the available data simply the past history of the series to be forecast, or are other series available that may be related to the series of interest?

6. (**Methods and Complexity,** the **Parsimony Principle,** and the **Shrinkage Principle**) What forecasting method is best suited to the needs of a particular forecasting problem? How complex should the forecasting model be? More generally, what sorts of models, in terms of complexity, tend to do best for forecasting in business, finance, economics, and government? The phenomena that we model and forecast are often tremendously complex, but does it necessarily follow that our forecasting models should be complex?

1. THE DECISION ENVIRONMENT AND LOSS FUNCTION

Forecasts are not made in a vacuum. The key to generating good and useful forecasts, which we will stress now and throughout this book, is recognizing that forecasts are made to guide decisions. The link between forecasts and decisions sounds obvious—and it is—but it is worth thinking about in some depth. Forecasts are made in a wide variety of situations, but in every case forecasts are made and are of value because they aid in decision making. Quite simply, good forecasts help to produce good decisions. Recognition and awareness of the decision-making environment is the key to effective design, use, and evaluation of forecasting models.

Consider the following stylized problem. You have started a firm and must decide how much inventory to hold going into the next sales period. If you knew that demand would be high next period, then you would like to have a lot of inventory on hand. If you knew that demand would be slack, then you would like to deplete your inventories because it costs money to store unnecessary inventories. The problem, of course, is that you don't know next period's demand, and you've got to make your inventory stocking decision *now!*

Let us make a chart showing your two possible inventory decisions and the two possible demand outcomes, as in Table 2.1. There are four possible outcomes, two good and two bad. The two good outcomes correspond to the diagonal entries in the table—you build inventories and demand turns out to

TABLE 2.1   Decision Making with Symmetric Loss

	Demand High	**Demand Low**
Build inventory	0	$10,000
Reduce inventory	$10,000	0

be high, or you reduce inventories and demand turns out to be low. In either case, it is clear that you made the right decision. The two bad outcomes correspond to the off-diagonal entries in the table—you reduce inventories and demand turns out to be high (lower-left table entry), or you build inventories and demand turns out to be low (upper-right table entry). In either case, it is clear that you made the wrong decision.

Each entry of the table contains a "cost" or "loss" to you corresponding to the associated decision/outcome pair. The good pairs, on the diagonal, have zero loss—after all, you did the right thing! The bad pairs, off the diagonal, have positive loss—you did the wrong thing, and you must suffer the consequences.

In Table 2.1, the loss associated with each incorrect decision is $10,000. We call such a loss structure *symmetric* because the loss is the same for both of the bad outcomes. In many important decision environments, a symmetric loss structure closely approximates the true losses of the forecaster. In other decision environments, however, **symmetric loss** may *not* be realistic; in general, there is no reason for loss to be symmetric.

In Table 2.2, we summarize a decision environment with **asymmetric loss** structure. As before, each entry of the table contains a loss corresponding to the associated decision/outcome pair. The "good" pairs, on the diagonal, have zero loss for the same reason as before—when you do the right thing, you incur no loss. The "bad" pairs, off the diagonal, again have positive loss— when you do the wrong thing, you suffer—but now the amount of the loss differs depending on what sort of mistake you make. If you reduce inventories and demand turns out to be high, then you have insufficient inventories to meet demand and you miss out on a lot of business, which is very costly ($20,000). On the other hand, if you build inventories and demand turns out to be low, then you must carry unneeded inventories, which is not as costly ($10,000).

TABLE 2.2   Decision Making with Asymmetric Loss

	Demand High	**Demand Low**
Build inventory	0	$10,000
Reduce inventory	$20,000	0

TABLE 2.3　　Forecasting with Symmetric Loss

	High Actual Sales	Low Actual Sales
High forecast sales	0	$10,000
Low forecast sales	$10,000	0

TABLE 2.4　　Forecasting with Asymmetric Loss

	High Actual Sales	Low Actual Sales
High forecast sales	0	$10,000
Low forecast sales	$20,000	0

To recap: for every decision-making problem there is an associated *loss structure;* for each decision/outcome pair there is an associated loss. We can think of the loss associated with the correct decision as zero, with incorrect decisions leading to positive loss.

Recall that *forecasts* are made to help *guide decisions.* Thus the loss structure associated with a particular decision induces a similar loss structure for forecasts used to inform that decision. Continuing with our example, we might forecast sales to help us decide whether to build or reduce inventory, and the loss we incur depends on the divergence between actual and predicted sales. To keep things simple, imagine that sales forecasts and sales realizations are either "high" or "low." Table 2.3 illustrates a symmetric forecasting loss structure, and Table 2.4 illustrates an asymmetric forecasting loss structure. Note that a forecast of high sales implies the decision "build inventory" (likewise for low sales and "reduce inventory"); thus we derive the loss structure associated with a forecast from the loss structure of decisions based on the forecasts.

The above example is highly simplified: forecasts are either "up" or "down" and realizations are similarly "up" or "down." In the important (practical) case of time series forecasting, both the forecast and the realization can typically assume a continuous range of values, so a more general notion of loss function is needed.

Let y denote a series and $\hat{y}$ its forecast. The corresponding **forecast error,** e, is the difference between the realization and the previously made forecast:

$$e = y - \hat{y}$$

We consider loss functions of the form $L(e)$. This means that the loss associated with a forecast depends only on the size of the forecast error. There are three minimal requirements that most reasonable loss functions of this form satisfy:

FIGURE 2.1   Quadratic Loss

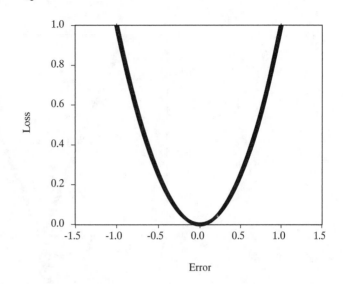

1. $L(0) = 0$. That is, no loss is incurred when the forecast error is zero. (A zero forecast error, after all, corresponds to a perfect forecast!)
2. $L(e)$ is continuous. That is, nearly identical forecast errors should produce nearly identical losses.
3. $L(e)$ increases as the absolute value of e increases. That is, the bigger the absolute size of the error, the bigger the loss.

Apart from these three requirements, we impose no restrictions on the form of the loss function.

As before, we distinguish between symmetric and asymmetric loss functions. A particular symmetric loss function that is tremendously important in practice, both because it is often an adequate approximation to realistic loss structures and because it is mathematically convenient, is

$$L(e) = e^2$$

This is called **quadratic loss,** or **squared-error loss,** illustrated in Figure 2.1. Note that because of the squaring associated with quadratic loss, large errors are *much* more costly than small ones. Equivalently, loss is increasing at an increasing rate on each side of the origin.

Another important symmetric loss function is **absolute loss,** or **absolute error loss,** given by

$$L(e) = |e|$$

FIGURE 2.2   Absolute Loss

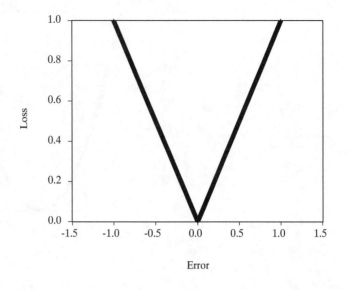

Like quadratic loss, absolute loss is increasing on each side of the origin, but loss increases at a constant (linear) rate with the size of the error. We illustrate absolute loss in Figure 2.2.

In certain contexts, symmetric loss functions may not be an adequate distillation of the forecast/decision environment. In Figure 2.3, for example, we show a particular asymmetric loss function for which negative forecast errors are less costly than positive errors.

In some situations even the $L(e)$ form of the loss function is too restrictive. Although loss will always be of the form $L(y, \hat{y})$, there is no reason why y and $\hat{y}$ should necessarily enter as $y - \hat{y}$. In predicting financial asset returns, for example, interest sometimes focuses on direction of change. A **direction-of-change forecast** takes one of two values—up or down. The loss function associated with a direction-of-change forecast might be:[2]

$$L(y, \hat{y}) = \begin{cases} 0, \text{ if sign}(\Delta y) = \text{sign}(\Delta \hat{y}) \\ 1, \text{ if sign}(\Delta y) \neq \text{sign}(\Delta \hat{y}) \end{cases}$$

With this loss function, if you predict the direction of change correctly, you incur no loss; but if your prediction is wrong, you are penalized.

Much of this book is about how to produce **optimal forecasts.** What precisely do we mean by an optimal forecast? That is where the loss function

2. The operator "Δ" means "change." Thus Δy_t is the change in y from period $t -$ 1 to period t, or $y_t - y_{t-1}$.

FIGURE 2.3   Asymmetric Loss

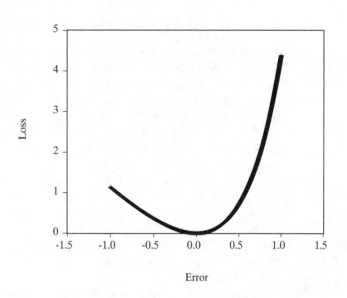

comes in—for a wide class of loss functions, we will figure out how to produce forecasts that are optimal in the sense that they minimize expected loss.

2. THE FORECAST OBJECT

There are many objects that we might want to forecast. In business and economics, the forecast object is typically one of three types: **event outcome, event timing,** or **time series.**

Event outcome forecasts are relevant to situations in which an event is certain to take place at a given time but the outcome of that event is uncertain. For example, many people are interested in whether the current chairman of the board of governors of the U.S. Federal Reserve System will eventually be reappointed. The "event" is the reappointment decision; the decision will occur at the end of the term. The outcome of this decision is confirmation or denial of the reappointment.

Event timing forecasts are relevant when an event is certain to take place and the outcome is known, but the timing is uncertain. A classic example of an event timing forecast concerns business cycle turning points, which are of two types: peaks and troughs. A peak occurs when the economy moves from expansion into recession, and a trough occurs when the economy moves from recession into expansion. If, for example, the economy is currently in an expansion, then there is no doubt that the next turning point will be a peak, but there is substantial uncertainty as to its *timing*. Will the peak occur this quarter? This year? More than four years from now?

Time series forecasts involve projecting the future value of a time series of interest. As we shall see, there are many ways to make such forecasts, but the basic forecasting setup doesn't change much. Based upon the history of the time series (and possibly a variety of other types of information as well, such as the histories of related time series, or subjective considerations), we want to project future values of the series. For example, we may have data on the number of Apple computers sold in Germany in each of the last 60 months, and we may want to use that data to forecast the number of Apple computers to be sold in Germany in each month of the next year.

There are at least two reasons why time series forecasts are by far the most frequently encountered in practice. First, most business, economic, and financial data are time series; thus, the general scenario of projecting the future of a series for which we have historical data arises constantly. Second, the technology for making and evaluating time series forecasts is sufficiently well developed, and the typical time series forecasting scenario is sufficiently precise, such that time series forecasts can routinely be made and evaluated. The situations associated with event outcome and event timing forecasts, in contrast, arise less frequently and are often less amenable to quantitative treatment.

Ultimately, the object to be forecast is a data series of some form or another, and the available quantity of data has important implications for the way we construct forecasting models. When the data sample is very long, for example, we can sometimes afford more intricate forecasting models. In situations of time series forecasting, a related issue concerns the number of series being forecast and the frequency at which forecasts are made. Clearly there is much less opportunity for providing "tender loving care" when forecasting 7,000 series each week than when forecasting 25 series each quarter.

The quality of the data also has implications for the construction of forecasting models. For example, time series data sometimes have missing observations—the data may not exist at certain times (due, for example, to holidays), or may be lost, or may have accidentally not been recorded. One way or another, such defects must be addressed in the construction of forecasting models. Similarly, when multiple series are forecast, in addition to having internally missing observations, the various series may have different starting or ending dates. In addition, unusual observations, whether due to mistakes such as recording errors or simply due to unusual circumstances, are sometimes present and must be addressed.

3. THE FORECAST STATEMENT

When we make a forecast, we must decide if the forecast will be (1) a single number (a "best guess"), (2) a range of numbers into which the future value can be expected to fall a certain percentage of the time, or (3) an entire probability distribution for the future value. In short, we need to decide upon the forecast type.

More precisely, we must decide if the forecast will be (1) a **point forecast,** (2) an **interval forecast,** or (3) a **density forecast.** A point forecast is a single number. For example, one possible point forecast of the growth rate of the total number of web pages over the next year might be + 23.3%; likewise, a point forecast of the growth rate of U.S. real gross domestic product (GDP) over the next year might be + 1.3%. Point forecasts are made routinely in numerous applications, and the methods used to construct them vary in difficulty from simple to sophisticated. The defining characteristic of a point forecast is simply that it is a single number.

A good point forecast provides a simple and easily digested guide to the future of a time series. However, random and unpredictable "shocks" affect all of the series that we forecast. As a result of such shocks, we expect nonzero forecast errors, even from very good forecasts. Thus, we may want to know the degree of confidence we have in a particular point forecast. Stated differently, we may want to know how much uncertainty is associated with a particular point forecast. The uncertainty surrounding point forecasts suggests the usefulness of an interval forecast.

An interval forecast is not a single number; rather, it is a range of values in which we expect the realized value of the series to fall with some (prespecified) probability.[3] Continuing with our examples, a 90% interval forecast for the growth rate of web pages might be the interval [11.3%, 35.3%] (23.3% ± 12%). That is, the forecast states that with probability 90% the future growth rate of web pages will be in the interval [11.3%, 35.3%]. Similarly, a 90% interval forecast for the growth rate of U.S. real GDP might be [−2.3%, 4.3%] (1.3% ± 3%); that is, the forecast states that with probability 90% the future growth rate of U.S. real GDP will be in the interval [−2.3%, 4.3%].

A number of remarks are in order regarding interval forecasts. First, the length (size) of the intervals conveys information regarding forecast uncertainty. The GDP growth rate interval is much shorter then the web page growth rate interval; this reflects the fact that there is less uncertainty associated with the real GDP growth rate forecast than the web page growth rate forecast. Second, interval forecasts convey more information than point forecasts: given an interval forecast, you can construct a point forecast by using

---

3. An interval forecast is very similar to the more general idea of a *confidence interval* in the field of statistics. An interval forecast is simply a confidence interval for the true (but unknown) future value of a series, computed using a sample of historical data. We will say that $[a, b]$ is a $100(1 − \alpha)\%$ interval forecast if the probability of the future value being less than a is $\alpha/2$ and the probability of the future value being greater than b is also $\alpha/2$.

FIGURE 2.4   Web Page Growth: Point, Interval, and Density Forecasts

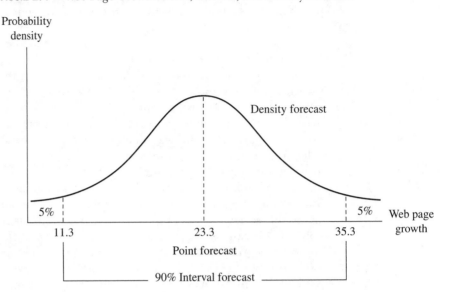

the midpoint of the interval.[4] Conversely, given only a point forecast, there is no way to infer an interval forecast.

Finally, we consider density forecasts. A density forecast gives the entire density (or probability distribution) of the future value of the series of interest. For example, the density forecast of future web page growth might be normally distributed with a mean of 23.3% and a standard deviation of 7.32%. Likewise, the density forecast of future real GDP growth might be normally distributed with a mean of 1.3% and a standard deviation of 1.83%.

As with interval forecasts, density forecasts convey more information than point forecasts. Density forecasts also convey more information than interval forecasts, because given a density, interval forecasts at any desired confidence level are readily constructed. For example, if the future value of some series x is distributed as $N(\mu,\sigma^2)$, then a 95% interval forecast of x is $\mu \pm 1.96\sigma$, a 90% interval forecast of x is $\mu \pm 1.64\sigma$, and so forth. Continuing with our example, the relationships between density, interval, and point forecasts are made clear in Figure 2.4 (web page growth) and Figure 2.5 (U.S. real GDP growth).

To recap, there are three time series forecast types: point, interval, and density. Density forecasts convey more information than interval forecasts, which in turn convey more information than point forecasts. This may seem

---

4. An interval forecast doesn't *have* to be symmetric around the point forecast, so we wouldn't *necessarily* infer a point forecast as the midpoint of the interval forecast, but in many cases such a procedure is appropriate.

FIGURE 2.5   U.S. Real GDP Growth: Point, Interval, and Density Forecasts

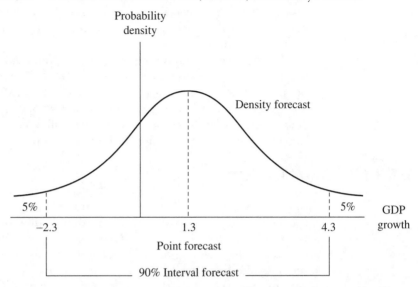

to suggest that density forecasts are always the preferred forecast, that density forecasts are the most commonly used forecasts in practice, and that we should focus most of our attention in this book on density forecasts.

In fact, the opposite is true. Point forecasts are the most commonly used forecasts in practice, interval forecasts are a rather distant second, and density forecasts are rarely made. There are at least two reasons for this. First, the construction of interval and density forecasts requires either (a) additional and possibly incorrect assumptions relative to those required for the construction of point forecasts, or (b) advanced and computer-intensive methods involving, for example, extensive simulation. Second, it is often easier to understand and take action based upon point forecasts relative to interval or density forecasts. The extra information provided by interval and density forecasts is not necessarily an advantage if information processing is costly.

Thus far we have focused exclusively on types of time series forecasts, in light of the tremendous importance of time series throughout the field of forecasting. Another forecast type of particular relevance to event outcome and event timing forecasting is the **probability forecast.** To understand the idea of a probability forecast, consider forecasting which of two politicians, Mr. Liar or Ms. Cheat, will win an election. (This is an event outcome forecasting situation.) If our calculations tell us that the odds favor Mr. Liar, we might issue the forecast simply as "Mr. Liar will win." This is roughly analogous to the time series point forecasts discussed earlier in the sense that we are not reporting any measure of the *uncertainty* associated with our forecast. Alternatively, we could report the probabilities associated with each of the possible outcomes; for example, "Mr. Liar will win with probability 0.6, and

Ms. Cheat will win with probability 0.4." This is roughly analogous to the time series interval or density forecasts discussed earlier in the sense that it explicitly quantifies the uncertainty associated with the future event with a probability distribution.

Event outcome and timing forecasts, although not as common as time series forecasts, do nevertheless arise in certain important situations and are often stated as probabilities. For example, when a bank assesses the probability of default on a new loan, or when a macroeconomist assesses the probability that a business cycle turning point will occur in the next six months, the banker or macroeconomist will often use a probability forecast.

4. THE FORECAST HORIZON

The forecast horizon is defined as the number of periods between today and the date of the forecast we make. For example, if we have annual data, and it is now year T, then a forecast of GDP for year $T + 2$ has a forecast horizon of two steps. The meaning of a step depends on the frequency of observation of the data. For monthly data, a step is one month; for quarterly data, a step is one quarter (three months); and so forth. In general, we speak of an **h-step-ahead forecast,** for which the horizon h is at the discretion of the user.[5]

The horizon is important for at least two reasons. First, of course, the forecast changes with the forecast horizon. Second, the best forecasting model will often change with the forecasting horizon as well. All of our forecasting models are approximations to the underlying dynamic patterns in the series we forecast; there is no reason why the best approximation for one purpose (e.g., short-term forecasting) should be the same as the best approximation for another purpose (e.g., long-term forecasting).

In closing this section, let us distinguish between what we call *h*-step-ahead forecasts and what we call **h-step-ahead extrapolation forecasts.** In *h*-step-ahead forecasts, the horizon is always fixed at the same value, *h*. For example, every month we might make a 4-month-ahead forecast. Alternatively, in extrapolation forecasts, the horizon includes all steps from 1-step-ahead to *h*-steps-ahead. There is nothing particularly deep or difficult about the distinction, but it is useful to make it, and we will use it subsequently.

Suppose, for example, that you observe a series from some initial time 1 to some final time T, and you plan to forecast the series.[6] We illustrate the

---

5. The choice of h depends on the decision that the forecast will guide. The nature of the decision environment typically dictates whether "short-term," "medium-term," or "long-term" forecasts are needed.

6. For a sample of data on a series y, we typically write $\{y_t\}_{t=1}^{T}$. This notation means, "we observe the series y from some beginning time "$t = 1$" to some ending time "$t = T$".

FIGURE 2.6   4-Step-Ahead Point Forecast

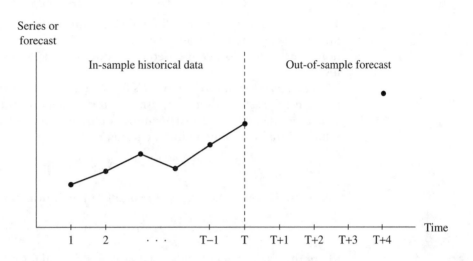

difference between *h*-step-ahead and *h*-step-ahead extrapolation forecasts in Figures 2.6 and 2.7. In Figure 2.6 we show a 4-step-ahead point forecast, and in Figure 2.7 we show a 4-step-ahead extrapolation point forecast. The extrapolation forecast is nothing more than a set consisting of 1-, 2-, 3-, and 4-step-ahead forecasts.

FIGURE 2.7   4-Step-Ahead Extrapolation Point Forecast

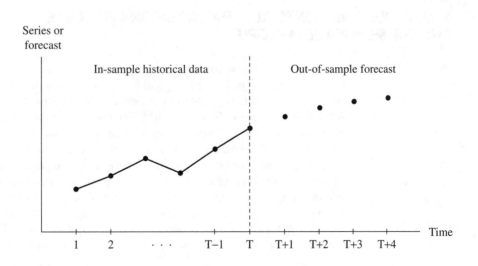

5. THE INFORMATION SET

The quality of our forecasts is limited by the quality and quantity of information available when forecasts are made. Any forecast we produce is conditional upon the information used to produce it, whether explicitly or implicitly.

The idea of an information set is fundamental to constructing good forecasts. In forecasting a series, y, using historical data from time 1 to time T, sometimes we use the univariate information set, which is the set of historical values of y up to and including the present,

$$\Omega_T^{univariate} = \left\{ y_T, y_{T-1}, \ldots, y_1 \right\}$$

Alternatively, sometimes we use the multivariate information set

$$\Omega_T^{multivariate} = \left\{ y_T, x_T, y_{T-1}, x_{T-1}, \ldots, y_1, x_1 \right\}$$

where the x's are a set of additional variables potentially related to y. Regardless, it is always important to seriously consider what information is available, what additional information could be collected or made available, the form of the information (e.g., quantitative or qualitative), and so on.

The idea of an information set is also fundamental for evaluating forecasts. When evaluating a forecast, we are sometimes interested in whether the forecast could be improved by using a given set of information more efficiently, and we are sometimes interested in whether the forecast could be improved by using more information. Either way, the ideas of information and information sets play crucial roles in forecasting.

6. METHODS AND COMPLEXITY, THE PARSIMONY PRINCIPLE, AND THE SHRINKAGE PRINCIPLE

It is crucial to tailor forecasting tools to forecasting tasks, and doing so is partly a matter of judgment. Typically the specifics of the situation (e.g., decision environment, forecast object, forecast statement, forecast horizon, information set, and so forth) will indicate the desirability of a specific method or modeling strategy. Moreover, as we shall see, formal statistical criteria exist to guide model selection within certain classes of models.

We have stressed that a variety of forecasting applications use a small set of common tools and models. You might guess that those models are tremendously complex, in light of the obvious complexity of the real-world phenomena we seek to forecast. Fortunately, such is not the case. In fact, decades of professional experience suggest just the opposite—simple, parsimonious models tend to be best for out-of-sample forecasting in business, finance, and economics. Hence, the **parsimony principle:** other things the same, simple models are preferable to complex models.

There are a number of reasons why smaller, simpler models are often more attractive than larger, more complicated ones. First, by virtue of their parsimony, we can estimate the parameters of simpler models more precisely. Second, because simpler models are more easily interpreted, understood, and scrutinized, anomalous behavior is more easily spotted. Third, it is easier to communicate an intuitive feel for the behavior of simple models, which makes them more useful in the decision-making process. Finally, enforcing simplicity lessens the scope for "data mining"—tailoring a model to maximize its fit to historical data. Data mining often results in models that fit historical data beautifully (by construction) but perform miserably in out-of-sample forecasting, because it tailors models in part to the *idiosyncracies* of historical data, which have no relationship to future, as-yet-unrealized, data.

The parsimony principle is related to, but distinct from, the **shrinkage principle,** which codifies the idea that imposing restrictions on forecasting models often improves forecast performance. The name "shrinkage" comes from the notion of coaxing, or "shrinking," forecasts in certain directions by imposing restrictions of various sorts on the models used to produce the forecasts.[7] It seems obvious that imposing *correct* restrictions should be helpful; the shrinkage principle, however, goes further: it may also be helpful to impose *incorrect* restrictions. The reasoning behind the shrinkage principle is subtle, and it permeates forecasting; by the time you have completed this book you will have a firm grasp of it.

Finally, note that simple models, of course, should not be confused with naive models. All of this is well formalized in the **KISS principle** (appropriately modified for forecasting): "Keep it Sophisticatedly Simple." We attempt to do so throughout this book.

7. CONCLUDING REMARKS

This chapter, like chapter 1, deals with broad issues of general relevance. For the most part, it avoids detailed discussion of specific modeling or forecasting techniques. In the next chapter, we begin to change the mix toward specific tools with specific applications. In the broad-brush tradition of chapters 1 and 2, we next focus on principles of statistical graphics that are relevant in any forecasting situation; but in contrast to chapters 1 and 2, we also introduce a number of specific graphical techniques that are useful in a variety of situations.

---

7. One such restriction is that, loosely speaking, forecasting models be simple; hence the link to the parsimony principle.

PROBLEMS AND COMPLEMENTS

1. (Forecasting as an ongoing process in organizations) We could add another very important item to this chapter's list of considerations basic to successful forecasting—forecasting in organizations is an ongoing process of building, using, evaluating, and improving forecast models. Provide a concrete example of a forecasting model used in business, finance, economics, or government, and discuss ways in which each of the following questions might be resolved prior to, during, or after its construction.

   (a) Are the data "dirty"? For example, are there **"ragged edges"**? That is, do the starting and ending dates of relevant series differ? Are there **missing observations**? Are there aberrant observations, called **outliers,** perhaps due to **measurement error**? Are the data in a format that inhibits computer analysis?

   (b) Has software been written for importing the data in an ongoing forecasting operation?

   (c) Who will build and maintain the model?

   (d) Are sufficient resources (time, money, staff) available to facilitate model building, use, evaluation, and improvement on a routine and ongoing basis?

   (e) How much time remains before the first forecast must be produced?

   (f) How many series must be forecast, and how often must ongoing forecasts be produced?

   (g) What level of **aggregation** or **disaggregation** is desirable?

   (h) To whom does the forecaster or forecasting group report and how will the forecasts be communicated?

   (i) How might you conduct a "forecasting audit"?

2. (Assessing forecasting situations) For each of the following scenarios, discuss the decision environment, the nature of the object to be forecast, the forecast type, the forecast horizon, the loss function, the information set, and what sorts of simple or complex forecasting approaches you might entertain.

   (a) You work for Airborne Analytics, a highly specialized mutual fund investing exclusively in airline stocks. The stocks held by the fund are chosen based on your recommendations. You learn that a newly rich oil-producing country has requested bids on a huge contract to deliver 30 state-of-the-art fighter planes, and moreover, that only two companies have submitted bids. The stock of the successful bidder is likely to rise.

   (b) You work for the Office of Management and Budget in Washington, D.C., and must forecast tax revenues for the upcoming fiscal year. You work for a president who wants to maintain funding for his pilot social programs, and high revenue forecasts ensure that the programs keep their funding. However, if the forecast is too high, and the president runs a large deficit at the end of the year, he will be seen as fiscally irresponsible, which will lessen his probability of re-election. Furthermore, your forecast will be scrutinized by the more conservative members of Congress; if they find fault with your procedures, they might have fiscal grounds to undermine the president's planned budget.

(c) You work for D&D, a major Los Angeles advertising firm, and you must create an ad for a client's product. The ad must be targeted toward teenagers, because they constitute the primary market for the product. You must (somehow) find out what teens currently think is "cool," incorporate that information into your ad, and make your client's product attractive to the new generation. If your hunch is right— Michael Jackson has still got it!—your firm basks in glory, and you can expect multiple future clients from this one advertisement. If you miss, however, and the teens don't respond to the ad, then your client's sales fall and the client may reduce or even close its account with you.

BIBLIOGRAPHICAL AND COMPUTATIONAL NOTES

Klein (1971) and Granger and Newbold (1986) contain a wealth of insightful (but more advanced) discussion of many of the topics presented in this chapter. The links between forecasts and decisions are clearly displayed in many of the chapters of Makridakis and Wheelwright (1987). Armstrong (1978) provides entertaining and insightful discussion of many of the specialized issues and techniques relevant in long-horizon forecasting. Several of the papers in Diebold and Watson (1996) concern the use of loss functions tailored to the decision-making situation of interest, both with respect to the forecast horizon and with respect to the shape of the loss function. Zellner (1992) provides an insightful statement of the KISS principle, which is very much related to the parsimony principle of Box and Jenkins (see Box, Jenkins, and Reinsel, 1994). Levenbach and Cleary (1984) contains useful discussion of forecasting as an ongoing process.

CONCEPTS FOR REVIEW

Absolute error loss   Interval forecast
Absolute loss   KISS principle
Aggregation   Loss function
Asymmetric loss   Measurement error

Decision environment
Density forecast
Direction-of-change forecast
Disaggregation
Event outcome forecast
Event timing forecast
Forecast error
Forecast horizon
Forecast object
Forecast statement
h-step-ahead extrapolation
   forecast
h-step-ahead forecast
Information set

Methods and complexity
Missing observations
Optimal forecast
Outlier
Parsimony principle
Point forecast
Probability forecast
Quadratic loss
Ragged edges
Shrinkage principle
Squared-error loss
Symmetric loss
Time series forecast

REFERENCES AND ADDITIONAL READINGS

Armstrong, J. S. (1978), *Long Run Forecasting: From Crystal Ball to Computer.* New York: Wiley.

Box, G. E. P., Jenkins, G. W., and Reinsel, G. (1994), *Time Series Analysis, Forecasting and Control,* third edition. Englewood Cliffs, N.J.: Prentice Hall.

Diebold, F. X., and Watson, M. W., eds. (1996), New Developments in Economic Forecasting, special issue of *Journal of Applied Econometrics,* 11, 453–594.

Granger, C. W. J., and Newbold, P. (1986), *Forecasting Economic Time Series,* second edition. Orlando, Fla.: Academic Press.

Klein, L. R. (1971), *An Essay on the Theory of Economic Prediction.* Chicago: Markham Publishing Company.

Levenbach, H., and Cleary, J. P. (1984), *The Modern Forecaster.* Belmont, Calif.: Lifetime Learning Publications.

Makridakis, S., and Wheelwright, S. (1987), *The Handbook of Forecasting: A Manager's Guide,* second edition. New York: Wiley.

Zellner, A. (1992), "Statistics, Science and Public Policy," *Journal of the American Statistical Association,* 87, 1–6.

STATISTICAL GRAPHICS FOR FORECASTING

1. WHY GRAPHICAL ANALYSIS IS IMPORTANT

It is almost always a good idea to begin forecasting projects with graphical analysis. When compared to the modern array of statistical modeling methods, graphical analysis might seem so simple and straightforward as to be incapable of delivering serious insights into the series to be forecast. Such is not the case: In many respects the human eye is a far more sophisticated tool for data analysis and modeling than the most sophisticated of modern modeling techniques. That is certainly not to say that graphical analysis alone will get the job done—graphics has plenty of limitations of its own—but it is usually the best place to *start*.

The four datasets shown in Table 3.1, known as **Anscombe's quartet,** provide stark illustration of the power of statistical graphics. Each dataset consists of 11 observations on two variables. Simply glancing at the data—or even studying it with some care—yields little insight. Of course, you say, but that is why we have powerful modern statistical techniques, such as the linear regression model. So let us regress y on x for each of the four datasets. The results appear in Table 3.2. Interestingly enough, although the four datasets certainly contain different numerical data values, the standard linear regression output is identical in each case. First, the fitted regression line is the same in each case, $y = 3 + \frac{1}{2}x$. Second, the uncertainty associated with the estimated parameters, as summarized by standard errors, is also the same in

TABLE 3.1   Anscombe's Quartet

(1)		(2)		(3)		(4)	
x1	y1	x2	y2	x3	y3	x4	y4
10.0	8.04	10.0	9.14	10.0	7.46	8.0	6.58
8.0	6.95	8.0	8.14	8.0	6.77	8.0	5.76
13.0	7.58	13.0	8.74	13.0	12.74	8.0	7.71
9.0	8.81	9.0	8.77	9.0	7.11	8.0	8.84
11.0	8.33	11.0	9.26	11.0	7.81	8.0	8.47
14.0	9.96	14.0	8.10	14.0	8.84	8.0	7.04
6.0	7.24	6.0	6.13	6.0	6.08	8.0	5.25
4.0	4.26	4.0	3.10	4.0	5.39	19.0	12.50
12.0	10.84	12.0	9.13	12.0	8.15	8.0	5.56
7.0	4.82	7.0	7.26	7.0	6.42	8.0	7.91
5.0	5.68	5.0	4.74	5.0	5.73	8.0	6.89

each dataset. Hence the t statistics, which are simply ratios of estimated coefficients to their standard errors, are also identical across datasets. Third, R^2, which is the percentage of variation in y explained by variation in x, is identical across datasets. Fourth, the sum of squared residuals, and hence the standard error of the regression (the estimated standard deviation of the stochastic disturbance to the linear regression relationship) is the same in each dataset.

That's all fine, too, you say—the relationship between y and x is simply the same in each dataset, even though the specific data differ due to random influences. The assertion that the relationship between y and x is the same in each dataset *could* be correct, but graphical examination of the data reveals immediately that it is *not* correct. In Figure 3.1, we show graphs of y vs. x (called **pairwise scatterplots,** or **bivariate scatterplots**) for each of the four datasets, with fitted regression lines superimposed. Although the fitted regression line *is* the same in each case, the reasons differ greatly, and it is clear that for most of the datasets the linear regression model is not appropriate.

In dataset 1, all looks well. $y1$ and $x1$ are clearly positively correlated, and they appear to conform rather well to a linear relationship, although the relationship is certainly not perfect. In short, all the conditions of the classical linear regression model appear satisfied in dataset 1.

In dataset 2, the situation is very different. The graph reveals that there is certainly a relationship between $y2$ and $x2$—perhaps even a deterministic

TABLE 3.2   Anscombe's Quartet: Regressions of yi on xi, $i = 1, \ldots, 4$

LS // Dependent Variable is Y1

Variable	Coefficient	Std. Error	T-Statistic
C	3.00	1.12	2.67
X1	0.50	0.12	4.24

R-squared	0.67	S.E. of regression	1.24

LS // Dependent Variable is Y2

Variable	Coefficient	Std. Error	T-Statistic
C	3.00	1.12	2.67
X2	0.50	0.12	4.24

R-squared	0.67	S.E. of regression	1.24

LS // Dependent Variable is Y3

Variable	Coefficient	Std. Error	T-Statistic
C	3.00	1.12	2.67
X3	0.50	0.12	4.24

R-squared	0.67	S.E. of regression	1.24

LS // Dependent Variable is Y4

Variable	Coefficient	Std. Error	T-Statistic
C	3.00	1.12	2.67
X4	0.50	0.12	4.24

R-squared	0.67	S.E. of regression	1.24

relationship—but it also makes clear that the relationship is not at all linear. Thus, the use of the linear regression model is not desirable in dataset 2.

In dataset 3, the graphics indicate that although y and x do seem to conform to a linear relationship, there is one key $(y3, x3)$ pair that doesn't conform well to the linear relationship. Most likely you never noticed that data

FIGURE 3.1   Anscombe's Quartet: Bivariate Scatterplots

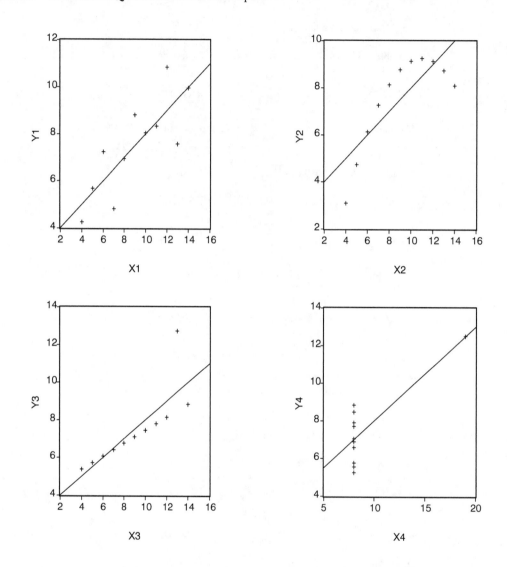

point when you simply examined the raw data in tabular form, in spite of the fact that it is visually obvious when we make use of graphics.

Datset 4 is rather odd—the (y4,x4) pairs are all stacked vertically, with the exception of one point, which exerts a huge influence on the fitted regression line. At any rate, the graphics once again makes the anomalous nature of this situation immediately apparent.

Let us summarize what we have learned about the power of graphics:

1. *Graphics helps us summarize and reveal patterns in data,* as, for example, with linear versus nonlinear functional form in the first and second Anscombe datasets. That is key in any forecasting project.

2. *Graphics helps us identify anomalies in data,* as in the third Anscombe dataset. That is also key in forecasting, because we will produce our forecasts from models fit to the historical data, and the dictum "garbage in, garbage out" most definitely applies.

3. Less obvious, but most definitely relevant, is the fact that *graphics facilitates and encourages comparison of different pieces of data.* That is why, for example, we graphed all four datasets in one figure. By doing so, we facilitate effortless and instantaneous cross-dataset comparison of statistical relationships. This technique is called **multiple comparisons.**

4. There is one more aspect of the power of statistical graphics. It comes into play in the analysis of large datasets, so it wasn't revealed in the analysis of the Anscombe datasets, which are not large, but it is nevertheless tremendously important. *Graphics enables us to present a huge amount of data in a small space, and it enables us to make huge datasets coherent.* We might, for example, have supermarket-scanner data, recorded in five-minute intervals for a year, on the quantities of goods sold in each of four food categories—dairy, meat, grains, and vegetables. Tabular or similar analysis of such data is simply out of the question, but graphics are straightforward and can reveal important patterns.

2. SIMPLE GRAPHICAL TECHNIQUES

As we discussed in chapter 2, time series are by far the most common objects for which forecasts are made. Thus, we will focus primarily on graphics useful for modeling and forecasting time series. The dimensionality of the data—the number of time series we wish to examine—plays a key role. Because graphical analysis "lets the data speak for themselves," it is most useful when the dimensionality of the data is low. We segment the following discussion into two parts: univariate and multivariate.

Univariate Graphics

First and foremost, graphics is used to reveal the patterns in time series data. We use graphical analysis to get a preliminary and informal idea of the nature of trend, seasonality, and cycles, as well as the nature and location of any unusual or aberrant observations, structural breaks, and so forth. The great workhorse of univariate time series graphics is the simple **time series plot,** in which the series of interest is graphed against time.

FIGURE 3.2   1-Year Treasury Bond Rate

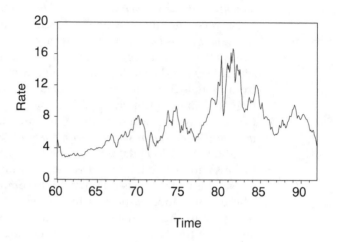

In Figure 3.2, for example, we present a time series plot of the 1-year U.S. Treasury bond rate, 1960.01–1991.12.[1] A number of important features of the series are apparent. Among other things, its movements appear sluggish and persistent, it appears to trend gently upward until about 1980, and it appears to trend gently downward thereafter.

Figure 3.3 provides a different perspective; we plot the *change* in the 1-year T-bond rate, which highlights volatility fluctuations. Interest rate volatility appears low in the 1960s, a bit higher in the 1970s, and very high from late 1979 through late 1982 (the period during which the Federal Reserve targeted a monetary aggregate, which had the side effect of increasing interest rate volatility), after which volatility gradually declines.

Time series plots are helpful for learning about other features of time series as well. In Figure 3.4, for example, we show a time series plot of U.S. liquor sales, 1967.01–1994.12. Clearly they are trending upward, but the plot indicates that there may be a break in the trend sometime during the 1980s. In addition, the plot makes clear the pronounced seasonality in the series— liquor sales skyrocket every December—and moreover that the volatility of the seasonal fluctuations grows over time as the level of the series increases.

Univariate graphical techniques are also routinely used to assess distributional shape. A **histogram,** for example, provides a simple estimate of the probability density of a random variable. The observed range of variation of the series is split into a number of segments of equal length, and the height of the bar placed at a segment is the percentage of observations falling in

---

1. The notation "1960.01–1991.12" means the first month of 1960 through the twelfth month of 1991.

FIGURE 3.3   Change in 1-Year Treasury Bond Rate

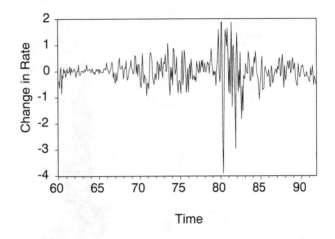

FIGURE 3.4   Liquor Sales

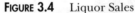

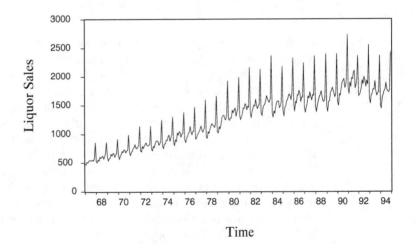

that segment.[2] In Figure 3.5 we show a histogram for the change in the 1-year T-bond rate with related diagnostic information. The histogram indicates that the series is roughly symmetrically distributed, and the additional statis-

---

2. In some software packages (e.g., Eviews), the height of the bar placed at a segment is simply the number, not the percentage, of observations falling in that segment. Strictly speaking, such histograms are not density estimators because the "area under the curve" doesn't add to one, but they are equally useful for summarizing the shape of the density.

FIGURE 3.5   Change in 1-Year Treasury Bond Rate:
Histogram and Descriptive Statistics

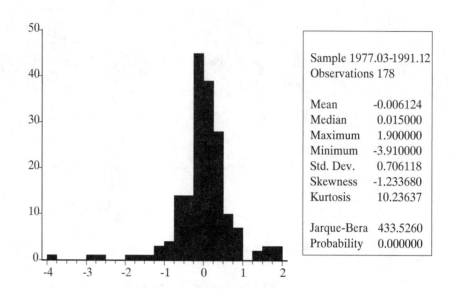

tics such as the sample mean, median, maximum, minimum, and standard deviation convey important additional information about the distribution.

For example, a key feature of the distribution of T-bond rate changes, which may not have been immediately apparent from the histogram, is that it has fatter tails than would be the case under normality. This is at once apparent from the kurtosis statistic, which would be approximately 3 if the data were normally distributed. Instead, it is about 10, indicating much fatter tails than the normal, which is very common in high-frequency financial data. The skewness statistic is modestly negative, indicating a rather long left tail. The Jarque-Bera normality test rejects the hypothesis of independent normally distributed observations. The rejection occurs because the interest rate changes are not independent, not normally distributed, or both. It is likely both, and the deviation from normality is due more to leptokurtosis than to asymmetry.[3]

Multivariate Graphics

When two or more variables are available, the possibility of relations among the variables becomes important, and we use graphics to uncover the existence and nature of such relationships. We use **relational graphics** to display

---

3. The rejection could also occur because the sample size is too small to invoke the large-sample theory on which the Jarque-Bera test is based, but that is not likely in the present application, for which we have quite a large sample of data.

FIGURE 3.6   Scatterplot: 1-Year vs. 10-Year Treasury Bond Rate

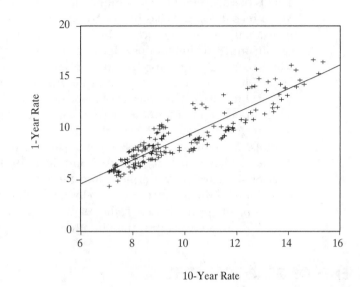

relationships and flag anomalous observations. You already understand the idea of a bivariate scatterplot—we used it extensively to uncover relationships and anomalies in the Anscombe data.[4] In Figure 3.6, for example, we show a bivariate scatterplot of the 1-year U.S. Treasury bond rate versus the 10-year U.S. Treasury bond rate, 1977.03–1991.12. The scatterplot indicates that the two move closely together. Although each of the rates is individually highly persistent, the deviations from the superimposed regression line appear transient. You can think of the line as perhaps representing long-run equilibrium relationships, to which the variables tend to cling.

The regression line that we superimpose on a scatterplot of y vs. x is an attempt to summarize how the conditional mean of y varies with x. Under certain conditions that we discuss in later chapters, this conditional mean is the best point forecast of y. Thus, you can think of the regression line as summarizing how our best point forecast of y varies with x. The linear regression model involves a lot of structure (it assumes that $E(y \mid x)$ is a linear function of x), but less structured approaches exist and are often used to provide potentially nonlinear estimates of conditional mean functions for superimposition on scatterplots.

---

4. Just as in our analysis of the Anscombe data, we often make bivariate scatterplots with fitted regression lines superimposed, to help us visually assess the adequacy of a linear model. Note that although superimposing a regression line is helpful in bivariate scatterplots, "connecting the dots" is not. This contrasts to time series plots, for which connecting the dots is fine and is typically done.

Thus far all of our discussion of multivariate graphics has been bivariate. That is because graphical techniques are best suited to low-dimensional data. Much recent research has been devoted to graphical techniques for high-dimensional data, but all such high-dimensional graphical analysis is subject to certain inherent limitations. Here we discuss just one simple and popular scatterplot technique for high-dimensional data—and one that has been around for a long time—the **scatterplot matrix,** or **multiway scatterplot.** The scatterplot matrix is just the set of all possible bivariate scatterplots, arranged in the upper right or lower left part of a matrix to facilitate multiple comparisons. If we have data on N variables, there are $(N^2 - N)/2$ such pairwise scatterplots. In Figure 3.7, for example, we show a scatterplot matrix for the 1-, 10-, 20-, and 30-year U.S. Treasury bond rates, 1977.03–1991.12. There are a total of six pairwise scatterplots, and the multiple comparison makes clear that although the interest rates are closely related in each case, with a regression slope of approximately 1, the relationship is more precise in some cases (e.g., 20- and 30-year rates) than in others (e.g., 1- and 30-year rates).

3. ELEMENTS OF GRAPHICAL STYLE

In the preceding section we discussed various graphical tools. As with all tools, however, graphical tools can be used effectively or ineffectively. In this section you will learn what makes good graphics good and bad graphics bad. In so doing you will also learn to use graphical tools effectively.

Bad graphics is like obscenity: it is hard to define, but you know it when you see it. Conversely, producing good graphics is like good writing: it is an iterative, trial-and-error procedure, and very much an art rather than a science. But that is not to say that anything goes; as with good writing, good graphics requires discipline. There are at least three keys to good graphics:

1. Know your audience, and know your goals.
2. Understand and follow two fundamental principles: Show the data and appeal to the viewer.
3. Revise and edit, again and again.

We can use a number of devices to *show the data.* First, avoid distorting the data or misleading the viewer. Thus, for example, avoid changing scales in midstream, use common scales when performing multiple comparisons, and so on. Second, minimize, within reason, **nondata ink.**[5] Avoid **chartjunk**

---

5. Nondata ink is ink used to depict anything other than data points.

FIGURE 3.7 Scatterplot Matrix: 1-, 10-, 20-, and 30-Year Treasury Bond Rates

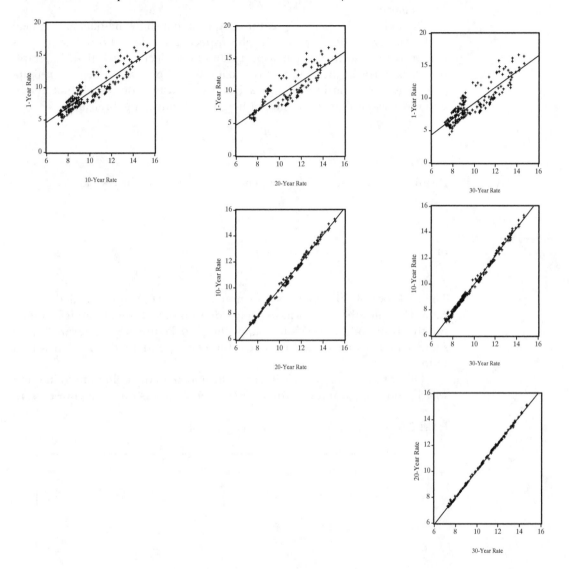

(elaborate shadings and grids, decoration, and related nonsense), erase unnecessary axes, refrain from using an artificial three-dimensional perspective,
and so forth.

Other guidelines help us *appeal to the viewer*. First, use clear and modest
type, avoid mnemonics and abbreviations, and use labels rather then legends
when possible. Second, make graphics self-contained; a knowledgeable
reader should be able to understand your graphics without reading pages of

accompanying text. Third, as with our prescriptions for showing the data, avoid chartjunk.

An additional aspect of creating graphics that show the data and appeal to the viewer is selection of a graph's **aspect ratio,** the ratio of the graph's height, h, to its width, w. The aspect should be selected such that the graph reveals patterns in the data and is visually appealing. One time-honored approach geared toward visual appeal is to use an aspect ratio such that height is to width as width is to the sum of height and width. Algebraically,

$$\frac{h}{w} = a = \frac{w}{h + w}$$

Dividing numerator and denominator of the right side by w yields

$$a = \frac{1}{a + 1}$$

or

$$a^2 + a - 1 = 0$$

The real root of this quadratic polynomial is $a = 0.618$, the so-called **golden ratio.** Graphics that conform to the golden ratio, with height a bit less than two-thirds of width, are visually appealing. In Figure 3.8, for example, we show a plot whose dimensions roughly correspond to the golden aspect ratio.

Other things the same, it is a good idea to keep the golden ratio in mind when producing graphics. Other things are not always the same, however. In

FIGURE 3.8   Time Series Plot with Aspect Ratio 1:1.6

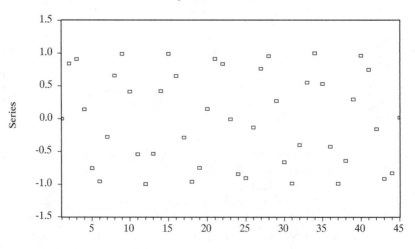

Time

FIGURE 3.9 Time Series Plot of Figure 3.8 Banked to 45 Degrees

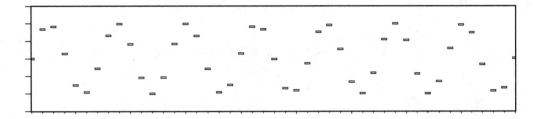

particular, the golden aspect ratio may not be the one that maximizes pattern revelation. Consider Figure 3.9, for example, in which we plot exactly the same data as in Figure 3.8, but with a smaller aspect ratio. The new plot reveals an obvious pattern in the data, which you probably didn't notice before, and is therefore a superior graphic.

The improved aspect ratio of Figure 3.9 was selected to make the average absolute slope of the line segments connecting the data points approximately equal to 45 degrees. This procedure, **banking to 45 degrees,** is useful for selecting a revealing aspect ratio. As in Figure 3.9, the most revealing aspect ratio for time series—especially long time series—is often less than the golden ratio. Sometimes, however, various devices can be used to maintain the golden aspect ratio while nevertheless clearly revealing patterns in the data. In Figure 3.10, for example, we use the golden aspect ratio but connect the data points, which makes the pattern clear.

FIGURE 3.10 Time Series Plot with Aspect Ratio 1:1.6 and Data Points Connected

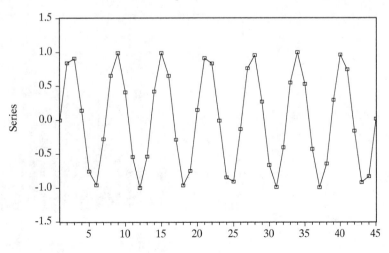

Time

4. APPLICATION: GRAPHING FOUR COMPONENTS OF REAL GDP

As with writing, the best way to learn graphics is to do it, so let us proceed immediately with an application that illustrates various points of graphical style. We examine four key components of U.S. real GDP: manufacturing, retail, services and agriculture, recorded annually 1960–1989 in millions of 1982 dollars.

We begin in Figure 3.11 with a set of bar graphs. The value of each series in each year is represented by the height of a vertical bar, with different bar shadings for the different series. The graph is unappealing and unreadable, with no title, no axis numbering or labels, bad mnemonics, and so on. The good news is that there is plenty of room for improvement.

We continue in Figure 3.12 with a set of stacked bar graphs, which are a bit easier to read because there is only one bar at each time point rather than four, but otherwise they suffer from all the defects of the bar graphs in Figure 3.11. Typically, bar graphs are simply not good graphical tools for time series. We therefore switch in Figure 3.13 to a time series plot with different types of lines and symbols for each series, which is a big improvement, but there is plenty of room for additional improvement.

In Figure 3.14 we drop the symbols and we add axis numbering. This is a major improvement, but the plot is still poor. In particular, it still has bad mnemonics, no title, and no axis labels. Moreover, it is not clear that dropping the plotting symbols produced an improvement, even though they are nondata ink. (Why?)

FIGURE 3.11

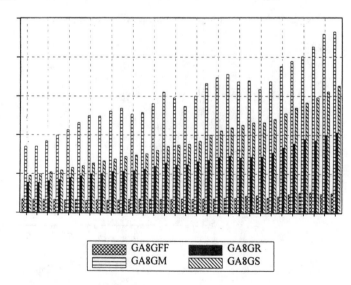

FIGURE 3.12

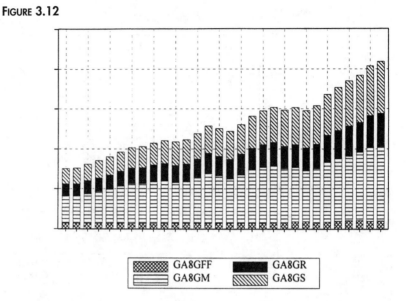

In Figure 3.15, we drop the different plotting lines and symbols alto-
gether. Instead, we simply plot all the series with solid lines and label them
directly. This approach produces a much more informative and appealing
plot, in large part because there no longer is a need for the hideous legend
and associated mnemonics. However, a new annoyance has been introduced:
the CAPITAL series labeling is unappealing.

FIGURE 3.13

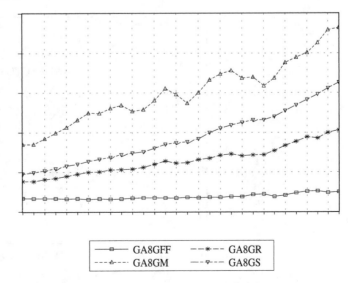

FIGURE 3.14

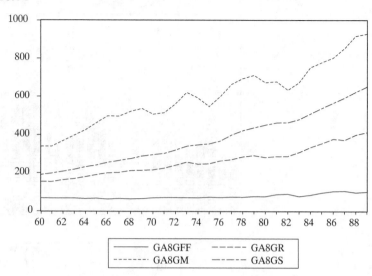

In Figure 3.16 we attempt to remedy the remaining defects of the plot. Both the horizontal and vertical axes are labeled, all labeling makes use of both capital and lower-case type as appropriate, the northern and eastern box lines have been eliminated (they are nondata ink and serve no useful purpose), the plot has a descriptive title, and, for visual reference, we have added shading to indicate recessions.

FIGURE 3.15

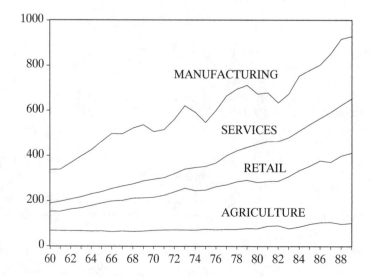

FIGURE **3.16**   Components of Real GDP (Millions of 1982 Dollars, Annual)

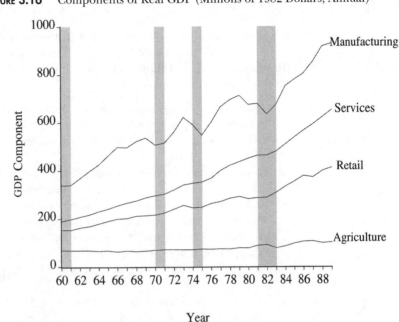

Year

5. CONCLUDING REMARKS

We have emphasized in this chapter that graphics is a powerful tool with a variety of uses in the construction and evaluation of forecasts and forecasting models. We hasten to add, however, that graphics has its limitations. In particular, graphics loses a lot of its power as the dimension of the data grows. If we have data in 10 dimensions, and we try to squash it into two or three dimensions to make a graph, there is bound to be some information loss. That is also true of the models we fit—a linear regression model with 10 right-hand-side variables, for example, assumes that the data tend to lie in a small subset of 10-dimensional space.

Thus, in contrast to the analysis of data in two or three dimensions—in which case learning about data by fitting models involves a loss of information whereas graphical analysis does not—graphical methods lose their comparative advantage in higher dimensions. In higher dimensions, *both* graphics and models lose information, and graphical analysis can become comparatively laborious and less insightful. The conclusion, however, is straightforward: graphical analysis and model fitting are complements, not substitutes, and when used together they can make valuable contributions to forecasting.

PROBLEMS AND COMPLEMENTS

1. (**Outliers**) Recall the lower-left panel of the multiple comparison plot of the Anscombe data (Figure 3.1), which made clear that dataset number three contained a severely anomalous observation. We call such data points "outliers."

   (a) Outliers require special attention because they can have substantial influence on the fitted regression line. Regression parameter estimates obtained by least squares are particularly susceptible to such distortions. Why?

   (b) Outliers can arise for a number of reasons. Perhaps the outlier is simply a mistake due to a clerical recording error, in which case you would want to replace the incorrect data with the correct data. We call such outliers **measurement outliers,** because they simply reflect measurement errors. If a particular value of a recorded series is plagued by a measurement outlier, there is no reason why observations at other times should necessarily be affected. But they *might* be affected. Why?

   (c) Alternatively, outliers in time series may be associated with large un-anticipated shocks, the effects of which may linger. If, for example, an adverse shock hits the U.S. economy this quarter (e.g., the price of oil on the world market triples) and the United States plunges into a severe depression, then it is likely that the depression will persist for some time. Such outliers are called **innovation outliers** because they are driven by shocks, or "innovations," whose effects naturally last more than one period due to the dynamics operative in business, economic, and financial series.

   (d) How to identify and treat outliers is a time-honored problem in data analysis, and there is no easy answer. What factors would you, as a forecaster, examine when deciding what to do with an outlier?

2. (Simple versus partial correlation) The set of pairwise scatterplots that comprises a multiway scatterplot provides useful information about the joint distribution of the N variables, but this is incomplete information and should be interpreted with care. A pairwise scatterplot summarizes information regarding the **simple correlation** between, say, x and y. But x and y may appear highly related in a pairwise scatterplot even if they are in fact unrelated, if each depends on a third variable, say z. The crux of the problem is that there is no way in a pairwise scatterplot to examine the correlation between x and y *controlling* for z, which we call **partial correlation.** When interpreting a scatterplot matrix, keep in mind that the pairwise scatterplots provide information only on simple correlation.

3. (Graphical regression diagnostic I: time series plot of y_t, $\hat{y}_t$, and e_t) After estimating a forecasting model, we often make use of graphical tech-

niques to provide important diagnostic information regarding the adequacy of the model. Often these graphical techniques involve the residuals from the model. Throughout, let the regression model be

$$y_t = \sum_{i=1}^{k} \beta_i \, x_{it} + \varepsilon_t$$

and let the fitted values be

$$\hat{y}_t = \sum_{i=1}^{k} \hat{\beta}_i \, x_{it}$$

The difference between the actual and fitted values is the residual,

$$e_t = y_t - \hat{y}_t$$

(a) Superimposed time series plots of y_t and $\hat{y}_t$ help us to assess the overall fit of a forecasting model and to assess variations in its performance at different times (e.g., performance in tracking peaks versus
troughs in the business cycle).

(b) A time series plot of e_t (a so-called residual plot) helps to reveal patterns in the residuals. Most important, it helps us assess whether the
residuals are correlated over time—that is, whether the residuals are
serially correlated—as well as whether there are any anomalous residuals. Note that even though there might be many right-hand-side
variables in this regression model, the actual values of y, the fitted
values of y, and the residuals are simple univariate series, which can
be plotted easily. We make use of such plots throughout this book.

4. (Graphical regression diagnostic II: time series plot of e_t^2 or $|e_t|$) Plots of
e_t^2 or $|e_t|$ reveal patterns (most notably serial correlation) in the *squared*
or *absolute* residuals, which correspond to nonconstant volatility, or heteroskedasticity, in the levels of the residuals. As with the standard residual
plot, the squared or absolute residual plot is always a simple univariate
plot, even when there are many right-hand-side variables. Such plots feature prominently, for example, in tracking and forecasting time-varying
volatility.

5. (Graphical regression diagnostic III: scatterplot of e_t vs. x_t) A plot of e_t versus x_t helps us assess whether the relationship between y and the set of x's
is truly linear, as assumed in linear regression analysis. If not, the linear
regression residuals will depend on x. If there is only one right-hand-side
variable, as above, we can simply make a scatterplot of e_t vs. x_t. If there is
more than one right-hand-side variable, we can make separate plots for

each, although the procedure loses some of its simplicity and transparency.

6. (Graphical analysis of foreign exchange rate data) Magyar Select, a marketing firm representing a group of Hungarian wineries, is considering entering into a contract to sell 8,000 cases of premium Hungarian dessert wine to AMI Imports, a worldwide distributer based in New York and London. The contract must be signed now, but payment and delivery is 90 days hence. Payment is to be in U.S. dollars; Magyar is therefore concerned about the U.S. dollar/Hungarian forint ($/Ft) exchange rate volatility over the next 90 days. Magyar has hired you to analyze and forecast the exchange rate, on which it has collected data for the last 620 days. Naturally, you suggest that Magyar begin with a graphical examination of the data. (The $/Ft exchange rate data are on the data disk.)

   (a) Why might we be interested in examining data on the log rather than the level of the $/Ft exchange rate?

   (b) Take logs and produce a time series plot of the log of the $/Ft exchange rate. Discuss.

   (c) Produce a scatterplot of the log of the $/Ft exchange rate against the lagged log of the $/Ft exchange rate. Discuss.

   (d) Produce a time series plot of the change in the log $/Ft exchange rate, and also produce a histogram, normality test, and other descriptive statistics. Discuss. (For small changes, the change in the logarithm is approximately equal to the percent change, expressed as a decimal.) Do the log exchange rate changes appear normally distributed? If not, what is the nature of the deviation from normality? Why do you think we computed the histogram and other statistics for the differenced log data rather than for the original series?

   (e) Produce a time series plot of the *square* of the change in the log $/Ft exchange rate. Discuss and compare to the earlier series of log changes. What do you conclude about the volatility of the exchange rate, as proxied by the squared log changes?

7. (**Common scales**) Redo the multiple comparison of the Anscombe data in Figure 3.1 using common scales. Do you prefer the original or your newly created graphic? Why or why not?

8. (Graphing real GDP, continued)

   (a) Consider Figure 3.16, the final plot at which we arrived in our application to graphing four components of U.S. real GDP. What do you like about the plot? What do you dislike about the plot? How could you make it even better? Do it!

   (b) In order to help sharpen your eye (or so I claim), some of the graphics in this book fail to adhere strictly to the elements of graphical style that we emphasized. Pick and critique three graphs from anywhere in the book (apart from this chapter), and produce improved versions.

9. (Color)

   (a) Color can aid graphics both in showing the data and in appealing to the viewer. How?

   (b) Color can also confuse. How?

   (c) Keeping in mind the principles of graphical style, formulate as many guidelines for color graphics as you can.

10. (Regression, regression diagnostics, and regression graphics in action) Let us say you are a new financial analyst at a major investment house, tracking and forecasting earnings of the health care industry. At the end of each quarter, you forecast industry earnings for the next quarter. Experience has revealed that your clients care about your forecast accuracy— that is, they want only small errors—but that they are not particularly concerned with the sign of your error. (Your clients use your forecast to help allocate their portfolios, and if your forecast is way off, they lose money, regardless of whether you are too optimistic or too pessimistic.) Your immediate predecessor has bequeathed you a forecasting model in which current earnings (y_t) are explained by one variable lagged by one quarter (x_{t-1}). (Data for both are on the data disk.)

    (a) Suggest and defend some candidate "x" variables. Why might lagged x, rather than current x, be included in the model?

    (b) Graph y_t vs. x_{t-1} and discuss.

    (c) Regress y_t on x_{t-1} and discuss (including related regression diagnostics that you deem relevant).

    (d) Assess the entire situation in light of seven key points: decision environment, loss function, forecast object, forecast statement, forecast horizon, information set, and parsimony principle.

    (e) Consider as many variations as you deem relevant on the general theme. At a minimum, you will want to consider the following:

       Does it appear necessary to include an intercept in the regression? Why care?

       Does the functional form appear adequate? Might the relationship be nonlinear? Why care?

       Do the regression residuals seem random; in particular, do they appear serially correlated or heteroskedastic? Why care?

       Are there any outliers? If so, does the estimated model appear robust to their inclusion or exclusion? Why care?

       Do the regression disturbances appear normally distributed? Why care?

       How might you assess whether the estimated model is structurally stable? Why care?

BIBLIOGRAPHICAL AND COMPUTATIONAL NOTES

A subfield of statistics called **exploratory data analysis** (EDA) focuses on learning about patterns in data without pretending to have too much a priori theory. As you would guess, EDA makes heavy use of graphical and related techniques. For an introduction, see Tukey (1977), a well-known book by a pioneer in the area.

This chapter has been heavily influenced by Tufte (1983)—as are all modern discussions of statistical graphics. Tufte's book is an insightful and entertaining masterpiece on graphical style that I recommend enthusiastically. Our discussion of Anscombe's quartet follows Tufte's; the original paper is Anscombe (1973).

Cleveland (1993, 1994) and Cook and Weisberg (1994) are fine examples of modern graphical techniques. Cleveland (1993) stresses tools for revealing information in high-dimensional data, as well as techniques that aid in showing the data and appealing to the viewer in standard low-dimensional situations. It also contains extensive discussion of banking to 45 degrees. Cook and Weisberg (1994) develop powerful graphical tools useful in the specification and evaluation of regression models.

Details of the Jarque-Bera test may be found in Jarque and Bera (1987).

All graphics in this chapter were done using Eviews. S+ implements a variety of more sophisticated graphical techniques and in many respects represents the cutting edge of statistical graphics software.

CONCEPTS FOR REVIEW

Anscombe's quartet	Multiple comparison
Aspect ratio	Multiway scatterplot
Banking to 45 degrees	Nondata ink
Bivariate scatterplot	Outlier
Chartjunk	Pairwise scatterplot
Common scales	Partial correlation
Exploratory data analysis	Relational graphics
Golden ratio	Scatterplot matrix
Histogram	Simple correlation
Innovation outlier	Time series plot
Measurement outlier	

REFERENCES AND ADDITIONAL READINGS

Anscombe, F. J. (1973), "Graphs in Statistical Analysis," *American Statistician,* 27, 17–21.

Cleveland, W. S. (1993), *Visualizing Data.* Summit, N.J.: Hobart Press.

Cleveland, W. S. (1994), *The Elements of Graphing Data,* second edition. Belmont, Calif.: Wadsworth.

Cook, R. D., and Weisberg, S. (1994), *An Introduction to Regression Graphics.* New York: Wiley.

Jarque, C. M., and Bera, A. K. (1987), "A Test for Normality of Observations and Regression Residuals," *International Statistical Review,* 55, 163–172.

Tufte, E. R. (1983), *The Visual Display of Quantitative Information.* Cheshire, Conn.: Graphics Press.

Tukey, J. W. (1977), *Exploratory Data Analysis.* Reading, Mass.: Addison-Wesley.

MODELING AND FORECASTING TREND

1. MODELING TREND

The series that we want to forecast vary over time, and we often mentally attribute that variation to unobserved underlying components, such as trends, seasonals, and cycles. In this chapter we focus on **trend.**[1] Trend is slow, long-run evolution in the variables that we want to model and forecast. In business, finance, and economics, for example, trend is produced by slowly evolving preferences, technologies, institutions, and demographics. We focus here on models of **deterministic trend,** in which the trend evolves in a perfectly predictable way. Deterministic trend models are tremendously useful in practice.[2]

Existence of trend is empirically obvious. Numerous series in diverse fields display trends. In Figure 4.1 we show the U.S. labor force participation rate for females aged 16 and over, in which the trend appears roughly *linear,* meaning that it increases or decreases like a straight line. That is, a simple linear function of time,

$$T_t = \beta_0 + \beta_1 \; TIME_t$$

---

1. Later we define and study seasonals and cycles. Not all components need be present in all observed series.

2. Later we broaden our discussion to allow for **stochastic trend.**

FIGURE 4.1   Labor Force Participation Rate for Females

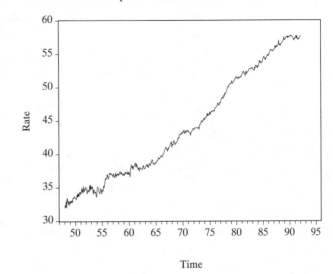

Time

provides a good description of the trend. The variable *TIME* is constructed artificially and is called a time trend or **time dummy.** Time equals 1 in the first period of the sample, 2 in the second period, and so on. Thus, for a sample of size T, $TIME = (1, 2, 3, \ldots, T-1, T)$; put differently, $TIME_t = t$. β_0 is the **intercept;** it is the value of the trend at time $t = 0$. β_1 is the **slope;** it is positive if the trend is increasing and negative if the trend is decreasing. The larger the absolute value of β_1, the steeper the trend's slope. In Figure 4.2, for example, we show two linear trends, one increasing and one decreasing. The increasing trend has an intercept of $\beta_0 = -50$ and an slope of $\beta_1 = 0.8$, whereas the decreasing trend has an intercept of $\beta_0 = 10$ and a gentler absolute slope of $\beta_1 = -0.25$.

In business, finance, and economics, linear trends are typically increasing, corresponding to growth, but this trend need not be the case. In Figure 4.3, for example, we show the U.S. labor force participation rate for *males* aged 16 and over, which displays a linearly *decreasing* trend.

To provide a visual check of the adequacy of linear trends for the labor force participation rates, we show them with linear trends superimposed in Figures 4.4 and 4.5.[3] In each case, we show the actual participation rate series together with the fitted trend, and we also show the residual—the deviation of the actual participation rate from the trend. The linear trends seem adequate. There are still obvious dynamic patterns in the residuals, but that is to

---

3. Shortly we discuss how we estimated the trends. For now, just take them as given.

FIGURE 4.2   Increasing and Decreasing Linear Trends

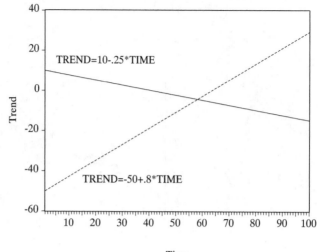

be expected—persistent dynamic patterns are typically observed in the deviations of variables from the trend.

Sometimes trend appears *nonlinear,* or curved, as for example when a variable increases at an increasing or decreasing rate. Ultimately, we don't require that trends be linear, only that they be *smooth.* Figure 4.6 shows the

FIGURE 4.3   Labor Force Participation Rate for Males

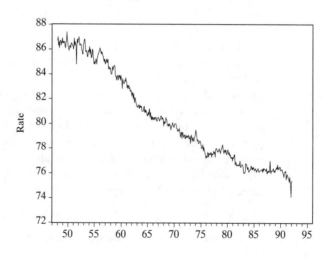

FIGURE 4.4 Linear Trend: Labor Force Participation Rate for Females

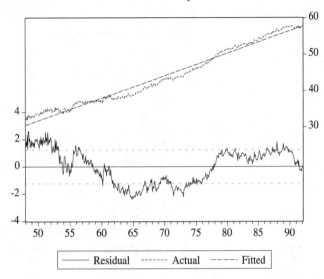

monthly volume of shares traded on the New York Stock Exchange (NYSE). Volume increases at an increasing rate; the trend is therefore nonlinear.

Quadratic trend models can potentially capture nonlinearities such as those observed in the volume series. Such trends are quadratic, as opposed to linear, functions of time,

$$T_t = \beta_0 + \beta_1 \; TIME_t + \beta_2 \; TIME_t^2$$

FIGURE 4.5 Linear Trend: Labor Force Participation Rate for Males

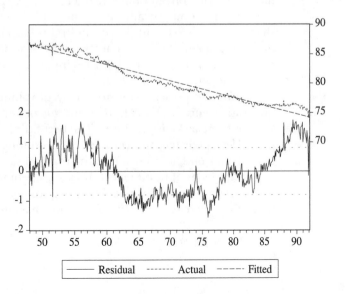

FIGURE **4.6**   Volume on the New York Stock Exchange

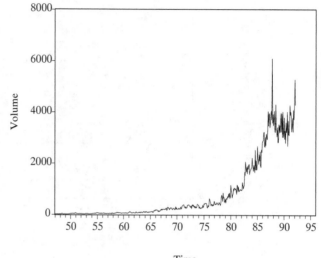

Linear trend emerges as a special (and potentially restrictive) case when $\beta_2 = 0$. Higher-order polynomial trends are sometimes entertained, but it is important to use low-order polynomials to maintain smoothness.

A variety of different nonlinear quadratic trend shapes are possible, depending on the signs and sizes of the coefficients; we show several in Figure 4.7. In particular, if $\beta_1 > 0$ and $\beta_2 > 0$, as in the upper-left panel, the trend is monotonically, but nonlinearly, increasing, Conversely, if $\beta_1 < 0$ and $\beta_2 < 0$, the trend is monotonically decreasing. If $\beta_1 < 0$ and $\beta_2 > 0$, the trend has a U shape, and if $\beta_1 > 0$ and $\beta_2 < 0$, the trend has an inverted U shape. Keep in mind that quadratic trends are used to provide local approximations; one rarely has a U-shaped trend, for example. Instead, all of the data may lie on one or the other side of the U.

Figure 4.8 presents the stock market volume data with a superimposed quadratic trend. The quadratic trend fits better than the linear trend, but it still has some awkward features. The best-fitting quadratic trend is still a little more U-shaped than the volume data, resulting in an odd pattern of deviations from trend, as reflected in the residual series.

Other types of nonlinear trend are sometimes appropriate. Consider the NYSE volume series once again. In Figure 4.9 we show the *logarithm* of volume, for which the trend appears approximately *linear*.[4] This situation, in

---

4. Throughout this book, logarithms are *natural* (base *e*) logarithms, denoted as ln.

FIGURE 4.7   Various Shapes of Quadratic Trends

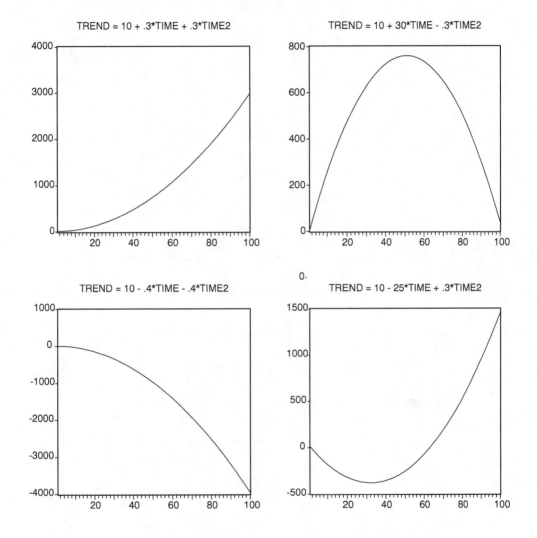

which a trend appears nonlinear in levels but linear in logarithms, is called **exponential trend,** or **log linear trend,** and is very common in business, finance, and economics because economic variables often display roughly constant growth rates (e.g., 3 percent per year). If trend is characterized by constant growth at rate β_1, then we can write

$$T_t = \beta_0 \, e^{\beta_1 \, TIME_t}$$

FIGURE 4.8   Quadratic Trend: Volume on the New York Stock Exchange

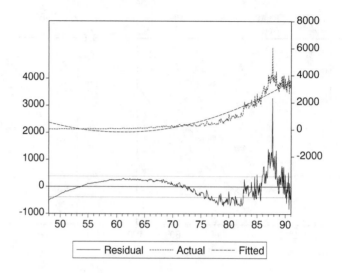

The trend is a nonlinear (exponential) function of time in levels, but in logarithms we have

$$\ln(T_t) = \ln(\beta_0) + \beta_1 \; TIME_t$$

Thus, $\ln(T_t)$ is a linear function of time.

FIGURE 4.9   Log Volume on the New York Stock Exchange

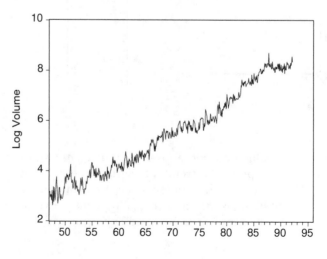

Figure 4.10 shows the variety of exponential trend shapes that can be obtained, depending on the parameters. As with quadratic trend, depending on the signs and sizes of the parameter values, exponential trend can achieve a variety of patterns, increasing or decreasing at an increasing or decreasing rate.

It is important to note that, although the same sorts of qualitative trend shapes can be achieved with quadratic and exponential trend, there are subtle differences between them. The nonlinear trends in some series are well approximated by quadratic trend, whereas the trends in other series are bet-

FIGURE 4.10 Various Shapes of Exponential Trends

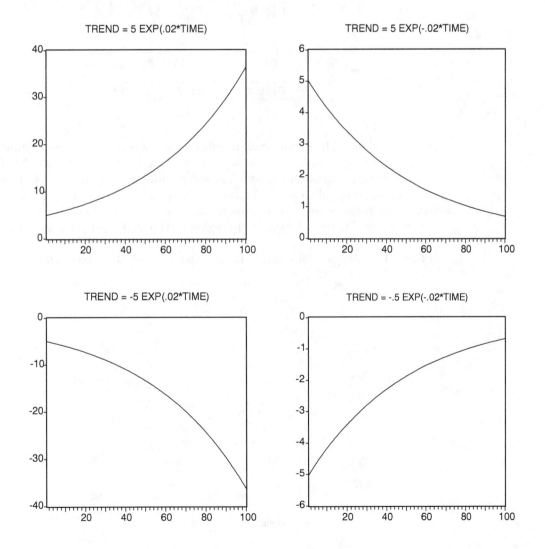

FIGURE **4.11**   Linear Trend: Log Volume on the New York Stock Exchange

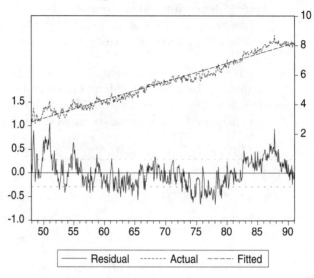

ter approximated by exponential trend. We have already seen, for example, that although quadratic trend looked better than linear trend for the NYSE volume data, the quadratic fit still had some undesirable features. Let us see how an exponential trend compares. In Figure 4.11 we plot the *log* volume data with linear trend superimposed; the log-linear trend looks quite good. Equivalently, Figure 4.12 shows the volume data in *levels* with exponential

FIGURE **4.12**   Exponential Trend: Volume on the New York Stock Exchange

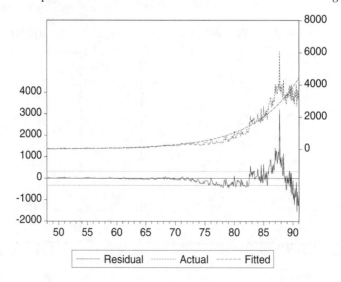

trend superimposed; the exponential trend looks much better than did the quadratic.

2. ESTIMATING TREND MODELS

Before we can estimate trend models we need to create and store on the computer variables such as *TIME* and its square. Fortunately, we don't have to type in the trend values $(1, 2, 3, 4, \ldots)$ by hand; most good software packages have a command to create the trend automatically, after which we can immediately compute derived variables such as the square of *TIME*, or $TIME^2$. Because, for example, $TIME = (1, 2, \ldots, T)$, $TIME^2 = (1, 4, \ldots, T^2)$; that is, $TIME_t^2 = t^2$.

We fit our various trend models to data on a time series y using **least squares regression.**[5] That is, we use a computer to find

$$\hat{\theta} = \underset{\theta}{\operatorname{argmin}} \sum_{t=1}^{T} \left[y_t - T_t(\theta) \right]^2$$

where θ denotes the set of parameters to be estimated. A linear trend, for example, has $T_t(\theta) = \beta_0 + \beta_1 \, TIME_t$ and $\theta = (\beta_0, \beta_1)$, in which case the computer finds

$$(\hat{\beta}_0, \hat{\beta}_1) = \underset{\beta_0, \beta_1}{\operatorname{argmin}} \sum_{t=1}^{T} \left[y_t - \beta_0 - \beta_1 \, TIME_t \right]^2$$

Similarly, in the quadratic trend case the computer finds

$$(\hat{\beta}_0, \hat{\beta}_1, \hat{\beta}_2) = \underset{\beta_0, \beta_1, \beta_2}{\operatorname{argmin}} \sum_{t=1}^{T} \left[y_t - \beta_0 - \beta_1 \, TIME_t - \beta_2 \, TIME_t^2 \right]^2$$

We can estimate an exponential trend in two ways. First, we can proceed directly from the exponential representation and let the computer find

$$(\hat{\beta}_0, \hat{\beta}_1) = \underset{\beta_0, \beta_1}{\operatorname{argmin}} \sum_{t=1}^{T} \left[y_t - \beta_0 \, e^{\beta_1 \, TIME_t} \right]^2$$

---

5. **"Argmin"** just means "the argument that minimizes." Least squares proceeds by finding the argument (in this case, the value of θ) that minimizes the sum of squared residuals; thus the least squares estimator is the "argmin" of the sum of squared residuals function.

Alternatively, because the nonlinear exponential trend is nevertheless linear in logs, we can estimate it by regressing ln y on an intercept and *TIME*. Thus we let the computer find

$$(\hat{\beta}_0, \hat{\beta}_1) = \underset{\beta_0, \beta_1}{\operatorname{argmin}} \; \sum_{t=1}^{T} \left[\ln y_t - \ln \beta_0 - \beta_1 \; TIME_t \right]^2$$

Note that the fitted values from this regression are the fitted values of ln y, so they must be exponentiated to get the fitted values of y.

3. FORECASTING TREND

Consider first the construction of point forecasts. Suppose we are presently at time T, and we want to use a trend model to forecast the h-step-ahead value of a series y. For illustrative purposes, we will work with a linear trend, but the procedures are identical with more complicated trends. The linear trend model, which holds for any time t, is

$$y_t = \beta_0 + \beta_1 \; TIME_t + \varepsilon_t$$

In particular, at time $T + h$, the future time of interest,

$$y_{T+h} = \beta_0 + \beta_1 \; TIME_{T+h} + \varepsilon_{T+h}$$

Two future values of series appear on the right side of the equation, $TIME_{T+h}$ and ε_{T+h}. If $TIME_{T+h}$ and ε_{T+h} were known at time T, we could immediately crank out the forecast. In fact, $TIME_{T+h}$ is known at time T because the artificially constructed time variable is perfectly predictable; specifically, $TIME_{T+h} = T + h$. Unfortunately ε_{T+h} is not known at time T, so we replace it with an optimal forecast of ε_{T+h} constructed using information only up to time T.[6] Under the assumption that ε is simply independent zero-mean, serially uncorrelated random noise, the optimal forecast of ε_{T+h} for any future period is 0, yielding the point forecast,[7]

$$y_{T+h,T} = \beta_0 + \beta_1 \; TIME_{T+h}$$

---

6. More formally, we say that we are "projecting ε_{T+h} on the time T information set," which we discuss in detail in chapter 8.

7. "Independent zero-mean random noise" is just a fancy way of saying that the regression disturbances satisfy the usual assumptions—they are identically and independently distributed.

The subscript "$T + h, T$" on the forecast reminds us that the forecast is for time $T + h$ and is made at time T.

The point forecast formula given above is not of practical use because it assumes known values of the trend parameters β_0 and β_1. But it is a simple matter to make it operational—we just replace unknown parameters with their least squares estimates, yielding

$$\hat{y}_{T+h,T} = \hat{\beta}_0 + \hat{\beta}_1 \; TIME_{T+h}$$

To form an interval forecast we assume further that the trend regression disturbance is normally distributed, in which case a 95% interval forecast ignoring parameter estimation uncertainty is $y_{T+h,T} \pm 1.96\sigma$, where σ is the standard deviation of the disturbance in the trend regression.[8] To make this operational, we use $\hat{y}_{T+h,T} \pm 1.96\hat{\sigma}$, where $\hat{\sigma}$ is the standard error of the trend regression, an estimate of σ.

To form a density forecast, we again assume that the trend regression disturbance is normally distributed. Then, ignoring parameter estimation uncertainty, we have the density forecast $N(y_{T+h,T}, \sigma^2)$, where σ is the standard deviation of the disturbance in the trend regression. To make this operational, we use the density forecast $N(\hat{y}_{T+h,T}, \hat{\sigma}^2)$.

4. SELECTING FORECASTING MODELS USING THE AKAIKE AND SCHWARZ CRITERIA

We have introduced a number of trend models, but how do we select among them when fitting a trend to a specific series? What are the consequences, for example, of fitting a number of trend models and selecting the model with highest R^2? Is there a better way? This issue of **model selection** is of tremendous importance in all of forecasting, so we introduce it now.

It turns out that model-selection strategies such as selecting the model with highest R^2 do *not* produce good out-of-sample forecasting models. Fortunately, however, a number of powerful modern tools exist to assist with model selection. Here we digress to discuss some of the available methods, which will be immediately useful in selecting among alternative trend models, as well as many other situations.

Most model selection criteria attempt to find the model with the smallest out-of-sample 1-step-ahead mean squared prediction error. The criteria we examine fit this general approach; the differences among criteria amount to

---

8. When we say that we ignore parameter estimation uncertainty, we mean that we use the estimated parameters as if they were the true values, ignoring the fact that they are only estimates, and subject to sampling variability. Later we see how to account for parameter estimation uncertainty by using simulation techniques.

different penalties for the number of degrees of freedom used in estimating the model (that is, the number of parameters estimated). Because all of the criteria are effectively estimates of out-of-sample mean square prediction error, they have a negative orientation—the smaller the better.

First consider the **mean squared error,**

$$MSE = \frac{\sum_{t=1}^{T} e_t^2}{T}$$

where T is the sample size and

$$e_t = y_t - \hat{y}_t$$

where

$$\hat{y}_t = \hat{\beta}_0 + \hat{\beta}_1 \ TIME_t$$

MSE is intimately related to two other diagnostic statistics routinely computed by regression software, the **sum of squared residuals** and R^2. Looking at the *MSE* formula reveals that the model with the smallest MSE is also the model with smallest sum of squared residuals, because scaling the sum of squared residuals by $1/T$ doesn't change the ranking. So selecting the model with the smallest *MSE* is equivalent to selecting the model with the smallest sum of squared residuals. Similarly, recall the formula for R^2,

$$R^2 = 1 - \frac{\sum_{t=1}^{T} e_t^2}{\sum_{t=1}^{T} (y_t - \bar{y})^2}$$

The denominator of the ratio that appears in the formula is just the sum of squared deviations of y from its sample mean (the so-called "total sum of squares"), which depends only on the data, not on the particular model fit. Thus, selecting the model that minimizes the sum of squared residuals—which as we saw is equivalent to selecting the model that minimizes *MSE*—is also equivalent to selecting the model that maximizes R^2.

Selecting forecasting models on the basis of *MSE* or any of the equivalent forms discussed above—that is, using in-sample *MSE* to estimate the out-of-sample 1-step-ahead *MSE*—turns out to be a bad idea. In-sample *MSE cannot* rise when more variables are added to a model, and typically it will fall continuously as more variables are added. To see why, consider the fitting of polynomial trend models. In that context, the number of variables in the model is linked to the degree of the polynomial (call it p):

$$T_t = \beta_0 + \beta_1 \ TIME_t + \beta_2 \ TIME_t^2 + \ldots + \beta_p \ TIME_t^p$$

We have already considered the cases of $p = 1$ (linear trend) and $p = 2$ (quadratic trend), but there is nothing to stop us from fitting models with higher powers of time included. As we include higher powers of time, the sum of squared residuals *cannot* rise because the estimated parameters are explicitly chosen to *minimize* the sum of squared residuals. The last-included power of time could always wind up with an estimated coefficient of zero; to the extent that the estimate is anything else, the sum of squared residuals must have fallen. Thus, the more variables we include in a forecasting model, the lower the sum of squared residuals will be, and therefore the lower MSE will be, and the higher R^2 will be. The reduction in MSE as higher powers of time are included in the model occurs even if they are in fact of no use in forecasting the variable of interest. Again, the sum of squared residuals cannot rise, and due to sampling error it is very unlikely that we would get a coefficient of exactly zero on a newly included variable, even if the coefficient is zero in population.

The effects described above have various names, including **in-sample overfitting** and **data mining,** reflecting the idea that including more variables in a forecasting model won't necessarily improve its out-of-sample forecasting performance, although it will improve the model's "fit" on historical data. The upshot is that MSE is a biased estimator of **out-of-sample 1-step-ahead prediction error variance,** and the size of the bias increases with the number of variables included in the model. The direction of the bias is downward—in-sample MSE provides an overly optimistic (that is, too small) assessment of out-of-sample prediction error variance.

To reduce the bias associated with MSE and its relatives, we need to penalize for degrees of freedom used. Thus let us consider the mean squared error corrected for degrees of freedom,

$$s^2 = \frac{\sum\limits_{t=1}^{T} e_t^2}{T - k}$$

where k is the number of degrees of freedom used in model fitting.[9] s^2 is just the usual unbiased estimate of the regression disturbance variance. That is, it

---

9. The degrees of freedom used in model fitting is simply the number of parameters estimated.

is the square of the usual standard error of the regression. So selecting the model that minimizes s^2 is also equivalent to selecting the model that minimizes the standard error of the regression. s^2 is also intimately connected to the R^2 adjusted for degrees of freedom (the "**adjusted R^2**," or $\overline{R}^2$). Recall that

$$\overline{R}^2 = 1 - \frac{\displaystyle\sum_{t=1}^{T} e_t^2 / (T-k)}{\displaystyle\sum_{t=1}^{T} (y_t - \overline{y})^2 / (T-1)} = 1 - \frac{s^2}{\displaystyle\sum_{t=1}^{T} (y_t - \overline{y})^2 / T - 1}$$

The denominator of the $\overline{R}^2$ expression depends only on the data, not the particular model fit, so the model that minimizes s^2 is also the model that maximizes $\overline{R}^2$. In short, the strategies of selecting the model that minimizes s^2, or the model that minimizes the standard error of the regression, or the model that maximizes $\overline{R}^2$, are equivalent, and they *do* penalize for degrees of freedom used.

To highlight the degree-of-freedom penalty, let us rewrite s^2 as a penalty factor times the *MSE*,

$$s^2 = \left(\frac{T}{T-k}\right) \frac{\displaystyle\sum_{t=1}^{T} e_t^2}{T}$$

Note in particular that including more variables in a regression will not necessarily lower s^2 or raise $\overline{R}^2$ —the *MSE* will fall, but the degrees-of-freedom penalty will rise, so the product could go either way.

As with s^2, many of the most important forecast model selection criteria are of the form "penalty factor times *MSE*." The idea is simply that if we want to get an accurate estimate of the 1-step-ahead out-of-sample prediction error variance, we need to penalize the in-sample residual variance (the *MSE*) to reflect the degrees of freedom used. Two very important such criteria are the **Akaike information criterion (AIC)** and the **Schwarz information criterion (SIC).** Their formulas are:

$$AIC = \exp\left(\frac{2k}{T}\right) \frac{\displaystyle\sum_{t=1}^{T} e_t^2}{T}$$

and

$$SIC = T^{\left(\frac{k}{T}\right)} \frac{\sum\limits_{t=1}^{T} e_t^2}{T}$$

How do the penalty factors associated with *MSE*, s^2, *AIC*, and *SIC* compare in terms of severity? All of the penalty factors are functions of k/T, the number of parameters estimated per sample observation, and we can compare the penalty factors graphically as k/T varies. In Figure 4.13 we show the penalties as k/T moves from 0 to 0.25, for a sample size of $T = 100$. The s^2 penalty is small and rises slowly with k/T; the *AIC* penalty is a bit larger and still rises only slowly with k/T. The *SIC* penalty, on the other hand, is substantially larger and rises at a slightly increasing rate with k/T.

It is clear that the different criteria penalize degrees of freedom differently. In addition, we could propose many other criteria by altering the penalty. How, then, do we select among the criteria? More generally, what properties might we expect a "good" model selection criterion to have? Are s^2, *AIC*, and *SIC* "good" model selection criteria?

We evaluate model selection criteria in terms of a key property called **consistency.** A model selection criterion is consistent if:

1. When the true model (that is, the **data-generating process,** or **DGP**) is among the models considered, the probability of selecting the true DGP approaches 1 as the sample size gets large.

FIGURE 4.13 Degrees-of-Freedom Penalties for Various Model Selection Criteria

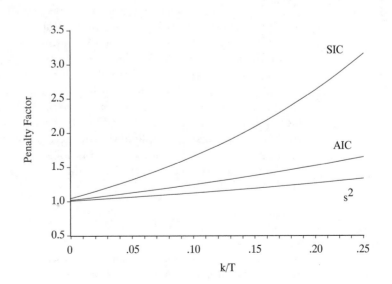

2. When the true model is *not* among those considered, so that it is impossible to select the true DGP, the probability of selecting the best *approximation* to the true DGP approaches 1 as the sample size gets large.[10]

Consistency is, of course, desirable. If the DGP is among those considered, then we hope that as the sample size gets large we would eventually select it. Of course, all of our models are false—they are intentional simplifications of a much more complex reality. Thus the second notion of consistency is the more compelling.

MSE is inconsistent because it doesn't penalize for degrees of freedom; that is why it is unattractive. s^2 does penalize for degrees of freedom, but, as it turns out, not enough to render it a consistent model selection procedure. *AIC* penalizes degrees of freedom more heavily than s^2, but it too remains inconsistent; even as the sample size gets large, *AIC* selects models that are too large ("overparameterized"). However, *SIC*, which penalizes degrees of freedom most heavily, *is* consistent.

The discussion thus far conveys the impression that *SIC* is unambiguously superior to *AIC* for selecting forecasting models, but such is not the case. Until now, we have implicitly assumed that either the true DGP or the best approximation to the true DGP is in the fixed set of models considered. In that case, *SIC is* a superior model selection criterion. However, a potentially more compelling view for forecasters is that both the true DGP and the best approximation to it are much more complicated than any model we fit, in which case we may want to expand the set of models we entertain as the sample size grows. We are then led to a different optimality property, called **asymptotic efficiency.** An asymptotically efficient model selection criterion chooses a sequence of models, as the sample size gets large, whose 1-step-ahead forecast error variances approach the one that would be obtained using the true model with known parameters at a rate at least as fast as that of any other model selection criterion. *AIC*, although inconsistent, *is* asymptotically efficient, whereas *SIC* is not.

In practical forecasting we usually report and examine both *AIC* and *SIC*. Most often they select the same model. When they don't, and in spite of the theoretical asymptotic efficiency property of *AIC*, I recommend use of the more parsimonious model selected by *SIC*, other things being equal. This accords with the KISS principle and with the results of studies comparing out-of-sample forecasting performance of models selected by various criteria.

Some authors (and software) examine and report the logarithms of *AIC* and *SIC*,

---

10. Most model selection criteria—including all of those discussed here—assess goodness of approximation in terms of 1-step-ahead mean squared forecast error.

$$\ln(AIC) = \ln\left(\frac{\sum_{t=1}^{T} e_t^2}{T}\right) + \left(\frac{2k}{T}\right)$$

$$\ln(SIC) = \ln\left(\frac{\sum_{t=1}^{T} e_t^2}{T}\right) + \frac{k\ln(T)}{T}$$

The practice is so common that $\ln(AIC)$ and $\ln(SIC)$ are often simply called "AIC" and "SIC."[11] AIC and SIC must be greater than zero, so $\ln(AIC)$ and $\ln(SIC)$ are always well defined and can take on any real value. Other authors (and software) use other variants, based, for example, on the value of the maximized likelihood or log likelihood function. Some software packages have even changed definitions of AIC and SIC across releases! The important insight, however, is that although these variations will, of course, change the numerical values of AIC and SIC by your computer "spits out," they will not change the *rankings* of models under the various criteria. Consider, for example, selecting among three models. If $AIC_1 < AIC_2 < AIC_3$, then it must be true as well that $\ln(AIC_1) < \ln(AIC_2) < \ln(AIC_3)$, so we would select model 1 regardless of the "definition" of the information criterion used.

AIC and SIC have enjoyed widespread popularity, but they are not universally applicable, and we are still learning about their performance in specific situations. However, the general principle that we need to correct somehow for degrees of freedom when estimating out-of-sample MSE on the basis of in-sample MSE *is* universally applicable. Judicious use of criteria such as AIC and SIC, in conjunction with knowledge about the nature of the system being forecast, is helpful in a variety of forecasting situations.

5. APPLICATION: FORECASTING RETAIL SALES

We illustrate trend modeling with an application to forecasting U.S. current-dollar retail sales. The data are monthly from 1955.01 through 1994.12 and have been seasonally adjusted.[12] We use the period 1955.01–1993.12 to esti-

---

11. Eviews, for example, reports $\ln(AIC)$ and $\ln(SIC)$ under the names "AIC" and "SIC."

12. When we say that the data have been "seasonally adjusted," we simply mean that they have been smoothed in a way that eliminates seasonal variation. We discuss seasonality in detail in chapter 5.

FIGURE **4.14**   Retail Sales

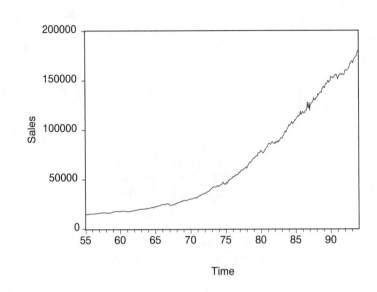

mate our forecasting models, and we use the "holdout sample" 1994.01–1994.12 to examine their out-of-sample forecasting performance.

In Figure 4.14 we provide a time series plot of the retail sales data, which display a clear nonlinear trend and not much else. Cycles are probably present but are not easily visible because they account for a comparatively minor share of the series' variation.

In Table 4.1 we show the results of fitting a linear trend model by regressing retail sales on a constant and a linear time trend. The trend appears highly significant as judged by the p-value of the t-statistic on the time trend, and the regression's R^2 is high. Moreover, the Durbin-Watson statistic indicates that the disturbances are positively serially correlated, so that the disturbance at any time t is positively correlated with the disturbance at time $t - 1$. In later chapters we show how to model such residual serial correlation and exploit it for forecasting purposes, but for now we ignore it and focus only on the trend.[13]

The residual plot in Figure 4.15 makes clear what is happening. The linear trend is simply inadequate because the actual trend is nonlinear. That is one key reason why the residuals are so highly serially correlated—first the

---

13. Such **residual serial correlation** may, however, render the standard errors of estimated coefficients (and the associated t statistics) untrustworthy. Here that is not a big problem, because it is visually obvious that trend is important in retail sales, but in other situations it may well be. Typically, when constructing forecasting models, we are concerned more with point estimation than with inference.

TABLE 4.1 Retail Sales: Linear Trend Regression

Dependent Variable is RTRR
Sample: 1955:01 1993:12
Included observations: 468

Variable	Coefficient	Std. Error	T-Statistic	Prob.
C	-16391.25	1469.177	-11.15676	0.0000
TIME	349.7731	5.428670	64.43073	0.0000

R-squared	0.899076	Mean dependent var	65630.56
Adjusted R-squared	0.898859	S.D. dependent var	49889.26
S.E. of regression	15866.12	Akaike info criterion	19.34815
Sum squared resid	1.17E+11	Schwarz criterion	19.36587
Log likelihood	-5189.529	F-statistic	4151.319
Durbin-Watson stat	0.004682	Prob(F-statistic)	0.000000

FIGURE 4.15 Retail Sales: Linear Trend Residual Plot

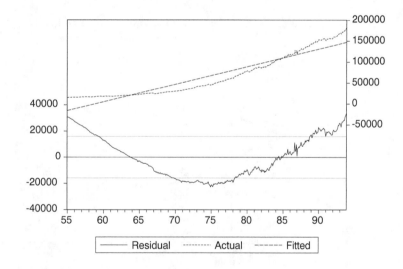

data are all above the linear trend, then below, and then above. Along with the residuals, we have plotted plus-or-minus one standard error of the regression, for visual reference.

Table 4.2 presents the results of fitting a quadratic trend model. Both the linear and quadratic terms appear highly significant.[14] R^2 is now almost 1.

---

14. The earlier caveat regarding the effects of serial correlation on inference applies, however.

TABLE 4.2   Retail Sales: Quadratic Trend Regression

Dependent Variable is RTRR
Sample: 1955:01 1993:12
Included observations: 468

Variable	Coefficient	Std. Error	T-Statistic	Prob.
C	18708.70	379.9566	49.23905	0.0000
TIME	-98.31130	3.741388	-26.27669	0.0000
TIME2	0.955404	0.007725	123.6754	0.0000

R-squared	0.997022	Mean dependent var	65630.56
Adjusted R-squared	0.997010	S.D. dependent var	49889.26
S.E. of regression	2728.205	Akaike info criterion	15.82919
Sum squared resid	3.46E+09	Schwarz criterion	15.85578
Log likelihood	-4365.093	F-statistic	77848.80
Durbin-Watson stat	0.151089	Prob(F-statistic)	0.000000

FIGURE 4.16   Retail Sales: Quadratic Trend Residual Plot

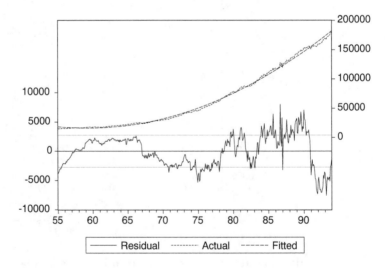

Figure 4.16 shows the residual plot, which now looks very nice, as the fitted nonlinear trend tracks the evolution of retail sales well. The residuals still display persistent dynamics (indicated as well by the still-low Durbin-Watson statistic), but there is little scope for explaining such dynamics with trend because they are related to the business cycle and not the growth trend.

TABLE 4.3   Retail Sales: Log Linear Trend Regression

Dependent Variable is LRTRR
Sample: 1955:01 1993:12
Included observations: 468

Variable	Coefficient	Std. Error	T-Statistic	Prob.
C	9.389975	0.008508	1103.684	0.0000
TIME	0.005931	3.14E-05	188.6541	0.0000

R-squared	0.987076	Mean dependent var	10.78072
Adjusted R-squared	0.987048	S.D. dependent var	0.807325
S.E. of regression	0.091879	Akaike info criterion	-4.770302
Sum squared resid	3.933853	Schwarz criterion	-4.752573
Log likelihood	454.1874	F-statistic	35590.36
Durbin-Watson stat	0.019949	Prob(F-statistic)	0.000000

FIGURE 4.17   Retail Sales: Log Linear Trend Residual Plot

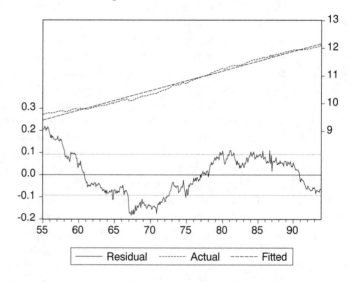

Now let us estimate a different type of nonlinear trend model, the exponential trend. First we do it by OLS regression of the log of retail sales on a constant and linear time trend variable. We show the estimation results and residual plot in Table 4.3 and Figure 4.17. As with the quadratic nonlinear trend, the exponential nonlinear trend model seems to fit well, apart from the low Durbin-Watson statistic.

TABLE 4.4   Retail Sales: Exponential Trend Regression

Dependent Variable is RTRR
Sample: 1955:01 1993:12
Included observations: 468
Convergence achieved after 1 iterations
RTRR=C(1)*EXP(C(2)*TIME)

	Coefficient	Std. Error	T-Statistic	Prob.
C(1)	11967.80	177.9598	67.25003	0.0000
C(2)	0.005944	3.77E-05	157.7469	0.0000

R-squared	0.988796	Mean dependent var	65630.56
Adjusted R-squared	0.988772	S.D. dependent var	49889.26
S.E. of regression	5286.406	Akaike info criterion	17.15005
Sum squared resid	1.30E+10	Schwarz criterion	17.16778
Log likelihood	-4675.175	F-statistic	41126.02
Durbin-Watson stat	0.040527	Prob(F-statistic)	0.000000

In sharp contrast to the results of fitting a linear trend to retail sales, which were poor, the results of fitting a linear trend to the *log* of retail sales seem much improved. But it is difficult to compare the log-linear trend model to the linear and quadratic models because the latter are in levels, not logs, which renders diagnostic statistics such as R^2 and the standard error of the regression incomparable. One way around this problem is to estimate the exponential trend model directly in levels, using nonlinear least squares. In Table 4.4 and Figure 4.18 we show the nonlinear least squares estimation results and residual plot for the exponential trend model. The diagnostic statistics and residual plot indicate that the exponential trend fits better than the linear but worse than the quadratic trend.

Thus far we have been informal in our comparison of the linear, quadratic, and exponential trend models for retail sales. We have noticed, for example, that the quadratic trend seems to fit the best. The quadratic trend model, however, contains one more parameter than the other two, so it is not surprising that it fits a little better, and there is no guarantee that its better fit on historical data will translate into better out-of-sample forecasting performance. (Recall the KISS principle from chapter 2.) To settle upon a final model, we examine *AIC* or *SIC*, which are summarized in Table 4.5 for the three trend models.[15] Both *AIC* and *SIC* indicate that nonlinearity is impor-

---

15. It is important that the exponential trend model be estimated in levels, in order to maintain comparability of the exponential trend model *AIC* and *SIC* with those of the other trend models.

FIGURE 4.18   Retail Sales: Exponential Trend Residual Plot

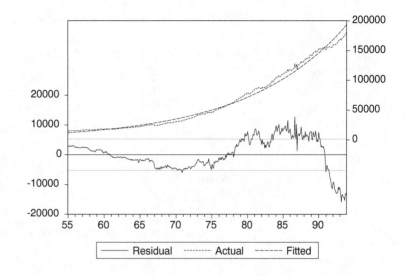

——— Residual   ········ Actual   ------ Fitted

tant in the trend, as both rank the linear trend last. Both, moreover, favor the quadratic trend model. So let us use the quadratic trend model.

Figure 4.19 shows the history of retail sales for the period, 1990.01–1993.12, together with out-of-sample point and 95% interval extrapolation forecasts for 1994.01–1994.12. The point forecasts look reasonable. These interval forecasts are computed under the (incorrect) assumption that the deviation of retail sales from trend is random noise, which is why they are of equal width throughout. Nevertheless, they look reasonable.

In Figure 4.20 we show the history of retail sales through 1993, the quadratic trend forecast for 1994, *and* the realization for 1994. The forecast is quite good—the realization hugs the forecast trend line quite closely. All of the realizations, moreover, fall inside the 95% forecast interval.

For comparison, we examine the forecasting performance of a simple linear trend model. Figure 4.21 presents the history of retail sales and the

TABLE 4.5   Model Selection Criteria: Linear, Quadratic, and
Exponential Trend Models

	Linear Trend	**Quadratic Trend**	**Exponential Trend**
AIC	19.35	15.83	17.15
SIC	19.37	15.86	17.17

FIGURE 4.19   Retail Sales History, 1990.01–1993.12, and Quadratic Trend Forecast, 1994.01–1994.12

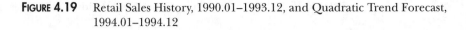

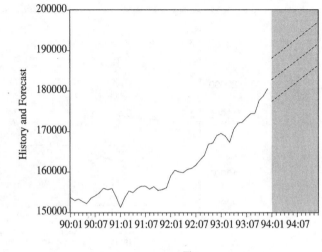

Time

out-of-sample point and 95% interval extrapolation forecasts for 1994. The point forecasts look very strange. The huge drop forecast relative to the historical sample path occurs because the linear trend is far below the sample path by the end of the sample. The confidence intervals are very wide, re-

FIGURE 4.20   Retail Sales History, 1990.01–1993.12, and Quadratic Trend Forecast and Realization, 1994.01–1994.12

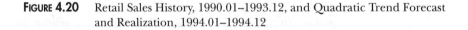

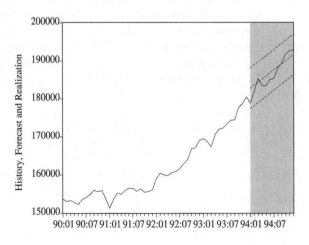

Time

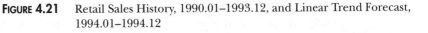

FIGURE 4.21   Retail Sales History, 1990.01–1993.12, and Linear Trend Forecast, 1994.01–1994.12

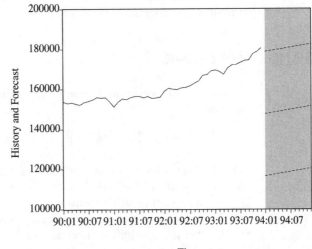

Time

flecting the large standard error of the linear trend regression relative to the quadratic trend regression.

Finally, Figure 4.22 shows the history, the linear trend forecast for 1994, and the realization. The forecast is terrible—far below the realization. Even the very wide interval forecasts fail to contain the realizations. The reason for

FIGURE 4.22   Retail Sales History, 1990.01–1993.12, and Linear Trend Forecast and Realization, 1994.01–1994.12

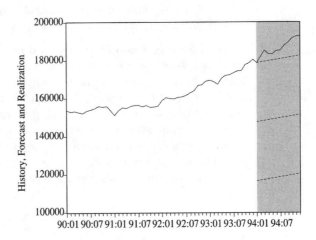

Time

the failure of the linear trend forecast is that the forecasts (point and interval) are computed under the assumption that the linear trend model is actually the true DGP, whereas in fact the linear trend model is a very poor approximation to the trend in retail sales.

PROBLEMS AND COMPLEMENTS

1. (Properties of **polynomial trends**) Consider a sixth-order deterministic polynomial trend:

$$T_t = \beta_0 + \beta_1 \ TIME_t + \beta_2 \ TIME_t^2 + \ldots + \beta_6 \ TIME_t^6$$

   (a) How many local maxima or minima may such a trend display?
   (b) Plot the trend for various values of the parameters to reveal some of the different possible trend shapes.
   (c) Is this an attractive trend model in general? Why or why not?
   (d) Fit the sixth-order polynomial trend model to the NYSE volume series. How does it perform in that particular case?

2. (Specialized nonlinear trends) The **logistic trend** is

$$T_t = \frac{1}{a + br^t}$$

   with $0 < r < 1$.

   (a) Display the trend shape for various a and b values. When might such a trend shape be useful?
   (b) Can you think of other specialized situations in which other specialized trend shapes might be useful? Produce mathematical formulas for the additional specialized trend shapes you suggest.

3. (Moving-average **smoothing** for trend estimation) The trend regression technique is one way to estimate and forecast trend. Another way to estimate trend is by *smoothing* techniques, which we briefly introduce here. We focus on three: two-sided moving averages, one-sided moving averages, and one-sided weighted moving averages. Here we present them as ways to estimate and examine the trend in a time series; later we see how they can actually be used to *forecast* time series.

   Denote the original data by $\{y_t\}_{t=1}^T$ and the smoothed data by $\{\bar{y}_t\}$. Then the **two-sided moving average** is

$$\bar{y}_t = (2m + 1)^{-1} \sum_{i=-m}^{m} y_{t-i}$$

the **one-sided moving average** is

$$\bar{y}_t = (m+1)^{-1} \sum_{i=0}^{m} y_{t-i}$$

and the **one-sided weighted moving average** is

$$\bar{y}_t = \sum_{i=0}^{m} w_i y_{t-i}$$

where the w_i are weights and m is an integer chosen by the user. The "standard" one-sided moving average corresponds to a one-sided weighted moving average with all weights equal to $(m+1)^{-1}$.

(a) For each of the smoothing techniques, discuss the role played by m. What happens as m gets very large? Very small? In what sense does m play a role similar to p, the order of a polynomial trend?

(b) If the original data run is from time 1 to time T, over what range can smoothed values be produced using each of the three smoothing methods? What are the implications for **"real-time,"** or **"on-line,"** **smoothing** versus **"ex post"** or **"off-line" smoothing**?

(c) You have been hired as a consultant by ICSB, a major international bank, to advise them on trends in North American and European stock markets, and to help them allocate their capital. You have extracted from your database the recent history of EUROStar, an index of eleven major European stock markets. Smooth the EUROStar data using equally weighted one-sided and two-sided moving averages, for a variety of m values, until you have found values of m that work well. What do we mean by "work well"? Must the chosen value of m be the same for the one- and two-sided smoothers? For your chosen m values, plot the two-sided smoothed series against the actual and plot the one-sided smoothed series against the actual. Do you notice any systematic difference in the relationship of the smoothed to the actual series depending on whether you do a two-sided or one-sided smoothing? Explain.

(d) Moving average procedures can also be used to **detrend** a series—we simply subtract the estimated trend from the series. Sometimes, but not usually, it is appropriate and desirable to detrend a series before modeling and forecasting it. Why might it sometimes be appropriate? Why is it not usually appropriate?

4. (**Bias corrections** when forecasting from logarithmic models)

(a) In chapter 2 we introduced squared error loss, $L(e) = e^2$. A popular measure of forecast accuracy is out-of-sample mean squared error,

$MSE = E(e^2).$[16] The more accurate the forecast, the smaller is MSE. Show that MSE is equal to the sum of the variance of the error and the square of the mean error.

(b) A forecast is *unbiased* if the mean forecast error is zero. Why might unbiased forecasts be desirable? Are they *necessarily* desirable?

(c) Suppose that $(\ln y)_{t+h,t}$ is an unbiased forecast of $(\ln y)_{t+h}$. Then $\exp((\ln y)_{t+h,t})$ is a *biased* forecast of y_{t+h}. More generally, if $(f(y))_{t+h,t}$ is an unbiased forecast of $(f(y))_{t+h}$, then $f^{-1}((f(y))_{t+h,t})$ is a biased forecast of y_{t+h}, for the arbitrary nonlinear function f. Why? (*Hint:* Is the expected value of a nonlinear function of the random variable the same as the nonlinear function of the expected value?)

(d) Various "corrections" for the bias in $\exp((\ln y)_{t+h,t})$ have been proposed. In practice, however, bias corrections may increase the variance of the forecast error even if they succeed in reducing bias. Why? (*Hint:* In practice, the corrections involve estimated parameters.)

(e) In practice, will bias corrections necessarily reduce the forecast MSE? Why or why not?

5. (Model selection for long-horizon forecasting) Suppose that you want to forecast a monthly series.

(a) Using the true data-generating process is best for forecasting at any horizon. Unfortunately, we never know the true data-generating process! All our models are approximations to the true but unknown data-generating process, in which case the best forecasting model may change with the horizon. Why?

(b) At what horizon are the forecasts generated by models selected by *AIC* and *SIC* likely to be most accurate? Why?

(c) How might you proceed to select a 1-month-ahead forecasting model? 2-month-ahead? 3-month-ahead? 4-month-ahead?

(d) What are the implications of your answer to part (c) for construction of an extrapolation forecast at horizons 1-month-ahead through 4-months-ahead?

(e) In constructing our extrapolation forecasts for retail sales, we used *AIC* and *SIC* to select one model, which we then used to forecast all horizons. Why do you think we didn't adopt a more sophisticated strategy?

---

16. The *MSE* introduced earlier in the context of model selection is the mean of the *in-sample* residuals, as opposed to out-of-sample prediction errors. The distinction is crucial.

BIBLIOGRAPHICAL AND COMPUTATIONAL NOTES

AIC and *SIC* trace at least to Akaike (1974) and Schwarz (1978). Granger, King, and White (1995) provide insightful discussion of consistency of model selection criteria, and the key (but difficult) reference on efficiency is Shibata (1980). Engle and Brown (1986) find that criteria with comparatively harsh degrees-of-freedom penalties (e.g., *SIC*) select the best forecasting models.

Kennedy (1992) reviews a number of corrections for the bias in exp $((\ln y)_{t+h,t})$.

A number of authors have begun to investigate the use of multiple models for multiple horizons, including Findley (1983) and Tiao and Tsay (1994). Findley (1985) develops criteria for selection of multi-step-ahead forecasting models.

CONCEPTS FOR REVIEW

Adjusted R^2	One-sided moving average
Akaike information criterion (AIC)	One-sided weighted moving average
Argmin	Out-of-sample 1-step-ahead
Asymptotic efficiency	prediction error variance
Bias correction	Polynomial trend
Consistency	Quadratic trend
Data-generating process (DGP)	R^2
Data mining	Real-time, or on-line, smoothing
Deterministic trend	Residual serial correlation
Detrending	s^2
Exponential trend	Schwarz information criterion (SIC)
Ex post, or off-line, smoothing	Slope
In-sample overfitting	Smoothing
Intercept	Stochastic trend
Least squares regression	Sum of squared residuals
Logistic trend	Time dummy
Log linear trend	Trend
Mean squared error	Two-sided moving average
Model selection	

REFERENCES AND ADDITIONAL READINGS

Akaike, H. (1974), "A New Look at the Statistical Model Identification," *IEEE Transactions on Automatic Control*, AC-19, 716–723.

Engle, R. F., and Brown, S. J. (1986), "Model Selection for Forecasting," *Applied Mathematics and Computation,* 20, 313–327.

Findley, D. F. (1983), "On the Use of Multiple Models for Multi-Period Forecasting," in *Proceedings of the American Statistical Association, Business, and Economic Statistics Section,* 528–531.

Findley, D. F. (1985), "Model Selection for Multi-Step-Ahead Forecasting," in *Identification and System Parameter Estimation,* 7th IFAC/FORS Symposium, 1039–1044.

Granger, C. W. J., King, M. L., and White, H. (1995), "Comments on the Testing of Economic Theories and the Use of Model Selection Criteria," *Journal of Econometrics,* 67, 173–187.

Kennedy, P. (1992), *A Guide to Econometrics,* third edition. Cambridge, Mass.: MIT Press.

Schwarz, G. (1978), "Estimating the Dimension of a Model," *Annals of Statistics,* 6, 461–464.

Shibata, R. (1980), "Asymptotically Efficient Selection of the Order of the Model for Estimating the Parameters of a Linear Process," *Annals of Statistics,* 8, 147–164.

Tiao, G. C., and Tsay, R. S. (1994), "Some Advances in Non-Linear and Adaptive Modeling in Time Series," *Journal of Forecasting,* 13, 109–131.

MODELING AND FORECASTING SEASONALITY

1. THE NATURE AND SOURCES OF SEASONALITY

In the last chapter we focused on the trends; now we focus on **seasonality.** A seasonal pattern is one that repeats itself every year.[1] The annual repetition can be *exact,* in which case we speak of **deterministic seasonality,** or approximate, in which case we speak of **stochastic seasonality.** Just as we focused exclusively on deterministic trend in chapter 4, reserving stochastic trend for subsequent treatment, so too shall we focus exclusively on deterministic seasonality here.

Seasonality arises from links of technologies, preferences, and institutions to the calendar. The weather (e.g., daily high temperature in Tokyo) is a trivial but very important seasonal series, because it is always hotter in the summer than in the winter. Any technology that involves the weather, such as production of agricultural commodities, is likely to be seasonal as well.

Preferences may also be linked to the calendar. Consider, for example, gasoline sales. In Figure 5.1 we show monthly U.S. current-dollar gasoline sales, 1980.02–1992.01. People want to do more vacation travel in the sum-

---

1. Note that seasonality is impossible, and therefore not an issue, in data recorded once per year or less often than once per year.

FIGURE 5.1   Gasoline Sales

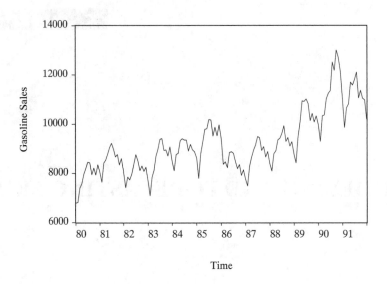

Time

mer, which tends to increase the price and quantity of summertime gasoline sales, both of which feed into higher current-dollar sales.

Finally, social institutions that are linked to the calendar, such as holidays, are responsible for seasonal variation in a variety of series. Purchases of retail goods skyrocket, for example, every Christmas season. In Figure 5.2, we plot monthly U.S. current-dollar liquor sales, 1980.01–1992.01, which are very high in November and December. In contrast, sales of durable goods fall in December, as Christmas purchases tend to be nondurables. This emerges clearly in Figure 5.3, in which we show monthly U.S. current-dollar durable goods sales, 1980.01–1992.01.

You might imagine that, although certain series are seasonal for obvious reasons, seasonality is nevertheless uncommon. On the contrary—and perhaps surprisingly—seasonality is pervasive in business and economics. Many industrialized economies, for example, expand briskly every fourth quarter and contract every first quarter.

One way to deal with seasonality in a series is simply to remove it, and then to model and forecast the **seasonally adjusted series.**[2] This strategy is perhaps appropriate in certain situations, such as when interest centers explicitly on forecasting **nonseasonal fluctuations,** as is often the case in macroeconomics. Seasonal adjustment is often inappropriate in business forecast-

---

2. Removal of seasonality is called **seasonal adjustment.**

FIGURE 5.2   Liquor Sales

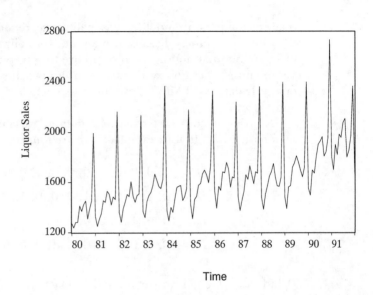

Time

ing situations, however, precisely because interest typically centers on forecasting *all* the variation in a series, not just the nonseasonal part. If seasonality is responsible for a large part of the variation in a series of interest, the last thing a forecaster wants to do is discard it and pretend it isn't there.

FIGURE 5.3   Durable Goods Sales

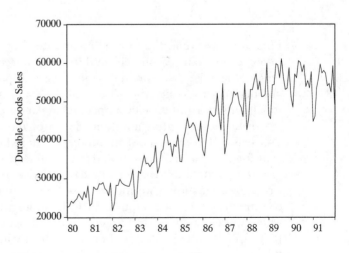

Time

2. MODELING SEASONALITY

A key technique for modeling seasonality is **regression on seasonal dummies.** Let s be the number of seasons in a year. Normally we think of four seasons in a year, but that notion is too restrictive for our purposes. Instead, think of s as the number of observations in a series in each year. Thus $s = 4$ if we have quarterly data, $s = 12$ if we have monthly data, $s = 52$ if we have weekly data, and so forth.

Now let us construct s **seasonal dummy variables,** which indicate what season we are in. If, for example, there are four seasons, we create:

$$D_1 = (1, 0, 0, 0, 1, 0, 0, 0, 1, 0, 0, 0, \ldots)$$
$$D_2 = (0, 1, 0, 0, 0, 1, 0, 0, 0, 1, 0, 0, \ldots)$$
$$D_3 = (0, 0, 1, 0, 0, 0, 1, 0, 0, 0, 1, 0, \ldots)$$
$$D_4 = (0, 0, 0, 1, 0, 0, 0, 1, 0, 0, 0, 1, \ldots)$$

D_1 indicates whether we are in the first quarter (it is 1 in the first quarter and 0 otherwise), D_2 indicates whether we are in the second quarter (it is 1 in the second quarter and 0 otherwise), and so on. At any given time, we can be in only one of the four quarters, so one seasonal dummy is 1, and all others are 0.

The pure seasonal dummy model is

$$y_t = \sum_{i=1}^{s} \gamma_i D_{it} + \varepsilon_t$$

Effectively, we are just regressing on an intercept, but we allow for a different intercept in each season. Those different intercepts, the γ_i's, are called the seasonal factors; they summarize the seasonal pattern over the year. In the absence of seasonality, the γ_i's are all the same, so we can drop all the seasonal dummies and instead simply include an intercept in the usual way.

Instead of including a full set of s seasonal dummies, we can include any $s - 1$ seasonal dummies and an intercept. Then the constant term is the intercept for the omitted season, and the coefficients on the seasonal dummies give the seasonal increase or decrease relative to the omitted season. In no case, however, should we include s seasonal dummies *and* an intercept. Including an intercept is equivalent to including a variable in the regression whose value is always 1, but note that the full set of s seasonal dummies sums to a variable whose value is always 1. Thus, inclusion of an intercept and a full set of seasonal dummies produces perfect multicollinearity, and your computer will scream at you if you run such a regression. (Try it!)

Trend may be included as well, in which case the model is[3]

$$y_t = \beta_1 \ TIME_t + \sum_{i=1}^{s} \gamma_i D_{it} + \varepsilon_t$$

In fact, you can think of what we are doing in this chapter as a generalization of what we did in the last chapter, in which we focused exclusively on trend. We *still* want to account for trend, if it is present, but we want to expand the model so that we can account for seasonality as well.

The idea of seasonality may be extended to allow for more general **calendar effects.** "Standard" seasonality is just one type of calendar effect. Two additional important calendar effects are **holiday variation** and **trading-day variation.**

Holiday variation refers to the fact that the dates of some holidays change over time. That is, although they arrive at approximately the same time each year, the exact dates differ. Easter is a common example. Because the behavior of many series, such as sales, shipments, inventories, hours worked, and so on, depends in part on the timing of such holidays, we may want to keep track of them in our forecasting models. As with seasonality, holiday effects may be handled with dummy variables. In a monthly model, for example, in addition to a full set of seasonal dummies, we might include an "Easter dummy," which is 1 if the month contains Easter and 0 otherwise.

Trading-day variation refers to the fact that different months contain different numbers of trading days or business days, which is an important consideration when modeling and forecasting certain series. For example, in a monthly forecasting model of volume traded on the London Stock Exchange, in addition to a full set of seasonal dummies, we might include a trading-day variable, whose value each month is the number of trading days that month.

Allowing for the possibility of holiday or trading-day variation gives the complete model

$$y_t = \beta_1 \ TIME_t + \sum_{i=1}^{s} \gamma_i D_{it} + \sum_{i=1}^{v_1} \delta_i^{HD} HDV_{it} + \sum_{i=1}^{v_2} \delta_i^{TD} TDV_{it} + \varepsilon_t$$

where the *HDV*s are the relevant holiday variables (there are v_1 of them) and the *TDV*s are the relevant trading day variables (here we have allowed for v_2 of them, but in most applications $v_2 = 1$ will be adequate). This is just a standard regression equation and can be estimated by ordinary least squares.

---

3. For simplicity we have included only a linear trend, but more complicated models of trend, such as quadratic, exponential, or logistic, could be used.

3. FORECASTING SEASONAL SERIES

Now consider constructing an h-step-ahead point forecast, $y_{T+h,T}$, at time T. As with the pure trend models discussed in the previous chapter, there is no problem in forecasting the right-hand-side variables, due to the special (perfectly predictable) nature of trend and seasonal variables, so point forecasts are easy to generate.

The full model is

$$y_t = \beta_1 \, TIME_t + \sum_{i=1}^{s} \gamma_i \, D_{it} + \sum_{i=1}^{v_1} \delta_i^{HD} HDV_{it} + \sum_{i=1}^{v_2} \delta_i^{TD} TDV_{it} + \varepsilon_t$$

so that at time $T + h$,

$$y_{T+h} = \beta_1 \, TIME_{T+h} + \sum_{i=1}^{s} \gamma_i \, D_{i,T+h} + \sum_{i=1}^{v_1} \delta_i^{HD} HDV_{i,T+h} + \sum_{i=1}^{v_2} \delta_i^{TD} TDV_{i,T+h} + \varepsilon_{T+h}$$

As with the pure trend model of chapter 4, we project the right side of the equation on what is known at time T (that is, the time-T information set, Ω_T) to obtain the forecast

$$y_{T+h,T} = \beta_1 \, TIME_{T+h} + \sum_{i=1}^{s} \gamma_i \, D_{i,T+h} + \sum_{i=1}^{v_1} \delta_i^{HD} HDV_{i,T+h} + \sum_{i=1}^{v_2} \delta_i^{TD} TDV_{i,T+h}$$

As always, we make this point forecast operational by replacing unknown parameters with estimates,

$$\hat{y}_{T+h,T} = \hat{\beta}_1 \, TIME_{T+h} + \sum_{i=1}^{s} \hat{\gamma}_i \, D_{i,T+h} + \sum_{i=1}^{v_1} \hat{\delta}_i^{HD} HDV_{i,T+h} + \sum_{i=1}^{v_2} \hat{\delta}_i^{TD} TDV_{i,T+h}$$

To form an interval forecast we proceed precisely as in pure trend models we studied earlier. We assume that the regression disturbance is normally distributed, in which case a 95% interval forecast ignoring parameter estimation uncertainty is $y_{T+h,T} \pm 1.96\sigma$, where σ is the standard deviation of the regression disturbance. To make the interval forecast operational, we use $\hat{y}_{T+h,T} \pm 1.96\hat{\sigma}$, where $\hat{\sigma}$ is the standard error of the regression.

To form a density forecast, we again assume that the trend regression disturbance is normally distributed. Then, ignoring parameter estimation uncertainty, the interval forecast is $N(y_{T+h,T}, \sigma^2)$, where σ is the standard deviation of the disturbance in the trend regression. The operational density forecast is then $N(\hat{y}_{T+h,T}, \hat{\sigma}^2)$.

4. APPLICATION: FORECASTING HOUSING STARTS

We now use the seasonal modeling techniques that we have developed in this chapter to build a forecasting model for housing starts. Housing starts are seasonal because it is usually preferable to start houses in the spring so that they are completed before winter arrives. Using monthly data on U.S. housing starts, we choose the 1946.01–1993.12 period for estimation and the 1994.01–1994.11 period for out-of-sample forecasting. We show the entire series in Figure 5.4, and we zoom in on the 1990.01–1994.11 period in Figure 5.5 to reveal the seasonal pattern in better detail.

The figures reveal that there is no trend, so we work with the pure seasonal model,

$$y_t = \sum_{i=1}^{s} \gamma_i D_{it} + \varepsilon_t$$

Table 5.1 shows the estimation results. The 12 seasonal dummies account for more than a third of the variation in housing starts, as $R^2 = 0.38$. At least some of the remaining variation is cyclical, which the model is not designed to capture. (Note the very low Durbin-Watson statistic.)

FIGURE 5.4 Housing Starts, 1994.01–1994.11

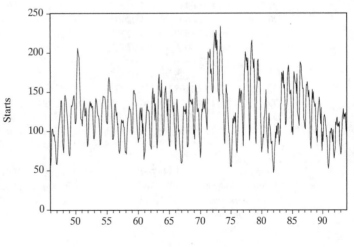

Time

FIGURE 5.5   Housing Starts, 1990.01–1994.11

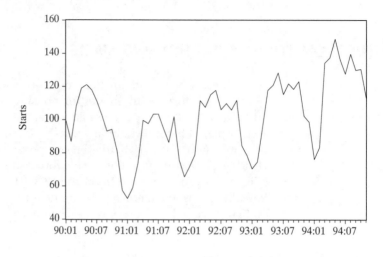

Time

TABLE 5.1   Regression Results: Seasonal Dummy Variable Model for Housing Starts

LS // Dependent Variable is STARTS
Sample: 1946:01 1993:12
Included observations: 576

Variable	Coefficient	Std. Error	t-Statistic	Prob.
D1	86.50417	4.029055	21.47009	0.0000
D2	89.50417	4.029055	22.21468	0.0000
D3	122.8833	4.029055	30.49929	0.0000
D4	142.1687	4.029055	35.28588	0.0000
D5	147.5000	4.029055	36.60908	0.0000
D6	145.9979	4.029055	36.23627	0.0000
D7	139.1125	4.029055	34.52733	0.0000
D8	138.4167	4.029055	34.35462	0.0000
D9	130.5625	4.029055	32.40524	0.0000
D10	134.0917	4.029055	33.28117	0.0000
D11	111.8333	4.029055	27.75671	0.0000
D12	92.15833	4.029055	22.87344	0.0000

R-squared	0.383780	Mean dependent var	123.3944	
Adjusted R-squared	0.371762	S.D. dependent var	35.21775	
S.E. of regression	27.91411	Akaike info criterion	6.678878	
Sum squared resid	439467.5	Schwarz criterion	6.769630	
Log likelihood	-2728.825	F-statistic	31.93250	
Durbin-Watson stat	0.154140	Prob(F-statistic)	0.000000	

FIGURE 5.6   Residual Plot

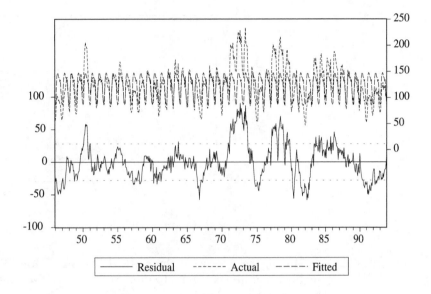

The residual plot in Figure 5.6 makes clear the strengths and limitations of the model. First, compare the actual and fitted values. The fitted values go through the same seasonal pattern every year—there is nothing in the model other than deterministic seasonal dummies—but that rigid seasonal pattern picks up a lot of the variation in housing starts. It doesn't pick up *all* of the variation, however, as evidenced by the serial correlation that is apparent in the residuals. Note the dips in the residuals, for example, in recessions (e.g., 1990, 1982, 1980, and 1975), and the peaks in booms.

The estimated seasonal factors are just the 12 estimated coefficients on the seasonal dummies, graphed in Figure 5.7. The seasonal effects are very low in January and February, and then rise quickly and peak in May, after which they decline, at first slowly and then abruptly in November and December.

In Figure 5.8 we see the history of housing starts through 1993, together with the out-of-sample point and 95% interval extrapolation forecasts for the first 11 months of 1994. The forecasts look reasonable, as the model has evidently done a good job of capturing the seasonal pattern. The forecast intervals are quite wide, however, reflecting the fact that the seasonal effects captured by the forecasting model are responsible for only about a third of the variation in the variable being forecast.

FIGURE 5.7   Estimated Seasonal Factors: Housing Starts

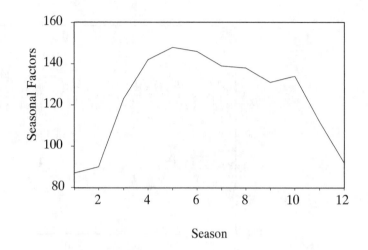

Season

In Figure 5.9, we include the 1994 realization. The forecast appears highly accurate, as the realization and forecast are quite close throughout. Moreover, the realization is everywhere well within the 95% interval.

FIGURE 5.8   Housing Starts: History (1990.01–1993.12) and Forecast (1994.01–1994.11)

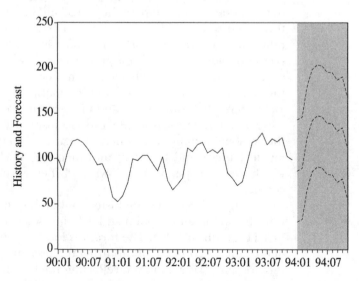

Time

FIGURE 5.9   Housing Starts: History (1990.01–1993.12) and Forecast and
Realization (1994.01–1994.11)

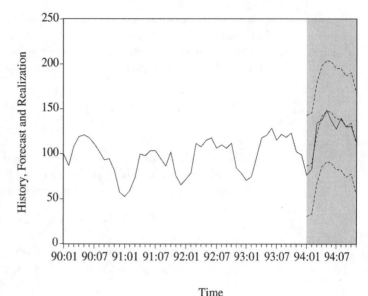

Time

PROBLEMS AND COMPLEMENTS

1. (Log transformations in seasonal models) Just as log transformations
    were useful in trend models to allow for nonlinearity, so too are they use-
    ful in seasonal models, although for a somewhat different purpose: **stabi-
    lization of variance.** Often log transformations stabilize seasonal patterns
    whose variance is growing over time. Explain and illustrate.

2. (Seasonal adjustment) Just as we sometimes want to remove the trend
    from a series, sometimes we want to seasonally adjust a series before mod-
    eling and forecasting it. Seasonal adjustment may be done with moving
    average methods analogous to those used for detrending in chapter 4, or
    with the dummy variable methods discussed in this chapter, or with so-
    phisticated hybrid methods like the X-11 procedure developed at the
    U.S. Census Bureau.

    (a) Discuss in detail how you would use dummy variable regression
        methods to seasonally adjust a series. (*Hint:* The seasonally adjusted
        series is closely related to the residual from the seasonal dummy vari-
        able regression.)

    (b) Seasonally adjust the housing starts series using dummy variable re-
        gression. Discuss the patterns present and absent from the seasonally
        adjusted series.

(c) Search the web (or the library) for information on the Census X-11
     seasonal adjustment procedure and report what you learned.

3. (Selecting forecasting models involving calendar effects) You are sure
    that a series you want to forecast is trending, and that a linear trend is
    adequate, but you are not sure whether seasonality is important. To be
    safe, you fit a forecasting model with both trend and seasonal dummies,

$$y_t = \beta_1 \, TIME_t + \sum_{i=1}^{s} \gamma_i \, D_{it} + \varepsilon_t$$

(a) The hypothesis of no seasonality, in which case you could drop the
     seasonal dummies, corresponds to equal seasonal coefficients across
     seasons, which is a set of $s - 1$ linear restrictions:

$$\gamma_1 = \gamma_2, \, \gamma_2 = \gamma_3, \, \ldots, \, \gamma_{s-1} = \gamma_s$$

     How would you perform an F test of the hypothesis? What assump-
     tions are you implicitly making about the regression's disturbance
     term?
(b) Alternatively, how would you use forecast model selection criteria to
     decide whether to include the seasonal dummies?
(c) What would you do in the event that the results of the "hypothesis
     testing" and "model selection" approaches disagree?
(d) How, if at all, would your answers change if instead of considering
     whether to include seasonal dummies you were considering whether
     to include holiday dummies? Trading-day dummies?

4. (Seasonal regressions with an intercept and $s - 1$ seasonal dummies) Re-
    estimate the housing starts model using an intercept and 11 seasonal
    dummies, rather than the full set of seasonal dummies as in the text.
    Compare and contrast your results with those reported in the text.

5. (Applied trend and seasonal modeling) Nile.com, a successful online
    bookseller, monitors and forecasts the number of "hits" per day to its web
    page. You have daily hits data for January 1, 1998 through September 28,
    1998.

(a) Fit and assess the standard linear, quadratic, and log linear trend
     models.
(b) For a few contiguous days roughly in late April and early May, hits
     were much higher than usual during a big sale. Do you find evidence
     of a corresponding group of outliers in the residuals from your
     trend models? Do they influence your trend estimates much? How
     should you treat them?

(c) Model and assess the significance of day-of-week effects in Nile.com web page hits.

(d) Select a final model, consisting only of trend and seasonal components, to use for forecasting. Assess its structural stability.

(e) Use your model to forecast Nile.com hits through the end of 1998.

(f) Compute your model's residual sample autocorrelations, sample partial autocorrelations, and related diagnostic statistics. Discuss.

BIBLIOGRAPHICAL AND COMPUTATIONAL NOTES

Nerlove, Grether, and Carvalho (1996) discuss various aspects of seasonality relevant for forecasting.

CONCEPTS FOR REVIEW

Calendar effect

Deterministic seasonality

Holiday variation

Nonseasonal fluctuations

Regression on seasonal dummies

Seasonal adjustment

Seasonal dummy variables

Seasonality

Seasonally adjusted series

Stabilization of variance

Stochastic seasonality

Trading-day variation

REFERENCES AND ADDITIONAL READINGS

Nerlove, M., Grether, D. M., and Carvalho, J. L. (1996), *Analysis of Economic Time Series: A Synthesis*, second edition. New York: Academic Press.

CHARACTERIZING CYCLES

We have already built forecasting models with trend and seasonal components. In this chapter, as well as the next two, we consider a crucial third component, **cycles.** When you think of a "cycle," you probably think of the sort of rigid up-and-down pattern depicted in Figure 6.1. Such cycles can sometimes arise, but cyclical fluctuations in business, finance, economics, and government are typically much less rigid. In fact, when we speak of cycles, we have in mind a much more general, all-encompassing notion of cyclicality: any sort of dynamics not captured by trends or seasonals.

Cycles, according to our broad interpretation, may display the sort of back-and-forth movement charactured in Figure 6.1, but they don't have to. All we require is that there be some dynamics, some persistence, some way in which the present is linked to the past, and the future to the present. Cycles are present in most of the series that concern us, and it is crucial that we know how to model and forecast them because their history conveys information regarding their future.

Trend and seasonal dynamics are simple, so we can capture them with simple models. Cyclical dynamics, however, are more complicated. Because of the wide variety of cyclical patterns, the sorts of models we need are substantially more involved. Thus we split the discussion into three parts. In this

FIGURE 6.1   A Rigid Cyclical Pattern

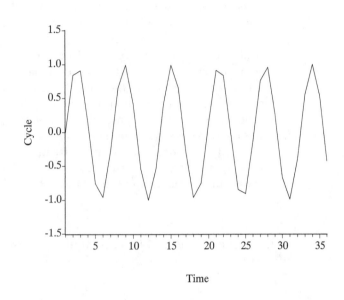

chapter we develop methods for *characterizing* cycles, in chapter 7 we discuss *models* of cycles, and following that, in chapter 8, we show how to use those models to *forecast* cycles. All of the material is crucial to a real understanding of forecasting and forecasting models. It is also a bit difficult the first time around because it is unavoidably rather mathematical, so careful, systematic study is required. The payoff will be large when we arrive at chapter 9, in which we assemble and apply extensively the ideas for modeling and forecasting trends, seasonals, and cycles developed in chapters 4 through 8.

1. COVARIANCE STATIONARY TIME SERIES

A **realization** of a time series is an ordered set, $\{\ldots, y_{-2}, y_{-1}, y_0, y_1, y_2, \ldots\}$. Typically the observations are ordered in time—hence the name **time series**—but they don't have to be. We could, for example, examine a spatial series, such as office space rental rates as we move along a line from a point in midtown Manhattan to a point in the New York suburbs 30 miles away. But the most important case for forecasting, by far, involves observations ordered in time, so that is what we stress here.

In theory, a time series realization begins in the infinite past and continues into the infinite future. This perspective may seem abstract and of limited practical applicability, but it will be useful in deriving certain very important properties of the forecasting models we will be using shortly. In practice, of course, the data we observe is just a finite subset of a realization, $\{y_1, \ldots, y_T\}$, called a **sample path.**

Shortly we will be building forecasting models for cyclical time series. If the underlying probabilistic structure of the series were changing over time, we would be doomed—there would be no way to predict the future accurately on the basis of the past because the laws governing the future would differ from those governing the past. If we want to forecast a series, at a minimum we would like its mean and its covariance structure (that is, the covariances between current and past values) to be stable over time; in that case we say that the series is covariance stationary.

Let us discuss **covariance stationarity** in greater depth. The first requirement for a series to be covariance stationary is that the mean of the series be stable over time. The mean of the series at time t is

$$Ey_t = \mu_t$$

If the mean is stable over time, as required by covariance stationarity, then we can write

$$Ey_t = \mu$$

for all t. Because the mean is constant over time, there is no need to put a time subscript on it.

The second requirement for a series to be covariance stationary is that its covariance structure be stable over time. Quantifying stability of the covariance structure is a bit tricky, but tremendously important, and we do it using the **autocovariance function.** The autocovariance at displacement τ is just the covariance between y_t and $y_{t-\tau}$. It will of course depend on τ, and it may also depend on t, so in general we write

$$\gamma(t,\tau) = \text{cov} (y_t, y_{t-\tau}) = E (y_t - \mu) (y_{t-\tau} - \mu)$$

If the covariance structure is stable over time, as required by covariance stationarity, then the autocovariances depend only on displacement, τ, not on time, t, and we write

$$\gamma(t,\tau) = \gamma(\tau)$$

for all t.

The autocovariance function is important because it provides a basic summary of cyclical dynamics in a covariance stationary series. By examining the autocovariance structure of a series, we learn about its dynamic behavior. We graph and examine the autocovariances as a function of τ. Note that the autocovariance function is symmetric; that is,

$$\gamma(\tau) = \gamma(-\tau)$$

for all τ. Typically, we consider only nonnegative values of τ. Symmetry reflects the fact that the autocovariance of a covariance stationary series depends only on displacement; it doesn't matter whether we go forward or backward. Note also that

$$\gamma(0) = \text{cov}\,(y_t,\, y_t) = \text{var}\,(y_t)$$

There is one more technical requirement of covariance stationarity; we require that the variance of the series—the autocovariance at displacement 0, $\gamma(0)$—be finite. It can be shown that no autocovariance can be larger in absolute value than $\gamma(0)$, so if $\gamma(0) < \infty$, then so too are all the other autocovariances.

It may seem that the requirements for covariance stationarity are quite stringent, which would bode poorly for our forecasting models, almost all of which invoke covariance stationarity in one way or another. It is certainly true that many economic, business, financial, and government series are not covariance stationary. An upward trend, for example, corresponds to a steadily increasing mean, and seasonality corresponds to means that vary with the season, both of which are violations of covariance stationarity.

But appearances can be deceptive. Although many series are not covariance stationary, it is frequently possible to work with models that give special treatment to nonstationary components such as trend and seasonality, so that the cyclical component left over is likely to be covariance stationary. We often adopt that strategy. Alternatively, simple transformations often appear to transform nonstationary series to covariance stationarity. For example, many series that are clearly nonstationary in levels appear covariance stationary in growth rates.

In addition, note that although covariance stationarity requires means and covariances to be stable and finite, it places no restrictions on other aspects of the distribution of the series, such as skewness and kurtosis.[1] The upshot is simple: Whether we work directly in levels and include special components for the nonstationary elements of our models, or we work on transformed data such as growth rates, the covariance stationarity assumption is not as unrealistic as it may seem.

Recall that the correlation between two random variables x and y is defined by

$$\text{corr}\,(x,\, y) = \frac{\text{cov}\,(x,\, y)}{\sigma_x \sigma_y}$$

---

1. For that reason, covariance stationarity is sometimes called **second-order stationarity** or **weak stationarity**.

That is, the correlation is simply the covariance, "normalized" or "standardized" by the product of the standard deviations of x and y. Both the correlation and the covariance are measures of linear association between two random variables. The correlation is often more informative and easily interpreted, however, because the construction of the correlation coefficient guarantees that $\text{corr}(x, y) \in [-1, 1]$, whereas the covariance between the same two random variables may take any value. The correlation, moreover, does not depend on the units in which x and y are measured, whereas the covariance does. Thus, for example, if x and y have a covariance of 10 million, they are not necessarily very strongly associated, whereas if they have a correlation of 0.95, it is unambiguously clear that they are very strongly associated.

In light of the superior interpretability of correlations as compared to covariances, we often work with the correlation, rather than the covariance, between y_t and $y_{t-\tau}$. That is, we work with the **autocorrelation function,** $\rho(\tau)$, rather than the autocovariance function, $\gamma(\tau)$. The autocorrelation function is obtained by dividing the autocovariance function by the variance,

$$\rho(\tau) = \frac{\gamma(\tau)}{\gamma(0)}, \ \tau = 0, 1, 2, \ldots$$

The formula for the autocorrelation is just the usual correlation formula, specialized to the correlation between y_t and $y_{t-\tau}$. To see why, note that the variance of y_t is $\gamma(0)$, and by covariance stationarity, the variance of y at any other time $y_{t-\tau}$ is also $\gamma(0)$. Thus,

$$\rho(\tau) = \frac{\text{cov}(y_t, y_{t-\tau})}{\sqrt{\text{var}(y_t)} \ \sqrt{\text{var}(y_{t-\tau})}} = \frac{\gamma(\tau)}{\sqrt{\gamma(0)} \ \sqrt{\gamma(0)}} = \frac{\gamma(\tau)}{\gamma(0)}$$

as claimed. Note that we always have $\rho(0) = \gamma(0)/\gamma(0) = 1$, because any series is perfectly correlated with itself. Thus the autocorrelation at displacement 0 isn't of interest; rather, only the autocorrelations *beyond* displacement 0 inform us about a series' dynamic structure.

Finally, the **partial autocorrelation function,** $p(\tau)$, is sometimes useful. $p(\tau)$ is just the coefficient on $y_{t-\tau}$ in a population linear regression of y_t on y_{t-} $1, \ldots, y_{t-\tau}$.[2] We call such regressions **autoregressions** because the variable is regressed on lagged values of itself. It is easy to see that the autocorrelations

---

2. To get a feel for what we mean by **"population regression,"** imagine that we have an infinite sample of data at our disposal, so that the parameter estimates in the regression are not contaminated by sampling variation—that is, they are the true population values. The thought experiment just described is a population regression.

FIGURE 6.2   Autocorrelation Function, Gradual One-Sided Damping

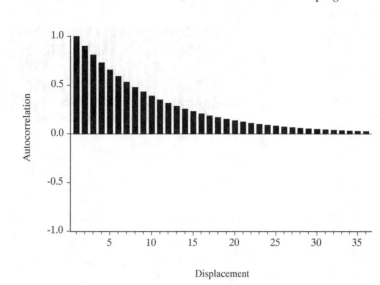

and partial autocorrelations, although related, differ in an important way. The autocorrelations are just the "simple" or "regular" correlations between y_t and $y_{t-\tau}$. The partial autocorrelations, on the other hand, measure the association between y_t and $y_{t-\tau}$ after *controlling* for the effects of $y_{t-1}, \ldots, y_{t-\tau+1}$; that is, they measure the partial correlation between y_t and $y_{t-\tau}$.

As with the autocorrelations, we often graph the partial autocorrelations as a function of τ and examine their qualitative shape, which we shall do soon. Like the autocorrelation function, the partial autocorrelation function provides a summary of a series' dynamics, but as we shall see, it does so in a different way.[3]

All of the covariance stationary processes that we will study subsequently have autocorrelation and partial autocorrelation functions that approach 0, one way or another, as the displacement gets large. In Figure 6.2 we show an autocorrelation function that displays gradual one-sided damping, and in Figure 6.3 we show a constant autocorrelation function; the latter could not be the autocorrelation function of a stationary process, whose autocorrelation function must eventually decay. The precise decay patterns of autocorrelations and partial autocorrelations of a covariance stationary series, however,

---

3. Also in parallel to the autocorrelation function, the partial autocorrelation at displacement 0 is always 1 and is therefore uninformative and uninteresting. Thus, when we graph the autocorrelation and partial autocorrelation functions, we begin at displacement 1 rather than displacement 0.

FIGURE 6.3   Autocorrelation Function, Nondamping

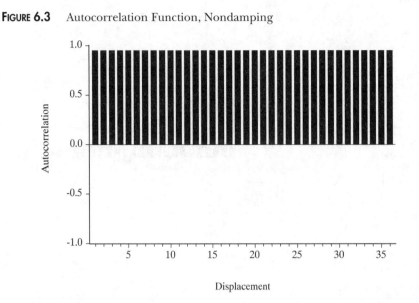

depend on the specifics of the series, as we shall see in detail in the next chapter. In Figure 6.4, for example, we show an autocorrelation function that displays damped oscillation—the autocorrelations are positive at first, then become negative for a while, then positive again, and so on, while continuously getting smaller in absolute value. Finally, in Figure 6.5 we show an autocorrelation function that differs in the way it approaches zero—the autocorrelations drop abruptly to 0 beyond a certain displacement.

FIGURE 6.4   Autocorrelation Function, Gradual Damped Oscillation

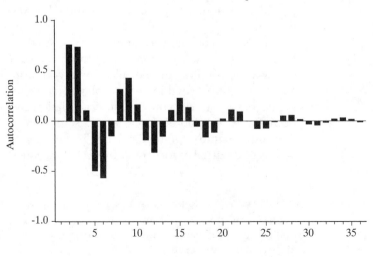

FIGURE 6.5   Autocorrelation Function, Sharp Cutoff

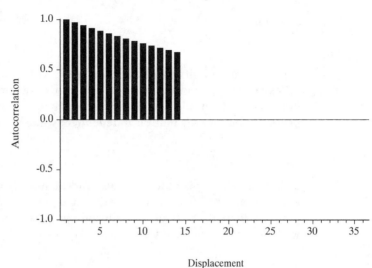

2. WHITE NOISE

In this section, and throughout the next chapter, we study the population properties of certain time series models, or **time series processes,** which are very important for forecasting. Before we estimate time series forecasting models, we need to understand their population properties, assuming that the postulated model is true. The simplest of all such time series processes is the fundamental building block from which all others are constructed. In fact, it is so important that we introduce it now. We use y to denote the observed series of interest. Suppose that

$$y_t = \varepsilon_t$$

$$\varepsilon_t \sim (0, \sigma^2)$$

where the "shock," ε_t, is uncorrelated over time. We say that ε_t, and hence y_t, is **serially uncorrelated.** Throughout, unless explicitly stated otherwise, we assume that $\sigma^2 < \infty$. Such a process, with zero mean, constant variance, and no serial correlation, is called **zero-mean white noise,** or simply **white noise.**[4] Sometimes for short we write

---

4.   White noise is analogous to white light, which is composed of all colors of the spectrum in equal amounts. We can think of white noise as being composed of a wide variety of cycles of differing periodicities in equal amounts.

$$\varepsilon_t \sim WN(0, \sigma^2)$$

and hence

$$y_t \sim WN(0, \sigma^2)$$

Note that, although ε_t and hence y_t are serially uncorrelated, they are not necessarily serially independent, because they are not necessarily normally distributed.[5] If in addition to being serially uncorrelated, y is serially independent, then we say that y is **independent white noise.** We write

$$y_t \overset{\text{iid}}{\sim} (0, \sigma^2)$$

and we say that "y is independently and identically distributed with 0 mean and constant variance." If y is serially uncorrelated and normally distributed, then it follows that y is also serially independent, and we say that y is **normal white noise,** or **Gaussian white noise.**[6] We write

$$y_t \overset{\text{iid}}{\sim} N(0, \sigma^2)$$

We read "y is independently and identically distributed as normal, with 0 mean and constant variance," or simply "y is Gaussian white noise." In Figure 6.6 we show a sample path of Gaussian white noise, of length $T = 150$, simulated on a computer. There are no patterns of any kind in the series due to the independence over time.

You already are familiar with white noise, although you may not realize it. Recall that the disturbance in a regression model is typically assumed to be white noise of one sort or another. There is a subtle difference here, however. Regression disturbances are not observable, whereas we are working with an observed series. Later, however, we shall see how all of our models for observed series can be used to model unobserved variables such as regression disturbances.

Let us characterize the dynamic stochastic structure of white noise, $y_t \sim WN(0, \sigma^2)$. By construction, the unconditional mean of y is

$$E(y_t) = 0$$

and the unconditional variance of y is

$$\text{var}(y_t) = \sigma^2$$

---

5. Recall that zero correlation implies independence only in the normal case.

6. Karl Friedrich Gauss, one of the greatest mathematicians of all time, discovered the normal distribution some 200 years ago; hence the adjective "Gaussian."

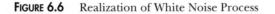

FIGURE 6.6   Realization of White Noise Process

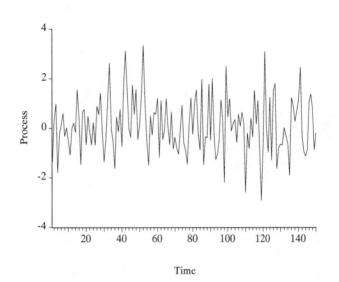

Time

Note that the unconditional mean and variance are constant. In fact, the unconditional mean and variance must be constant for any covariance stationary process. The reason is that constancy of the unconditional mean was our first explicit requirement of covariance stationarity, and that constancy of the unconditional variance follows implicitly from the second requirement of covariance stationarity—that the autocovariances depend only on displacement, not on time.[7]

To understand fully the linear dynamic structure of a covariance stationary time series process, we need to compute and examine its mean and its autocovariance function. For white noise, we have already computed the mean and the variance, which is the autocovariance at displacement 0. We have yet to compute the rest of the autocovariance function; fortunately, however, it is very simple. Because white noise is, by definition, uncorrelated over time, all the autocovariances, and hence all the autocorrelations, are 0 beyond displacement 0.[8] Formally, then, the autocovariance function for a white noise process is

$$\gamma(\tau) = \begin{cases} \sigma^2, \tau = 0 \\ 0, \tau \geq 1 \end{cases}$$

---

7. Recall that $\sigma^2 = \gamma(0)$.

8. If the autocovariances are all 0, so are the autocorrelations, because the autocorrelations are proportional to the autocovariances.

FIGURE **6.7**   Population Autocorrelation Function: White Noise Process

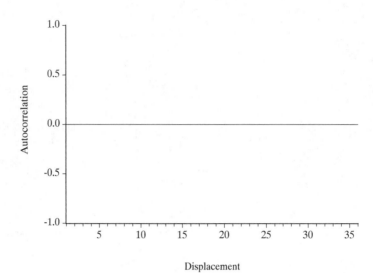

Displacement

and the autocorrelation function for a white noise process is

$$\rho(\tau) = \begin{cases} 1, \tau = 0 \\ 0, \tau \geq 1 \end{cases}$$

In Figure 6.7 we plot the white noise autocorrelation function.

Finally, consider the partial autocorrelation function for a white noise series. For the same reason that the autocorrelation at displacement 0 is always 1, so too is the partial autocorrelation at displacement 0. For a white noise process, all partial autocorrelations beyond displacement 0 are 0, which again follows from the fact that white noise, by construction, is serially uncorrelated. Population regressions of y_t on y_{t-1}, or on y_{t-1} and y_{t-2}, or on any other lags, produce nothing but zero coefficients, because the process is serially uncorrelated. Formally, the partial autocorrelation function of a white noise process is

$$p(\tau) = \begin{cases} 1, \tau = 0 \\ 0, \tau \geq 1 \end{cases}$$

We show the partial autocorrelation function of a white noise process in Figure 6.8. Again, it is degenerate, and exactly the same as the autocorrelation function!

By now you surely have noticed that if you were assigned the task of forecasting independent white noise, you would likely be doomed to failure.

FIGURE 6.8   Population Partial Autocorrelation Function: White Noise Process

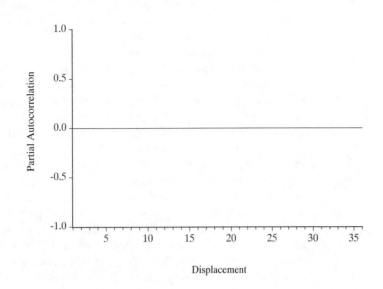

What happens to a white noise series at any time is uncorrelated with any-thing in the past, and similarly, what happens in the future is uncorrelated with anything in the present or past. But understanding white noise is tre-mendously important for at least two reasons. First, as already mentioned, processes with much richer dynamics are built up by taking simple transfor-mations of white noise. Second, 1-step-ahead forecast errors from good mod-els should be white noise. After all, if such forecast errors aren't white noise, then they are serially correlated, which means that they are forecastable, and if forecast errors are forecastable then the forecast cannot be very good. Thus it is important that we understand and be able to recognize white noise.

Thus far we have characterized white noise in terms of its mean, vari-ance, autocorrelation function, and partial autocorrelation function. An-other characterization of dynamics, with important implications for forecast-ing, involves the mean and variance of a process *conditional* upon its past. In particular, we often gain insight into the dynamics in a process by examining its conditional mean, which is a key object for forecasting.[9] In fact, through-out our study of time series, we will be interested in computing and contrast-ing the **unconditional mean and variance** and the **conditional mean and vari-ance** of various processes of interest. Means and variances, which convey information about location and scale of random variables, are examples of

9. If you need to refresh your memory on conditional means, consult any good introductory statistics book, such as Wonnacott and Wonnacott (1990).

what statisticians call **moments.** For the most part, our comparisons of the conditional and unconditional moment structure of time series processes will focus on means and variances (the most important moments), but sometimes we will be interested in higher-order moments, which are related to properties such as skewness and kurtosis.

For comparing conditional and unconditional means and variances, it will simplify our story to consider independent white noise, $y_t \overset{\text{iid}}{\sim} (0, \sigma^2)$. By the same arguments as before, the unconditional mean of y is 0 and the unconditional variance is σ^2. Now consider the conditional mean and variance, where the information set Ω_{t-1} upon which we condition contains either the past history of the observed series, $\Omega_{t-1} = \{y_{t-1}, y_{t-2}, \ldots\}$, or the past history of the shocks, $\Omega_{t-1} = \{\varepsilon_{t-1}, \varepsilon_{t-2}, \ldots\}$. (They are the same in the white noise case.) In contrast to the unconditional mean and variance, which must be constant by covariance stationarity, the conditional mean and variance need not be constant, and in general we would expect them *not* to be constant. The unconditionally expected growth of laptop computer sales next quarter may be 10 percent, but expected sales growth may be much higher, *conditional* upon knowledge that sales grew this quarter by 20 percent. For the independent white noise process, the conditional mean is

$$E(y_t \mid \Omega_{t-1}) = 0$$

and the conditional variance is

$$\text{var}(y_t \mid \Omega_{t-1}) = E\left[(y_t - E(y_t \mid \Omega_{t-1}))^2 \mid \Omega_{t-1}\right] = \sigma^2$$

Conditional and unconditional means and variances are identical for an independent white noise series; there are no dynamics in the process, and hence no dynamics in the conditional moments, to exploit for forecasting.

3. THE LAG OPERATOR

The **lag operator** and related constructs are the natural language in which forecasting models are expressed. If you want to understand and manipulate forecasting models—or even if you simply want to be able to read the software manuals—you have to be comfortable with the lag operator. The lag operator, L, is very simple. It "operates" on a series by lagging it; thus,

$$L\, y_t = y_{t-1}$$

Similarly,

$$L^2 y_t = L(L(y_t)) = L(y_{t-1}) = y_{t-2}$$

and so on. Typically we operate on a series not with the lag operator but with a **polynomial in the lag operator.** A lag operator polynomial of degree m is just a linear function of powers of L, up through the mth power,

$$B(L) = b_0 + b_1 L + b_2 L^2 + \ldots b_m L^m$$

To take a very simple example of a lag operator polynomial operating on a series, consider the mth order lag operator polynomial L^m, for which

$$L^m y_t = y_{t-m}$$

A well-known operator, the first-difference operator Δ, is actually a first-order polynomial in the lag operator; you can readily verify that

$$\Delta y_t = (1 - L)y_t = y_t - y_{t-1}$$

As a final example, consider the second-order lag operator polynomial $(1 + 0.9L + 0.6L^2)$ operating on y_t. We have

$$(1 + 0.9L + 0.6L^2)y_t = y_t + 0.9y_{t-1} + 0.6y_{t-2}$$

which is a weighted sum, or **distributed lag,** of current and past values. All forecasting models, one way or another, must contain such distributed lags, because they have to quantify how the past evolves into the present and future; hence lag operator notation is a useful shorthand for stating and manipulating forecasting models.

Thus far we have considered only finite-order polynomials in the lag operator; it turns out that infinite-order polynomials are also of great interest. We write the infinite-order lag operator polynomial as

$$B(L) = b_0 + b_1 L + b_2 L^2 + \ldots = \sum_{i=0}^{\infty} b_i L^i$$

Thus, for example, to denote an infinite distributed lag of current and past shocks we might write

$$B(L)\varepsilon_t = b_0 \varepsilon_t + b_1 \varepsilon_{t-1} + b_2 \varepsilon_{t-2} + \ldots = \sum_{i=0}^{\infty} b_i \varepsilon_{t-i}$$

At first sight, infinite distributed lags may seem esoteric and of limited practical interest because models with infinite distributed lags have infinitely many parameters $(b_0, b_1, b_2, \ldots)$ and therefore cannot be estimated with a finite sample of data. On the contrary, and surprisingly, it turns out that models involving infinite distributed lags are central to time series modeling and forecasting. Wold's theorem, to which we now turn, establishes that centrality.

4. WOLD'S THEOREM, THE GENERAL LINEAR PROCESS, AND RATIONAL DISTRIBUTED LAGS[10]

Wold's Theorem

Many different dynamic patterns are consistent with covariance stationarity. Thus, if we know only that a series is covariance stationary, it is not at all clear what sort of model we might fit to describe its evolution. The trend and seasonal models that we have studied aren't of use; they are models of specific nonstationary components. Effectively, what we need now is an appropriate model for what is left after fitting the trend and seasonal components—a model for a covariance stationary residual. **Wold's representation theorem** points to the appropriate model.

Theorem

Let $\{y_t\}$ be any zero-mean covariance-stationary process.[11] Then we can write it as

$$y_t = B(L)\varepsilon_t = \sum_{i=0}^{\infty} b_i \varepsilon_{t-i}$$

$$\varepsilon_t \sim WN(0, \sigma^2)$$

where $b_0 = 1$ and $\sum_{i=0}^{\infty} b_i^2 < \infty$. In short, the right "model" for any covariance stationary series is some infinite distributed lag of white noise, called the **Wold representation.** The ε_t's are often called innovations, because (as we shall see in chapter 8) they correspond to the 1-step-ahead forecast errors that we would make if we were to use a particularly good forecast. That is, the ε_t's represent that part of the evolution of y that is linearly unpredictable on the basis of the past of y. Note also that the ε_t's, although uncorrelated, are not necessarily independent. Again, it is only for Gaussian random variables that lack of correlation implies independence, and the innovations are not necessarily Gaussian.

In our statement of Wold's theorem we assumed a zero mean. That may seem restrictive, but it isn't. Rather, whenever you see y_t, just read $y_t - \mu$, so

---

10. This section is a bit more abstract than others, but don't be put off by it. On the contrary, you may want to read it several times. The material in it is crucially important for time series modeling and forecasting and is therefore central to our concerns.

11. Moreover, we require that the covariance stationary processes not contain any deterministic components.

that the process is expressed in deviations from its mean. The deviation from the mean has a zero mean, by construction. Working with zero-mean processes therefore involves no loss of generality while facilitating notational economy. We use this device frequently.

The General Linear Process

Wold's theorem tells us that when formulating forecasting models for covariance stationary time series we need consider only models of the form

$$y_t = B(L)\varepsilon_t = \sum_{i=0}^{\infty} b_i \varepsilon_{t-i}$$

$$\varepsilon_t \sim WN(0, \sigma^2)$$

where the b_i are coefficients with

$$b_0 = 1 \text{ and } \sum_{i=0}^{\infty} b_i^2 < \infty$$

We call this the **general linear process**—"general" because any covariance stationary series can be written that way, and "linear" because the Wold representation expresses the series as a linear function of its innovations.

The general linear process is so important that it is worth examining its unconditional and conditional moment structure in some detail. Taking means and variances, we obtain the unconditional moments

$$E(y_t) = E\left(\sum_{i=0}^{\infty} b_i \varepsilon_{t-i}\right) = \sum_{i=0}^{\infty} b_i E \varepsilon_{t-i} = \sum_{i=0}^{\infty} b_i \cdot 0 = 0$$

and

$$\text{var}(y_t) = \text{var}\left(\sum_{i=0}^{\infty} b_i \varepsilon_{t-i}\right) = \sum_{i=0}^{\infty} b_i^2 \text{var}(\varepsilon_{t-i}) = \sum_{i=0}^{\infty} b_i^2 \sigma^2 = \sigma^2 \sum_{i=0}^{\infty} b_i^2$$

At this point, in parallel to our discussion of white noise, we could compute and examine the autocovariance and autocorrelation functions of the general linear process. Those calculations, however, are rather involved, and not particularly revealing, so we proceed instead to examine the conditional mean and variance, where the information set Ω_{t-1} upon which we condition contains past innovations; that is, $\Omega_{t-1} = \{\varepsilon_{t-1}, \varepsilon_{t-2}, \ldots\}$. In this manner we can see how dynamics are modeled via conditional moments.[12] The conditional mean is

$$E(y_t \mid \Omega_{t-1}) = E(\varepsilon_t \mid \Omega_{t-1}) + b_1 E(\varepsilon_{t-1} \mid \Omega_{t-1}) + b_2 E(\varepsilon_{t-2} \mid \Omega_{t-1}) + \ldots$$

$$= 0 + b_1 \varepsilon_{t-1} + b_2 \varepsilon_{t-2} + \ldots = \sum_{i=1}^{\infty} b_i \varepsilon_{t-i}$$

and the conditional variance is

$$\text{var}(y_t \mid \Omega_{t-1}) = E[(y_t - E(y_t \mid \Omega_{t-1}))^2 \mid \Omega_{t-1}] = E(\varepsilon_t^2 \mid \Omega_{t-1}) = E(\varepsilon_t^2) = \sigma^2$$

The key insight is that the conditional mean *moves* over time in response to the evolving information set. The model captures the dynamics of the process, and the evolving conditional mean is one crucial way of summarizing them. An important goal of time series modeling, especially for forecasters, is capturing such conditional mean dynamics—the unconditional mean is constant (a requirement of stationarity), but the conditional mean varies in response to the evolving information set.[13]

Rational Distributed Lags

As we have seen, the Wold representation points to the crucial importance of models with infinite distributed lags. Infinite distributed lag models, in turn, are stated in terms of infinite polynomials in the lag operator, which are therefore very important as well. Infinite distributed lag models are not of immediate practical use, however, because they contain infinitely many parameters, which certainly inhibits practical application! Fortunately, infinite polynomials in the lag operator need not contain infinitely many free parameters. The infinite polynomial $B(L)$ may, for example, be a ratio of finite-order (and perhaps very low-order) polynomials. Such polynomials are called **rational polynomials,** and distributed lags constructed from them are called **rational distributed lags.**

---

12. Although Wold's theorem guarantees only serially uncorrelated white noise innovations, we sometimes make a stronger assumption of independent white noise innovations in order to focus the discussion. We do so, for example, in the following characterization of the conditional moment structure of the general linear process.

13. Note, however, an embarrassing asymmetry: the conditional variance, like the unconditional variance, is a fixed constant. Models that allow the conditional variance to change with the information set have recently attracted attention, however, and are an exciting area of current forecasting research. See the Problems and Complements for this chapter, as well as those for chapters 7 and 8.

Suppose, for example, that

$$B(L) = \frac{\Theta(L)}{\Phi(L)}$$

where the numerator polynomial is of degree q,

$$\Theta(L) = \sum_{i=0}^{q} \theta_i L^i$$

and the denominator polynomial is of degree p,

$$\Phi(L) = \sum_{i=0}^{p} \varphi_i L^i$$

There are *not* infinitely many free parameters in the $B(L)$ polynomial; instead, there are only $p + q$ parameters (the θ's and the φ's). If p and q are small, say 0, 1, or 2, then what seems like a hopeless task—estimation of $B(L)$—may actually be easy.

More realistically, suppose that $B(L)$ is not exactly rational, but is approximately rational,

$$B(L) \approx \frac{\Theta(L)}{\Phi(L)}$$

Then we can **approximate the Wold representation** using a rational distributed lag. Rational distributed lags produce models of cycles that economize on parameters (they are **parsimonious**), while nevertheless providing accurate approximations to the Wold representation. The popular ARMA and ARIMA forecasting models, which we will study shortly, are simply rational approximations to the Wold representation.

5. ESTIMATION AND INFERENCE FOR THE MEAN, AUTOCORRELATION, AND PARTIAL AUTOCORRELATION FUNCTIONS

Now suppose we have a sample of data on a time series, and we don't know the true model that generated the data, or the mean, autocorrelation function, or partial autocorrelation function associated with that true model. Instead, we want to use the data to *estimate* the mean, autocorrelation function, and partial autocorrelation function, which we might then use to help us learn about the underlying dynamics, and to decide upon a suitable model or set of models to fit to the data.

Sample Mean

The mean of a covariance stationary series is $\mu = Ey_t$. A fundamental principle of estimation, called the **analog principle,** suggests that we develop estimators by replacing expectations with sample averages. Thus our estimator for the population mean, given a sample of size T, is the **sample mean,**

$$\bar{y} = \frac{1}{T} \sum_{t=1}^{T} y_t$$

Typically we are not directly interested in the estimate of the mean, but it is needed for estimation of the autocorrelation function.

Sample Autocorrelations

The autocorrelation at displacement τ for the covariance stationary series y is

$$\hat{\rho}(\tau) = \frac{E\left[(y_t - \mu)(y_{t-\tau} - \mu)\right]}{E\left[(y_t - \mu)^2\right]}$$

Application of the analog principle yields a natural estimator,

$$\hat{\rho}(\tau) = \frac{\frac{1}{T} \sum_{t=\tau+1}^{T} \left[(y_t - \bar{y})(y_{t-\tau} - \bar{y})\right]}{\frac{1}{T} \sum_{t=1}^{T} (y_t - \bar{y})^2} = \frac{\sum_{t=\tau+1}^{T} \left[(y_t - \bar{y})(y_{t-\tau} - \bar{y})\right]}{\sum_{t=1}^{T} (y_t - \bar{y})^2}$$

This estimator, viewed as a function of τ, is called the **sample autocorrelation function,** or correlogram. Note that some of the summations begin at $t = \tau + 1$, not at $t = 1$; this is necessary because of the appearance of $y_{t-\tau}$ in the sum. Note that we divide those same sums by T, even though only $(T - \tau)$ terms appear in the sum. When T is large relative to τ (which is the relevant case), division by T or by $T - \tau$ yields approximately the same result, so it won't make much difference for practical purposes; moreover, there are good mathematical reasons for preferring division by T.[14]

It is often of interest to assess whether a series is reasonably approximated as white noise, which is to say whether all its autocorrelations are zero

---

14. For additional discussion, consult any of the more advanced time series texts mentioned in chapter 1.

in population. A key result, which we simply assert, is that if a series is white noise, then the distribution of the sample autocorrelations in large samples is

$$\hat{\rho}(\tau) \sim N\left(0, \frac{1}{T}\right)$$

Note how simple the result is. The sample autocorrelations of a white noise series are approximately normally distributed, and the normal is always a convenient distribution. The mean of the sample autocorrelations is 0, which is to say that they are unbiased estimators of the true autocorrelations, which are in fact 0. Finally, the variance of the sample autocorrelations is approximately $1/T$ (equivalently, the standard deviation is $1/\sqrt{T}$), which is easy to construct and remember. Under normality, taking ± 2 standard errors yields an approximate 95% confidence interval. Thus, if the series is white noise, approximately 95% of the sample autocorrelations should fall in the interval $\pm 2/\sqrt{T}$. In practice, when we plot the sample autocorrelations for a sample of data, we typically include the "two-standard-error bands," which are useful for making informal graphical assessments of whether and how the series deviates from white noise.

The two-standard-error bands, although very useful, provide 95% bounds only for the sample autocorrelations taken one at a time. Ultimately, we often are interested in whether a series is white noise, that is, whether *all* its autocorrelations are *jointly* 0. A simple extension lets us test that hypothesis. Rewrite the expression

$$\hat{\rho}(\tau) \sim N\left(0, \frac{1}{T}\right)$$

as

$$\sqrt{T}\hat{\rho}(\tau) \sim N(0, 1)$$

Squaring both sides yields[15]

$$T\hat{\rho}^2(\tau) \sim \chi_1^2$$

It can be shown that, in addition to being approximately normally distributed, the sample autocorrelations at various displacements are approximately independent of one another. Recalling that the sum of independent χ^2 variables is also χ^2 with degrees of freedom equal to the sum of the degrees of freedom of the variables summed, we show that the **Box-Pierce Q-statistic,**

---

15. Recall that the square of a standard normal random variable is a χ^2 random variable with one degree of freedom.

$$Q_{BP} = T \sum_{\tau=1}^{m} \hat{\rho}^2(\tau)$$

is approximately distributed as a χ^2_m random variable under the null hypothesis that y is white noise.[16] A slight modification of this, designed to follow more closely the χ^2 distribution in small samples, is

$$Q_{LB} = T(T+2) \sum_{\tau=1}^{m} \left(\frac{1}{T-\tau}\right) \hat{\rho}^2(\tau)$$

Under the null hypothesis that y is white noise, Q_{LB} is approximately distributed as a χ^2_m random variable. Note that the **Ljung-Box Q-statistic** is the same as the Box-Pierce Q-statistic, except that the sum of squared autocorrelations is replaced by a weighted sum of squared autocorrelations, where the weights are $(T + 2/T - \tau)$. For moderate and large T, the weights are approximately 1, so that the Ljung-Box statistic differs little from the Box-Pierce statistic.

Selection of m is done to balance competing criteria. On the one hand, we don't want m too small because, after all, we are trying to do a joint test on a large part of the autocorrelation function. On the other hand, as m grows relative to T, the quality of the distributional approximations we have invoked deteriorates. In practice, focusing on m in the neighborhood of $\sqrt{T}$ is often reasonable.

Sample Partial Autocorrelations

Recall that the partial autocorrelations are obtained from population linear regressions, which correspond to a thought experiment involving linear regression using an infinite sample of data. The sample partial autocorrelations correspond to the same thought experiment, except that the linear regression is now done on the (feasible) sample of size T. If the fitted regression is

$$\hat{y}_t = \hat{c} + \hat{\beta}_1 y_{t-1} + \ldots + \hat{\beta}_\tau y_{t-\tau}$$

then the **sample partial autocorrelation** at displacement τ is

$$\hat{p}(\tau) \equiv \hat{\beta}_\tau$$

---

16. The variable m is a maximum displacement selected by the user. Shortly we will discuss how to choose it.

FIGURE 6.9   Canadian Employment Index

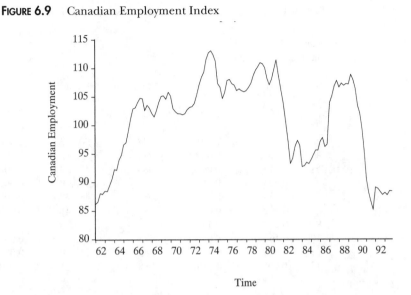

Distributional results identical to those we discussed for the sample autocorrelations hold as well for the sample *partial* autocorrelations. That is, if the series is white noise, approximately 95% of the sample partial autocorrelations should fall in the interval $\pm 2/\sqrt{T}$. As with the sample autocorrelations, we typically plot the sample partial autocorrelations along with their two-standard-error bands.

6. APPLICATION: CHARACTERIZING CANADIAN EMPLOYMENT DYNAMICS

To illustrate the ideas we have introduced, we examine a quarterly, seasonally adjusted index of Canadian employment, 1962.1–1993.4, which we plot in Figure 6.9. The series displays no trend, and, of course, it displays no seasonality because it is seasonally adjusted. It does, however, appear highly serially correlated. It evolves in a slow, persistent fashion—high in business cycle booms and low in recessions.

To get a feel for the dynamics operating in the employment series we perform a correlogram analysis.[17] The results appear in Table 6.1. Consider first the Q-statistic.[18] We compute the Q-statistic and its p-value under the null

17. A **correlogram analysis** simply means examination of the sample autocorrelation and partial autocorrelation functions (with two-standard-error bands), together with related diagnostics, such as Q-statistics.

18. We show the Ljung-Box version of the Q-statistic.

TABLE 6.1   Canadian Employment Index Correlogram

Sample: 1962:1 1993:4
Included observations: 128

	Acorr.	P. Acorr.	Std. Error	Ljung-Box	p-value
1	0.949	0.949	.088	118.07	0.000
2	0.877	-0.244	.088	219.66	0.000
3	0.795	-0.101	.088	303.72	0.000
4	0.707	-0.070	.088	370.82	0.000
5	0.617	-0.063	.088	422.27	0.000
6	0.526	-0.048	.088	460.00	0.000
7	0.438	-0.033	.088	486.32	0.000
8	0.351	-0.049	.088	503.41	0.000
9	0.258	-0.149	.088	512.70	0.000
10	0.163	-0.070	.088	516.43	0.000
11	0.073	-0.011	.088	517.20	0.000
12	-0.005	0.016	.088	517.21	0.000

hypothesis of white noise for values of m (the number of terms in the sum that underlies the Q-statistic) ranging from 1 through 12. The p-value is consistently 0 to four decimal places, so the null hypothesis of white noise is decisively rejected.

Now we examine the sample autocorrelations and partial autocorrelations. The sample autocorrelations are very large relative to their standard errors and display slow one-sided decay.[19] The sample partial autocorrelations, in contrast, are large relative to their standard errors at first (particularly for the 1-quarter displacement) but are statistically negligible beyond a displacement of 2.[20] In Figure 6.10 we plot the sample autocorrelations and partial autocorrelations along with their two-standard-error bands.

It is clear that employment has a strong cyclical component; all diagnostics reject the white noise hypothesis immediately. Moreover, the sample

---

19. We don't show the sample autocorrelation or partial autocorrelation at displacement 0 because as we mentioned earlier, they equal 1.0, by construction and therefore convey no useful information. We adopt this convention throughout.

20. Note that the sample autocorrelation and partial autocorrelation are identical at a displacement of 1. That is because at a displacement of 1, there are no earlier lags to control for when computing the sample partial autocorrelation, so it equals the sample autocorrelation. At higher displacements, of course, the two diverge.

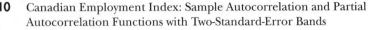

FIGURE 6.10   Canadian Employment Index: Sample Autocorrelation and Partial
Autocorrelation Functions with Two-Standard-Error Bands

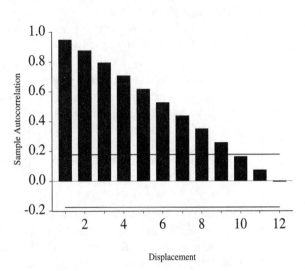

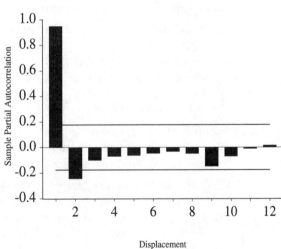

autocorrelation and partial autocorrelation functions have particular
shapes—the autocorrelation function displays slow one-sided damping, while
the partial autocorrelation function cuts off at a displacement of 2. You
might guess that such patterns, which summarize the dynamics in the series,
might be useful for suggesting candidate forecasting models. Such is indeed
the case, as we shall see in the next chapter.

PROBLEMS AND COMPLEMENTS

1. (Selecting an employment forecasting model with *AIC* and *SIC*) Use *AIC* and *SIC* to assess the necessity and desirability of including trend and seasonal components in a forecasting model for Canadian employment.

    (a) Display *AIC* and *SIC* for a variety of specifications of trend and seasonality. Which would you select using *AIC*? Using *SIC*? Do *AIC* and *SIC* select the same model? If not, which do you prefer?

    (b) Discuss the estimation results and residual plot from your preferred model, and perform a correlogram analysis of the residuals. Discuss, in particular, the patterns of the sample autocorrelations and partial autocorrelations, and their statistical significance.

    (c) How, if at all, are your results different from those reported in the text? Are the differences important? Why or why not?

2. (**Simulating time series processes**) Many cutting-edge estimation and forecasting techniques involve simulation. Moreover, simulation is often a good way to get a feel for a model and its behavior. White noise can be simulated on a computer using **random number generators,** which are available in most statistics, econometrics, and forecasting packages.

    (a) Simulate a Gaussian white noise realization of length 200. Call the white noise ε_t. Compute the correlogram. Discuss.

    (b) Form the distributed lag $y_t = \varepsilon_t + 0.9\varepsilon_{t-1}$, $t = 2, 3, \ldots, 200$. Compute the sample autocorrelations and partial autocorrelations. Discuss.

    (c) Let $y_1 = 1$ and $y_t = 0.9y_{t-1} + \varepsilon_t$, $t = 2, 3, \ldots, 200$. Compute the sample autocorrelations and partial autocorrelations. Discuss.

3. (Sample autocorrelation functions for trending series) A tell-tale sign of the slowly evolving nonstationarity associated with trend is a sample autocorrelation function that damps extremely slowly.

    (a) Find three trending series, compute their sample autocorrelation functions, and report your results. Discuss.

    (b) Fit appropriate trend models, obtain the model residuals, compute their sample autocorrelation functions, and report your results. Discuss.

4. (Sample autocorrelation functions for seasonal series) A tell-tale sign of seasonality is a sample autocorrelation function with sharp peaks at the seasonal displacements (4, 8, 12, . . . for quarterly data; 12, 24, 36, . . . for monthly data; and so on).

    (a) Find a series with both trend and seasonal variation, and detrend it. Discuss.

(b) Compute the sample autocorrelation function of the detrended series. Discuss.

(c) Compute the sample autocorrelation function of the original, non-detrended series, and contrast it to that of the detrended series. Discuss.

5. (Volatility dynamics: correlograms of squares) In the Problems and Complements of chapter 3, we suggested that a time series plot of a squared residual, e_t^2, can reveal serial correlation in squared residuals, which corresponds to nonconstant volatility, or heteroskedasticity, in the levels of the residuals. Financial asset returns often display little systematic variation, so instead of examining residuals from a model of returns, we often examine returns directly. In what follows, we will continue to use the notation e_t, but you should interpret e_t as an observed asset return.

(a) Find a high-frequency (e.g., daily) financial asset return series, e_t, plot it, and discuss your results.

(b) Perform a correlogram analysis of e_t and discuss your results.

(c) Plot e_t^2 and discuss your results.

(d) In addition to plotting e_t^2, examining the correlogram of e_t^2 often proves information for assessing volatility persistence. Why might that be so? Perform a correlogram analysis of e_t^2 and discuss your results.

BIBLIOGRAPHICAL AND COMPUTATIONAL NOTES

Wold's theorem was originally proved in a 1938 monograph, later revised as Wold (1954). Rational distributed lags have long been used in engineering, and their use in econometric modeling extends at least to Jorgenson (1966).

Bartlett (1946) derived the standard errors of the sample autocorrelations and partial autocorrelations of white noise. In fact, the plus-or-minus two-standard-error bands are often called the **Bartlett bands.**

The two variants of the Q-statistic that we introduced were developed in the 1970s by Box and Pierce (1970) and by Ljung and Box (1978). Some packages compute both variants, and some compute only one (typically Ljung-Box, because it is designed to be more accurate in small samples). In practice, the Box-Pierce and Ljung-Box statistics usually lead to the same conclusions.

For concise and insightful discussion of random number generation, as well as a variety of numerical and computational techniques, see Press et al. (1992).

CONCEPTS FOR REVIEW

Approximation of the Wold representation	Partial autocorrelation function
Analog principle	Polynomial in the lag operator
Autocorrelation function	Population regression
Autocovariance function	Random number generator
Autoregression	Rational distributed lag
Bartlett bands	Rational polynomial
Box-Pierce Q-statistic	Realization
Conditional mean and variance	Sample autocorrelation function
Correlogram analysis	Sample mean
Covariance stationarity	Sample partial autocorrelation
Cycle	Sample path
Distributed lag	Second-order stationarity
Gaussian white noise	Serially uncorrelated
General linear process	Simulating a time series process
Independent white noise	Time series
Innovation	Time series process
Lag operator	Unconditional mean and variance
Ljung-Box Q-statistic	Weak stationarity
Moments	White noise
Normal white noise	Wold representation
Parsimonious	Wold's representation theorem
	Zero-mean white noise

REFERENCES AND ADDITIONAL READINGS

Bartlett, M. (1946), "On the Theoretical Specification of Sampling Properties of Autocorrelated Time Series," *Journal of the Royal Statistical Society B,* 8, 27–41.

Box, G. E. P., and Pierce, D. A. (1970), "Distribution of Residual Autocorrelations in ARIMA Time-Series Models," *Journal of the American Statistical Association,* 65, 1509–1526.

Jorgenson, D. (1966), "Rational Distributed Lag Functions," *Econometrica,* 34, 135–149.

Ljung, G. M., and Box, G. E. P. (1978), "On a Measure of Lack of Fit in Time-Series Models," *Biometrika,* 65, 297–303.

Press, W. H., et al. (1992), *Numerical Recipes: The Art of Scientific Computing.* Cambridge: Cambridge University Press.

Wold, H. O. (1954), *A Study in the Analysis of Stationary Time Series,* second edition. Uppsala, Sweden: Almquist and Wicksell.

Wonnacott, T. H., and Wonnacott, R. J. (1990), *Introductory Statistics,* fifth edition. New York: Wiley.

CHAPTER 7

MODELING CYCLES: MA, AR, AND ARMA MODELS

When building forecasting models, we don't want to pretend that the model we fit is true. Instead, we want to be aware that we are *approximating* a more complex reality. That is the modern view of modeling, and it has important implications for forecasting. In particular, we have seen that the key to successful time series modeling and forecasting is parsimonious, yet accurate, approximation of the Wold representation. In this chapter we consider three approximations: **moving-average (MA) models, autoregressive (AR) models,** and **autoregressive moving-average (ARMA) models.**

The three models, all **approximations to the Wold representation,** nevertheless differ in their specifics. Although two very different looking models sometimes provide equally good approximations to the Wold representation, certainly it is not the case that we can simply assert, say, an autoregressive model for a series and be confident that it is going to perform as well as any other. The three models vary in their strengths in capturing different sorts of autocorrelation behavior.

We begin by characterizing the autocorrelation functions and related quantities associated with each model under the assumption that the model is "true." We do this separately for autoregressive, moving-average, and

ARMA models.[1] These characterizations have nothing to do with data or estimation, but they are crucial for developing a basic understanding of the properties of the models, which is necessary to perform intelligent modeling and forecasting. They enable us to make statements such as, "If the data were really generated by an autoregressive process, then we would expect its autocorrelation function to have property x." Armed with that knowledge, we use the sample autocorrelations and partial autocorrelations, in conjunction with *AIC* and *SIC*, to suggest candidate forecasting models, which we then estimate.

1. MOVING-AVERAGE (MA) MODELS

The finite-order moving-average process is a natural and obvious approximation to the Wold representation, which is an infinite-order moving-average process. Finite-order moving-average processes also have direct motivation: the fact that all variation in time series, one way or another, is driven by shocks of various sorts suggests the possibility of modeling time series directly as distributed lags of current and past shocks, that is, as moving-average processes.[2]

The MA(1) Process

The first-order moving-average, or MA(1), process is

$$y_t = \varepsilon_t + \theta \varepsilon_{t-1} = (1 + \theta L)\varepsilon_t$$

$$\varepsilon_t \sim WN(0, \sigma^2)$$

The defining characteristic of the MA process in general, and the MA(1) in particular, is that the current value of the observed series is expressed as a function of current and lagged unobservable shocks—think of it as a regression model with nothing but current and lagged disturbances on the right-hand side.

To help develop a feel for the behavior of the MA(1) process, we show two simulated realizations of length 150 in Figure 7.1. The processes are

$$y_t = \varepsilon_t + 0.4\varepsilon_{t-1}$$

---

1. Sometimes, especially when characterizing population properties under the assumption that the models are correct, we refer to them as processes, which is short for **stochastic processes;** hence the terms "moving-average process," "autoregressive process," and "ARMA process."

2. Economic equilibria, for example, may be disturbed by shocks that take some time to be fully assimilated.

FIGURE 7.1   Realizations of Two MA(1) Processes

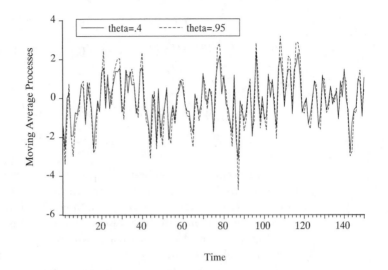

and

$$y_t = \varepsilon_t + 0.95\varepsilon_{t-1}$$

where in each case $\varepsilon_t \overset{iid}{\sim} N(0,1)$. To construct the realizations, we used the same series of underlying white noise shocks; the only difference in the realizations comes from the different coefficients. Past shocks feed *positively* into the current value of the series, with a small weight of $\theta = 0.4$ in one case and a large weight of $\theta = 0.95$ in the other. You might think that $\theta = 0.95$ would induce much more persistence than $\theta = 0.4$, but it doesn't. The structure of the MA(1) process, in which only the first lag of the shock appears on the right, forces it to have a very short memory, and hence weak dynamics, regardless of the parameter value.

The unconditional mean and variance are

$$Ey_t = E(\varepsilon_t) + \theta E(\varepsilon_{t-1}) = 0$$

and

$$\text{var}(y_t) = \text{var}(\varepsilon_t) + \theta^2 \text{var}(\varepsilon_{t-1}) = \sigma^2 + \theta^2 \sigma^2 = \sigma^2(1 + \theta^2)$$

Note that for a fixed value of σ, as θ increases in absolute value so too does the unconditional variance. That is why the MA(1) process with parameter $\theta = 0.95$ varies a bit more than the process with parameter $\theta = 0.4$.

The conditional mean and variance of an MA(1), where the conditioning information set is $\Omega_{t-1} = \{\varepsilon_{t-1}, \varepsilon_{t-2}, \ldots\}$, are

$$E(y_t \mid \Omega_{t-1}) = E((\varepsilon_t + \theta\varepsilon_{t-1}) \mid \Omega_{t-1})$$

$$= E(\varepsilon_t \mid \Omega_{t-1}) + \theta E(\varepsilon_{t-1} \mid \Omega_{t-1}) = \theta\varepsilon_{t-1}$$

and

$$\text{var}(y_t \mid \Omega_{t-1}) = E[(y_t + E(y_t \mid \Omega_{t-1}))^2 \mid \Omega_{t-1}]$$

$$= E(\varepsilon_t^2 \mid \Omega_{t-1}) = E(\varepsilon_t^2) = \sigma^2$$

The conditional mean explicitly adapts to the information set, in contrast to the unconditional mean, which is constant. Note, however, that only the first lag of the shock enters the conditional mean—more distant shocks have no effect on the current conditional expectation. This is indicative of the one-period memory of MA(1) processes, which we now characterize in terms of the autocorrelation function.

To compute the autocorrelation function for the MA(1) process, we must first compute the autocovariance function. We have

$$\gamma(\tau) = E(y_t\, y_{t-\tau}) = E((\varepsilon_t + \theta\varepsilon_{t-1})\,(\varepsilon_{t-\tau} + \theta\varepsilon_{t-\tau-1})) = \begin{cases} \theta\sigma^2, & \tau = 1 \\ 0, & \text{otherwise} \end{cases}$$

(The proof is left as a problem.) The autocorrelation function is just the autocovariance function scaled by the variance,

$$\rho(\tau) = \frac{\gamma(\tau)}{\gamma(0)} = \begin{cases} \dfrac{\theta}{1 + \theta^2}, & \tau = 1 \\ 0, & \text{otherwise} \end{cases}$$

The key feature here is the sharp **cutoff in the autocorrelations.** All autocorrelations are zero beyond displacement 1, the order of the MA process. In Figures 7.2 and 7.3, we show the autocorrelation functions for our two MA(1) processes with parameters $\theta = 0.4$ and $\theta = 0.95$, respectively. At displacement 1, the process with parameter $\theta = 0.4$ has a smaller autocorrelation than the process with parameter $\theta = 0.95$, but both drop to 0 beyond displacement 1.

Note that the requirements of covariance stationarity (constant unconditional mean, constant and finite unconditional variance, and autocorrelation depends only on displacement) are met for any MA(1) process, *regardless* of the values of its parameters. If, moreover, $|\theta| < 1$, then we say that the MA(1) process is **invertible.** In that case, we can "invert" the MA(1) process and express the current value of the series not in terms of a current shock and a

FIGURE **7.2**   Population Autocorrelation Function: MA(1) Process, $\theta = 0.4$

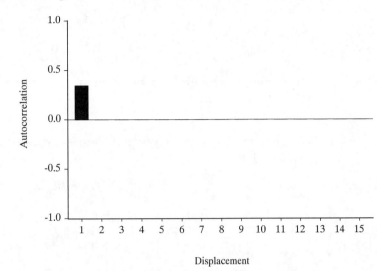

lagged shock, but rather in terms of a current shock *and lagged values of the series.* This is called an **autoregressive representation.** An autoregressive representation has a current shock and lagged observable values of the series on the right, whereas a moving average representation has a current shock and lagged unobservable shocks on the right.

FIGURE **7.3**   Population Autocorrelation Function: MA(1) Process, $\theta = 0.95$

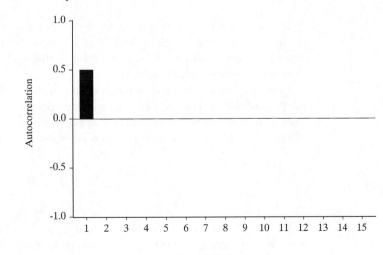

Let us compute the autoregressive representation. The process is

$$y_t = \varepsilon_t + \theta \varepsilon_{t-1}$$

$$\varepsilon_t \sim WN(0, \sigma^2)$$

Thus we can solve for the innovation as

$$\varepsilon_t = y_t - \theta \varepsilon_{t-1}$$

Lagging by successively more periods gives expressions for the innovations at various dates,

$$\varepsilon_{t-1} = y_{t-1} - \theta \varepsilon_{t-2}$$

$$\varepsilon_{t-2} = y_{t-2} - \theta \varepsilon_{t-3}$$

$$\varepsilon_{t-3} = y_{t-3} - \theta \varepsilon_{t-4}$$

and so forth. Making use of these expressions for lagged innovations, we can substitute backward in the MA(1) process, yielding

$$y_t = \varepsilon_t + \theta y_{t-1} - \theta^2 y_{t-2} + \theta^3 y_{t-3} - \ldots$$

In lag-operator notation, we write the infinite autoregressive representation as

$$\frac{1}{1 + \theta L} y_t = \varepsilon_t$$

Note that the back substitution used to obtain the autoregressive representation makes sense—and in fact that a convergent autoregressive representation exists—only if $|\theta| < 1$, because in the back substitution we raise θ to progressively higher powers.

We can restate the invertibility condition in another way: the inverse of the root of the moving-average lag operator polynomial $(1 + \theta L)$ must be less than 1 in absolute value. Recall that a polynomial of degree m has m roots. Thus the MA(1) lag operator polynomial has one root, which is the solution to

$$1 + \theta L = 0$$

The root is $L = -1/\theta$, so its inverse will be less than 1 in absolute value if $|\theta| < 1$, and the two invertibility conditions are equivalent. The "inverse root" way of stating invertibility conditions seems tedious, but it turns out to be of greater applicability than the $|\theta| < 1$ condition, as we shall see shortly.

Autoregressive representations are appealing to forecasters because, one way or another, if a model is to be used for real-world forecasting, it has to link the present observables to the past history of observables, so that we can extrapolate to form a forecast of future observables based on present and past observables. Superficially, moving-average models don't seem to meet that requirement because the current value of a series is expressed in terms of current and lagged unobservable shocks, not observable variables. But under the invertibility conditions that we have described, moving average processes have equivalent autoregressive representations. Thus, although we want autoregressive representations for forecasting, we don't have to start with an autoregressive model. We typically restrict ourselves to invertible processes, however, because for forecasting purposes we want to be able to express current observables as functions of past observables.

Let us now consider the partial autocorrelation function for the MA(1) process. From the infinite autoregressive representation of the MA(1) process, we see that the partial autocorrelation function will decay gradually to zero. As we discussed in chapter 6, the partial autocorrelations are just the coefficients on the last included lag in a sequence of progressively higher order autoregressive approximations. If $\theta > 0$, then the pattern of decay will be one of damped oscillation; otherwise, the decay will be one-sided.

In Figures 7.4 and 7.5 we show the partial autocorrelation functions for our example MA(1) processes. For each process, $|\theta| < 1$, so that an autoregressive representation exists, and $\theta > 0$, so that the coefficients in the

FIGURE 7.4 Population Partial Autocorrelation Function: MA(1) Process, $\theta = 0.4$

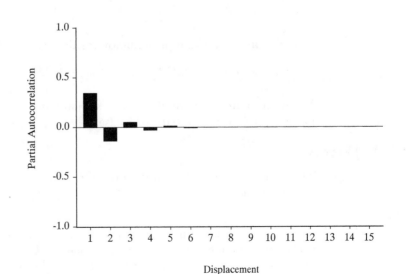

Displacement

FIGURE 7.5   Population Partial Autocorrelation Function: MA(1) Process, $\theta = 0.95$

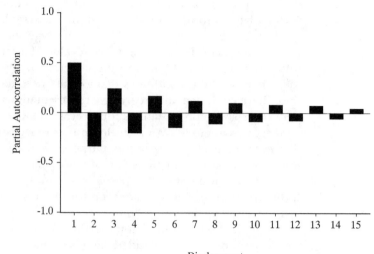

autoregressive representations alternate in sign. Specifically, we showed the general autoregressive representation to be

$$y_t = \varepsilon_t + \theta y_{t-1} - \theta^2 \, y_{t-2} + \theta^3 \, y_{t-3} - \ldots$$

so the autoregressive representation for the process with $\theta = 0.4$ is

$$y_t = \varepsilon_t + 0.4 y_{t-1} - 0.4^2 y_{t-2} + \ldots = \varepsilon_t + 0.4 y_{t-1} - 0.16 y_{t-2} + \ldots$$

and the autoregressive representation for the process with $\theta = 0.95$ is

$$y_t = \varepsilon_t + 0.95 y_{t-1} - 0.95^2 \, y_{t-2} + \ldots \;=\; \varepsilon_t + 0.95 y_{t-1} - 0.9025 y_{t-2} + \ldots$$

The partial autocorrelations display a similar damped oscillation.[3] The decay, however, is slower for the $\theta = 0.95$ case.

The MA(q) Process

Now consider the general finite-order moving-average process of order q, or MA(q) for short,

---

3. Note, however, that the partial autocorrelations are *not* the successive coefficients in the infinite autoregressive representation. Rather, they are the coefficients on the last included lag in sequence of progressively longer autoregressions. The two are related but distinct.

$$y_t = \varepsilon_t + \theta_1 \varepsilon_{t-1} + \ldots + \theta_q \varepsilon_{t-q} = \Theta(L)\varepsilon_t$$

$$\varepsilon_t \sim WN(0, \sigma^2)$$

where

$$\Theta(L) = 1 + \theta_1 L + \ldots + \theta_q L^q$$

is a qth-order lag operator polynomial. The $MA(q)$ process is a natural generalization of the $MA(1)$. By allowing for more lags of the shock on the right side of the equation, the $MA(q)$ process can capture richer dynamic patterns, which we can potentially exploit for improved forecasting. The $MA(1)$ process is, of course, a special case of the $MA(q)$, corresponding to $q = 1$.

The properties of the $MA(q)$ processes parallel those of the $MA(1)$ process in all respects, so in what follows we refrain from grinding through the mathematical derivations. Instead we focus on the key features of practical importance. Just as the $MA(1)$ process was covariance stationary for any value of its parameters, so too is the finite-order $MA(q)$ process. As with the $MA(1)$ process, the $MA(q)$ process is *invertible* only if a root condition is satisfied. The $MA(q)$ lag operator polynomial has q roots; when $q > 1$, the possibility of **complex roots** arises. The **condition for invertibility of the $MA(q)$ process** is that the inverses of all of the roots must be inside the unit circle, in which case we have the convergent autoregressive representation,

$$\frac{1}{\Theta(L)} y_t = \varepsilon_t$$

The conditional mean of the $MA(q)$ process evolves with the information set, in contrast to the unconditional moments, which are fixed. In contrast to the $MA(1)$ case, in which the conditional mean depends on only the first lag of the innovation, in the $MA(q)$ case the conditional mean depends on q lags of the innovation. Thus the $MA(q)$ process has the potential for longer memory.

The potentially longer memory of the $MA(q)$ process emerges clearly in its autocorrelation function. In the $MA(1)$ case, all autocorrelations beyond displacement 1 are 0; in the $MA(q)$ case, all autocorrelations beyond displacement q are 0. This autocorrelation cutoff is a distinctive property of moving-average processes. The partial autocorrelation function of the $MA(q)$ process, in contrast, decays gradually, in accord with the infinite autoregressive representation, in either an oscillating or one-sided fashion, depending on the parameters of the process.

In closing this section, let us step back for a moment and consider in greater detail the precise way in which finite-order moving-average processes approximate the Wold representation. The Wold representation is

$$y_t = B(L)\varepsilon_t$$

where $B(L)$ is of infinite order. The MA(1), in contrast, is simply a first-order moving average, in which a series is expressed as a one-period moving average of current and past innovations. Thus when we fit an MA(1) model we are using the first-order polynomial $1 + \theta L$ to approximate the infinite-order polynomial $B(L)$. Note that $1 + \theta L$ is a rational polynomial with numerator polynomial of degree 1 and degenerate denominator polynomial (degree 0).

MA(q) processes have the potential to deliver better approximations to the Wold representation, but at the cost of more parameters having to be estimated. The Wold representation involves an infinite moving average; the MA(q) process approximates the infinite moving average with a *finite-order* moving average,

$$y_t = \Theta(L)\varepsilon_t$$

whereas the MA(1) process approximates the infinite moving average with only a *first-order* moving average, which can sometimes be very restrictive.

2. AUTOREGRESSIVE (AR) MODELS

The autoregressive process is also a natural approximation to the Wold representation. We have seen, in fact, that under certain conditions a moving-average process has an autoregressive representation, so an autoregressive process is in a sense the same as a moving-average process. Like the moving-average process, the autoregressive process has direct motivation; it is simply a *stochastic difference equation*, a simple mathematical model in which the current value of a series is linearly related to its past values, plus an additive stochastic shock. Stochastic difference equations are a natural vehicle for discrete-time stochastic dynamic modeling.

The AR(1) Process

The first-order autoregressive process, AR(1) for short, is

$$y_t = \varphi y_{t-1} + \varepsilon_t$$

$$\varepsilon_t \sim WN(0, \sigma^2)$$

In lag operator form, we write

$$(1 - \varphi L)\, y_t = \varepsilon_t$$

Let us verify that the lag operator representation makes sense. Note that

$$(1 - \varphi L)y_t = y_t - \varphi L y_t = y_t - \varphi y_{t-1}$$

Thus the model

$$(1 - \varphi L)\, y_t = \varepsilon_t.$$

is equivalent to

$$y_t - \varphi y_{t-1} = \varepsilon_t$$

or

$$y_t = \varphi y_{t-1} + \varepsilon_t$$

as claimed.

In Figure 7.6 we show simulated realizations of length 150 of two AR(1) processes; the first is

$$y_t = 0.4 y_{t-1} + \varepsilon_t$$

and the second is

$$y_t = 0.95 y_{t-1} + \varepsilon_t$$

where in each case $\varepsilon_t \overset{iid}{\sim} N(0,1)$, and the same innovation sequence underlies each realization. The fluctuations in the AR(1) process with parameter $\phi = 0.95$ appear much more persistent that those of the AR(1) process with parameter $\phi = 0.4$. This contrasts sharply with the MA(1) process, which has a very short memory regardless of parameter value. Thus the AR(1) model is

FIGURE 7.6   Realizations of Two AR(1) Processes

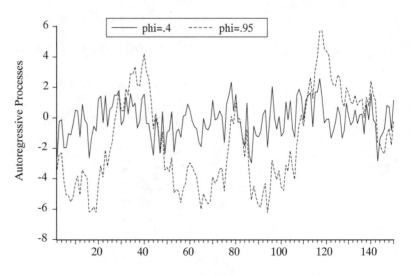

Time

capable of capturing much more persistent dynamics than is the MA(1) model.

Recall that a finite-order moving-average process is always covariance stationary, but that certain conditions must be satisfied for invertibility, in which case an autoregressive representation exists. For autoregressive processes, the situation is precisely the reverse. Autoregressive processes are always invertible—in fact, invertibility isn't even an issue, as finite-order autoregressive processes *already are* in autoregressive form—but certain conditions must be satisfied for an autoregressive process to be covariance stationary.

If we begin with the AR(1) process,

$$y_t = \varphi y_{t-1} + \varepsilon_t$$

and substitute backward for lagged y's on the right side, we obtain

$$y_t = \varepsilon_t + \varphi \varepsilon_{t-1} + \varphi^2 \varepsilon_{t-2} + \ldots$$

In lag operator form we write

$$y_t = \frac{1}{1 - \varphi L} \varepsilon_t$$

This moving-average representation for y is convergent if and only if $|\varphi| < 1$; thus, $|\varphi| < 1$ is the condition for covariance stationarity in the AR(1) case. Equivalently, the condition for covariance stationarity is that the inverse of the root of the autoregressive lag operator polynomial be less than 1 in absolute value.

From the moving-average representation of the covariance stationary AR(1) process, we can compute the unconditional mean and variance,

$$E(y_t) = E(\varepsilon_t + \varphi \varepsilon_{t-1} + \varphi^2 \varepsilon_{t-2} + \ldots)$$

$$= E(\varepsilon_t) + \varphi E(\varepsilon_{t-1}) + \varphi^2 E(\varepsilon_{t-2}) + \ldots$$

$$= 0$$

and

$$\text{var}(y_t) = \text{var}(\varepsilon_t + \varphi \varepsilon_{t-1} + \varphi^2 \varepsilon_{t-2} + \ldots)$$

$$= \sigma^2 + \varphi^2 \sigma^2 + \varphi^4 \sigma^2 + \ldots$$

$$= \sigma^2 \sum_{i=0}^{\infty} \varphi^{2i}$$

$$= \frac{\sigma^2}{1 - \varphi^2}$$

The conditional moments, in contrast, are

$$
\begin{aligned}
E\left(y_t \mid y_{t-1}\right) &= E\left(\left(\varphi y_{t-1} + \varepsilon_t\right) \mid y_{t-1}\right) \\
&= \varphi E\left(y_{t-1} \mid y_{t-1}\right) + E\left(\varepsilon_t \mid y_{t-1}\right) \\
&= \varphi y_{t-1} + 0 \\
&= \varphi y_{t-1}
\end{aligned}
$$

and

$$
\begin{aligned}
\operatorname{var}\left(y_t \mid y_{t-1}\right) &= \operatorname{var}\left(\left(\left(\varphi y_{t-1} + \varepsilon_t\right) \mid y_{t-1}\right)\right) \\
&= \varphi^2 \operatorname{var}\left(y_{t-1} \mid y_{t-1}\right) + \operatorname{var}\left(\varepsilon_t \mid y_{t-1}\right) \\
&= 0 + \sigma^2 \\
&= \sigma^2
\end{aligned}
$$

Note in particular that the simple way that the conditional mean adapts to the changing information set as the process evolves.

To find the autocovariances, we proceed as follows. The process is

$$
y_t = \varphi y_{t-1} + \varepsilon_t
$$

so that multiplying both sides of the equation by $y_{t-\tau}$, we obtain

$$
y_t\, y_{t-\tau} = \varphi y_{t-1}\, y_{t-\tau} + \varepsilon_t\, y_{t-\tau}
$$

For $\tau \geq 1$, taking expectations of both sides gives

$$
\gamma(\tau) = \varphi \gamma(\tau - 1)
$$

This is called the **Yule-Walker equation.** It is a recursive equation; that is, given $\gamma(\tau)$, for any τ, the Yule-Walker equation immediately tells us how to get $\gamma(\tau + 1)$. If we knew $\gamma(0)$ to start things off (an "initial condition"), we could use the Yule-Walker equation to determine the entire autocovariance sequence. And we do know $\gamma(0)$; it is just the variance of the process, which we already showed to be $\gamma(0) = \sigma^2/(1 - \varphi^2)$. Thus we have

$$
\gamma(0) = \frac{\sigma^2}{1 - \varphi^2}
$$

$$
\gamma(1) = \varphi\, \frac{\sigma^2}{1 - \varphi^2}
$$

$$
\gamma(2) = \varphi^2\, \frac{\sigma^2}{1 - \varphi^2}
$$

and so on. In general, then,

$$\gamma(\tau) = \varphi^\tau \frac{\sigma^2}{1 - \varphi^2}, \ \tau = 0, 1, 2, \ldots$$

Dividing through by $\gamma(0)$ gives the autocorrelations,

$$\rho(\tau) = \varphi^\tau, \ \tau = 0, 1, 2, \ldots$$

Note the gradual autocorrelation decay, which is typical of autoregressive processes. The autocorrelations approach zero, but only in the limit as the displacement approaches infinity. In particular, they don't cut off to zero, as is the case for moving-average processes. If φ is positive, the autocorrelation decay is one-sided. If φ is negative, the decay involves back-and-forth oscillations. The relevant case in business and economics is $\varphi > 0$, but either way, the autocorrelations damp gradually, not abruptly. In Figure 7.7 and 7.8 we show the autocorrelation functions for AR(1) processes with parameters $\phi = 0.4$ and $\phi = 0.95$, respectively. The persistence is much stronger when $\phi = 0.95$, in contrast to the MA(1) case, in which the persistence was weak regardless of the parameter.

Finally, the partial autocorrelation function for the AR(1) process cuts off abruptly; specifically,

$$p(\tau) = \begin{cases} \varphi, \tau = 1 \\ 0, \tau > 1 \end{cases}$$

It is easy to see why the cutoff occurs. The partial autocorrelations are just the last coefficients in a sequence of successively longer population autoregres-

FIGURE 7.7   Population Autocorrelation Function: AR(1) Process, $\varphi = 0.4$

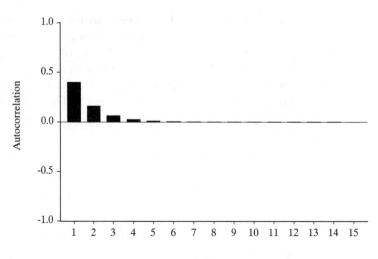

Displacement

FIGURE **7.8**   Population Autocorrelation Function: AR(1) Process, $\varphi = 0.95$

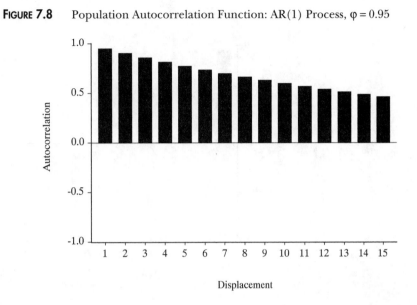

sions. If the true process is in fact AR(1), the first partial autocorrelation is just the autoregressive coefficient, and coefficients on all longer lags are zero.

In Figures 7.9 and 7.10 we show the partial autocorrelation functions for our two AR(1) processes. At displacement 1, the partial autocorrelations are simply the parameters of the process (0.4 and 0.95, respectively, in Figures 7.9 and 7.10), and at longer displacements, the partial autocorrelations are zero.

FIGURE **7.9**   Population Partial Autocorrelation Function: AR(1) Process, $\varphi = 0.4$

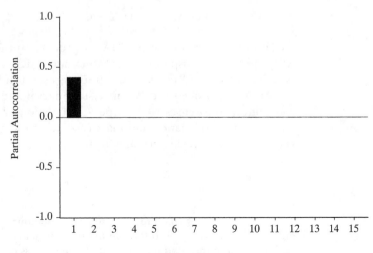

FIGURE **7.10**   Population Partial Autocorrelation Function: AR(1) Process, $\varphi = 0.95$

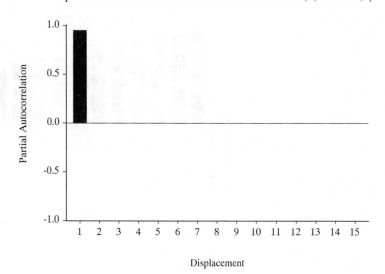

The AR(p) Process

The general pth order autoregressive process, or **AR(p)** for short, is

$$y_t = \varphi_1\, y_{t-1} + \varphi_2\, y_{t-2} + \ldots + \varphi_p\, y_{t-p} + \varepsilon_t$$

$$\varepsilon_t \sim WN(0, \sigma^2)$$

In lag operator form, we write

$$\Phi(L)y_t = (1 - \varphi_1\, L - \varphi_2\, L^2 - \ldots - \varphi_p\, L^p)\, y_t = \varepsilon_t$$

As with our discussion of the MA(q) process, in our discussion here of the AR(p) process we dispense with mathematical derivations and instead rely on parallels with the AR(1) case to intuitively establish its key properties.

An AR(p) process is covariance stationary if and only if the inverses of all roots of the autoregressive lag operator polynomial $\Phi(L)$ are inside the unit circle.[4] In the covariance stationary case we can write the process in the convergent infinite moving-average form

$$y_t = \frac{1}{\Phi(L)}\, \varepsilon_t$$

---

4. A necessary **condition for covariance stationarity**, which is often useful as a quick check, is $\Sigma_{i=1}^{p}\, \varphi_i < 1$. If the condition is satisfied, the process may or may not be stationary, but if the condition is violated, the process cannot be stationary.

The autocorrelation function for the general AR(p) process, as with that of the AR(1) process, decays gradually with displacement. Finally, the AR(p) partial autocorrelation function has a sharp cutoff at displacement p, for the same reason that the AR(1) partial autocorrelation function has a sharp cutoff at displacement 1.

Let us discuss the AR(p) autocorrelation function in a bit greater depth. The key insight is that, in spite of the fact that its qualitative behavior (gradual damping) matches that of the AR(1) autocorrelation function, it can nevertheless display a richer variety of patterns, depending on the order and parameters of the process. It can, for example, have damped monotonic decay, as in the AR(1) case with a positive coefficient, but it can also have damped oscillation in ways that AR(1) cannot. In the AR(1) case, the only possible oscillation occurs when the coefficient is negative, in which case the autocorrelations switch signs at each successively longer displacement. In higher-order autoregressive models, however, the autocorrelations can oscillate with much richer patterns reminiscent of cycles in the more traditional sense. This occurs when some roots of the autoregressive lag operator polynomial are complex.[5]

Consider, for example, the AR(2) process,

$$y_t = 1.5y_{t-1} - 0.9y_{t-2} + \varepsilon_t$$

The corresponding lag operator polynomial is $1 - 1.5L + 0.9L^2$, with two complex conjugate roots, $0.83 \pm 0.65i$. The inverse roots are $0.75 \pm 0.58i$, both of which are close to, but inside, the unit circle; thus the process is covariance stationary. It can be shown that the autocorrelation function for an AR(2) process is

$$\rho(0) = 1$$

$$\rho(1) = \frac{\varphi_1}{1 - \varphi_2}$$

$$\rho(\tau) = \varphi_1 \, \rho(\tau - 1) + \varphi_2 \, \rho(\tau - 2), \, \tau = 2, 3, \ldots$$

By using this formula, we can evaluate the autocorrelation function for the process at hand. We plot the AR(2) process in Figure 7.11. Because the roots are complex, the autocorrelation function oscillates, and because the roots are close to the unit circle, the oscillation damps slowly.

Finally, let us step back once again to consider in greater detail the precise way that finite-order autoregressive processes approximate the Wold representation. As always, the Wold representation is

$$y_t = B(L)\varepsilon_t$$

---

5. Note that complex roots cannot occur in the AR(1) case.

FIGURE 7.11   Population Autocorrelation Function: AR(2) Process with
               Complex Roots

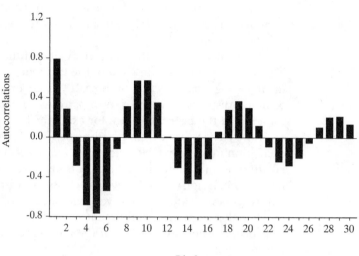

where $B(L)$ is of infinite order. The AR(1), as compared to the MA(1), is simply a different approximation to the Wold representation. The moving-average representation associated with the AR(1) process is

$$y_t = \frac{1}{1 - \varphi L} \, \varepsilon_t$$

Thus, when we fit an AR(1) model, we are using $1/(1 - \varphi L)$, a rational polynomial with degenerate numerator polynomial (degree 0) and denominator polynomial of degree 1, to approximate $B(L)$. The moving-average representation associated with the AR(1) process is of infinite order, as is the Wold representation, but it does not have infinitely many free coefficients. In fact, only one parameter, φ, underlies it.

The AR(p) is an obvious generalization of the AR(1) strategy for approximating the Wold representation. The moving-average representation associated with the AR(p) process is

$$y_t = \frac{1}{\Phi(L)} \, \varepsilon_t$$

When we fit an AR(p) model to approximate the Wold representation, we are still using a rational polynomial with degenerate numerator polynomial (degree 0), but the denominator polynomial is of higher degree.

3. AUTOREGRESSIVE MOVING-AVERAGE (ARMA) MODELS

Autoregressive and moving-average models are often combined in attempts to obtain better and more parsimonious approximations to the Wold representation, yielding the autoregressive moving-average process, **ARMA(p,q)** for short. As with moving-average and autoregressive processes, ARMA processes also have direct motivation.[6] First, if the random shock that drives an autoregressive process is itself a moving-average process, then it can be shown that we obtain an ARMA process. Second, ARMA processes can arise from aggregation. For example, sums of AR processes, or sums of AR and MA processes, can be shown to be ARMA processes. Finally, AR processes observed subject to measurement error also turn out to be ARMA processes.

The simplest ARMA process that is not a pure autoregression or pure moving-average process is the ARMA(1,1), given by

$$y_t = \varphi y_{t-1} + \varepsilon_t + \theta \varepsilon_{t-1}$$

$$\varepsilon_t \sim WN(0, \sigma^2)$$

or, in lag operator form,

$$(1 - \varphi L)\, y_t = (1 + \theta L)\, \varepsilon_t$$

where $|\varphi| < 1$ is required for stationarity and $|\theta| < 1$ is required for invertibility.[7] If the covariance stationarity condition is satisfied, then we have the moving-average representation

$$y_t = \frac{(1 + \theta L)}{(1 - \varphi L)} \varepsilon_t$$

which is an infinite distributed lag of current and past innovations. Similarly, if the invertibility condition is satisfied, then we have the infinite autoregressive representation,

$$\frac{(1 - \varphi L)}{(1 + \theta L)} y_t = \varepsilon_t$$

The ARMA(p,q) process is a natural generalization of the ARMA(1,1) that allows for multiple moving-average and autoregressive lags. We write

$$y_t = \varphi_1 y_{t-1} + \ldots + \varphi_p y_{t-p} + \varepsilon_t + \theta_1 \varepsilon_{t-1} + \ldots + \theta_q \varepsilon_{t-q}$$

$$\varepsilon_t \sim WN(0, \sigma^2)$$

---

6. For a more extensive discussion, see Granger and Newbold (1986).

7. Both stationarity and invertibility need to be checked in the ARMA case, because both autoregressive and moving-average components are present.

or

$$\Phi(L)y_t = \Theta(L)\varepsilon_t$$

If the inverses of all roots of $\Phi(L)$ are inside the unit circle, then the process is covariance stationary and has the convergent infinite moving-average representation

$$y_t = \frac{\Theta(L)}{\Phi(L)}\varepsilon_t$$

If the inverses of all roots of $\Theta(L)$ are inside the unit circle, then the process is invertible and has the convergent infinite autoregressive representation

$$\frac{\Phi(L)}{\Theta(L)}y_t = \varepsilon_t$$

As with autoregressions and moving averages, ARMA processes have a fixed unconditional mean but a time-varying conditional mean. In contrast to pure moving-average or pure autoregressive processes, however, neither the autocorrelation nor partial autocorrelation functions of ARMA processes cut off at any particular displacement. Instead, each damps gradually, with the precise pattern depending on the process.

ARMA models approximate the Wold representation by a ratio of two finite-order lag-operator polynomials, neither of which is degenerate. Thus ARMA models use ratios of full-fledged polynomials in the lag operator to approximate the Wold representation,

$$y_t = \frac{\Theta(L)}{\Phi(L)}\varepsilon_t$$

ARMA models, by allowing for both moving-average and autoregressive components, often provide accurate approximations to the Wold representation that nevertheless have just a few parameters. That is, ARMA models are often both highly accurate and highly parsimonious. In a particular situation, for example, it might take an AR(5) to get the same approximation accuracy as could be obtained with an ARMA(2,1), but the AR(5) has five parameters to be estimated, whereas the ARMA(2,1) has only three.

4. APPLICATION: SPECIFYING AND ESTIMATING MODELS FOR EMPLOYMENT FORECASTING

In chapter 6, we examined the correlogram for the Canadian employment series, and we saw that the sample autocorrelations damp slowly and the sample partial autocorrelations cut off, just the opposite of what is expected for a moving average. Thus the correlogram indicates that a finite-order moving-average process would not provide a good approximation to employment dynamics. Nevertheless, nothing stops us from fitting moving-average models, so let us fit them and use *AIC* and *SIC* to guide model selection.

Moving-average models are nonlinear in the parameters; thus, estimation proceeds by nonlinear least squares (numerical minimization). The idea is the same as when we encountered nonlinear least squares in our study of nonlinear trends—pick the parameters to minimize the sum of squared residuals—but finding an expression for the residual is a little bit trickier. To understand why moving-average models are nonlinear in the parameters, and to get a feel for how they are estimated, consider an invertible MA(1) model, with a nonzero mean explicitly included for added realism,

$$y_t = \mu + \varepsilon_t + \theta \varepsilon_{t-1}$$

Substitute backward m times to obtain the autoregressive approximation

$$y_t \approx \frac{\mu}{1+\theta} + \theta y_{t-1} - \theta^2 y_{t-2} + \ldots + (-1)^{m+1} \theta^m y_{t-m} + \varepsilon_t$$

Thus an invertible moving average can be approximated as a finite-order autoregression. The larger m is, the better the approximation. This lets us (approximately) express the residual in terms of observed data, after which we can use a computer to solve for the parameters that minimize the sum of squared residuals,

$$\hat{\mu}, \hat{\theta} = \underset{\mu, \theta}{\text{argmin}} \sum_{t=1}^{T} \left[y_t - \left(\frac{\mu}{1+\theta} + \theta y_{t-1} - \theta^2 y_{t-2} + \ldots + (-1)^{m+1} \theta^m y_{t-m} \right) \right]^2$$

$$\hat{\sigma}^2 = \frac{1}{T} \sum_{t=1}^{T} \left[y_t - \left(\frac{\hat{\mu}}{1+\hat{\theta}} + \hat{\theta} y_{t-1} - \hat{\theta}^2 y_{t-2} + \ldots + (-1)^{m+1} \hat{\theta}^m y_{t-m} \right) \right]^2$$

The parameter estimates must be found using numerical optimization methods, because the parameters of the autoregressive approximation are restricted. The coefficient of the second lag of y is the square of the coefficient on the first lag of y, and so on. The parameter restrictions must be imposed in estimation, which is why we cannot simply run an ordinary least squares regression of y on lags of itself.

The next step would be to estimate MA(q) models, $q = 1, 2, 3, 4$. Both *AIC* and *SIC* suggest that the MA(4) is best. To save space, we report only the results of the MA(4) estimation in Table 7.1. The results of the MA(4) estimation, although better than lower-order MAs, are nevertheless poor. The R^2 of 0.84 is rather low, for example, and the Durbin-Watson statistic indicates that

TABLE 7.1   Employment MA(4) Model

LS // Dependent Variable is CANEMP
Sample: 1962:1 1993:4
Included observations: 128
Convergence achieved after 49 iterations

Variable	Coefficient	Std. Error	t-Statistic	Prob.
C	100.5438	0.843322	119.2234	0.0000
MA(1)	1.587641	0.063908	24.84246	0.0000
MA(2)	0.994369	0.089995	11.04917	0.0000
MA(3)	-0.020305	0.046550	-0.436189	0.6635
MA(4)	-0.298387	0.020489	-14.56311	0.0000

R-squared	0.849951	Mean dependent var	101.0176
Adjusted R-squared	0.845071	S.D. dependent var	7.499163
S.E. of regression	2.951747	Akaike info criterion	2.203073
Sum squared resid	1071.676	Schwarz criterion	2.314481
Log likelihood	-317.6208	F-statistic	174.1826
Durbin-Watson stat	1.246600	Prob(F-statistic)	0.000000

Inverted MA Roots	.41	-.56+.72i	-.56 -.72i	-.87

the MA(4) model fails to account for all the serial correlation in employment. The residual plot, which we show in Figure 7.12, clearly indicates a neglected cycle, an impression confirmed by the residual correlogram (Table 7.2, Figure 7.13).

FIGURE 7.12   Employment: MA(4) Model, Residual Plot

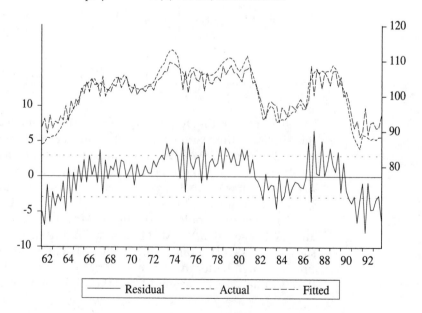

TABLE 7.2   Employment: MA(4) Model, Residual Correlogram

Sample: 1962:1 1993:4
Included observations: 128
Q-statistic probabilities adjusted for 4 ARMA term(s)

	Acorr.	P. Acorr.	Std. Error	Ljung-Box	p-value
1	0.345	0.345	.088	15.614	
2	0.660	0.614	.088	73.089	
3	0.534	0.426	.088	111.01	
4	0.427	-0.042	.088	135.49	
5	0.347	-0.398	.088	151.79	0.000
6	0.484	0.145	.088	183.70	0.000
7	0.121	-0.118	.088	185.71	0.000
8	0.348	-0.048	.088	202.46	0.000
9	0.148	-0.019	.088	205.50	0.000
10	0.102	-0.066	.088	206.96	0.000
11	0.081	-0.098	.088	207.89	0.000
12	0.029	-0.113	.088	208.01	0.000

If we insist on using a moving-average model, we would want to explore orders greater than four, but all the results thus far indicate that moving average processes don't provide good approximations to employment dynamics. Thus let us consider alternative approximations, such as autoregressions. Autoregressions can be conveniently estimated by ordinary least squares regression. Consider, for example, the AR(1) model,

$$(y_t - \mu) = \varphi(y_{t-1} - \mu) + \varepsilon_t$$

$$\varepsilon_t \sim (0, \sigma^2)$$

which can be written as

$$y_t = c + \varphi y_{t-1} + \varepsilon_t$$

where $c = \mu(1 - \varphi)$. The least squares estimators are

$$\hat{c}, \hat{\varphi} = \underset{c, \varphi}{\operatorname{argmin}} \sum_{t=1}^{T} \left[y_t - c - \varphi y_{t-1} \right]^2$$

$$\hat{\sigma}^2 = \frac{1}{T} \sum_{t=1}^{T} \left[y_t - \hat{c} - \hat{\varphi} y_{t-1} \right]^2$$

FIGURE 7.13   Employment: MA(4) Model, Residual Sample Autocorrelation and
                Partial Autocorrelation Functions, with Two Standard-Error Bands

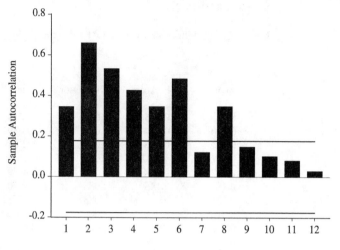

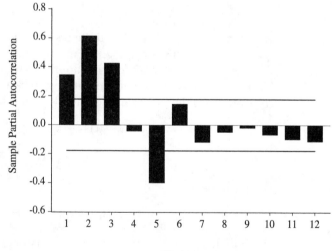

The implied estimate of μ is $\hat{\mu} = \hat{c}/(1 - \hat{\phi})$. Unlike the moving-average case, for which the sum of squares function is nonlinear in the parameters and requires the use of numerical minimization methods, the sum of squares function for autoregressive processes is linear in the parameters, so that estimation is particularly stable and easy. In the AR(1) case, we simply run an ordinary least squares regression of y on one lag of y; in the AR(p) case, we regress y on p lags of y.

We estimate AR(p) models, p = 1, 2, 3, 4. Both *AIC* and *SIC* suggest that AR(2) is best. To save space, we report only the results of AR(2) estimation in Table 7.3. The estimation results look good, and the residuals (Figure 7.14)

TABLE 7.3   Employment: AR(2) Model

LS // Dependent Variable is CANEMP
Sample: 1962:1 1993:4
Included observations: 128
Convergence achieved after 3 iterations

Variable	Coefficient	Std. Error	t-Statistic	Prob.
C	101.2413	3.399620	29.78017	0.0000
AR(1)	1.438810	0.078487	18.33188	0.0000
AR(2)	-0.476451	0.077902	-6.116042	0.0000

R-squared	0.963372	Mean dependent var	101.0176
Adjusted R-squared	0.962786	S.D. dependent var	7.499163
S.E. of regression	1.446663	Akaike info criterion	0.761677
Sum squared resid	261.6041	Schwarz criterion	0.828522
Log likelihood	-227.3715	F-statistic	1643.837
Durbin-Watson stat	2.067024	Prob(F-statistic)	0.000000

Inverted AR Roots	.92	.52

FIGURE 7.14   Employment: AR(2) Model, Residual Plot

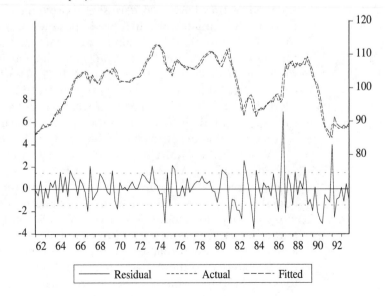

TABLE 7.4   Employment: AR(2) Model, Residual Correlogram

Sample: 1962:1 1993:4
Included observations: 128
Q-statistic probabilities adjusted for 2 ARMA term(s)

	Acorr.	P. Acorr.	Std. Error	Ljung-Box	p-value
1	-0.035	-0.035	.088	0.1606	
2	0.044	0.042	.088	0.4115	
3	0.011	0.014	.088	0.4291	0.512
4	0.051	0.050	.088	0.7786	0.678
5	0.002	0.004	.088	0.7790	0.854
6	0.019	0.015	.088	0.8272	0.935
7	-0.024	-0.024	.088	0.9036	0.970
8	0.078	0.072	.088	1.7382	0.942
9	0.080	0.087	.088	2.6236	0.918
10	0.050	0.050	.088	2.9727	0.936
11	-0.023	-0.027	.088	3.0504	0.962
12	-0.129	-0.148	.088	5.4385	0.860

look like white noise. The residual correlogram (Table 7.4, Figure 7.15) supports that conclusion.

Finally, we consider ARMA(p,q) approximations to the Wold representation. ARMA models are estimated in a fashion similar to moving-average models; they have autoregressive approximations with nonlinear restrictions on the parameters, which we impose when doing a numerical sum of squares minimization. We examine all ARMA(p,q) models with p and q less than or equal to 4; the *AIC* and *SIC* values appear in Tables 7.5 and 7.6, respectively. *SIC* selects the AR(2) (an ARMA(2,0)), which we have already discussed. *AIC*, which penalizes degrees of freedom less harshly, selects an ARMA(3,1) model. The ARMA(3,1) model looks good; the estimation results appear in Table 7.7, the residual plot is shown in Figure 7.16, and the residual correlogram is given in Table 7.8 and Figure 7.17.

Although the ARMA(3,1) looks good, apart from its lower *AIC* it looks no better than the AR(2), which basically seemed perfect. In fact, there are at least three reasons to prefer the AR(2). First, for the reasons that we discussed in chapter 4, when *AIC* and *SIC* disagree we recommend using the more parsimonious model selected by *SIC*. Second, if we consider a model selection strategy involving not just examination of *AIC* and *SIC*, but also examination of autocorrelations and partial autocorrelations, which we advocate, we are led to the AR(2). Finally, and importantly, the impression that the ARMA(3,1) provides a richer approximation to employment dynamics is

FIGURE 7.15   Employment: AR(2) Model, Residual Sample Autocorrelation, and
               Partial Autocorrelation Functions, with Two Standard-Error Bands

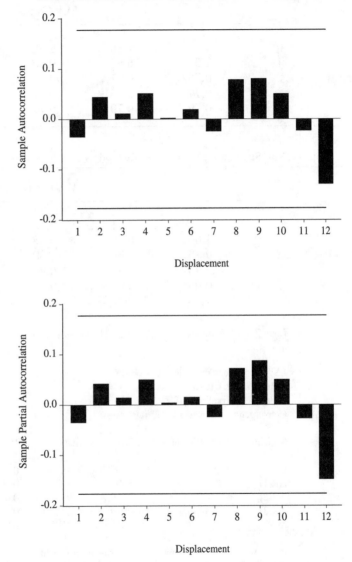

likely spurious in this case. The ARMA(3,1) has an inverse autoregressive
root of −0.94 and an inverse moving-average root of −0.97. Those roots are,
of course, just *estimates*, subject to sampling uncertainty. They are likely to be
statistically indistinguishable from one another, in which case we can *cancel*
them, which brings us down to an ARMA(2,0), or AR(2), model with roots
virtually indistinguishable from those of our earlier-estimated AR(2) process!

TABLE 7.5   Employment: AIC Values, Various ARMA Models

		MA Order				
		0	1	2	3	4
	0		2.86	2.32	2.47	2.20
	1	1.01	0.83	0.79	0.80	0.81
AR Order	2	0.762	0.77	0.78	0.80	0.80
	3	0.77	0.761	0.77	0.78	0.79
	4	0.79	0.79	0.77	0.79	0.80

TABLE 7.6   Employment: SIC Values, Various ARMA Models

		MA Order				
		0	1	2	3	4
	0		2.91	2.38	2.56	2.31
	1	1.05	0.90	0.88	0.91	0.94
AR Order	2	0.83	0.86	0.89	0.92	0.96
	3	0.86	0.87	0.90	0.94	0.96
	4	0.90	0.92	0.93	0.97	1.00

TABLE 7.7   Employment: ARMA(3,1) Model

LS // Dependent Variable is CANEMP
Sample: 1962:1 1993:4
Included observations: 128
Convergence achieved after 17 iterations

Variable	Coefficient	Std. Error	t-Statistic	Prob.
C	101.1378	3.538602	28.58130	0.0000
AR(1)	0.500493	0.087503	5.719732	0.0000
AR(2)	0.872194	0.067096	12.99917	0.0000
AR(3)	-0.443355	0.080970	-5.475560	0.0000
MA(1)	0.970952	0.035015	27.72924	0.0000

R-squared	0.964535	Mean dependent var	101.0176
Adjusted R-squared	0.963381	S.D. dependent var	7.499163
S.E. of regression	1.435043	Akaike info criterion	0.760668
Sum squared resid	253.2997	Schwarz criterion	0.872076
Log likelihood	-225.3069	F-statistic	836.2912
Durbin-Watson stat	2.057302	Prob(F-statistic)	0.000000

Inverted AR Roots	.93	.51	-.94
Inverted MA Roots	-.97		

FIGURE 7.16   Employment: ARMA(3,1) Model, Residual Plot

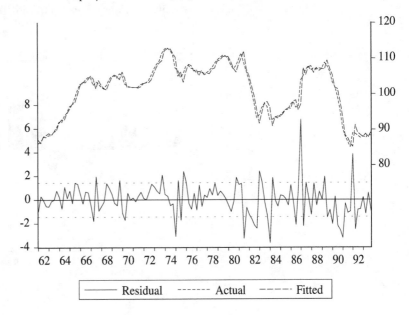

TABLE 7.8   Employment: ARMA (3,1) Model, Residual Correlogram

Sample: 1962:1 1993:4
Included observations: 128
Q-statistic probabilities adjusted for 4 ARMA term(s)

	Acorr.	P. Acorr.	Std. Error	Ljung-Box	p-value
1	-0.032	-0.032	.09	0.1376	
2	0.041	0.040	.09	0.3643	
3	0.014	0.017	.09	0.3904	
4	0.048	0.047	.09	0.6970	
5	0.006	0.007	.09	0.7013	0.402
6	0.013	0.009	.09	0.7246	0.696
7	-0.017	-0.019	.09	0.7650	0.858
8	0.064	0.060	.09	1.3384	0.855
9	0.092	0.097	.09	2.5182	0.774
10	0.039	0.040	.09	2.7276	0.842
11	-0.016	-0.022	.09	2.7659	0.906
12	-0.137	-0.153	.09	5.4415	0.710

FIGURE 7.17   Employment: ARMA(3,1) Model, Residual Sample Autocorrelation and Partial Autocorrelation Functions, with Two-Standard-Error Bands

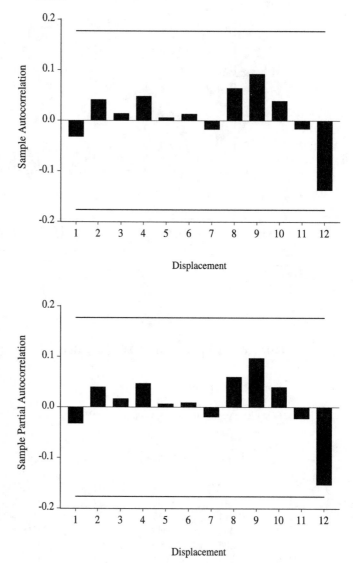

We refer to this situation as one of **common factors** in an ARMA model. Be on the lookout for such situations, which arise frequently and can lead to substantial model simplification.

Thus we arrive at an AR(2) model for employment. In the next chapter we learn how to use it to produce point and interval forecasts.

PROBLEMS AND COMPLEMENTS

1. (The mechanics of fitting ARMA models) The data disk contains data for daily transfers over BankWire, a financial wire transfer system in a country responsible for much of the world's finance, over a recent span of 200 business days.

   (a) Is trend or seasonality operative? Defend your answer.
   (b) Using the methods developed in chapters 6 and 7, find a parsimonious ARMA(p,q) model that fits well, and defend its adequacy.

2. (Diagnostic checking of model residuals) If a forecasting model has extracted all the systematic information from the data, then what is left—the residual—should be white noise. More precisely, the true innovations are white noise, and if a model is a good approximation to the Wold representation, then its 1-step-ahead forecast errors should be approximately white noise. The model residuals are the in-sample analog of out-of-sample 1-step-ahead forecast errors. Hence we see the usefulness of various tests of the hypothesis that residuals are white noise.

   The Durbin-Watson test is the most popular of these tests. Recall the Durbin-Watson test statistic, discussed in the appendix to chapter 1,

$$DW = \frac{\sum_{t=2}^{T}(e_t - e_{t-1})^2}{\sum_{t=1}^{T} e_t^2}$$

Note that

$$\sum_{t=2}^{T}(e_t - e_{t-1})^2 \approx 2\sum_{t=2}^{T} e_t^2 - 2\sum_{t=2}^{T} e_t e_{t-1}$$

Thus

$$DW \approx 2(1 - \hat{\rho}(1))$$

so that the Durbin-Watson test is effectively based only on the first sample autocorrelation and really tests only whether the first autocorrelation is zero. We therefore say that the Durbin-Watson is a test for **first-order se-**

rial correlation. In addition, the Durbin-Watson test is not valid in the presence of lagged dependent variables.[8] On both counts, we would like a more general and flexible framework for diagnosing serial correlation. The residual correlogram, comprised of the residual sample autocorrelations, the sample partial autocorrelations, and the associated Q-statistics, fills this role.

(a) When we discussed the correlogram in the text, we focused on the case of an observed time series, in which case we showed that the Q-statistics are distributed as χ^2_m. Now, however, we want to assess whether unobserved model disturbances are white noise. To do so, we use the model residuals, which are estimates of the unobserved disturbances. Because we fit a model to get the residuals, we need to account for the degrees of freedom used. The upshot is that the distribution of the Q-statistics under the white noise hypothesis is better approximated by a χ^2_{m-k} random variable, where k is the number of parameters estimated. That is why, for example, we don't report (and in fact the software doesn't compute) the p-values for the Q-statistics associated with the residual correlogram of our employment forecasting model until $m > k$.

(b) **Durbin's h test** is an alternative to the Durbin-Watson test. As with the Durbin-Watson test, it is designed to detect first-order serial correlation, but it is valid in the presence of lagged dependent variables. Do some background reading as well on Durbin's h test and report what you learned.

(c) The **Breusch-Godfrey test** is another alternative to the Durbin-Watson test. It is designed to detect pth-order serial correlation, where p is selected by the user, and is also valid in the presence of lagged dependent variables. Do some background reading on the Breusch-Godfrey procedure and report what you learned.

(d) Which do you think is likely to be most useful to you in assessing the properties of residuals from forecasting models: the residual correlogram, Durbin's h test, or the Breusch-Godfrey test? Why?

3. (The autocovariance function of the MA(1) process, revisited) In the text we wrote

$$\gamma(\tau) = E\left(y_t\, y_{t-\tau}\right) = E\left((\varepsilon_t + \theta\varepsilon_{t-1})\,(\varepsilon_{t-\tau} + \theta\varepsilon_{t-\tau-1})\right) = \begin{cases} \theta\sigma^2, & \tau = 1 \\ 0, & \text{otherwise} \end{cases}$$

---

8. Following standard—if not strictly appropriate—practice, in this book we often report and examine the Durbin-Watson statistic even when lagged dependent variables are included. We always supplement the Durbin-Watson statistic, however, with other diagnostics such as the residual correlogram, which remain valid in the presence of lagged dependent variables, and which almost always produce the same inference as the Durbin-Watson statistic.

Fill in the missing steps by evaluating explicitly the expectation $E((\varepsilon_t + \theta\varepsilon_{t-1})(\varepsilon_{t-\tau} + \theta\varepsilon_{t-\tau-1}))$.

4. (**Aggregation** and **disaggregation: top-down** versus **bottom-up forecasting models**) Related to the issue of methods and complexity discussed in chapter 2 is the question of aggregation. Often we want to forecast an aggregate, such as total sales of a manufacturing firm, but we can take either an aggregated or disaggregated approach.

   Suppose, for example, that total sales is composed of sales of three products. The aggregated, or top-down, or macro, approach is simply to model and forecast total sales. The disaggregated, or bottom-up, or micro, approach is to model and forecast separately the sales of the individual products, and then to add them together.

   (a) Perhaps surprisingly, it is impossible to know in advance whether the aggregated or disaggregated approach is better. It all depends on the specifics of the situation; the only way to tell is to try both approaches and compare the forecasting results.

   (b) However, in real-world situations characterized by likely model misspecification and parameter estimation uncertainty, there are reasons to suspect that the aggregated approach may be preferable. First, standard (e.g., linear) models fit to aggregated series may be less prone to specification error because aggregation can produce approximately linear relationships even when the underlying disaggregated relationships are not linear. Second, if the disaggregated series depends in part on a common factor (e.g., general business conditions), then it will emerge more clearly in the aggregate data. Finally, modeling and forecasting of one aggregated series, as opposed to many disaggregated series, relies on far fewer parameter estimates.

   (c) Of course, if our interest centers on the disaggregated components, then we have no choice but to take a disaggregated approach.

5. (Nonlinear forecasting models: regime switching) In this chapter we have studied dynamic **linear models,** which are tremendously important in practice. They are called "linear" because y_t is a simple linear function of past y's or past ε's. In some forecasting situations, however, good statistical characterization of dynamics may require some notion of regime switching, as between "good" and "bad" states, which is a type of **nonlinear model.**

   Models incorporating **regime switching** have a long tradition in business-cycle analysis, in which expansion is the good state, and contraction (recession) is the bad state. This idea is also manifest in the great interest in the popular press, for example, in identifying and forecasting turning points in economic activity. It is only within a regime-switching framework that the concept of a turning point has intrinsic meaning; turning points are naturally and immediately defined as the times separating expansions and contractions.

Threshold models are squarely in line with the regime-switching tradition. The following threshold model, for example, has three regimes, two thresholds, and a d-period delay regulating the switches:

$$y_t = \begin{cases} c^{(u)} + \varphi^{(u)} y_{t-1} + \varepsilon_t^{(u)}, & \theta^{(u)} < y_{t-d} \\ c^{(m)} + \varphi^{(m)} y_{t-1} + \varepsilon_t^{(m)}, & \theta^{(l)} < y_{t-d} < \theta^{(u)} \\ c^{(l)} + \varphi^{(l)} y_{t-1} + \varepsilon_t^{(l)}, & \theta^{(l)} > y_{t-d} \end{cases}$$

The superscripts indicate "upper," "middle," and "lower" regimes, and the regime operative at any time t depends on the observable past history of y—in particular, on the value of y_{t-d}.

Although observable threshold models are of interest, models with *latent* (or unobservable) states as opposed to observed states may be more appropriate in many business, economic, and financial contexts. In such a setup, time-series dynamics are governed by a finite-dimensional parameter vector that switches (potentially each period) depending upon which of two unobservable states is realized, with state transitions governed by a first-order Markov process (meaning that the state at any time t depends only on the state at time $t-1$, not at time $t-2, t-3, \ldots$).

To make matters concrete, let us take a simple example. Let $\{s_t\}_{t=1}^T$ be the (latent) sample path of a two-state first-order autoregressive process, taking just the two values 0 or 1, with the transition probability matrix given by

$$M = \begin{pmatrix} p_{00} & 1 - p_{00} \\ 1 - p_{11} & p_{11} \end{pmatrix}$$

The ijth element of M gives the probability of moving from state i (at time $t-1$) to state j (at time t). Note that there are only two free parameters, the staying probabilities, p_{00} and p_{11}. Let $\{y_t\}_{t=1}^T$ be the sample path of an observed time series that depends on $\{s_t\}_{t=1}^T$ such that the density of y_t conditional upon s_t is

$$f(y_t \mid s_t; \theta) = \frac{1}{\sqrt{2\pi}\,\sigma} \exp\left(\frac{-(y_t - \mu_{s_t})^2}{2\,\sigma^2} \right)$$

Thus, y_t is Gaussian white noise with a potentially switching mean. The two means around which y_t moves are of particular interest and may, for example, correspond to episodes of differing growth rates ("booms" and "recessions," "bull" and "bear" markets, and so forth).

6. (Volatility dynamics: ARCH and GARCH models) Here we introduce the ARCH and GARCH models, which have proved extremely useful for modeling and forecasting volatility fluctuations. For a detailed discussion, see Diebold and Lopez (1995), on which this complement draws heavily.

(a) The ARCH process, proposed by Engle (1982), is given by

$$\varepsilon_t \,|\, \Omega_{t-1} \sim N(0, h_t)$$

$$h_t = \omega + \gamma(L)\,\varepsilon_t^2$$

$$\omega > 0, \ \gamma(L) = \sum_{i=1}^{p} \gamma_i\, L^i, \ \gamma_i \geq 0 \text{ for all } i, \ \gamma(1) < 1$$

The process is parameterized in terms of the conditional density of $\varepsilon_t \,|\, \Omega_{t-1}$, which is assumed to be normal with a zero conditional mean and a conditional variance that depends linearly on past squared innovations. Thus, although the ε_t's are serially uncorrelated, they are not independent (unless $\gamma(L)$ is zero, in which case ε_t is simply iid noise with variance ω). In particular, the conditional variance, a common measure of *volatility*, fluctuates and is forecastable. How would you expect the correlogram of ε_t^2 to look? Why?

(b) The generalized ARCH, or GARCH, process proposed by Bollerslev (1986) approximates conditional variance dynamics in the same way that ARMA models approximate conditional mean dynamics:

$$\varepsilon_t \,|\, \Omega_{t-1} \sim N(0, h_t)$$

$$h_t = \omega + \alpha(L)\varepsilon_t^2 + \beta(L)h_t$$

$$\alpha(L) = \sum_{i=1}^{p} \alpha_i\, L^i \quad \beta(L) = \sum_{i=1}^{q} \beta_i\, L^i$$

$$\omega > 0 \ \ \alpha_i \geq 0 \ \ \beta_i \geq 0 \text{ for all } i \ \ \alpha(1) + \beta(1) < 1$$

Engle's (1982) ARCH model emerges when $\beta(L) = 0$. How would you expect the correlogram of ε_t^2 to look? Why? Do you expect the ARCH model or the GARCH model to provide more parsimonious approximations to volatility dynamics? Why?

(c) GARCH and related models have found wide application in financial settings, in which market volatility often fluctuates in a predictable way. They are also consistent with the fat-tailed unconditional distributions typically found for high-frequency asset returns. For detailed discussion, see Bollerslev, Chou, and Kroner (1992) and Taylor (1996).

7. (Difficulties with nonlinear optimization) Nonlinear optimization is a tricky business, fraught with problems. Some eye-opening reading includes Newbold, Agiakloglou, and Miller (1994) and McCullough and Vinod (1999).

(a) Some problems are generic. It is relatively easy to find a global optimum, for example, but much harder to be confident that the local optimum is global. Simple checks, such as trying a variety of startup values and checking the optimum to which convergence occurs, are used routinely, but the problem nevertheless remains.

(b) Some problems may be software specific. For example, some software may use highly accurate analytic derivatives, whereas other software uses approximate numerical derivatives.

(c) Software for ARMA model estimation is unavoidably exposed to such problems because estimation of any model involving MA terms requires numerical optimization of a likelihood or sum-of-squares function.

BIBLIOGRAPHICAL AND COMPUTATIONAL NOTES

Characterization of time series by means of autoregressive, moving-average, or ARMA models was suggested, more or less simultaneously, by the Russian statistician and economist E. Slutsky and the British statistician G.U. Yule. Slutsky (1927) remains a classic. The Slutsky-Yule framework was modernized, extended, and made part of an innovative and operational modeling and forecasting paradigm in a more recent classic, a 1970 book by Box and Jenkins, the latest edition of which is Box, Jenkins, and Reinsel (1994). In fact, ARMA and related models are often called **Box-Jenkins models.**

Granger and Newbold (1986) contains a more detailed discussion of a number of topics in this chapter, including the idea of moving-average processes as describing economic equilibrium disturbed by transient shocks, the Yule-Walker equation, and the insight that aggregation and measurement error lead naturally to ARMA processes.

The sample autocorrelations and partial autocorrelations, together with related diagnostics, provide graphical aids to model selection that complement the Akaike and Schwarz information criteria introduced earlier. Not long ago, the sample autocorrelation and partial autocorrelation functions were often used *alone* to guide forecast model selection, a tricky business that was more art than science. Use of the Akaike and Schwarz criteria results in more systematic and replicable model selection, but the sample autocorrelation and partial autocorrelation functions nevertheless remain important

as basic graphical summaries of dynamics in time series data. The two approaches are complements, not substitutes.

Our discussion of estimation was a bit fragmented; we discussed estimation of moving-average and ARMA models using nonlinear least squares, whereas we discussed estimation of autoregressive models using ordinary least squares. A more unified approach proceeds by writing each model as a regression on an intercept, with a serially correlated disturbance. Thus the moving-average model is

$$y_t = \mu + \varepsilon_t$$

$$\varepsilon_t = \Theta(L)v_t$$

$$v_t \sim WN(0, \sigma^2)$$

The autoregressive model is

$$y_t = \mu + \varepsilon_t$$

$$\Phi(L)\varepsilon_t = v_t$$

$$v_t \sim WN(0, \sigma^2)$$

And the ARMA model is

$$y_t = \mu + \varepsilon_t$$

$$\Phi(L)\varepsilon_t = \Theta(L)v_t$$

$$v_t \sim WN(0, \sigma^2)$$

We can estimate each model in identical fashion using nonlinear least squares. Eviews and other forecasting packages proceed in precisely that way.[9]

This framework—regression on a constant with serially correlated disturbances—has a number of attractive features. First, the mean of the process is the regression constant term.[10] Second, it leads us naturally toward regression on more than just a constant; other right-hand-side variables can be added as desired. Finally, it exploits the fact that because autoregressive and moving-average models are special cases of the ARMA model, their estimation is also a special case of estimation of the ARMA model.

---

9. That is why, for example, information on the number of iterations required for convergence is presented even for estimation of the autoregressive model.

10. Hence the notation "μ" for the intercept.

Our description of estimating ARMA models—compute the autoregressive representation, truncate it, and estimate the resulting approximate model by nonlinear least squares—is conceptually correct but intentionally simplified. The actual estimation methods implemented in modern software are more sophisticated, and the precise implementations vary across software packages. Beneath it all, however, all estimation methods are closely related to our discussion, whether implicitly or explicitly. You should consult your software manual for details.

Pesaran, Pierse, and Kumar (1989) and Granger (1990) study the question of top-down versus bottom-up forecasting.

Our discussion of regime-switching models draws heavily on Diebold and Rudebusch (1996). Tong (1990) is a key reference on observable-state threshold models, as is Hamilton (1989) for latent-state threshold models. There are a number of extensions of those basic regime-switching models of potential interest for forecasters, such as allowing for smooth as opposed to abrupt transitions in threshold models with observed states (Granger and Teräsvirta, 1993), and allowing for time-varying transition probabilities in threshold models with latent states (Diebold, Lee, and Weinbach, 1994).

CONCEPTS FOR REVIEW

Aggregation
Approximation to the Wold
  representation
ARMA(p,q) process
AR(p) process
Autoregressive (AR) model
Autoregressive moving average
  (ARMA) model
Autoregressive representation
Bottom-up forecasting model
Box-Jenkins model
Breusch-Godfrey test
Common factors
Complex roots
Condition for covariance
  stationarity
Condition for invertibility of
  the MA(q) process

Cutoff in the autocorrelation
  function
Disaggregation
Durbin's h test
First-order serial correlation
Invertibility
Linear model
MA(1) process
MA(q) process
Moving-average (MA) model
Nonlinear model
Regime switching
Stochastic process
Threshold model
Top-down forecasting model
Yule-Walker equation

REFERENCES AND ADDITIONAL READINGS

Bollerslev, T. (1986), "Generalized Autoregressive Conditional Heteroskedasticity," *Journal of Econometrics,* 31, 307–327.

Bollerslev, T., Chou, R. Y., and Kroner, K. F. (1992), "ARCH Modeling in Finance: A Selective Review of the Theory and Empirical Evidence," *Journal of Econometrics,* 52, 5–59.

Box, G. E. P., Jenkins, G. W., and Reinsel, G. (1994), *Time Series Analysis, Forecasting and Control,* third edition. Englewood Cliffs, N.J.: Prentice Hall.

Burns, A. F., and Mitchell, W. C. (1946), *Measuring Business Cycles.* New York: National Bureau of Economic Research.

Diebold, F. X., Lee, J.-H., and Weinbach, G. (1994), "Regime Switching with Time-Varying Transition Probabilities," in C. Hargreaves (ed.), *Nonstationary Time Series Analysis and Cointegration.* Oxford: Oxford University Press, 283–302. Reprinted in Diebold and Rudebusch (1999).

Diebold, F. X., and Lopez, J. (1995), "Modeling Volatility Dynamics," in Kevin Hoover (ed.), *Macroeconometrics: Developments, Tensions and Prospects.* Boston: Kluwer Academic Press, 427–472.

Diebold, F. X., and Rudebusch, G. D. (1996), "Measuring Business Cycles: A Modern Perspective," *Review of Economics and Statistics,* 78, 67–77. Reprinted in Diebold and Rudebusch (1999).

Diebold, F. X., and Rudebusch, G. D. (1999), *Business Cycles: Durations, Dynamics, and Forecasting.* Princeton, N.J.: Princeton University Press.

Engle, R. F. (1982), "Autoregressive Conditional Heteroskedasticity with Estimates of the Variance of U.K. Inflation," *Econometrica,* 50, 987–1008.

Granger, C. W. J. (1990), "Aggregation of Time Series Variables: A Survey," in T. Barker and M. H. Pesaran (eds.), *Disaggregation in Econometric Modelling.* London and New York: Routledge.

Granger, C. W. J., and Newbold, P. (1986), *Forecasting Economic Time Series,* second edition. Orlando, Fla.: Academic Press.

Granger, C. W. J., and Teräsvirta, Y. (1993), *Modelling Nonlinear Economic Relationships.* Oxford: Oxford University Press.

Hamilton, J. D. (1989), "A New Approach to the Economic Analysis of Nonstationary Time Series and the Business Cycle," *Econometrica,* 57, 357–384.

McCullough, B. D., and Vinod, H. D. (1999), "The Numerical Reliability of Econometric Software," *Journal of Economic Literature,* 37, 633–665.

Newbold, P., Agiakloglou, C., and Miller, J. P. (1994), "Adventures with ARIMA Software," *International Journal of Forecasting,* 10, 573–581.

Pesaran, M. H., Pierse, R. G., and Kumar, M. S. (1989), "Econometric Analysis of Aggregation in the Context of Linear Prediction Models," *Econometrica,* 57, 861–888.

Slutsky, E. (1927), "The Summation of Random Causes as the Source of Cyclic Processes," *Econometrica,* 5, 105–146.

Taylor, S. (1996), *Modeling Financial Time Series,* second edition. New York: Wiley.

Tong, H. (1990), *Non-linear Time Series.* Oxford: Clarendon Press.

CHAPTER

FORECASTING CYCLES

1. OPTIMAL FORECASTS

By now you should be comfortable with the idea of an **information set.** Here we use that idea extensively. We denote the time-T information set by Ω_T. At first pass it seems most natural to think of the information set as containing the available past history of the series,

$$\Omega_T = \{y_T, y_{T-1}, y_{T-2}, \ldots\}$$

where for theoretical purposes we imagine history as having begun in the infinite past.

As long as y is covariance stationary, however, we can just as easily express the information available at time T in terms of current and past shocks,

$$\Omega_T = \{\varepsilon_T, \varepsilon_{T-1}, \varepsilon_{T-2}, \ldots\}$$

Suppose, for example, that the process to be forecast is a covariance stationary AR(1),

$$y_t = \varphi y_{t-1} + \varepsilon_t$$

Then immediately,

$$\varepsilon_T = y_T - \varphi y_{T-1}$$

$$\varepsilon_{T-1} = y_{T-1} - \varphi y_{T-2}$$

$$\varepsilon_{T-2} = y_{T-2} - \varphi y_{T-3}$$

and so on. In other words, we can figure out the current and lagged ε's from the current and lagged y's. Even if a series is MA or ARMA, if it is invertible we can write it as an AR, which is to say we can express the ε's in terms of the y's.

Assembling the discussion thus far, we can view the time-T information set as containing the current and past values of y and ε,

$$\Omega_T = \{y_T, y_{T-1}, y_{T-2}, \ldots, \varepsilon_T, \varepsilon_{T-1}, \varepsilon_{T-2}, \ldots\}$$

Based upon that information set, we want to find the **optimal forecast** of y at some future time $T + h$. The optimal forecast is the one with the smallest loss on average, that is, the forecast that minimizes **expected loss.** It turns out that under reasonably weak conditions the optimal forecast is the **conditional mean,** $E(y_{T+h} \mid \Omega_T)$, the expected value of the future value of the series being forecast, conditional upon available information.

In general, the conditional mean need not be a linear function of the elements of the information set. Because linear functions are particularly tractable, we prefer to work with **linear forecasts**—forecasts that are linear in the elements of the information set—by finding the best linear approximation to the conditional mean, called the **linear projection,** denoted $P(y_{T+h} \mid \Omega_T)$. This explains the common term, **linear least squares forecast.** The linear projection is often very useful and accurate because the conditional mean is often close to linear. In fact, in the Gaussian case the conditional expectation is exactly linear, so that $E(y_{T+h} \mid \Omega_T) = P(y_{T+h} \mid \Omega_T)$.

2. FORECASTING MOVING-AVERAGE PROCESSES

Optimal Point Forecasts for Finite-Order Moving Averages

Our forecasting method is always the same: we write out the process for the future time period of interest, $T + h$, and project it on what is known at time T, when the forecast is made. This process is best learned by example. Consider an MA(2) process,

$$y_t = \varepsilon_t + \theta_1 \varepsilon_{t-1} + \theta_2 \varepsilon_{t-2}$$

$$\varepsilon_t \sim WN(0, \sigma^2)$$

Suppose we are standing at time T and we want to forecast y_{T+1}. First we write out the process for $T+1$,

$$y_{T+1} = \varepsilon_{T+1} + \theta_1 \varepsilon_T + \theta_2 \varepsilon_{T-1}$$

Then we project on the time-T information set, which simply means that all future innovations are replaced by zeros. Thus

$$y_{T+1,T} = P(y_{T+1} \mid \Omega_T) = \theta_1 \varepsilon_T + \theta_2 \varepsilon_{T-1}$$

To forecast two steps ahead, we note that

$$y_{T+2} = \varepsilon_{T+2} + \theta_1 \varepsilon_{T+1} + \theta_2 \varepsilon_T$$

and we project on the time-T information set to get

$$y_{T+2,T} = \theta_2 \varepsilon_T$$

Continuing in this fashion, we see that

$$y_{T+h,T} = 0$$

for all $h > 2$.

Now let us compute the corresponding **forecast errors.**[1] We have:

$$e_{T+1,T} = \varepsilon_{T+1} \qquad \text{(white noise)}$$

$$e_{T+2,T} = \varepsilon_{T+2} + \theta_1 \varepsilon_{T+1} \qquad \text{(MA(1))}$$

$$\cdot$$
$$\cdot$$
$$\cdot$$

$$e_{T+h,T} = \varepsilon_{T+h} + \theta_1 \varepsilon_{T+h-1} + \theta_2 \varepsilon_{T+h-2} \quad \text{(MA(2))}$$

for all $h > 2$.

Finally, the **forecast error variances** are:

$$\sigma_1^2 = \sigma^2$$

$$\sigma_2^2 = \sigma^2(1 + \theta_1^2)$$

$$\cdot$$
$$\cdot$$
$$\cdot$$

$$\sigma_h^2 = \sigma^2(1 + \theta_1^2 + \theta_2^2)$$

---

1. Recall that the forecast error is simply the difference between the actual and forecasted values. That is, $e_{T+h,T} = y_{T+h} - y_{T+h,T}$.

for all $h > 2$. Moreover, the forecast error variance for $h > 2$ is just the unconditional variance of y_t.

Now consider the general MA(q) case. The model is

$$y_t = \varepsilon_t + \theta_1 \varepsilon_{t-1} + \ldots + \theta_q \varepsilon_{t-q}$$

First, consider the forecasts. If $h \leq q$, the forecast has the form

$$y_{T+h,T} = 0 + \text{adjustment}$$

whereas if $h > q$ the forecast is

$$y_{T+h,T} = 0$$

Thus, an MA(q) process is not forecastable (apart from the unconditional mean) more than q steps ahead. All the dynamics in the MA(q) process, which we exploit for forecasting, "wash out" by the time we get to horizon q—a reflection of the autocorrelation function of the MA(q) process, which we showed in chapter 7 to cut off at displacement q.

Second, consider the corresponding forecast errors. They are

$$e_{T+h,T} = \text{MA}(h-1)$$

for $h \leq q$ and

$$e_{T+h,T} = \text{MA}(q)$$

for $h > q$. The h-step-ahead forecast error for $h > q$ is just the process itself, minus its mean.

Finally, consider the forecast error variances. For $h \leq q$,

$$\sigma_h^2 \leq \text{var}(y_t)$$

whereas for $h > q$,

$$\sigma_h^2 = \text{var}(y_t)$$

In summary, we have thus far studied the MA(1), and then the general MA(q), process, computing the optimal h-step-ahead forecast, the corresponding forecast error, and the forecast error variance. As we now see, the emerging patterns that we cataloged turn out to be quite general.

Optimal Point Forecasts for Infinite-Order Moving Averages

By now you should be getting the hang of it, so let us consider the general case of an infinite-order MA process. The infinite-order moving-average process may seem like a theoretical curiosity, but precisely the opposite is true. Any covariance stationary process can be written as a (potentially infinite-order) moving-average process, and moving-average processes are easy to understand and manipulate because they are written in terms of white noise shocks, which have very simple statistical properties. Thus, if you take the time to understand the mechanics of constructing optimal forecasts for infinite moving-average processes, you will understand everything, and you will have some powerful technical tools and intuition at your command.

Recall from chapter 6 that the general linear process is

$$y_t = \sum_{i=0}^{\infty} b_i \varepsilon_{t-i}$$

where $\varepsilon_t \sim WN(0, \sigma^2)$, $b_0 = 1$, and $\sigma^2 \sum_{i=0}^{\infty} b_i^2 < \infty$. We proceed in the usual way. We first write out the process at the future time of interest:

$$y_{T+h} = \varepsilon_{T+h} + b_1 \varepsilon_{T+h-1} + \ldots + b_h \varepsilon_T + b_{h+1} \varepsilon_{T-1} + \ldots$$

Then we project y_{T+h} on the time-T information set. The projection yields zeros for all of the future ε's (because they are white noise and hence unforecastable), leaving

$$y_{T+h,T} = b_h \varepsilon_T + b_{h+1} \varepsilon_{T-1} + \ldots$$

It follows that the h-step ahead forecast error is serially correlated; it follows an $MA(h-1)$ process,

$$e_{T+h,T} = (y_{T+h} - y_{T+h,T}) = \sum_{i=0}^{h-1} b_i \varepsilon_{t+h-i}$$

with mean 0 and variance

$$\sigma_h^2 = \sigma^2 \sum_{i=0}^{h-1} b_i^2$$

A number of remarks are in order concerning the optimal forecasts of the general linear process and the corresponding forecast errors and forecast error variances. First, the 1-step-ahead forecast error is simply ε_t. Again, ε_t is that part of y_{t+1} that can't be linearly forecast, which is why it is called the **innovation.** Second, although it might at first seem strange that an *optimal* forecast error would be serially correlated, as is the case when $h > 1$, nothing is awry. The serial correlation cannot be used to improve forecasting performance because the autocorrelations of the $MA(h-1)$ process cut off just before the beginning of the time-T information set $\{\varepsilon_T, \varepsilon_{T-1}, \ldots\}$. This is a general and tremendously important property of the errors associated with optimal forecasts: *errors from optimal forecasts cannot be forecast using information available when the forecast was made.* If you can forecast the forecast error, then you can improve the forecast, which means that it could not have been optimal. Finally, note that as h approaches infinity $y_{T+h,T}$ approaches zero, the unconditional mean of the process, and σ_h^2 approaches $\sigma^2 \Sigma_{i=0}^\infty b_i^2$, the unconditional variance of the process, which reflects the fact that as h approaches infinity the conditioning information on which the forecast is based becomes progressively less useful. In other words, the distant future is more difficult to forecast than the near future!

Interval and Density Forecasts

Now we construct interval and density forecasts. Regardless of whether the moving average is finite or infinite, we proceed in the same way, as follows. The definition of the h-step-ahead forecast error is

$$e_{T+h,T} = y_{T+h} - y_{T+h,T}$$

Equivalently, the h-step-ahead realized value, y_{T+h}, equals the forecast plus the error,

$$y_{T+h} = y_{T+h,T} + e_{T+h,T}$$

If the innovations are normally distributed, then the future value of the series of interest is also normally distributed, conditional upon the information set available at the time the forecast was made, and so we have the 95% h-step-ahead interval forecast $y_{T+h,T} \pm 1.96\sigma_h$.[2] In similar fashion, we construct the h-step-ahead density forecast as $N(y_{T+h,T}, \sigma_h^2)$. The mean of the conditional distribution of y_{T+h} is $y_{T+h,T}$, which, of course, must be the case because we constructed the point forecast as the conditional mean. The variance of the conditional distribution is σ_h^2, the variance of the forecast error.

As an example of interval and density forecasting, consider again the MA(2) process,

$$y_t = \varepsilon_t + \theta_1 \varepsilon_{t-1} + \theta_2 \varepsilon_{t-2}$$

$$\varepsilon_t \sim WN(0, \sigma^2)$$

---

2. Confidence intervals at any other desired confidence level may be constructed in similar fashion, by using a different critical point of the standard normal distribution. A 90% interval forecast, for example, is $y_{T+h,T} \pm 1.64\sigma_h$. In general, for a Gaussian process, a $(1 - \alpha)100\%$ confidence interval is $y_{T+h,T} \pm z_{\alpha/2}\sigma_h$, where $z_{\alpha/2}$ is that point on the $N(0,1)$ distribution such that $\text{prob}(z > z_{\alpha/2}) = \alpha/2$.

Assuming normality, the 1-step-ahead 95% interval forecast is $y_{T+1,T}=$ $(\theta_1\varepsilon_T + \theta_2\varepsilon_{T-1}) \pm 1.96\sigma$, and the 1-step-ahead density forecast is $N(\Theta_1\varepsilon_T + \theta_2\varepsilon_{T-1}, \sigma^2)$.

3. MAKING THE FORECASTS OPERATIONAL

So far we have assumed that the parameters of the process being forecast are known. In practice, of course, they must be estimated. To make our forecasting procedures operational, we simply replace the unknown parameters in our formulas with estimates and the unobservable innovations with residuals.

Consider, for example, the MA(2) process,

$$y_t = \varepsilon_t + \theta_1\varepsilon_{t-1} + \theta_2\varepsilon_{t-2}$$

As you can readily verify using the methods we have introduced, the 2-step-ahead optimal forecast, assuming known parameters, is

$$y_{T+2,T} = \theta_2\varepsilon_T$$

with corresponding forecast error

$$e_{T+2,T} = \varepsilon_{T+2} + \theta_1\varepsilon_{T+1}$$

and forecast-error variance

$$\sigma_2^2 = \sigma^2(1 + \theta_1^2)$$

To make the forecast operational, we replace unknown parameters with estimates and the time-T innovation with the time-T residual, yielding

$$\hat{y}_{T+2,T} = \hat{\theta}_2\hat{\varepsilon}_T$$

and forecast error variance

$$\hat{\sigma}_2^2 = \hat{\sigma}^2(1 + \hat{\theta}_1^2)$$

Then, if desired, we can construct operational 2-step-ahead interval and density forecasts, as $\hat{y}_{T+2,T} \pm z_{\alpha/2}\hat{\sigma}_2$ and $N(\hat{y}_{T+2,T}, \hat{\sigma}_2^2)$.

The strategy of taking a forecast formula derived under the assumption of known parameters and replacing unknown parameters with estimates is a natural way to operationalize the construction of point forecasts. However, using the same strategy to produce operational interval or density forecasts involves a subtlety that merits additional discussion. The forecast error variance estimate so obtained can be interpreted as one that ignores parameter estimation uncertainty, as follows. Recall once again that the actual future value of the series is

$$y_{T+2} = \varepsilon_{T+2} + \theta_1 \varepsilon_{T+1} + \theta_2 \varepsilon_T$$

and that the operational forecast is

$$\hat{y}_{T+2,T} = \hat{\theta}_2 \varepsilon_T$$

Thus the exact forecast error is

$$\hat{e}_{T+2,T} = y_{T+2} - \hat{y}_{T+2,T} = \varepsilon_{T+2} + \theta_1 \varepsilon_{T+1} + (\theta_2 - \hat{\theta}_2) \varepsilon_T$$

the variance of which is very difficult to evaluate. So we make a convenient approximation: we ignore parameter estimation uncertainty by assuming that estimated parameters equal true parameters. We therefore set $(\theta_2 - \hat{\theta}_2)$ to zero, which yields

$$\hat{e}_{T+2,T} = \varepsilon_{T+2} + \theta_1 \varepsilon_{T+1}$$

with variance

$$\sigma_2^2 = \sigma^2 (1 + \theta_1^2)$$

which we make operational as

$$\hat{\sigma}_2^2 = \hat{\sigma}^2 (1 + \hat{\theta}_1^2)$$

4. THE CHAIN RULE OF FORECASTING

Point Forecasts of Autoregressive Processes

Because any covariance stationary $AR(p)$ process can be written as an infinite moving average, there is no need for specialized forecasting techniques for autoregressions. Instead, we can simply transform the autoregression into a moving average, and then use the techniques we developed for forecasting moving averages. It turns out, however, that a very simple recursive method for computing the optimal forecast is available in the autoregressive case.

The recursive method, called the **chain rule of forecasting,** is best learned by example. Consider the AR(1) process,

$$y_t = \varphi y_{t-1} + \varepsilon_t$$

$$\varepsilon_t \sim WN(0, \sigma^2)$$

First we construct the optimal 1-step-ahead forecast, and then we construct the optimal 2-step-ahead forecast, which depends on the optimal 1-step-ahead forecast we have already constructed. Then we construct the optimal 3-step-ahead forecast, which depends on the already computed 2-step-ahead forecast, and so on.

To construct the 1-step-ahead forecast, we write out the process for time $T+1$,

$$y_{T+1} = \varphi y_T + \varepsilon_{T+1}$$

Then, projecting the right-hand side on the time-T information set, we obtain

$$y_{T+1,T} = \varphi y_T$$

Now let us construct the 2-step-ahead forecast. Write out the process for time $T+2$,

$$y_{T+2} = \varphi y_{T+1} + \varepsilon_{T+2}$$

Then project directly on the time-T information set to get

$$y_{T+2,T} = \varphi y_{T+1,T}$$

Note that the future innovation is replaced by 0, as always, and that we have directly replaced the time $T+1$ value of y with its earlier-constructed optimal forecast. Now let us construct the 3-step-ahead forecast. Write out the process for time $T+3$,

$$y_{T+3} = \varphi y_{T+2} + \varepsilon_{T+3}$$

Then project directly on the time-T information set,

$$y_{T+3,T} = \varphi y_{T+2,T}$$

The required 2-step-ahead forecast was already constructed.

Continuing in this way, we can recursively build up forecasts for any and all future periods. Hence the name "chain rule of forecasting." Note that, for the AR(1) process, only the most recent value of y is needed to construct optimal forecasts, for any horizon, and for the general AR(p) process only the p most recent values of y are needed.

Point Forecasts of ARMA Processes

Now we consider forecasting covariance stationary ARMA processes. Just as with autoregressive processes, we could always convert an ARMA process to an infinite moving average, and then use our earlier-developed methods for forecasting moving averages. But also as with autoregressive processes, a simpler method is available for forecasting ARMA processes directly, by *combining* our earlier approaches to moving-average and autoregressive forecasting.

As always, we write out the ARMA process for the future period of interest,

$$y_{T+h} = \varphi_1 y_{T+h-1} + \ldots + \varphi_p\, y_{T+h-p} + \varepsilon_{T+h} + \theta_1 \varepsilon_{T+h-1} + \ldots + \theta_q \varepsilon_{T+h-q}$$

On the right-hand side we have various future values of y and ε, and perhaps also past values, depending on the forecast horizon. We replace everything on the right-hand side with its projection on the time-T information set. That is, we replace all future values of y with optimal forecasts (built up recursively using the chain rule) and all future values of ε with optimal forecasts (0), yielding

$$y_{T+h,T} = \varphi_1\, y_{T+h-1,T} + \ldots + \varphi_p\, y_{T+h-p,T} + \varepsilon_{T+h,T}$$
$$+ \theta_1\, \varepsilon_{T+h-1,T} + \ldots + \theta_q\, \varepsilon_{T+h-q,T}$$

When evaluating this formula, note that the optimal time-T "forecast" of any value of y or ε dated time T or earlier is just y or ε itself.

As an example, consider forecasting the ARMA(1,1) process,

$$y_t = \varphi y_{t-1} + \varepsilon_t + \theta\varepsilon_{t-1}$$
$$\varepsilon_t \sim WN(0, \sigma^2)$$

Let us find $y_{T+1,T}$. The process at time $T+1$ is

$$y_{T+1} = \varphi y_T + \varepsilon_{T+1} + \theta\varepsilon_T$$

Projecting the right-hand side on Ω_T yields

$$y_{T+1,T} = \varphi y_T + \theta\varepsilon_T$$

Now let us find $y_{T+2,T}$. The process at time $T+2$ is

$$y_{T+2} = \varphi y_{T+1} + \varepsilon_{T+2} + \theta\varepsilon_{T+1}$$

Projecting the right-hand side on Ω_T yields

$$y_{T+2,T} = \varphi y_{T+1,T}$$

Substituting our earlier-computed 1-step-ahead forecast yields

$$y_{T+2,T} = \varphi(\varphi y_T + \theta\varepsilon_T)$$
$$= \varphi^2 y_T + \varphi\theta\varepsilon_T$$

Continuing, it is clear that

$$y_{T+h,T} = \varphi y_{T+h-1,T}$$

for all $h > 1$.

Interval and Density Forecasts

The chain rule, whether applied to pure autoregressive models or to ARMA models, is a device for simplifying the computation of *point* forecasts. Interval and density forecasts require the *h*-step-ahead forecast error variance, which we get from the moving-average representation, as discussed earlier. It is

$$\sigma_h^2 = \sigma^2 \sum_{i=0}^{h-1} b_i^2$$

which we operationalize as

$$\hat{\sigma}_h^2 = \hat{\sigma}^2 \sum_{i=0}^{h-1} \hat{b}_i^2$$

Note that we do not actually estimate the moving-average representation; rather, we solve backward for as many b's as we need, *in terms of the original model parameters*, which we replace with estimates.

Let us illustrate by constructing a 2-step-ahead 95% interval forecast for the ARMA(1,1) process. We already constructed the 2-step-ahead point forecast, $y_{T+2,T}$; we need only compute the 2-step-ahead forecast error variance. The process is

$$y_t = \varphi y_{t-1} + \varepsilon_t + \theta \varepsilon_{t-1}$$

Substitute backward for y_{t-1} to get

$$y_t = \varphi(\varphi y_{t-2} + \varepsilon_{t-1} + \theta \varepsilon_{t-2}) + \varepsilon_t + \theta \varepsilon_{t-1}$$

$$= \varepsilon_t + (\varphi + \theta)\varepsilon_{t-1} + \ldots$$

We need not substitute back any farther, because the 2-step-ahead forecast error variance is $\sigma_2^2 = \sigma^2(1 + b_1^2)$, where b_1 is the coefficient on ε_{t-1} in the moving-average representation of the ARMA(1,1) process, which we just calculated to be $(\varphi + \theta)$. Thus the 2-step-ahead interval forecast is $y_{T+2,T} \pm 1.96\sigma_2$, or

$$(\varphi^2 y_T + \varphi\theta\varepsilon_T) \pm 1.96\sigma \sqrt{1 + (\varphi + \theta)^2}$$

We make this operational as

$$(\hat{\phi}^2 y_T + \hat{\phi}\hat{\theta}\varepsilon_T) \pm 1.96\,\hat{\sigma}\,\sqrt{1 + (\hat{\phi} + \hat{\theta})^2}$$

5. APPLICATION: FORECASTING EMPLOYMENT

Now we put our forecasting technology to work to produce point and interval forecasts for Canadian employment. Recall that the best moving-average model was an MA(4), whereas the best autoregressive model, as well as the best ARMA model and the best model overall, was an AR(2).

First, consider forecasting with the MA(4) model. In Figure 8.1, we show the employment history together with operational 4-quarter-ahead point and interval extrapolation forecasts. The 4-quarter-ahead extrapolation forecast reverts very quickly to the mean of the employment index, which is 100.2. In 1993.4, the last quarter of historical data, employment is well below its mean, but the forecast calls for a quick rise. The forecast quick rise seems unnatural, because employment dynamics are historically very persistent. If employment is well below its mean in 1993.4, we would expect it to stay well below its mean for some time.

The MA(4) model is unable to capture such persistence. The quick reversion of the MA(4) forecast to the mean is a manifestation of the short

FIGURE 8.1   Employment History and Forecast: MA(4) Model

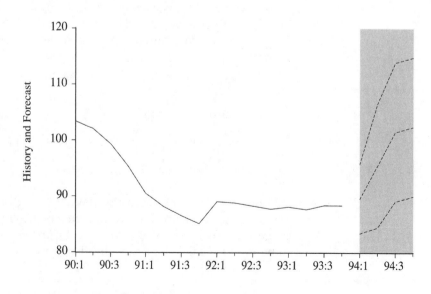

Time

FIGURE 8.2   Employment History and Long-Horizon Forecast: MA(4) Model

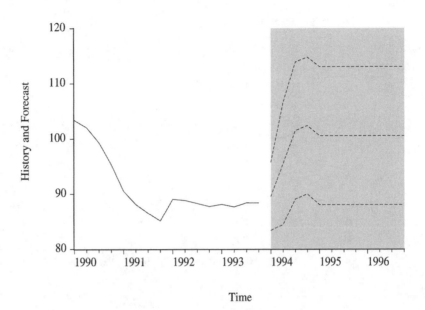

Time

memory of moving-average processes. Recall, in particular, that an MA(4) process has a four-period memory—all autocorrelations are zero beyond displacement 4. Thus, all forecasts more than four steps ahead are simply equal to the unconditional mean (100.2), and all 95% interval forecasts more than four steps ahead are ±1.96 unconditional standard deviations. All of this is made clear in Figure 8.2, in which we show the employment history together with 12-step-ahead point and interval extrapolation forecasts.

In Figure 8.3 we show the 4-quarter-ahead forecast and realization. Our suspicions are confirmed. The actual employment series stays well below its mean over the forecast period, whereas the forecast rises quickly back to the mean. The mean squared forecast error is a large 55.9.

Now consider forecasting with the AR(2) model. In Figure 8.4 we show the 4-quarter-ahead extrapolation forecast, which reverts to the unconditional mean much less quickly, as seems natural given the high persistence of employment. The 4-quarter-ahead point forecast is, in fact, still well below the mean. Similarly, the 95% error bands grow gradually and have not approached their long-horizon values by four quarters out.

Figures 8.5 and 8.6 make clear the very different nature of the autoregressive forecasts. Figure 8.5 presents the 12-step-ahead extrapolation forecast, and Figure 8.6 presents a much longer horizon extrapolation forecast. Eventually the unconditional mean is approached, and eventually the error bands *do* go flat, but only for very long horizon forecasts, due to the high persistence in employment, which the AR(2) model captures.

FIGURE 8.3   Employment History, Forecast, and Realization: MA(4) Model

FIGURE 8.4   Employment History and Forecast: AR(2) Model

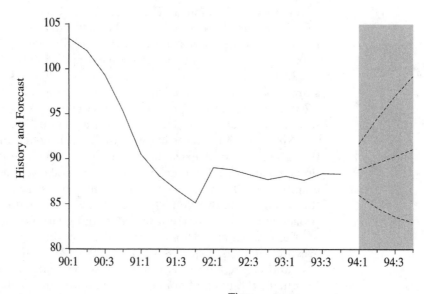

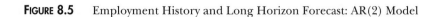

FIGURE 8.5   Employment History and Long Horizon Forecast: AR(2) Model

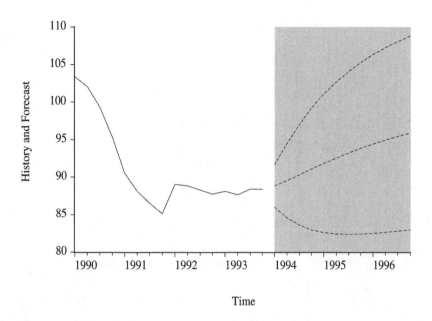

FIGURE 8.6   Employment History and Very Long Horizon Forecast: AR(2) Model

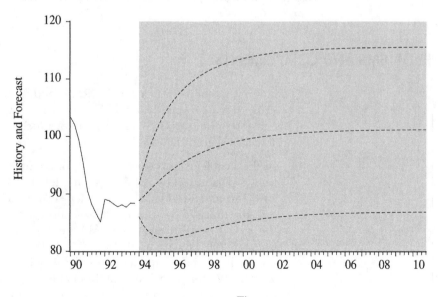

FIGURE 8.7   Employment History, Forecast, and Realization: AR(2) Model

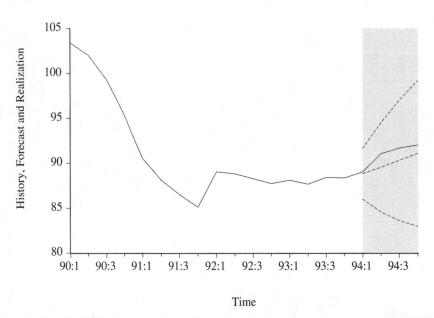

Time

    In Figure 8.7 we show the employment history, 4-quarter-ahead AR(2) extrapolation forecast, and the realization. The AR(2) forecast appears quite accurate; the mean squared forecast error is 1.3, drastically smaller than that of the MA(4) forecast.

PROBLEMS AND COMPLEMENTS

1. (The mechanics of forecasting with ARMA models: BankWire continued) The data disk contains data for daily transfers over BankWire, a wire transfer system in a country responsible for much of the world's finance, over a recent span of 200 business days.

   (a) In the Problems and Complements of chapter 7, you were asked to find a parsimonious ARMA(p,q) model that fits the transfer data well, and to defend its adequacy. Repeat the exercise, this time using only the first 175 days for model selection and fitting. Is it necessarily the case that the selected ARMA model will remain the same as when all 200 days are used? Does yours?

   (b) Use your estimated model to produce point and interval forecasts for days 176 through 200. Plot them and discuss the forecast pattern.

   (c) Compare your forecasts to the actual realizations. Do the forecasts perform well? Why or why not?

(d) Discuss precisely how your software constructs point and interval forecasts. It should certainly match our discussion in spirit, but it may differ in some of the details. Are you uncomfortable with any of the assumptions made? How, if at all, could the forecasts be improved?

2. (Forecasting an AR(1) process with known and unknown parameters) Use the chain rule to forecast the AR(1) process,

$$y_t = \varphi y_{t-1} + \varepsilon_t$$

For now, assume that all parameters are known.

(a) Show that the optimal forecasts are

$$y_{T+1,T} = \varphi y_T$$

$$y_{T+2,T} = \varphi^2 y_T$$

$$\cdot$$
$$\cdot$$
$$\cdot$$

$$y_{T+h,T} = \varphi^h y_T$$

(b) Show that the corresponding forecast errors are

$$e_{T+1,T} = (y_{T+1} - y_{T+1,T}) = \varepsilon_{T+1}$$

$$e_{T+2,T} = (y_{T+2} - y_{T+2,T}) = \varphi \varepsilon_{T+1} + \varepsilon_{T+2}$$

$$\cdot$$
$$\cdot$$
$$\cdot$$

$$e_{T+h,T} = (y_{T+h} - y_{T+h,T}) = \varepsilon_{T+h} + \varphi \varepsilon_{T+h-1} + \ldots + \varphi^{h-1} \varepsilon_{T+1}$$

(c) Show that the forecast error variances are

$$\sigma_1^2 = \sigma^2$$

$$\sigma_2^2 = \sigma^2(1 + \varphi^2)$$

$$\cdot$$
$$\cdot$$
$$\cdot$$

$$\sigma_h^2 = \sigma^2 \sum_{i=0}^{h-1} \varphi^{2i}$$

(d) Show that the limiting forecast error variance is

$$\lim_{h \to \infty} \sigma_h^2 = \frac{\sigma^2}{1 - \varphi^2}$$

the unconditional variance of the AR(1) process. Now assume that the parameters are unknown and so must be estimated.

(e) Make your expressions for both the forecasts and the forecast error variances operational by inserting least squares estimates where unknown parameters appear, and use them to produce an operational point forecast and an operational 90% interval forecast for y_{T+2}.

3. (Forecasting an ARMA(2,2) process) Consider the ARMA(2,2) process:

$$y_t = \varphi_1 y_{t-1} + \varphi_2 y_{t-2} + \varepsilon_t + \theta_1 \varepsilon_{t-1} + \theta_2 \varepsilon_{t-2}$$

(a) Verify that the optimal 1-step-ahead forecast made at time T is

$$y_{T+1,T} = \varphi_1 y_T + \varphi_2 y_{T-1} + \theta_1 \varepsilon_T + \theta_2 \varepsilon_{T-1}$$

(b) Verify that the optimal 2-step-ahead forecast made at time T is

$$y_{T+2,T} = \varphi_1 y_{T+1,T} + \varphi_2 y_T + \theta_2 \varepsilon_T$$

and express it purely in terms of elements of the time-T information set.

(c) Verify that the optimal 3-step-ahead forecast made at time T is

$$y_{T+3,T} = \varphi_1 y_{T+2,T} + \varphi_2 y_{T+1,T}$$

and express it purely in terms of elements of the time-T information set.

(d) Show that for any forecast horizon $h \geq 3$,

$$y_{T+h,T} = \varphi_1 y_{T+h-1,T} + \varphi_2 y_{T+h-2,T}$$

4. (Optimal forecasting under asymmetric loss) One of the conditions required for optimality of the conditional mean forecast is **symmetric loss.** We make that assumption for a number of reasons. First, the conditional mean is usually easy to compute. In contrast, optimal forecasting under **asymmetric loss** is rather involved, and the tools for doing so are still under development. Second, and more important, symmetric loss often provides a good approximation to the loss structure relevant in a particular decision environment.

Symmetric loss is not *always* appropriate, however. Here we discuss some aspects of forecasting under asymmetric loss. Under asymmetric loss, optimal forecasts are biased, whereas the conditional mean forecast is unbiased.[3] Bias is optimal under asymmetric loss because we can gain on average by pushing the forecasts in the direction such that we make relatively few errors of the more costly sign.

There are many possible asymmetric loss functions. A few, however, have proved particularly useful because of their flexibility and tractability. One is the **linex loss function,**

$$L(e) = b[\exp(ae) - ae - 1], \quad a \neq 0, \quad b > 0$$

This function is called "linex" because when $a > 0$, loss is approximately linear to the left of the origin and approximately exponential to the right, and conversely when $a < 0$. Another is the **linlin loss function,** given by

$$L(e) = \begin{cases} a\,|\,e\,|\,, \text{ if } e > 0 \\ b\,|\,e\,|\,, \text{ if } e \leq 0 \end{cases}$$

Its name comes from the linearity on each side of the origin.

(a) Discuss three practical forecasting situations in which the loss function might be asymmetric. Give detailed reasons for the asymmetry, and discuss how you might produce and evaluate forecasts.

(b) Explore and graph the linex and linlin loss functions for various values of a and b. Discuss the roles played by a and b in each loss function. In particular, which parameter or combination of parameters governs the degree of asymmetry? What happens to the linex loss function as a gets smaller? What happens to the linlin loss function as a/b approaches 1?

5. (Truncation of infinite distributed lags, state-space representations, and the Kalman filter) This complement concerns practical implementation of formulae that involve innovations (ε's). Earlier we noted that as long as a process is invertible we can express the ε's in terms of the y's. If the process involves a moving-average component, however, the ε's will depend on the infinite past history of the y's, so we need to truncate to make it operational. Suppose, for example, that we are forecasting the MA(1) process,

$$y_t = \varepsilon_t + \theta\varepsilon_{t-1}$$

---

3. A forecast is unbiased if its error has a mean of 0. The error from the conditional mean forecast has mean 0, by construction.

The operational 1-step-ahead forecast is

$$y_{t+1,T} = \hat{\theta}\hat{\varepsilon}_T$$

But what, precisely, do we insert for the residual, $\hat{\varepsilon}_T$? Back substitution yields the autoregressive representation,

$$\varepsilon_t = y_t + \theta y_{t-1} - \theta^2 y_{t-2} + \ldots$$

Thus,

$$\varepsilon_T = y_T + \theta y_{T-1} - \theta^2 y_{T-2} + \ldots$$

which we are forced to truncate at time $T = 1$, when the data begin. This yields the approximation

$$\varepsilon_T \approx y_T + \theta y_{T-1} - \theta^2 y_{T-2} + \ldots + \theta^T y_1$$

Unless the sample size is very small, or θ is very close to 1, the approximation will be very accurate, because θ is less than 1 in absolute value (by invertibility), and we are raising it to higher and higher powers. Finally, we make the expression operational by replacing the unknown moving-average parameter with an estimate, yielding

$$\hat{\varepsilon}_T \approx y_T + \hat{\theta} y_{T-1} - \hat{\theta}^2 y_{T-2} + \ldots + \hat{\theta}^T y_1$$

In the engineering literature of the 1960s, and then in the statistics and econometrics literatures of the 1970s, important tools called "state-space representations" and the "Kalman filter" were developed. Those tools provide a convenient and powerful framework for estimating a wide variety of forecasting models and constructing optimal forecasts, and they enable us to tailor the forecasts precisely to the sample of data at hand, so that no truncation is necessary.

6. (**Bootstrap simulation** to acknowledge **innovation distribution uncertainty** and **parameter estimation uncertainty**) A variety of simulation-based methods fall under the general heading of "bootstrap." Their common element, and the reason for the name "bootstrap," is that they build up an approximation to an object of interest (for example, the distribution of a random disturbance, which then translates into an interval or density forecast) directly from the data, rather than making a possibly erroneous assumption such as normality. Hence they "pull themselves up by their own bootstraps."

   (a) The density and interval forecasts that we have discussed rely crucially on normality. In many situations, normality is a perfectly reasonable and useful assumption; after all, that is why we call it the "normal" distribution. Sometimes, however, such as when forecasting high-frequency financial asset returns, normality may be unrealistic. Using bootstrap methods we can relax the normality assumption. Suppose, for example, that we want a 1-step-ahead interval forecast for an AR(1) process. We know that the future observation of interest is

$$y_{T+1} = \varphi y_T + \varepsilon_{T+1}$$

We know y_T, and we can estimate φ and then proceed as if φ were known, using the operational point forecast, $\hat{y}_{T+1,T} = \hat{\varphi} y_T$. If we want an operational interval forecast, however, we have thus far relied on a normality assumption, in which case we use $\hat{y}_{T+1,T} \pm z_{\alpha/2} \hat{\sigma}$. To relax the normality assumption, we can proceed as follows. Imagine that we could sample from the distribution of ε_{T+1}—whatever that distribution might be. Take R draws, $\{\varepsilon_{T+1}^{(i)}\}_{i=1}^{R}$, where R is a large number, such as 10,000. For each such draw, construct the corresponding forecast of y_{T+1} as

$$\hat{y}_{T+1,T}^{(i)} = \hat{\varphi} y_T + \varepsilon_{T+1}^{(i)}$$

Then form a histogram of the $\hat{y}_{T+1,T}^{(i)}$ values, which is the density forecast. Given the density forecast, we can, of course, construct interval forecasts at any desired level. If, for example, we want a 90% interval, we can sort the $\hat{y}_{T+1,T}^{(i)}$ values from smallest to largest, and find the 5th percentile (call it a) and the 95th percentile (call it b), and use the 90% interval forecast $[a, b]$.

(b) The only missing link in the strategy in part (a) is how to sample from the distribution of ε_{T+1}. It turns out that it is easy to do—we simply assign probability $1/T$ to each of the observed residuals (which are estimates of the unobserved ε's) and draw from them R times with replacement. Describe how you might do so.

(c) Note that the interval and density forecasts we have constructed thus far—even the one in part (a) based on bootstrap techniques—make no attempt to account for parameter estimation uncertainty. Intuitively, we would expect confidence intervals obtained by ignoring parameter estimation uncertainty to be more narrow than they would be if parameter uncertainty were taken into account, thereby producing an artificial appearance of precision. In spite of this defect, parameter uncertainty is usually ignored in practice, for a number of reasons. The uncertainty associated with estimated parameters vanishes as the sample size grows, and in fact it vanishes quickly. Furthermore, the fraction of forecast error attributable to the difference between estimated and true parameters is likely to be small compared to the fraction of forecast error coming from other sources, such as using a model that does a poor job of approximating the dynamics of the variable being forecast.

(d) Quite apart from the reasons given above for ignoring parameter estimation uncertainty, the biggest reason is probably that, until very recently, mathematical and computational difficulties made attempts to account for parameter uncertainty infeasible in many situations of practical interest. Modern computing speed, however, lets us use the bootstrap to approximate the effects of parameter estimation uncertainty. To continue with the AR(1) example, suppose that we know that the disturbances are Gaussian, but that we want to attempt to account for the effects of parameter estimation uncertainty when we produce our 1-step-ahead density forecast. How could we use the bootstrap to do so?

(e) The "real sample" of data ends with observation y_T, and the optimal point forecast depends only on y_T. It would therefore seem desirable that all of your R "bootstrap samples" of data also end with y_T. Do you agree? How might you enforce that property while still respecting the AR(1) dynamics? (This is tricky.)

(f) Can you think of a way to assemble the results thus far to produce a density forecast that acknowledges both innovation distribution uncertainty and parameter estimation uncertainty? (This is very challenging.)

BIBLIOGRAPHICAL AND COMPUTATIONAL NOTES

The methods discussed in this chapter were developed by Wiener, Kolmogorov, and Wold more than 50 years ago, and they underlie all modern forecasting software. It is important to understand them so that you are the master of your software, and not the other way around.

For a proof of our assertion of optimality of the conditional mean forecast, as well as a precise statement of the conditions under which the result holds, see any good advanced text, such as Hamilton (1994).

Linex loss was introduced by Varian (1974) in the context of real estate assessment, and further studied by Zellner (1986). Harvey (1993) gives a lucid exposition of state-space representations and the Kalman filter. Efron and Tibshirani (1993) is a good introduction to the bootstrap and its many uses. Stine (1987) and Breidt, Davis, and Dunsmuir (1995) show how to use the bootstrap to produce interval and density forecasts under weak assumptions. Chatfield (1993, 1995) argues that the fraction of forecast error attributable to the difference between estimated and true parameters is likely much smaller than the fraction of forecast error coming from other sources, such as model misspecification. Clements and Hendry (1994, 1997) provide insightful discussion of a variety of advanced topics in applied forecasting.

CONCEPTS FOR REVIEW

Asymmetric loss	Linear forecast
Bootstrap simulation	Linear least squares forecast
Chain rule of forecasting	Linear projection
Conditional mean	Linex loss function
Expected loss	Linlin loss function
Forecast error	Optimal forecast
Forecast error variance	Parameter estimation
Information set	uncertainty
Innovation	Symmetric loss
Innovation distribution	
uncertainty	

REFERENCES AND ADDITIONAL READINGS

Breidt, F. J., Davis, R. A., and Dunsmuir, W. T. M. (1995), "Improved Bootstrap Prediction Intervals for Autoregressions," *Journal of Time Series Analysis,* 16, 177–200.

Chatfield, C. (1993), "Calculating Interval Forecasts (with Discussion)," *Journal of Business and Economic Statistics,* 11, 121–144.

Chatfield, C. (1995), "Model Uncertainty, Data Mining and Statistical Inference (with Discussion)," *Journal of the Royal Statistical Society A,* 158, Part 3, 419–466.

Clements, M. P., and Hendry, D. F. (1994), "Towards a Theory of Economic Forecasting," in C. P. Hargreaves (ed.), *Nonstationary Times Series Analysis and Cointegration.* Oxford: Oxford University Press.

Clements, M. P., and Hendry, D. F. (1997), *The Marshall Lectures in Economic Forecasting.* Cambridge: Cambridge University Press.

Efron, B., and Tibshirani, R. J. (1993), *An Introduction to the Bootstrap.* London: Chapman and Hall.

Hamilton, J. D. (1994), *Time Series Analysis.* Princeton, N.J.: Princeton University Press.

Harvey, A. C. (1993), *Time Series Models,* second edition. Cambridge, Mass.: MIT Press.

Stine, R. A. (1987), "Estimating Properties of Autoregressive Forecasts," *Journal of the American Statistical Association,* 82, 1072–1078.

Varian, H. (1974), "A Bayesian Approach to Real Estate Assessment," in S. E. Feinberg and A. Zellner (eds.), *Studies in Bayesian Econometrics and Statistics in Honor of L. J. Savage.* Amsterdam: North-Holland.

Wonnacott, T. H., and Wonnacott, R. J. (1990), *Introductory Statistics,* fifth edition. New York: Wiley.

Zellner, A. (1986), "Bayesian Estimation and Prediction Using Asymmetric Loss Functions," *Journal of the American Statistical Association,* 81, 446–451.

PUTTING IT ALL TOGETHER:
A FORECASTING MODEL WITH TREND,
SEASONAL, AND CYCLICAL COMPONENTS

1. ASSEMBLING WHAT WE HAVE LEARNED

Thus far we have focused on modeling trend, seasonals, and cycles one at a time. In chapter 4, we introduced models and forecasts of trend. We forecast retail sales, and we used a model that included only trend. The data were seasonally adjusted, so it wasn't necessary to model seasonality, and although cycles were likely present, we simply ignored them. In chapter 5, we introduced models and forecasts of seasonality. We forecast housing starts, and we used a model that included only seasonal dummies. We didn't need a trend, and again we simply ignored cycles. In chapters 6 through 8, we introduced models and forecasts of cycles. We forecast employment, and we used autoregressive, moving-average, and ARMA models. We didn't need trends or seasonals because employment had no trend and had been seasonally adjusted.

In many forecasting situations, however, more than one component is needed to capture the dynamics in a series to be forecast—frequently they are *all* needed. Here we assemble our tools for forecasting trends, seasonals, and cycles; we use regression on a trend and seasonal dummies, and we capture cyclical dynamics by allowing for ARMA effects in the regression disturbances. The full model is

$$y_t = T_t(\theta) + \sum_{i=1}^{s} \gamma_i D_{it} + \sum_{i=1}^{v_1} \delta_i^{HD} HDV_{it} + \sum_{i=1}^{v_2} \delta_i^{TD} TDV_{it} + \varepsilon_t$$

$$\Phi(L)\varepsilon_t = \Theta(L)v_t$$

$$\Theta(L) = 1 + \theta_1 L + \ldots + \theta_q L^q$$

$$\Phi(L) = 1 - \varphi_1 L - \ldots - \varphi_p L^p$$

$$v_t \sim WN(0, \sigma^2)$$

$T_t(\theta)$ is a trend, with underlying parameters θ. For example, linear trend has $\theta = \beta_1$ and

$$T_t(\theta) = \beta_1 TIME_t$$

and quadratic trend has $\theta = (\beta_1, \beta_2)$ and

$$T_t(\theta) = \beta_1 TIME_t + \beta_2 TIME_t^2$$

In addition to the trend, we include seasonal dummies, holiday dummies, and trading-day dummies.[1] The disturbances follow an ARMA(p,q) process, of which pure autoregressions and pure moving averages are special cases. In any particular application, of course, various trend effects, seasonal and other calendar effects, and ARMA cyclical effects may not be needed and therefore could be dropped.[2] Finally, v_t is the underlying innovation that drives everything.

Now consider constructing an h-step-ahead point forecast at time T, $y_{T+h,T}$. At time $T+h$,

$$y_{T+h} = T_{T+h}(\theta) + \sum_{i=1}^{s} \gamma_i D_{i,T+h} + \sum_{i=1}^{v_1} \delta_i^{HD} HDV_{i,T+h}$$

$$+ \sum_{i=1}^{v_2} \delta_i^{TD} TDV_{i,T+h} + \varepsilon_{T+h}$$

---

1. Note that, because we include a full set of seasonal dummies, the trend does not contain an intercept, and we don't include an intercept in the regression.

2. If the seasonal dummies were dropped, then we would include an intercept in the regression.

Projecting the right-hand-side variables on what is known at time T (that is, the time-T information set, Ω_T) yields the point forecast

$$y_{T+h,T} = T_{T+h}(\theta) + \sum_{i=1}^{s} \gamma_i D_{i,T+h} + \sum_{i=1}^{v_1} \delta_i^{HD} HDV_{i,T+h}$$

$$+ \sum_{i=1}^{v_2} \delta_i^{TD} TDV_{i,T+h} + \varepsilon_{T+h,T}$$

As with the pure trend and seasonal models discussed earlier, the trend and seasonal variables on the right-hand side are perfectly predictable. The only twist concerns the cyclical behavior that may be lurking in the disturbance term, future values of which don't necessarily project to zero because the disturbance is not necessarily white noise. Instead, we construct $\varepsilon_{T+h,T}$ using the methods we developed for forecasting cycles.

As always, we make the point forecast operational by replacing unknown parameters with estimates, yielding

$$\hat{y}_{T+h,T} = T_{T+h}(\hat{\theta}) + \sum_{i=1}^{s} \hat{\gamma}_i D_{i,T+h} + \sum_{i=1}^{v_1} \hat{\delta}_i^{HD} HDV_{i,T+h}$$

$$+ \sum_{i=1}^{v_2} \hat{\delta}_i^{TD} TDV_{i,T+h} + \hat{\varepsilon}_{T+h,T}$$

To construct $\hat{\varepsilon}_{T+h,T}$, in addition to replacing the parameters in the formula for $\varepsilon_{T+h,T}$ with estimates, we replace the unobservable disturbances, the ε_t's, with the observable residuals, the e_t's.

We use our earlier-developed operational expressions for cycle forecast error variances to produce an h-step-ahead interval forecast; it is simply $\hat{y}_{T+h,T} \pm z_{\alpha/2}\hat{\sigma}_h$, where $\hat{\sigma}_h^2$ is the operational estimate of the variance of the error in forecasting ε_{T+h}, and $z_{\alpha/2}$ is the appropriate critical point of the $N(0,1)$ density. For example, a 95% interval forecast is $\hat{y}_{T+h,T} \pm 1.96\hat{\sigma}_h$. Finally, the complete h-step-ahead density forecast is $N(\hat{y}_{T+h,T}, \hat{\sigma}_h^2)$.

Once again, we don't actually have to *do* any of the computations just discussed; rather, the computer does them all for us. So let us get on with an application, now that we know what we're doing.

FIGURE **9.1**   Liquor Sales, 1968.01–1993.12

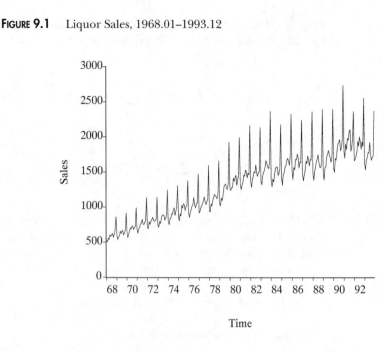

2. APPLICATION: FORECASTING LIQUOR SALES

Here we forecast monthly U.S. liquor sales. We graphed a short span of the series in chapter 5 and noted its pronounced seasonality—sales skyrocket during the Christmas season. In Figure 9.1, we show a longer history of liquor sales, 1968.01–1993.12. In Figure 9.2 we show log liquor sales; we take logs to stabilize the variance, which grows over time.[3] The variance of log liquor sales is more stable, and it is the series for which we will build forecasting models.[4]

Liquor sales dynamics also feature prominent trend and cyclical effects. Liquor sales trend upward, and the trend appears nonlinear in spite of the fact that we are working in logs. To handle the nonlinear trend, we adopt a quadratic trend model (in logs). The estimation results are shown in Table 9.1. The residual plot (Figure 9.3) shows that the fitted trend increases at a decreasing rate; both the linear and quadratic terms are highly significant. The adjusted R^2 is 89%, reflecting the fact that trend is responsible for a

---

3. The nature of the logarithmic transformation is such that it "compresses" an increasing variance. Make a graph of $\log(x)$ as a function of x to see why.

4. From this point onward, for brevity we simply refer to "liquor sales," but remember that we have taken logs.

FIGURE 9.2   Log Liquor Sales, 1968.01–1993.12

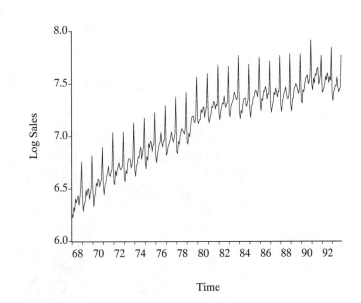

TABLE 9.1   Log Liquor Sales: Quadratic Trend Regression

LS // Dependent Variable is LSALES
Sample: 1968:01 1993:12
Included observations: 312

Variable	Coefficient	Std. Error	t-Statistic	Prob.
C	6.237356	0.024496	254.6267	0.0000
TIME	0.007690	0.000336	22.91552	0.0000
TIME2	-1.14E-05	9.74E-07	-11.72695	0.0000

R-squared	0.892394	Mean dependent var	7.112383
Adjusted R-squared	0.891698	S.D. dependent var	0.379308
S.E. of regression	0.124828	Akaike info criterion	-4.152073
Sum squared resid	4.814823	Schwarz criterion	-4.116083
Log likelihood	208.0146	F-statistic	1281.296
Durbin-Watson stat	1.752858	Prob(F-statistic)	0.000000

FIGURE 9.3   Log Liquor Sales: Quadratic Trend Regression, Residual Plot

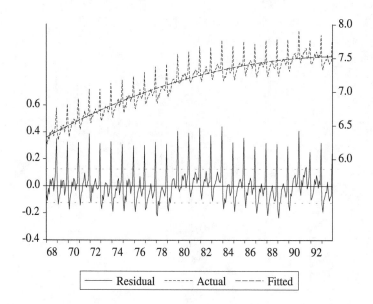

large part of the variation in liquor sales. The standard error of the regression is 0.125; it is an estimate of the standard deviation of the error we would expect to make in forecasting liquor sales if we accounted for trend but ignored seasonality and serial correlation. The Durbin-Watson statistic provides no evidence against the hypothesis that the regression disturbance is white noise.

The residual plot, however, shows obvious residual seasonality. The Durbin-Watson statistic missed it, evidently because it is not designed to have power against seasonal dynamics.[5] The residual plot also suggests that there may be a cycle in the residual, although it is difficult to tell (difficult for the Durbin-Watson statistic as well), because the pervasive seasonality swamps the picture and makes it hard to infer much of anything.

The residual correlogram (Table 9.2) and its graph (Figure 9.4) confirm the importance of the neglected seasonality. The residual sample autocorrelation function has large spikes, far exceeding the Bartlett bands, at the seasonal displacements, 12, 24, and 36. It indicates some cyclical dynamics as well; apart from the seasonal spikes, the residual sample autocorrelation

5. Recall that the Durbin-Watson test is designed to detect simple AR(1) dynamics. It also has the ability to detect other sorts of dynamics, but evidently not those relevant to the present application, which are very different from a simple AR(1).

TABLE 9.2   Log Liquor Sales: Quadratic Trend Regression, Residual Correlogram

	Acorr.	P. Acorr.	Std. Error	Ljung-Box	p-value
1	0.117	0.117	.056	4.3158	0.038
2	-0.149	-0.165	.056	11.365	0.003
3	-0.106	-0.069	.056	14.943	0.002
4	-0.014	-0.017	.056	15.007	0.005
5	0.142	0.125	.056	21.449	0.001
6	0.041	-0.004	.056	21.979	0.001
7	0.134	0.175	.056	27.708	0.000
8	-0.029	-0.046	.056	27.975	0.000
9	-0.136	-0.080	.056	33.944	0.000
10	-0.205	-0.206	.056	47.611	0.000
11	0.056	0.080	.056	48.632	0.000
12	0.888	0.879	.056	306.26	0.000
13	0.055	-0.507	.056	307.25	0.000
14	-0.187	-0.159	.056	318.79	0.000
15	-0.159	-0.144	.056	327.17	0.000
16	-0.059	-0.002	.056	328.32	0.000
17	0.091	-0.118	.056	331.05	0.000
18	-0.010	-0.055	.056	331.08	0.000
19	0.086	-0.032	.056	333.57	0.000
20	-0.066	0.028	.056	335.03	0.000
21	-0.170	0.044	.056	344.71	0.000
22	-0.231	0.180	.056	362.74	0.000
23	0.028	0.016	.056	363.00	0.000
24	0.811	-0.014	.056	586.50	0.000
25	0.013	-0.128	.056	586.56	0.000
26	-0.221	-0.136	.056	603.26	0.000
27	-0.196	-0.017	.056	616.51	0.000
28	-0.092	-0.079	.056	619.42	0.000
29	0.045	-0.094	.056	620.13	0.000
30	-0.043	0.045	.056	620.77	0.000
31	0.057	0.041	.056	621.89	0.000
32	-0.095	-0.002	.056	625.07	0.000
33	-0.195	0.026	.056	638.38	0.000
34	-0.240	0.088	.056	658.74	0.000
35	0.006	-0.089	.056	658.75	0.000
36	0.765	0.076	.056	866.34	0.000

and partial autocorrelation functions oscillate, and the Ljung-Box statistic rejects the white noise null hypothesis even at very small, nonseasonal, displacements.

In Table 9.3 we show the results of regression on quadratic trend and a full set of seasonal dummies. The quadratic trend remains highly significant.

Figure 9.4   Log Liquor Sales: Quadratic Trend Regression,
Residual Sample Autocorrelation, and
Partial Autocorrelation Functions

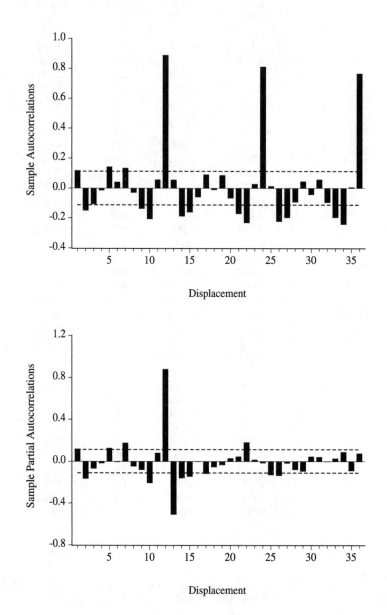

TABLE 9.3   Log Liquor Sales: Quadratic Trend Regression with Seasonal Dummies

LS // Dependent Variable is LSALES
Sample: 1968:01 1993:12
Included observations: 312

Variable	Coefficient	Std. Error	t-Statistic	Prob.
TIME	0.007656	0.000123	62.35882	0.0000
TIME2	-1.14E-05	3.56E-07	-32.06823	0.0000
D1	6.147456	0.012340	498.1699	0.0000
D2	6.088653	0.012353	492.8890	0.0000
D3	6.174127	0.012366	499.3008	0.0000
D4	6.175220	0.012378	498.8970	0.0000
D5	6.246086	0.012390	504.1398	0.0000
D6	6.250387	0.012401	504.0194	0.0000
D7	6.295979	0.012412	507.2402	0.0000
D8	6.268043	0.012423	504.5509	0.0000
D9	6.203832	0.012433	498.9630	0.0000
D10	6.229197	0.012444	500.5968	0.0000
D11	6.259770	0.012453	502.6602	0.0000
D12	6.580068	0.012463	527.9819	0.0000

R-squared	0.986111	Mean dependent var	7.112383
Adjusted R-squared	0.985505	S.D. dependent var	0.379308
S.E. of regression	0.045666	Akaike info criterion	-6.128963
Sum squared resid	0.621448	Schwarz criterion	-5.961008
Log likelihood	527.4094	F-statistic	1627.567
Durbin-Watson stat	0.586187	Prob(F-statistic)	0.000000

The adjusted R^2 rises to 99%, and the standard error of the regression falls to 0.046, which is an estimate of the standard deviation of the forecast error we expect to make if we account for trend and seasonality but ignore serial correlation. The Durbin-Watson statistic, however, has greater ability to detect serial correlation now that the residual seasonality has been taken into account, and it sounds a loud alarm.

The residual plot of Figure 9.5 shows no seasonality, which is now picked up by the model, but it confirms the Durbin-Watson's warning of serial correlation. The residuals are highly persistent, and hence predictable. We show the residual correlogram in tabular and graphical form in Table 9.4 and Figure 9.6, respectively. The residual sample autocorrelations oscillate and de-

FIGURE 9.5   Log Liquor Sales: Quadratic Trend Regression with Seasonal Dummies, Residual Plot

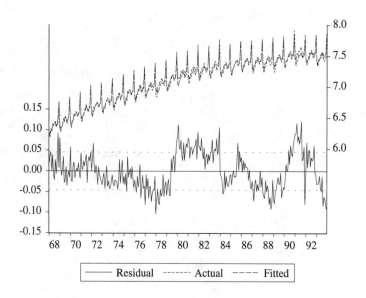

cay slowly, and they exceed the Bartlett standard errors throughout. The Ljung-Box test strongly rejects the white noise null at all displacements. Finally, the residual sample partial autocorrelations cut off at displacement 3. All of this suggests that an AR(3) would provide a good approximation to the disturbance's Wold representation.

In Table 9.5, then, we report the results of estimating a liquor sales model with quadratic trend, seasonal dummies, and AR(3) disturbances. The R^2 is now 100%, and the Durbin-Watson statistic is fine. One inverse root of the AR(3) disturbance process is estimated to be real and close to the unit circle (0.95), and the other two inverse roots are a complex conjugate pair farther from the unit circle. The standard error of this regression is an estimate of the standard deviation of the forecast error we would expect to make after modeling the residual serial correlation, as we have now done;

TABLE 9.4   Log Liquor Sales: Quadratic Trend Regression with Seasonal Dummies, Residual Correlogram

	Acorr.	P. Acorr.	Std. Error	Ljung-Box	p-value
1	0.700	0.700	.056	154.34	0.000
2	0.686	0.383	.056	302.86	0.000
3	0.725	0.369	.056	469.36	0.000
4	0.569	-0.141	.056	572.36	0.000
5	0.569	0.017	.056	675.58	0.000
6	0.577	0.093	.056	782.19	0.000
7	0.460	-0.078	.056	850.06	0.000
8	0.480	0.043	.056	924.38	0.000
9	0.466	0.030	.056	994.46	0.000
10	0.327	-0.188	.056	1029.1	0.000
11	0.364	0.019	.056	1072.1	0.000
12	0.355	0.089	.056	1113.3	0.000
13	0.225	-0.119	.056	1129.9	0.000
14	0.291	0.065	.056	1157.8	0.000
15	0.211	-0.119	.056	1172.4	0.000
16	0.138	-0.031	.056	1178.7	0.000
17	0.195	0.053	.056	1191.4	0.000
18	0.114	-0.027	.056	1195.7	0.000
19	0.055	-0.063	.056	1196.7	0.000
20	0.134	0.089	.056	1202.7	0.000
21	0.062	0.018	.056	1204.0	0.000
22	-0.006	-0.115	.056	1204.0	0.000
23	0.084	0.086	.056	1206.4	0.000
24	-0.039	-0.124	.056	1206.9	0.000
25	-0.063	-0.055	.056	1208.3	0.000
26	-0.016	-0.022	.056	1208.4	0.000
27	-0.143	-0.075	.056	1215.4	0.000
28	-0.135	-0.047	.056	1221.7	0.000
29	-0.124	-0.048	.056	1227.0	0.000
30	-0.189	0.086	.056	1239.5	0.000
31	-0.178	-0.017	.056	1250.5	0.000
32	-0.139	0.073	.056	1257.3	0.000
33	-0.226	-0.049	.056	1275.2	0.000
34	-0.155	0.097	.056	1283.7	0.000
35	-0.142	0.008	.056	1290.8	0.000
36	-0.242	-0.074	.056	1311.6	0.000

FIGURE 9.6   Log Liquor Sales: Quadratic Trend Regression with
              Seasonal Dummies, Residual Sample Autocorrelation,
              and Partial Autocorrelation Functions

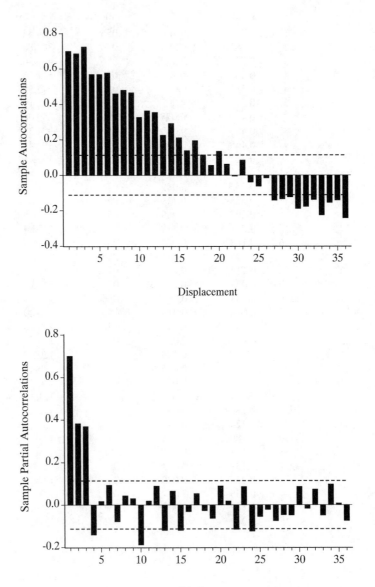

TABLE 9.5   Log Liquor Sales: Quadratic Trend Regression with Seasonal Dummies
and AR(3) Disturbances

LS // Dependent Variable is LSALES
Sample: 1968:01 1993:12
Included observations: 312
Convergence achieved after 4 iterations

Variable	Coefficient	Std. Error	t-Statistic	Prob.
TIME	0.008606	0.000981	8.768212	0.0000
TIME2	-1.41E-05	2.53E-06	-5.556103	0.0000
D1	6.073054	0.083922	72.36584	0.0000
D2	6.013822	0.083942	71.64254	0.0000
D3	6.099208	0.083947	72.65524	0.0000
D4	6.101522	0.083934	72.69393	0.0000
D5	6.172528	0.083946	73.52962	0.0000
D6	6.177129	0.083947	73.58364	0.0000
D7	6.223323	0.083939	74.14071	0.0000
D8	6.195681	0.083943	73.80857	0.0000
D9	6.131818	0.083940	73.04993	0.0000
D10	6.157592	0.083934	73.36197	0.0000
D11	6.188480	0.083932	73.73176	0.0000
D12	6.509106	0.083928	77.55624	0.0000
AR(1)	0.268805	0.052909	5.080488	0.0000
AR(2)	0.239688	0.053697	4.463723	0.0000
AR(3)	0.395880	0.053109	7.454150	0.0000

R-squared	0.995069	Mean dependent var	7.112383
Adjusted R-squared	0.994802	S.D. dependent var	0.379308
S.E. of regression	0.027347	Akaike info criterion	-7.145319
Sum squared resid	0.220625	Schwarz criterion	-6.941373
Log likelihood	688.9610	F-statistic	3720.875
Durbin-Watson stat	1.886119	Prob(F-statistic)	0.000000

Inverted AR Roots	.95	-.34+.55i	-.34 -.55i

that is, it is an estimate of the standard deviation of v.[6] It is a very small 0.027,
roughly half that obtained when we ignored serial correlation.

We show the residual plot in Figure 9.7 and the residual correlogram in
Table 9.6 and Figure 9.8. The residual plot reveals no patterns; instead, the
residuals look like white noise, as they should. The residual sample autocorrelations and partial autocorrelations display no patterns and are mostly inside the Bartlett bands. The Ljung-Box statistics also look good for small and

---

6. Recall that v is the innovation that drives the ARMA process for the regression disturbance, ε.

FIGURE 9.7 Log Liquor Sales: Quadratic Trend Regression with Seasonal Dummies and AR(3) Disturbances, Residual Plot

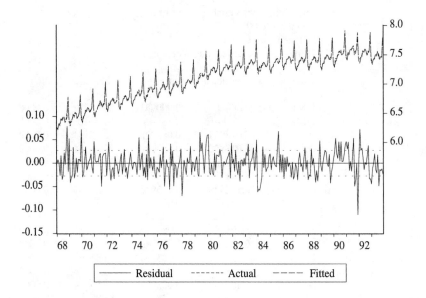

moderate displacements, although their *p*-values decrease for longer displacements.

All things considered, the quadratic trend, seasonal dummy, and AR(3) specification seems tentatively adequate. We also perform a number of additional checks. In Figure 9.9, we show a histogram and normality test applied to the residuals. The histogram looks symmetric, as confirmed by the skewness near zero. The residual kurtosis is a bit higher than 3, and causes the Jarque-Bera test to reject the normality hypothesis with a *p*-value of 0.02, but the residuals nevertheless appear to be fairly well approximated by a normal distribution, even if they may have slightly fatter tails.

Now we use the estimated model to produce forecasts. In Figure 9.10 we show the history of liquor sales and a 12-month-ahead extrapolation forecast for 1994.[7] To aid visual interpretation, we show only two years of history. The forecast looks reasonable. It is visually apparent that the model has done a good job of picking up the seasonal pattern, which dominates the local behavior of the series. In Figure 9.11, we show the history, the forecast, and the 1994 realization. The forecast was very good!

---

7. We show the point forecast together with 95% intervals.

TABLE 9.6   Log Liquor Sales: Quadratic Trend Regression with Seasonal Dummies and AR(3) Disturbances, Residual Correlogram

	Acorr.	P. Acorr.	Std. Error	Ljung-Box	p-value
1	0.056	0.056	.056	0.9779	0.323
2	0.037	0.034	.056	1.4194	0.492
3	0.024	0.020	.056	1.6032	0.659
4	-0.084	-0.088	.056	3.8256	0.430
5	-0.007	0.001	.056	3.8415	0.572
6	0.065	0.072	.056	5.1985	0.519
7	-0.041	-0.044	.056	5.7288	0.572
8	0.069	0.063	.056	7.2828	0.506
9	0.080	0.074	.056	9.3527	0.405
10	-0.163	-0.169	.056	18.019	0.055
11	-0.009	-0.005	.056	18.045	0.081
12	0.145	0.175	.056	24.938	0.015
13	-0.074	-0.078	.056	26.750	0.013
14	0.149	0.113	.056	34.034	0.002
15	-0.039	-0.060	.056	34.532	0.003
16	-0.089	-0.058	.056	37.126	0.002
17	0.058	0.048	.056	38.262	0.002
18	-0.062	-0.050	.056	39.556	0.002
19	-0.110	-0.074	.056	43.604	0.001
20	0.100	0.056	.056	46.935	0.001
21	0.039	0.042	.056	47.440	0.001
22	-0.122	-0.114	.056	52.501	0.000
23	0.146	0.130	.056	59.729	0.000
24	-0.072	-0.040	.056	61.487	0.000
25	0.006	0.017	.056	61.500	0.000
26	0.148	0.082	.056	69.024	0.000
27	-0.109	-0.067	.056	73.145	0.000
28	-0.029	-0.045	.056	73.436	0.000
29	-0.046	-0.100	.056	74.153	0.000
30	-0.084	0.020	.056	76.620	0.000
31	-0.095	-0.101	.056	79.793	0.000
32	0.051	0.012	.056	80.710	0.000
33	-0.114	-0.061	.056	85.266	0.000
34	0.024	0.002	.056	85.468	0.000
35	0.043	-0.010	.056	86.116	0.000
36	-0.229	-0.140	.056	104.75	0.000

In Figure 9.12 we show four years of history together with a 60-month-ahead (five-year-ahead) extrapolation forecast to provide a better feel for the dynamics in the forecast. The figure also makes clear the trend forecast is slightly *downward*. To put the long-horizon forecast in historical context, we show in Figure 9.13 the 60-month-ahead forecast together with the complete history. Finally, in Figure 9.14, we show the history and point forecast of the

FIGURE 9.8   Log Liquor Sales: Quadratic Trend Regression with Seasonal Dummies and AR(3) Disturbances, Residual Sample Autocorrelation and Partial Autocorrelation Functions

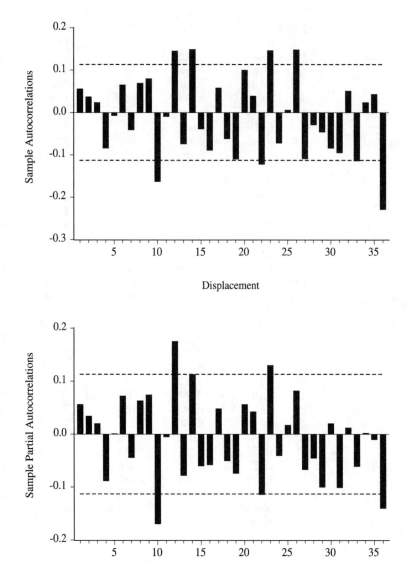

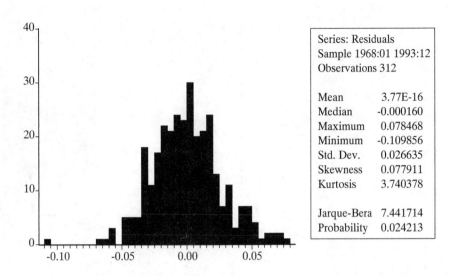

FIGURE 9.9   Log Liquor Sales: Quadratic Trend Regression with Seasonal Dummies and AR(3) Disturbances, Residual Histogram and Normality Test

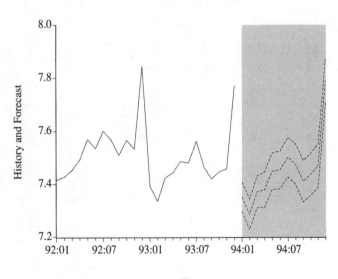

FIGURE 9.10   Log Liquor Sales: History and 12-Month-Ahead Forecast

FIGURE 9.11   Log Liquor Sales: History, 12-Month-Ahead Forecast, and Realization

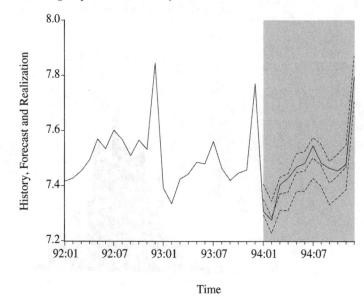

FIGURE 9.12   Log Liquor Sales: History and 60-Month-Ahead Forecast

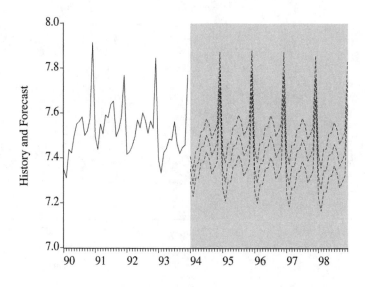

FIGURE 9.13   Log Liquor Sales: Long History and 60-Month-Ahead Forecast

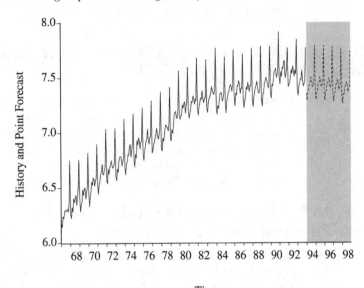

FIGURE 9.14   Liquor Sales: Long History and 60-Month-Ahead Forecast

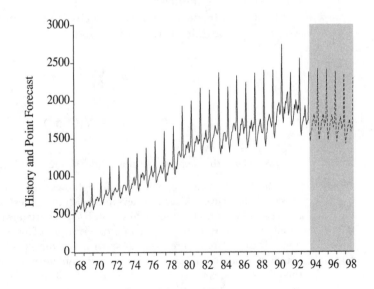

level of liquor sales (as opposed to log liquor sales), which we obtain by exponentiating the forecast of log liquor sales.[8]

3. RECURSIVE ESTIMATION PROCEDURES FOR DIAGNOSING AND SELECTING FORECASTING MODELS

Recursive estimation means beginning with a small sample of data, estimating a model, adding an observation, re-estimating the model, and continuing in that fashion until the sample is exhausted.[9] Recursive estimation and related techniques are useful in a variety of situations of importance in forecasting, including stability assessment and model selection. On both counts, it is natural to introduce them now.

Assessing the Stability of Forecasting Models: Recursive Parameter Estimation and Recursive Residuals

Business and economic relationships often vary over time; sometimes parameters evolve slowly and sometimes they break sharply. If a forecasting model displays such instability, it isn't likely to produce good forecasts, so it is important that we have tools that help us to diagnose the instability. Recursive estimation procedures, which allow us to assess and track time-varying parameters, are therefore useful in the construction and evaluation of a variety of forecasting models.

First we introduce the idea of recursive parameter estimation. We work with the standard linear regression model,

$$y_t = \sum_{i=1}^{k} \beta_i x_{i,t} + \varepsilon_t$$

$$\varepsilon_t \overset{iid}{\sim} N(0, \sigma^2)$$

---

8. Recall that exponentiating "undoes" a natural logarithm.

9. Strictly speaking, "sequential" might be a more descriptive adjective than "recursive." "Recursive updating" refers to the fact that an estimate based on $t + 1$ observations can sometimes be computed simply by appropriately combining the old estimate based on t observations with the new observation. (This is possible, for example, with linear least squares regression.) Recursive updating achieves a drastic reduction in computational requirements relative to complete re-estimation of the model each time the sample is updated, which we might call "brute force updating." For our purposes, it is inconsequential whether we do recursive updating or brute force updating (and the speed of modern computers often makes brute force attractive); we use "recursive estimation" as a blanket term for any sequential estimation procedure, whether the computations are done by recursive or brute force techniques.

$t = 1, \ldots, T$, and we estimate it using least squares. Instead of immediately using all the data to estimate the model, however, we begin with a small subset. If the model contains k parameters, we begin with the first k observations and estimate the model. Then we estimate the model using the first $k + 1$ observations, and so on, until the sample is exhausted. At the end we have a set of recursive parameter estimates $\hat{\beta}_{i,t}$, for $t = k, \ldots, T$ and $i = 1, \ldots, k$. It often pays to compute and examine recursive estimates because they convey important information about parameter stability—they show how the estimated parameters move as more and more observations are accumulated. It is often informative to plot the recursive estimates to help answer the obvious questions of interest. Do the coefficient estimates stabilize as the sample size grows? Or do they wander around, or drift in a particular direction, or break sharply at one or more points?

Now we introduce the **recursive residuals.** At each t, $t = k, \ldots, T-1$, we can compute a 1-step-ahead forecast,

$$\hat{y}_{t+1,t} = \sum_{i=1}^{k} \hat{\beta}_{i,t} x_{i,t+1}$$

The corresponding forecast errors, or recursive residuals, are $\hat{e}_{t+1,t} = y_{t+1} - \hat{y}_{t+1,t}$. The variance of these 1-step-ahead forecast errors changes as the sample size grows, because under the maintained assumptions the model parameters are estimated more precisely as the sample size grows. Specifically,

$$\hat{e}_{t+1,t} \sim N(0, \sigma^2 r_t)$$

where $r_t > 1$ for all t and r_t is a somewhat complicated function of the data.[10]

As with recursive parameter estimates, recursive residuals can reveal **parameter instability** in forecasting models. Often we examine a plot of the recursive residuals and estimated two standard error bands ($\pm 2\hat{\sigma}\sqrt{r_t}$).[11] This has an immediate forecasting interpretation and is sometimes called a sequence of 1-step forecast tests—we make recursive 1-step-ahead 95% interval forecasts and then check where the subsequent realizations fall. If many of them fall outside the intervals, one or more parameters may be unstable, and the

---

10. Derivation of a formula for r_t is beyond the scope of this book. Ordinarily we would ignore the inflation of var $(\hat{e}_{t+1,t})$ due to parameter estimation, which vanishes with sample size so that $r_t \to 1$, and simply use the large-sample approximation $\hat{e}_{t+1,t} \sim N(0, \sigma^2)$. Presently, however, we are estimating the regression recursively, so the initial regressions will always be performed on very small samples, thereby rendering large-sample approximations unpalatable.

11. $\hat{\sigma}$ is just the usual standard error of the regression, estimated from the full sample of data.

locations of the violations of the interval forecasts give some indication as to the nature of the instability.

Sometimes it is helpful to consider the **standardized recursive residuals,**

$$w_{t+1,t} \equiv \frac{\hat{e}_{t+1,t}}{\sigma \sqrt{r_t}}$$

$t = k, \ldots, T-1$. Under the maintained assumptions,

$$w_{t+1,t} \overset{iid}{\sim} N(0, 1)$$

If any of the maintained model assumptions are violated, the standardized recursive residuals will fail to be iid normal, so we can learn about various model inadequacies by examining them. The cumulative sum (*CUSUM*) of the standardized recursive residuals is particularly useful in assessing parameter stability. Because $w_{t+1,t} \overset{iid}{\sim} N(0, 1)$, it follows that

$$CUSUM_t \equiv \sum_{\tau = k}^{t} w_{\tau+1,\tau}$$

$t = k, \ldots, T-1$ is just a sum of iid $N(0, 1)$ random variables.[12] Probability bounds for the *CUSUM* have been tabulated, and we often examine time series plots of the *CUSUM* and its 95% probability bounds, which grow linearly and are centered at 0.[13] If the *CUSUM* violates the bounds at any point, there is evidence of parameter instability. Such an analysis is called a *CUSUM* analysis.

As an illustration of the use of recursive techniques for detecting structural change, we consider in Figures 9.15 through 9.17 three stylized data-generating processes (bivariate regression models, satisfying the classical assumptions apart from the possibility of a time-varying parameter). The first has a constant parameter, the second has a trending parameter, and the third has a sharply breaking parameter. For each we show a scatterplot of *y* versus *x*, recursive parameter estimates, recursive residuals, and a *CUSUM* **plot.**

We show the constant parameter model in Figure 9.15. As expected, the scatterplot shows no evidence of instability, the recursive parameter estimate stabilizes quickly, its variance decreases quickly, the recursive residuals look like zero-mean random noise, and the *CUSUM* plot shows no evidence of instability.

---

12. Sums of zero-mean iid random variables are very important. In fact, they are so important that they have their own name, **random walks.** We study them in detail in chapter 10.

13. To make the standardized recursive residuals—and hence the *CUSUM* statistic—operational, we replace σ with $\hat{\sigma}$.

FIGURE 9.15   Recursive Analysis: Constant Parameter Model

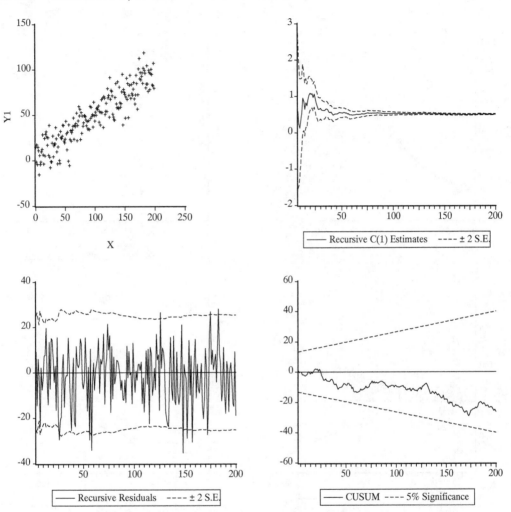

We show the trending parameter model in Figure 9.16; the results are very different from those of Figure 9.15. The true relationship between y and x is one of proportionality, with the constant of proportionality trending gradually upward. This shows up in the scatterplot as a nonlinear relationship between y and x.[14] The recursive residual is obviously not zero-mean ran-

---

14. Here the true model is linear with time-varying parameters, and the scatterplot looks nonlinear. The converse is often useful to remember when building forecasting models: linear models with time-varying parameters can often be used to provide good approximations to more complicated nonlinear relationships.

FIGURE 9.16   Recursive Analysis: Trending Parameter Model

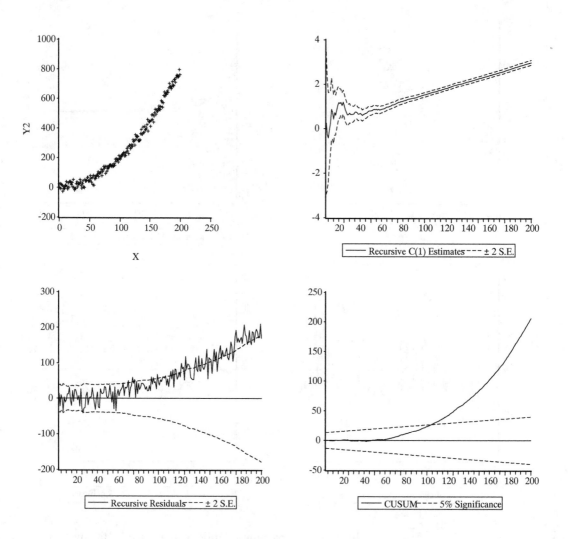

dom noise, and the recursive parameter estimate clearly reveals that the parameter is trending. The *CUSUM* grows gradually until it exceeds the 95% probability limit, indicating parameter instability.

We show the breaking parameter model in Figure 9.17; the results are different yet again. The true relationship between *y* and *x* is one of proportionality, with the constant of proportionality jumping in midsample. The jump is clearly evident in the scatterplot, in the recursive residuals, and in the recursive parameter estimate. The *CUSUM* remains near zero until midsample, at which time it shoots through the 95% probability limit.

FIGURE 9.17   Recursive Analysis: Breaking Parameter Model

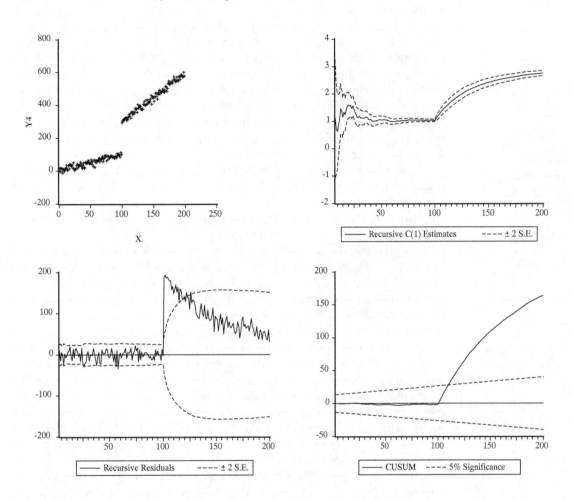

Model Selection Based on Simulated Forecasting Performance

All the forecast model selection strategies that we have studied thus far amount to strategies for finding the model that is most likely to perform well in terms of out-of-sample 1-step-ahead mean squared forecast error. In every case, we effectively estimate *out-of-sample* 1-step-ahead mean squared forecast error by adjusting the *in-sample* mean squared error with a degrees-of-freedom penalty. The important insight is that we estimate out-of-sample forecast accuracy by using in-sample residuals. Recursive estimation suggests a different approach, which is also more direct and flexible—recursive estimation lets us estimate out-of-sample forecast accuracy directly, using out-of-sample forecast errors.

We first introduce a procedure called **cross-validation,** in reference to the fact that the predictive ability of the model is evaluated on observations different from those on which the model is estimated, thereby incorporating an automatic degrees-of-freedom penalty. It is actually not based on recursive estimation because we don't let the estimation sample expand. Instead, we obtain the various estimation samples by sequentially deleting observations. As we shall see, however, it provides a natural introduction to a closely related recursive model selection procedure that we will introduce subsequently—recursive cross-validation.

Cross-validation proceeds as follows. Consider selecting among J forecasting models. Start with model 1, estimate it using all data observations except the first, use it to forecast the first observation, and compute the associated squared forecast error. Then estimate it using all observations except the second, use it to forecast the second observation, and compute the associated squared error. Keep doing this—estimating the model with one observation deleted and then using the estimated model to forecast the deleted observation—until each observation has been sequentially deleted, and then average the squared errors in predicting each of the T sequentially deleted observations. Repeat the procedure for the other models, $j = 2, \ldots, J$, and select the model with the smallest average squared forecast error.

As we describe it here, cross-validation is mainly of use in cross-section—as opposed to time series—forecasting environments because the "leave one out" estimations required for cross-validation make sense only in the absence of dynamics. That is, it is only in the absence of dynamics that we can simply pluck out an observation, discard it, and proceed to estimate the model with the remaining observations without further adjustment. It is easy to extend the basic idea of cross-validation to the time series case, however, which leads to the idea of recursive cross-validation.

Recursive cross-validation proceeds as follows. Let the initial estimation sample run $t = 1, \ldots, T^*$, and let the "holdout sample" used for comparing predictive performance run $t = T^* + 1, \ldots, T$. For each model, proceed as follows. Estimate the model using observations $t = 1, \ldots, T^*$. Then use it to forecast observation $T^* + 1$, and compute the associated squared error. Next, update the sample by one observation (observation $T^* + 1$), estimate the model using the updated sample $t = 1, \ldots, T^* + 1$, forecast observation $T^* + 2$, and compute the associated squared error. Continue this recursive re-estimation and forecasting until the sample is exhausted, and then average the squared errors in predicting observations $T^* + 1$ through T. Select the model with the smallest average squared forecast error.

4. LIQUOR SALES, CONTINUED

In Figures 9.18 through 9.20, we show the results of a recursive analysis. In Figure 9.18, we show the recursive residuals and their two-standard-error bands under the joint null hypothesis of correct specification and parameter constancy. The recursive residuals rarely violate the 95% bands. In Figure 9.19 we show the recursive parameter estimates together with recursively computed standard errors. The top row shows the two trend parameters, the next three rows show the twelve seasonal dummy parameters, and the last row shows the three autoregressive parameters. All parameter estimates seem to stabilize as the sample size grows. Finally, in Figure 9.20 we show a *CUSUM* chart, which reveals no evidence against the hypothesis of correct specification and structural stability; the *CUSUM* never even approaches the 5% significance boundary.

FIGURE 9.18   Log Liquor Sales: Quadratic Trend Regression with Seasonal Dummies and AR(3) Disturbances, Recursive Residuals and Two-Standard-Error Bands

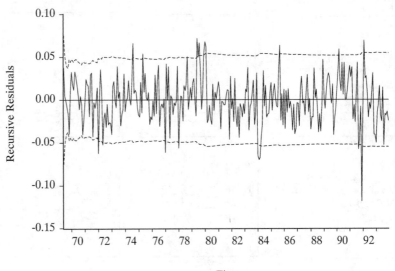

FIGURE 9.19   Log Liquor Sales: Quadratic Trend Regression with Seasonal Dummies and AR(3) Disturbances, Recursive Parameter Estimates

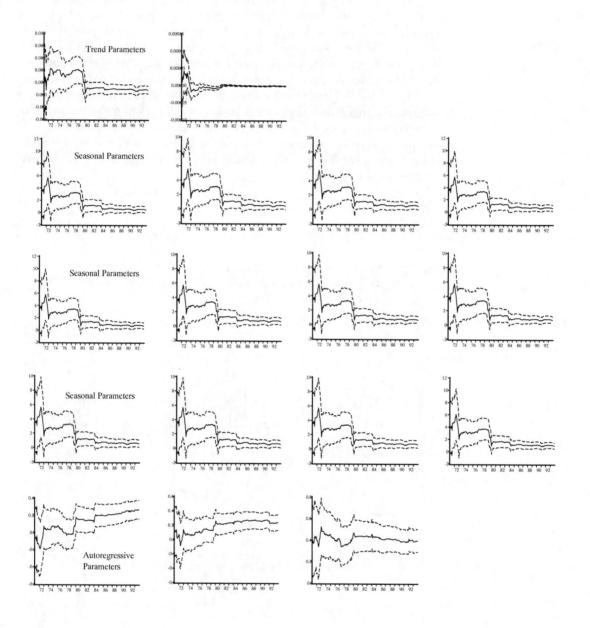

FIGURE 9.20 Log Liquor Sales: Quadratic Trend Regression with Seasonal Dummies and AR(3) Disturbances, *CUSUM* Analysis

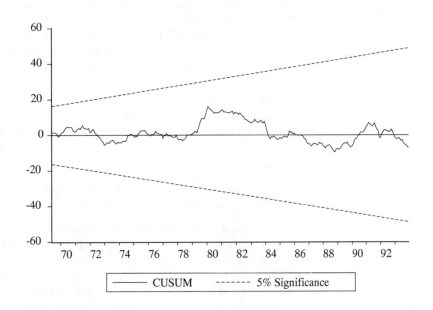

PROBLEMS AND COMPLEMENTS

1. (Serially correlated disturbances versus lagged dependent variables) Estimate the quadratic trend model for log liquor sales with seasonal dummies and three lags of the dependent variable included directly. Discuss your results and compare them to those we obtained when we instead allowed for AR(3) disturbances in the regression.

2. (Assessing adequacy of the liquor sales forecasting model) Critique the liquor sales forecasting model we adopted (log liquor sales with quadratic trend, seasonal dummies, and AR(3) disturbances), especially with respect to the adequacy of the log-quadratic trend and adequacy of the AR(3) disturbance dynamics.

   (a) If the trend is not a good approximation to the actual trend in the series, would it greatly affect short-run forecasts? Long-run forecasts?

   (b) Fit and assess the adequacy of a model with log-linear trend.

   (c) How might you fit and assess the adequacy of a *broken* linear trend? How might you decide on the location of the break point?

   (d) Return to the log-quadratic trend model with seasonal dummies, allow for ARMA(p,q) disturbances, and do a systematic selection of p and q using *AIC* and *SIC*. Do *AIC* and *SIC* select the same model? If not, which do you prefer? If your preferred forecasting model differs from the AR(3) that we used, replicate the analysis in the text using your preferred model, and discuss your results.

(e) Recall our earlier argument, made in the Problems and Complements of chapter 7, that best practice requires using a χ^2_{m-k} distribution rather than a χ^2_m distribution to assess the significance of Q-statistics for model residuals, where m is the number of autocorrelations included in the Box-Pierce statistic and k is the number of parameters estimated. In several places in this chapter, we failed to heed this advice when evaluating the liquor sales model. If we were instead to compare the residual Q-statistic p-values to a χ^2_{m-k} distribution, how, if at all, would our assessment of the model's adequacy change?

3. (*CUSUM* analysis of the housing starts model) Consider the housing starts forecasting model that we built in chapter 5.

   (a) Perform a *CUSUM* analysis of a housing starts forecasting model that does not account for cycles. (Recall that our model in chapter 5 did not account for cycles). Discuss your results.

   (b) Specify and estimate a model that *does* account for cycles.

   (c) Do a *CUSUM* analysis of the model that accounts for cycles. Discuss your results and compare them to those of part (a).

4. (Model selection based on simulated forecasting performance)

   (a) Return to the retail sales data of chapter 4 and use recursive cross-validation to select between the linear trend forecasting model and the quadratic trend forecasting model. Which do you select? How does it compare with the model selected by *AIC* and *SIC*?

   (b) How did you decide upon a value of T^* when performing the recursive cross-validation on the retail sales data? What are the relevant considerations?

   (c) One virtue of recursive cross validation procedures is their flexibility. Suppose that your loss function is not a 1-step-ahead mean squared error; instead, suppose it is an asymmetric function of the 1-step-ahead error. How would you modify the recursive cross-validation procedure to enforce the asymmetric loss function? How would you proceed if the loss function were a 4-step-ahead squared error? How would you proceed if the loss function were an average of the 1-step-ahead through 4-step-ahead squared errors?

5. (Seasonal models with **time-varying parameters:** forecasting Air Canada passenger-miles) Suppose you work for Air Canada and are modeling and forecasting the miles per person (passenger-miles) traveled on their flights through the four quarters of the year. During the past 15 years for

which you have data, it is well known in the industry that trend passenger-miles have been flat (that is, there is no trend), and similarly, there have been no cyclical effects. It is believed by industry experts, however, that there are strong seasonal effects, which you think might be very important for modeling and forecasting passenger-miles.

(a) Why might airline passenger-miles be seasonal?
(b) Fit a quarterly seasonal model to the Air Canada data and assess the importance of seasonal effects. Do the t and F tests indicate that seasonality is important? Do the Akaike and Schwarz criteria indicate that seasonality is important? What is the estimated seasonal pattern?
(c) Use recursive procedures to assess whether the seasonal coefficients are evolving over time. Discuss your results.
(d) If the seasonal coefficients are evolving over time, how might you model that evolution and thereby improve your forecasting model? (*Hint:* Allow for trends in the seasonal coefficients themselves.)
(e) Compare 4-quarter-ahead extrapolation forecasts from your models with and without evolving seasonality.

6. (**Formal models of unobserved-components**) We have used the idea of unobserved-components as informal motivation for our models of trends, seasonals, and cycles. Although we will not do so, it is possible to work with formal unobserved-components models, such as

$$y_t = T_t + S_t + C_t + I_t$$

where T is the trend component, S is the seasonal component, C is the cyclical component, and I is the remainder, or "irregular," component, which is white noise. Typically, we would assume that each component is uncorrelated with all other components at all leads and lags. Typical models for the various components include:

Trend

$$T_t = \beta_0 + \beta_1 TIME_t \qquad \text{(deterministic)}$$

$$T_t = \beta_1 + T_{t-1} + \varepsilon_{1t} \qquad \text{(stochastic)}$$

Seasonal

$$S_t = \sum_{i=1}^{s} \gamma_i D_{it} \qquad \text{(deterministic)}$$

$$S_t = \frac{1}{1 - \gamma L^s} \varepsilon_{2t} \qquad \text{(stochastic)}$$

Cycle

$$C_t = \frac{1}{(1 - \alpha_1 L)}\, \varepsilon_{3t} \qquad\qquad (\text{AR(1)})$$

$$C_t = \frac{1 + \beta_1 L + \beta_2 L^2}{(1 - \alpha_1 L)(1 - \alpha_2 L)}\, \varepsilon_{3t} \qquad (\text{ARMA(2,2)})$$

Irregular

$$I_t = \varepsilon_{4t}$$

7. (The restrictions associated with unobserved-components structures) The restrictions associated with formal unobserved-components models are surely false, in the sense that real-world dynamics are not likely to be decomposable in such a sharp and tidy way. Rather, the decomposition is effectively an accounting framework that we use simply because it is helpful to do so. Trend, seasonal, and cyclical variation are so different—and so important in business, economic, and financial series—that it is often helpful to model them separately to help ensure that we model each adequately. A consensus has not yet emerged as to whether it's more effective to exploit the unobserved-components perspective for intuitive motivation, as we do throughout this book, or to enforce formal unobserved-components decompositions in hopes of benefiting from considerations related to the shrinkage principle.

8. (**Additive and multiplicative unobserved-components decompositions**) We have already introduced the formal unobserved-components decomposition,

$$y_t = T_t + S_t + C_t + I_t$$

where T is the trend component, S is the seasonal component, C is the cyclical component, and I is the remainder, or "irregular," component. Alternatively, we could have introduced a *multiplicative* decomposition,

$$y_t = T_t\, S_t\, C_t\, I_t$$

(a) Begin with the multiplicative decomposition and take logs. How does your result relate to our original additive decomposition?

(b) Does the exponential (log-linear) trend fit more naturally in the additive or *multiplicative* decomposition framework? Why?

9. (**Signal, noise, and overfitting**) Using our unobserved-components perspective, we have discussed trends, seasonals, cycles, and noise. We have modeled and forecast each, with the exception of noise. Clearly we *cannot*

model or forecast the noise; by construction, it is unforecastable. Instead, the noise is what *remains* after accounting for the other components. We call the other components signals, and the signals are buried in noise. Good models fit signals, not noise. Data-mining expeditions, in contrast, lead to models that often fit very well over the historical sample, but fail miserably for out-of-sample forecasting. That is because such data mining effectively tailors the model to fit the idiosyncracies of the in-sample noise, which improves the in-sample fit but is of no help in out-of-sample forecasting.

(a) Choose your favorite trending (but not seasonal) series, and select a sample path of length 100. Graph it.

(b) Regress the first 20 observations on a fifth-order polynomial time trend, and allow for five autoregressive lags as well. Graph the actual and fitted values from the regression. Discuss.

(c) Use your estimated model to produce an 80-step-ahead extrapolation forecast. Graphically compare your forecast to the actual realization. Discuss.

BIBLIOGRAPHICAL AND COMPUTATIONAL NOTES

Nerlove, Grether, and Carvalho (1996) discuss unobserved components models and their relationship to ARMA models. They also provide an insightful history of the use of unobserved components decompositions for data description and forecasting.

Harvey (1990) derives and presents the formula for r_t, the key element of the variance of the recursive residual. We suggested using the standard error of the regression to estimate σ, the standard deviation of the nonrecursive regression disturbance, as suggested in the original work by Brown, Durbin, and Evans (1975). Since then, a number of authors have used an alternative estimator of σ based on the recursive residuals, which may lead to *CUSUM* tests with better small-sample power. For a discussion in the context of the dynamic models useful for forecasting, see Krämer, Ploberger, and Alt (1988).

Efron and Tibshirani (1993) give an insightful discussion of forecasting model selection criteria as estimates of out-of-sample MSE, and the natural attractiveness in that regard of numerical methods such as cross-validation and its relatives.

Recursive cross-validation is often called "predictive stochastic complexity"; the basic theory was developed by Rissanen (1989). Kuan and Liu (1995) make good use of recursive cross-validation to select models for forecasting exchange rates, and they provide additional references to the literature on the subject.

Recursive estimation and related techniques are implemented in a number of modern software packages.

CONCEPTS FOR REVIEW

Additive unobserved-components
   decomposition
Cross-validation
CUSUM
CUSUM plot
Formal model of unobserved
   components
Multiplicative unobserved-
   components decomposition

Parameter instability
Random walk
Recursive cross-validation
Recursive estimation
Recursive residuals
Signal, noise, and overfitting
Standardized recursive residuals
Time-varying parameters

REFERENCES AND ADDITIONAL READINGS

Brown, R. L., Durbin, J., and Evans, J. M. (1975), "Techniques for Testing the
   Constance of Regression Relationships Over Time," *Journal of the Royal
   Statistical Society* B, 37, 149–163.

Efron, B., and Tibshirani, R. J. (1993), *An Introduction to the Bootstrap.* New
   York: Chapman and Hall.

Harvey, A. C. (1990), *The Econometric Analysis of Time Series,* second edition.
   Cambridge, Mass.: MIT Press.

Krämer, W., Ploberger, W., and Alt, R. (1988), "Testing for Structural Change
   in Dynamic Models," *Econometrica,* 56, 1355–1369.

Kuan, C. M., and Liu, Y. (1995), "Forecasting Exchange Rates Using Feedforward and Recurrent Neural Networks," *Journal of Applied Econometrics,* 10,
   347–364.

Nerlove, M., Grether, D. M., and Carvalho, J. L. (1996), *Analysis of Economic
   Time Series: A Synthesis,* second edition. New York: Academic Press.

Rissanen, J. (1989), *Stochastic Complexity in Statistical Inquiry.* Singapore:
   World Science Publishing.

CHAPTER 10

FORECASTING WITH REGRESSION MODELS

The regression model is an explicitly multivariate model, in which variables are explained and forecast on the basis of their own history *and* the histories of other, related, variables. Exploiting such cross-variable linkages may lead to good and intuitive forecasting models, and to better forecasts than those obtained from univariate models.

Regression models are often called causal, or explanatory, models. For example, in the linear regression model,

$$y_t = \beta_0 + \beta_1\, x_t + \varepsilon_t$$

$$\varepsilon_t \sim WN(0, \sigma^2)$$

the presumption is that x helps determine, or cause, y, not the other way around. For this reason the left-hand-side variable is sometimes called the "endogenous" variable, and the right-hand-side variables are called "exogenous" or "explanatory" variables.

But ultimately, regression models, like all statistical models, are models of correlation, not causation. Except in special cases, all variables are endogenous, and it is best to admit as much from the outset. Toward the end of this chapter we will explicitly do so; we will work with systems of regression equations called vector autoregressions (VARs). For now, however, we will work with the standard single-equation linear regression model, a great workhorse of forecasting, which we can interpret as one equation of a larger system.

1. CONDITIONAL FORECASTING MODELS AND SCENARIO ANALYSIS

A **conditional forecasting model** is one that can be used to produce forecasts for a variable of interest, *conditional* upon assumptions about other variables. With the regression model,

$$y_t = \beta_0 + \beta_1 \, x_t + \varepsilon_t$$

$$\varepsilon_t \sim N(0, \sigma^2)$$

for example, we can forecast y conditional upon an assumed future value of x.[1] This sort of conditional forecasting is often called **scenario analysis,** or **contingency analysis,** because a conditional forecasting model helps us answer the "what if" questions that often arise. If we condition on the assumption, for example, that the h-step-ahead value of x is x^*_{T+h}, then our h-step-ahead conditional forecast for y is

$$y_{T+h,T} \mid x^*_{T+h} = \beta_0 + \beta_1 \, x^*_{T+h}$$

Assuming normality, we use the conditional density forecast $N(y_{T+h,T} \mid x^*_{T+h}, \sigma^2)$, and conditional interval forecasts follow immediately from the conditional density forecast. As always, we make the procedure operational by replacing unknown parameters with estimates.

2. ACCOUNTING FOR PARAMETER UNCERTAINTY IN CONFIDENCE INTERVALS FOR CONDITIONAL FORECASTS

Forecasts are, of course, subject to error, and scenario forecasts are no exception. There are at least three sources of such error. One important source of forecast error is **specification uncertainty.** All our models are intentional simplifications, which hopefully capture the salient properties of the data for forecasting purposes. By using modern tools such as information criteria, re-

---

1. To enhance pedagogical clarity, we work throughout this chapter with regression models containing only one right-hand-side variable. Extensions to models with more than one right-hand-side variable are straightforward.

sidual correlograms, and so on, in conjunction with intuition and theory, we attempt to minimize specification uncertainty.

A second source of forecast error is **innovation uncertainty,** which reflects the fact that future innovations are not known when the forecast is made. This is the source of forecast error that we have explicitly acknowledged in our computations of interval and density forecasts. We have seen, for example, that the cumulative effect of innovation uncertainty tends to grow with the forecast horizon, resulting in interval and density forecasts that widen with the horizon.

A third source of forecast error is **parameter uncertainty.** The coefficients that we use to produce forecasts are, of course, just *estimates,* and the estimates are subject to sampling variability. Specification and innovation uncertainty are likely more important than parameter uncertainty (which vanishes as the sample size grows), and, in addition, the effect of parameter uncertainty on forecast uncertainty is difficult to quantify in many situations. For both these reasons, parameter uncertainty is often ignored, as we have done thus far.

When using a conditional forecasting model, however, simple calculations allow us to quantify both innovation and parameter uncertainty. Consider, for example, the very simple case in which x has a 0 mean and

$$y_t = \beta x_t + \varepsilon_t$$

Suppose we want to predict y_{T+h} at $x_{T+h} = x^*_{T+h}$. If $x_{T+h} = x^*_{T+h}$, then

$$y_{T+h} = \beta x^*_{T+h} + \varepsilon_{T+h}$$

Thus

$$\hat{y}_{T+h,T} \mid x^*_{T+h} = \hat{\beta} x^*_{T+h}$$

with corresponding error

$$\hat{e}_{T+h,T} = y_{T+h} - \hat{y}_{T+h,T} = (\beta - \hat{\beta}) x^*_{T+h} + \varepsilon_{T+h}$$

Thus,

$$\mathrm{var}\,(\hat{e}_{T+h,T}) = x^{*2}_{T+h}\,\mathrm{var}\,(\hat{\beta}) + \sigma^2$$

We won't do so here, but it can be shown that[2]

---

2. See any of the elementary statistics or econometrics texts cited in chapter 1.

$$\text{var} (\hat{\beta}) = \frac{\sigma^2}{\displaystyle\sum_{t=1}^{T} x_t^2}$$

Thus, we arrive at the final formula,

$$\text{var} (\hat{e}_{T+h,T}) = \frac{\sigma^2}{\displaystyle\sum_{t=1}^{T} x_t^2} \, x_{T+h}^{*2} + \sigma^2$$

In this expression, the first term accounts for parameter uncertainty, while the second accounts for the usual innovation uncertainty. Taken together, the results suggest an operational density forecast that accounts for parameter uncertainty,

$$N\!\left(\hat{\beta} x_{T+h}^*, \ \frac{\hat{\sigma}^2}{\displaystyle\sum_{t=1}^{T} x_t^2} \, x_{T+h}^{*2} + \hat{\sigma}^2 \right)$$

from which interval forecasts may be constructed as well.

Note that when parameter uncertainty exists, the closer x_{T+h}^* is to its mean (0), the smaller is the prediction-error variance. The idea can be shown to carry over to more complicated situations when y and x don't necessarily have 0 means, and to models with more than one regressor: the closer x is to its mean, the tighter the prediction interval. We illustrate the situation in Figure 10.1; the top panel shows constant intervals ($\pm 1.96\sigma$) that fail to account for parameter uncertainty, and the bottom panel shows the intervals of varying width that account for parameter uncertainty. Finally, note that as the sample size gets large, $\Sigma_{t=1}^{T} x_t^2$ gets large as well, so the adjustment for parameter uncertainty vanishes, and the formula collapses to our old one.

The discussion of this section depends on the future value of x being known with certainty, which is acceptable in the case of conditional forecasts, in which case we are simply conditioning on an assumption about future x.[3]

---

3. The discussion also applies to forecasting in cross-sectional environments, in which forecasts are almost always conditional. Suppose, for example, that we estimate a regression model relating expenditure on restaurant meals to income, using cross-section data on 1,000 households for 1997. Then, if we get 1997 income data for an additional set of people, we can use it to forecast their restaurant expenditures.

FIGURE 10.1   Point and Interval Forecasts: Top Panel Interval Forecasts *Don't*
Acknowledge Parameter Uncertainty; Bottom Panel Interval Forecasts
Do Acknowledge Parameter Uncertainty

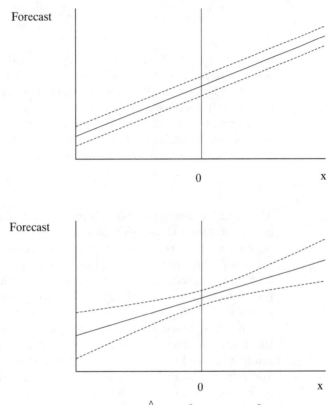

Note: To produce this figure, we set $\hat{\beta} = 0$, $\sigma^2 = 1$, and $\Sigma x_t^2 = 50$.

If we don't want to condition on an assumption about future x, or if we are
using certain more complicated models (with dynamics, for example), the
formula does not apply. We now turn to such situations and models.

3. UNCONDITIONAL FORECASTING MODELS

Notwithstanding the usefulness of scenario analyses, often we do not want to
make forecasts of y conditional upon assumptions about x; rather, we just
want the best possible forecast of y—an **unconditional forecast.** To get an unconditional forecast from a regression model, we often encounter the **forecasting the right-hand-side variables problem.** That is, to get an optimal un-

conditional point forecast for y, we cannot insert an arbitrary value for future x; rather, we need to insert the optimal point forecast, $x_{T+h,T}$, which yields the unconditional forecast

$$y_{T+h,T} = \beta_0 + \beta_1 x_{T+h,T}$$

Of course, we usually don't have such a forecast for x, and the model at hand doesn't help us. (It is a model for y—we don't have a model for x.)

One thing we might do is fit a univariate model to x (e.g., an autoregressive model), forecast x (that is, form $\hat{x}_{T+h,T}$), and then use that forecast of x to forecast y. But just as easily, and in fact preferably, we can estimate all the parameters simultaneously by regressing y on $x_{t-h}, x_{t-h-1}, \ldots$ If we want to forecast only one step ahead, we could use the model

$$y_t = \beta_0 + \delta x_{t-1} + \varepsilon_t$$

The right-hand-side variable is lagged by one period, so the model is immediately useful for 1-step-ahead unconditional forecasting. More lags of x can, of course, be included; the key is that all variables on the right are lagged by at least one period. Forecasting more than one step ahead, however, again leads to the forecasting the right-hand-side variables problem—if we want to forecast h steps ahead, all variables on the right must be lagged by at least h periods.

In a few important special cases, the problem of forecasting the right-hand-side variables doesn't arise because the regressors are perfectly deterministic, so we know exactly what they will be at any future time. The trend and seasonal models discussed in chapters 4 and 5 are leading examples. Such cases are atypical, however.

4. DISTRIBUTED LAGS, POLYNOMIAL DISTRIBUTED LAGS, AND RATIONAL DISTRIBUTED LAGS

An unconditional forecasting model such as

$$y_t = \beta_0 + \delta x_{t-1} + \varepsilon_t$$

can be immediately generalized to the **distributed lag model,**

$$y_t = \beta_0 + \sum_{i=1}^{N_x} \delta_i x_{t-i} + \varepsilon_t$$

We say that y depends on a distributed lag of past x's. The coefficients on the lagged x's are called *lag weights*, and their pattern is called the *lag distribution*.

One way to estimate a distributed lag model is simply to include all N_x lags of x in the regression, which can be estimated by least squares in the usual way. In many situations, however, N_x might be quite a large number, in which case we would have to use many degrees of freedom to estimate the model, violating the parsimony principle. Often we can recover many of those degrees of freedom without seriously worsening the model's fit by constraining the lag weights to lie on a low-order polynomial. Such **polynomial distributed lags** promote smoothness in the lag distribution and may lead to sophisticatedly simple models with improved forecasting performance.

Polynomial distributed lag models are estimated by minimizing the sum of squared residuals in the usual way, subject to the constraint that the lag weights follow a low-order polynomial whose degree must be specified. Suppose, for example, that we constrain the lag weights to follow a second-degree polynomial. Then we find the parameter estimates by solving the problem

$$\min_{\beta_0, \delta_i} \sum_{t=N_x+1}^{T} \left[y_t - \beta_0 - \sum_{i=1}^{N_x} \delta_i \, x_{t-i} \right]^2$$

subject to

$$\delta_i = P(i) = a + bi + ci^2, \ i = 1, \ldots, N_x$$

This converts the estimation problem from one of estimating $1 + N_x$ parameters, $\beta_0, \delta_1, \ldots, \delta_{N_x}$, to one of estimating four parameters, β_0, a, b, and c. Sometimes additional constraints are imposed on the shape of the polynomial, such as

$$P(N_x) = 0$$

which enforces the idea that the dynamics have been exhausted by lag N_x.

Polynomial distributed lags produce aesthetically appealing, but basically ad hoc, lag distributions. After all, why should the lag weights necessarily follow a low-order polynomial? An alternative and often preferable approach makes use of the **rational distributed lags** that we introduced in chapter 6 in the context of univariate ARMA modeling. Rational distributed lags promote parsimony, and hence smoothness in the lag distribution, but they do so in a way that is potentially much less restrictive than requiring the lag weights to follow a low-order polynomial. We might, for example, use a model such as

$$y_t = \frac{A(L)}{B(L)} x_t + \varepsilon_t$$

where $A(L)$ and $B(L)$ are low-order polynomials in the lag operator. Equivalently, we can write

$$B(L)y_t = A(L)x_t + B(L)\varepsilon_t$$

which emphasizes that the rational distributed lag of x actually brings both lags of x and lags of y into the model. One way or another, it is crucial to allow for lags of y, and we now study such models in greater depth.

5. REGRESSIONS WITH LAGGED DEPENDENT VARIABLES, REGRESSIONS WITH ARMA DISTURBANCES, AND TRANSFER FUNCTION MODELS

Something is missing in distributed lag models of the form

$$y_t = \beta_0 + \sum_{i=1}^{N_x} \delta_i \, x_{t-i} + \varepsilon_t$$

A multivariate model (in this case, a regression model) should relate the current value y to its own past and to the past of x. But as presently written, we have left out the past of y! Even in distributed lag models, we always want to allow for the presence of the usual univariate dynamics. Put differently, the included regressors may not capture all the dynamics in y, which we need to model one way or another. Thus, for example, a preferable model includes lags of the dependent variable,

$$y_t = \beta_0 + \sum_{i=1}^{N_y} \alpha_i \, y_{t-i} + \sum_{j=1}^{N_x} \delta_j \, x_{t-j} + \varepsilon_t$$

This model, a **distributed lag regression model with lagged dependent variables,** is closely related to, but not exactly the same as, the rational distributed lag model introduced earlier. (Why?) You can think of it as arising by beginning with a univariate autoregressive model for y, and then introducing additional explanatory variables. If the lagged y's don't play a role, as assessed with the usual tests, we can always delete them, but we never want to eliminate from the outset the possibility that lagged dependent variables play a role. Lagged dependent variables absorb residual serial correlation and can *dramatically* enhance forecasting performance.

Alternatively, we can capture own-variable dynamics in distributed lag regression models by using a **distributed lag regression model with ARMA disturbances.** Recall that our ARMA(p,q) models are equivalent to regression on a constant with ARMA(p,q) disturbances,

$$y_t = \beta_0 + \varepsilon_t$$

$$\varepsilon_t = \frac{\Theta(L)}{\Phi(L)} v_t$$

$$v_t \sim WN(0, \sigma^2)$$

We want to begin with the univariate model as a baseline, and then generalize it to allow for multivariate interaction, resulting in models such as

$$y_t = \beta_0 + \sum_{i=1}^{N_x} \delta_i x_{t-i} + \varepsilon_t$$

$$\varepsilon_t = \frac{\Theta(L)}{\Phi(L)} v_t$$

$$v_t \sim WN(0, \sigma^2)$$

Regressions with ARMA disturbances make clear that regression (a statistical and econometric tool with a long tradition) and the ARMA model of time-series dynamics (a more recent innovation) are not at all competitors; rather, when used appropriately they can be highly complementary.

It turns out that the distributed lag regression model with autoregressive disturbances—a great workhorse in econometrics—is a special case of the more general model with lags of both y and x and white noise disturbances. To see this, let us take the simple example of an unconditional (1-step-ahead) regression forecasting model with AR(1) disturbances:

$$y_t = \beta_0 + \beta_1 x_{t-1} + \varepsilon_t$$

$$\varepsilon_t = \varphi \varepsilon_{t-1} + v_t$$

$$v_t \sim WN(0, \sigma^2)$$

In lag operator notation, we write the AR(1) regression disturbance as

$$(1 - \varphi L)\varepsilon_t = v_t$$

or

$$\varepsilon_t = \frac{1}{(1 - \varphi L)} v_t$$

Thus, we can rewrite the regression model as

$$y_t = \beta_0 + \beta_1 x_{t-1} + \frac{1}{(1 - \varphi L)} v_t$$

Now multiply both sides by $(1 - \varphi L)$ to get

$$(1 - \varphi L) y_t = (1 - \varphi) \beta_0 + \beta_1 (1 - \varphi L) x_{t-1} + v_t$$

or

$$y_t = \varphi y_{t-1} + (1 - \varphi)\beta_0 + \beta_1 x_{t-1} - \varphi\beta_1 x_{t-2} + v_t$$

Thus, a model with one lag of x on the right and AR(1) disturbances is equivalent to a model with y_{t-1}, x_{t-1}, and x_{t-2} on the right-hand side and white noise errors, *subject to the restriction* that the coefficient on the second lag of x_{t-2} is the negative of the product of the coefficients on y_{t-1} and x_{t-1}.

Thus, distributed lag regressions with lagged dependent variables are more general than distributed lag regressions with dynamic disturbances. **Transfer function models** are more general still, and include both as special cases, as can be seen in Table 10.1, which displays a variety of important forecasting models, all special cases of the transfer function model. The basic idea is to exploit the power and parsimony of rational distributed lags in modeling both own-variable and cross-variable dynamics. Imagine beginning with a univariate ARMA model,

$$y_t = \frac{C(L)}{D(L)} \varepsilon_t$$

which captures own-variable dynamics using a rational distributed lag. Now extend the model to capture cross-variable dynamics using a rational distributed lag of the other variable, which yields the general transfer function model,

$$y_t = \frac{A(L)}{B(L)} x_t + \frac{C(L)}{D(L)} \varepsilon_t$$

TABLE 10.1 The Transfer Function Model and Various Special Cases

Name	Model	Restrictions
Transfer Function	$y_t = \dfrac{A(L)}{B(L)} x_t + \dfrac{C(L)}{D(L)} \varepsilon_t$	None
Standard Distributed Lag	$y_t = A(L) x_t + \varepsilon_t$	$B(L) = C(L) = D(L) = 1$
Rational Distributed Lag	$y_t = \dfrac{A(L)}{B(L)} x_t + \varepsilon_t$	$C(L) = D(L) = 1$
Univariate AR	$y_t = \dfrac{1}{D(L)} \varepsilon_t$	$A(L) = 0,\ C(L) = 1$
Univariate MA	$y_t = C(L) \varepsilon_t$	$A(L) = 0,\ D(L) = 1$
Univariate ARMA	$y_t = \dfrac{C(L)}{D(L)} \varepsilon_t$	$A(L) = 0$
Distributed Lag with Lagged Dependent Variables	$B(L) y_t = A(L) x_t + \varepsilon_t,$ or $y_t = \dfrac{A(L)}{B(L)} x_t + \dfrac{1}{B(L)} \varepsilon_t$	$C(L) = 1,\ D(L) = B(L)$
Distributed Lag with ARMA Disturbances	$y_t = A(L) x_t + \dfrac{C(L)}{D(L)} \varepsilon_t$	$B(L) = 1$
Distributed Lag with AR Disturbances	$y_t = A(L) x_t + \dfrac{1}{D(L)} \varepsilon_t$	$B(L) = C(L) = 1$

Distributed lag regression with lagged dependent variables is a potentially restrictive special case, which emerges when $C(L) = 1$ and $B(L) = D(L)$. (Why?) Distributed lag regression with ARMA disturbances is also a special case, which emerges when $B(L) = 1$. (Why?)

In practice, the important thing is to *somehow* allow for own-variable dynamics in order to account for dynamics in y not explained by the right-hand-side variables. Whether we do so by including lagged dependent variables, or by allowing for ARMA disturbances, or by estimating general transfer function models can occasionally be important, but usually it is a comparatively minor issue.

6. VECTOR AUTOREGRESSIONS

A univariate autoregression involves one variable. In a univariate autoregression of order p, we regress a variable on p lags of itself. In contrast, a multivariate autoregression—that is, a vector autoregression, or VAR—involves N variables. In an N-variable **vector autoregression of order p**, or VAR(p), we estimate N different equations. In each equation, we regress the relevant left-hand-side variable on p lags of itself, *and p lags of every other variable.*[4] Thus the right-hand-side variables are the same in every equation—p lags of every variable.

The key point is that, in contrast to the univariate case, vector autoregressions allow for **cross-variable dynamics.** Each variable is related not only to its own past, but also to the past of all the other variables in the system. In a two-variable VAR(1), for example, we have two equations, one for each variable (y_1 and y_2). We write

$$y_{1,t} = \varphi_{11}\, y_{1,t-1} + \varphi_{12}\, y_{2,t-1} + \varepsilon_{1,t}$$

$$y_{2,t} = \varphi_{21}\, y_{1,t-1} + \varphi_{22}\, y_{2,t-1} + \varepsilon_{2,t}$$

Each variable depends on one lag of the other variable in addition to one lag of itself; that is one obvious source of multivariate interaction captured by the VAR that may be useful for forecasting. In addition, the disturbances may be correlated, so that when one equation is shocked, the other will typically be shocked as well, which is another type of multivariate interaction that univariate models miss. We summarize the disturbance variance-covariance structure as

$$\varepsilon_{1,t} \sim WN(0, \sigma_1^2)$$

$$\varepsilon_{2,t} \sim WN(0, \sigma_2^2)$$

$$\mathrm{cov}\,(\varepsilon_{1,t}, \varepsilon_{2,t}) = \sigma_{12}$$

The innovations *could* be uncorrelated, which occurs when $\sigma_{12} = 0$, but they need not be.

You might guess that VARs would be difficult to estimate. After all, they are fairly complicated models, with potentially many equations and many right-hand-side variables in each equation. In fact, precisely the opposite is true. VARs are very easy to estimate because we need run only N linear regressions. That is one reason why VARs are so popular—OLS estimation of autoregressive models is simple and stable, in contrast to the numerical esti-

---

4. Trends, seasonals, and other exogenous variables may also be included, as long as they are all included in every equation.

mation required for models with moving-average components.[5] Equation-by-equation OLS estimation also turns out to have very good statistical properties when each equation has the same regressors, as is the case in standard VARs. Otherwise, a more complicated estimation procedure called seemingly unrelated regression, which explicitly accounts for correlation across equation disturbances, would be required to obtain estimates with good statistical properties.[6]

When fitting VARs to data, we use the Schwarz and Akaike criteria, just as in the univariate case. The formulas differ, however, because we are now working with a multivariate system of equations rather than a single equation. To get an *AIC* or *SIC* value for a VAR system, we could add up the equation-by-equation *AIC*s or *SIC*s, but, unfortunately, doing so is appropriate only if the innovations are uncorrelated across equations, which is a very special and unusual situation. Instead, explicitly multivariate versions of *AIC* and *SIC*—and more advanced formulas—that account for cross-equation innovation correlation are required. It is beyond the scope of this book to derive and present those formulas because they involve unavoidable use of matrix algebra, but fortunately we don't need to. They are preprogrammed in many computer packages, and we interpret the *AIC* and *SIC* values computed for VARs of various orders in exactly the same way as in the univariate case: we select that order p such that *AIC* or *SIC* is minimized.

We construct VAR forecasts in a way that precisely parallels the univariate case. We can construct 1-step-ahead point forecasts immediately, because all variables on the right-hand side are lagged by one period. Armed with the 1-step-ahead forecasts, we can construct the 2-step-ahead forecasts, from which we can construct the 3-step-ahead forecasts, and so on in the usual way, following Wold's chain rule. We construct interval and density forecasts in ways that also parallel the univariate case. The multivariate nature of VARs makes the derivations more tedious, however, so we bypass them. As always, to construct practical forecasts we replace unknown parameters by estimates.

7. PREDICTIVE CAUSALITY

An important statistical notion of causality is intimately related to forecasting and naturally introduced in the context of VARs. It is based on two key principles: first, cause should occur before effect, and second, a causal series

---

5. Estimation of MA and ARMA models is stable enough in the univariate case but rapidly becomes unwieldy in multivariate situations. Hence multivariate ARMA models are used infrequently in practice, in spite of the potential they hold for providing parsimonious approximations to the Wold representation.

6. For an exposition of seemingly unrelated regression, see Pindyck and Rubinfeld (1991), chapter 11.

should contain information useful for forecasting that is not available in the other series (including the past history of the variable being forecast). In the unrestricted VARs that we have studied thus far, *everything* causes everything else, because lags of every variable appear on the right side of every equation. Cause precedes effect because the right-hand-side variables are lagged, and each variable is useful in forecasting every other variable.

We stress from the outset that the notion of **predictive causality** contains little, if any, information about causality in the philosophical sense. Rather, the statement "y_i causes y_j" is just shorthand for the more precise, but long-winded, statement, "y_i contains useful information for predicting y_j (in the linear least squares sense), over and above the past histories of the other variables in the system." To save space, we simply say that y_i causes y_j.

To understand what predictive causality means in the context of a VAR(p), consider the jth equation, which has y_j on the left and p lags of each of the N variables on the right. If y_i causes y_j, then at least one of the lags of y_i that appear on the right side of the y_j equation must have a nonzero coefficient.

It is also useful to consider the opposite situation, in which y_i does not cause y_j. In that case, all of the lags of that y_i that appear on the right side of the y_j equation must have 0 coefficients.[7] Statistical causality tests are based on this formulation of noncausality. We use an *F*-test to assess whether all coefficients on lags of y_j are jointly 0.

Note that we have defined noncausality in terms of 1-step-ahead prediction errors. In the bivariate VAR, this implies noncausality in terms of *h*-step-ahead prediction errors, for all *h*. In higher dimensional cases, things are trickier: 1-step-ahead noncausality does not necessarily imply noncausality at other horizons. For example, variable *i* may 1-step cause variable *j*, and variable *j* may 1-step cause variable *k*. Thus, variable *i* 2-step causes variable *k*, but does not 1-step cause variable *k*.

Causality tests are often used when building and assessing forecasting models because they can inform us about those parts of the workings of complicated multivariate models that are particularly relevant for forecasting. Just staring at the coefficients of an estimated VAR (and in complicated systems there are *many* coefficients) rarely yields insights into its workings. Thus we need tools that help us to see through to the practical forecasting properties of the model that concerns us. And we often have keen interest in the answers to questions such as "Does y_i contribute toward improving forecasts of y_j?" and "Does y_j contribute toward improving forecasts of y_i?" If the results violate intuition or theory, then we might scrutinize the model more closely. In a situation in which we cannot reject a certain noncausality hypothesis,

---

7. Note that in such a situation the error variance in forecasting y_j using lags of all variables in the system will be the same as the error variance in forecasting y_j using lags of all variables in the system *except* y_i.

and neither intuition nor theory makes us uncomfortable with it, we might want to *impose* it, by omitting certain lags of certain variables from certain equations.

Various types of causality hypotheses are sometimes entertained. In any equation (the *j*th, say), we have already discussed testing the simple non-causality hypothesis that:

1. No lags of variable *i* aid in 1-step-ahead prediction of variable *j*.

We can broaden the idea, however. Sometimes we test stronger noncausality hypotheses such as:

2. No lags of a *set* of other variables aid in 1-step-ahead prediction of variable *j*.
3. No lags of *any other variables* aid in 1-step-ahead prediction of variable *j*.

Hypotheses 1, 2, and 3 all amount to assertions that various coefficients are 0. Finally, sometimes we test noncausality hypotheses that involve more than one equation, such as:

4. No variable in a set *A* causes any variable in a set *B*, in which case we say that the variables in *A* are block noncausal for those in *B*.

This particular noncausality hypothesis corresponds to exclusion restrictions that hold simultaneously in a number of equations. Again, however, standard test procedures are applicable.

8. IMPULSE-RESPONSE FUNCTIONS AND VARIANCE DECOMPOSITIONS

The **impulse-response function** is another device that helps us to learn about the dynamic properties of vector autoregressions of interest to forecasters. We introduce it first in the *univariate* context, and then move to VARs. The question of interest is simple and direct: How does a unit innovation to a series affect it, now and in the future? To answer this question, we simply read off the coefficients in the moving average representation of the process.

We are used to normalizing the coefficient on ε_t to unity in moving-average representations, but we don't have to do so; more generally, we can write

$$y_t = b_0\,\varepsilon_t + b_1\,\varepsilon_{t-1} + b_2\,\varepsilon_{t-2} + \ldots$$

$$\varepsilon_t \sim WN(0, \sigma^2)$$

The additional generality introduces ambiguity, however, because we can always multiply and divide every ε_t by an arbitrary constant *m*, yielding an equivalent model but with different parameters and innovations,

$$y_t = (b_0 \ m) \left(\frac{1}{m} \varepsilon_t\right) + (b_1 \ m) \left(\frac{1}{m} \varepsilon_{t-1}\right) + (b_2 \ m) \left(\frac{1}{m} \varepsilon_{t-2}\right) + \ldots$$

$$\varepsilon_t \sim WN(0, \sigma^2)$$

or

$$y_t = b_0' \ \varepsilon_t' + b_1' \ \varepsilon_{t-1}' + b_2' \ \varepsilon_{t-2}' + \ldots$$

$$\varepsilon_t' \sim WN\left(0, \frac{\sigma^2}{m^2}\right)$$

where $b_i' = b_i m$ and $\varepsilon_t' = \varepsilon_t / m$.

To remove the ambiguity, we must set a value of m. Typically we set $m = 1$, which yields the standard form of the moving-average representation. For impulse-response analysis, however, a different normalization turns out to be particularly convenient; we choose $m = \sigma$, which yields

$$y_t = (b_0 \ \sigma) \left(\frac{1}{\sigma} \varepsilon_t\right) + (b_1 \ \sigma) \left(\frac{1}{\sigma} \varepsilon_{t-1}\right) + (b_2 \ \sigma) \left(\frac{1}{\sigma} \varepsilon_{t-2}\right) + \ldots$$

$$\varepsilon_t \sim WN(0, \sigma^2)$$

or

$$y_t = b_0' \ \varepsilon_t' + b_1' \ \varepsilon_{t-1}' + b_2' \ \varepsilon_{t-2}' + \ldots$$

$$\varepsilon_t' \sim WN(0, 1)$$

where $b_i' = b_i \sigma$ and $\varepsilon_t' = \varepsilon_t / \sigma$. Taking $m = \sigma$ converts shocks to "standard deviation units," because a unit shock to ε_t' corresponds to a one-standard-deviation shock to ε_t.

To make matters concrete, consider the univariate AR(1) process,

$$y_t = \varphi y_{t-1} + \varepsilon_t$$

$$\varepsilon_t \sim WN(0, \sigma^2)$$

The standard moving-average form is

$$y_t = \varepsilon_t + \varphi \varepsilon_{t-1} + \varphi^2 \varepsilon_{t-2} + \ldots$$

$$\varepsilon_t \sim WN(0, \sigma^2)$$

and the equivalent representation in standard deviation units is

$$y_t = b_0 \ \varepsilon_t' + b_1 \ \varepsilon_{t-1}' + b_2 \ \varepsilon_{t-2}' + \ldots$$

$$\varepsilon_t' \sim WN(0, 1)$$

where $b_i = \varphi^i \sigma$ and $\varepsilon_i' = \varepsilon_i / \sigma$. The impulse-response function is $\{\, b_0, b_1, \ldots \,\}$. The parameter b_0 is the contemporaneous effect of a unit shock to ε_i', or, equivalently, a one-standard-deviation shock to ε_i; as must be the case, then, $b_0 = \sigma$. Note well that b_0 gives the effect of the shock at time t, when it hits. The parameter b_1, which multiplies ε_{t-1}', gives the effect of the shock one period later, and so on. The full set of impulse-response coefficients, $\{b_0, b_1, \ldots\}$, tracks the complete dynamic response of y to the shock.

Now we consider the multivariate case. The idea is the same, but there are more shocks to track. The key question is, "How does a unit shock to ε_i affect y_j, now and in the future, for all the various combinations of i and j?" Consider, for example, the bivariate VAR(1),

$$y_{1t} = \varphi_{11}\, y_{1,t-1} + \varphi_{12}\, y_{2,t-1} + \varepsilon_{1t}$$

$$y_{2t} = \varphi_{21}\, y_{1,t-1} + \varphi_{22}\, y_{2,t-1} + \varepsilon_{2t}$$

$$\varepsilon_{1,t} \sim WN(0, \sigma_1^2)$$

$$\varepsilon_{2,t} \sim WN(0, \sigma_2^2)$$

$$\mathrm{cov}\,(\varepsilon_1, \varepsilon_2) = \sigma_{12}$$

The standard moving-average representation, obtained by back substitution, is

$$y_{1t} = \varepsilon_{1t} + \varphi_{11}\, \varepsilon_{1,t-1} + \varphi_{12}\, \varepsilon_{2,t-1} + \cdots$$

$$y_{2t} = \varepsilon_{2t} + \varphi_{21}\, \varepsilon_{1,t-1} + \varphi_{22}\, \varepsilon_{2,t-1} + \cdots$$

$$\varepsilon_{1,t} \sim WN(0, \sigma_1^2)$$

$$\varepsilon_{2,t} \sim WN(0, \sigma_2^2)$$

$$\mathrm{cov}\,(\varepsilon_1, \varepsilon_2) = \sigma_{12}$$

Just as in the univariate case, it proves fruitful to adopt a different normalization of the moving-average representation for impulse-response analysis. The multivariate analog of our univariate normalization by σ is called normalization by the Cholesky factor.[8] The resulting VAR moving-average representation has a number of useful properties that parallel the univariate case precisely. First, the innovations of the transformed system are in standard deviation units. Second, although the current innovations in the standard representation have unit coefficients, the current innovations in the normalized

---

8. For detailed discussion and derivation of this advanced topic, see Hamilton (1994).

representation have nonunit coefficients. In fact, the first equation has only one current innovation, $\varepsilon_{1,t}$. (The other has a 0 coefficient.) The second equation has both current innovations. Thus, the ordering of the variables can matter.[9]

If y_1 is ordered first, the normalized representation is

$$y_{1,t} = b_{11}^0 \, \varepsilon_{1,t} + b_{11}^1 \, \varepsilon_{1,t-1} + b_{12}^1 \, \varepsilon_{2,t-1} + \ldots$$

$$y_{2,t} = b_{21}^0 \, \varepsilon_{1,t} + b_{22}^0 \, \varepsilon_{2,t} + b_{21}^1 \, \varepsilon_{1,t-1} + b_{22}^1 \, \varepsilon_{2,t-1} + \ldots$$

$$\varepsilon_{1,t} \sim WN(0, 1)$$

$$\varepsilon_{2,t} \sim WN(0, 1)$$

$$\mathrm{cov} \, (\varepsilon_1, \varepsilon_2) = 0$$

Alternatively, if y_2 is ordered first, the normalized representation is

$$y_{2,t} = b_{22}^0 \, \varepsilon_{2,t} + b_{21}^1 \, \varepsilon_{1,t-1} + b_{22}^1 \, \varepsilon_{2,t-1} + \ldots$$

$$y_{1,t} = b_{11}^0 \, \varepsilon_{1,t} + b_{12}^0 \, \varepsilon_{2,t} + b_{11}^1 \, \varepsilon_{1,t-1} + b_{12}^1 \, \varepsilon_{2,t-1} + \ldots$$

$$\varepsilon_{1,t} \sim WN(0, 1)$$

$$\varepsilon_{2,t} \sim WN(0, 1)$$

$$\mathrm{cov} \, (\varepsilon_1, \varepsilon_2) = 0$$

Finally, the normalization adopted yields a 0 covariance between the disturbances of the transformed system. This is crucial because it lets us perform the experiment of interest— shocking one variable in isolation of the others, which we can do if the innovations are uncorrelated but cannot do if they are correlated, as in the original representation.

After normalizing the system, for a given ordering, say y_1, first we compute four sets of impulse-response functions for the bivariate model: response of y_1 to a unit normalized innovation to y_1, $\{ b_{11}^0, b_{11}^1, b_{11}^2, \ldots\}$, response of y_1 to a unit normalized innovation to y_2, $\{b_{12}^1, b_{12}^2, \ldots\}$, response of y_2 to a unit normalized innovation to y_2, $\{ b_{22}^0, b_{22}^1, b_{22}^2, \ldots\}$, and response of y_2 to a unit normalized innovation to y_1, $\{ b_{21}^0, b_{21}^1, b_{21}^2, \ldots\}$. Typically, we examine the set of impulse-response functions graphically. Often it turns out that impulse-

---

9. In higher-dimensional VAR's, the equation that is first in the ordering has only one current innovation, $\varepsilon_{1,t}$. The equation that is second has only current innovations $\varepsilon_{1,t}$ and $\varepsilon_{2,t}$, and the equation that is third has only current innovations $\varepsilon_{1,t}, \varepsilon_{2,t}, \varepsilon_{3,t}$, and so on.

response functions are not sensitive to ordering, but the only way to be sure is to check.[10]

In practical applications of impulse-response analysis, we simply replace unknown parameters by estimates, which immediately yields point estimates of the impulse-response functions. Getting confidence intervals for impulse-response functions is trickier, however, and adequate procedures are still under development.

Another way of characterizing the dynamics associated with VARs, closely related to impulse-response functions, is the **variance decomposition.** Variance decompositions have an immediate link to forecasting—they answer the question, "How much of the h-step-ahead forecast error variance of variable i is explained by innovations to variable j, for $h = 1, 2, \ldots$?" As with impulse-response functions, we typically make a separate graph for every (i, j) pair. Impulse-response functions and the variance decompositions present the same information (although they do so in different ways). For that reason it is not strictly necessary to present both, and impulse-response analysis has gained greater popularity. Hence, we offer only this brief discussion of variance decomposition. In the application to housing starts and completions that follows, however, we examine both impulse-response functions and variance decompositions. The two are highly complementary, as with information criteria and correlograms for model selection, and the variance decompositions have a nice forecasting motivation.

9. APPLICATION: HOUSING STARTS AND COMPLETIONS

We estimate a bivariate VAR for U.S. seasonally adjusted housing starts and completions, two widely watched business cycle indicators, 1968.01–1996.06. We use the VAR to produce point extrapolation forecasts. We show housing starts and completions in Figure 10.2. Both are highly cyclical, increasing during business-cycle expansions and decreasing during contractions. Moreover, completions tend to lag behind starts, which makes sense because a house takes time to complete.

We split the data into an estimation sample, 1968.01–1991.12, and a hold-out sample, 1992.01–1996.06 for forecasting. We therefore perform all model specification analysis and estimation, to which we now turn, on the 1968.01–1991.12 data. We show the housing starts correlogram in Table 10.2 and Figure 10.3. The sample autocorrelation function decays slowly, whereas the sample partial autocorrelation function appears to cut off at displacement 2. The patterns in the sample autocorrelations and partial autocorrela-

---

10. Note well that the issues of normalization and ordering affect only impulse-response analysis; for forecasting we need only the unnormalized model.

FIGURE 10.2   U.S. Housing Starts and Completions, 1968.01–1996.06

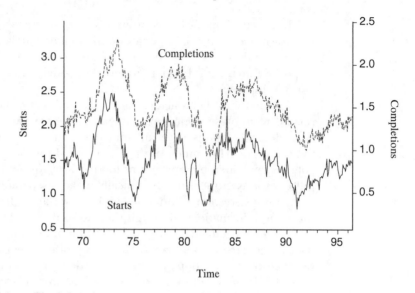

Time

Note: The left scale represents starts and the right scale represents completions.

tions are highly statistically significant, as evidenced by both the Bartlett standard errors and the Ljung-Box Q-statistics. The housing completions correlogram, shown in Table 10.3 and Figure 10.4, behaves similarly.

We have not yet introduced the **cross-correlation function.** There has been no need because it isn't relevant for univariate modeling. It provides important information, however, in the multivariate environments that now concern us. Recall that the autocorrelation function is the correlation between a variable and lags of itself. The cross-correlation function is a natural multivariate analog; it is simply the correlation between a variable and lags of *another* variable. We estimate those correlations using the usual estimator and graph them as a function of displacement along with the Bartlett two-standard-error bands, which apply just as in the univariate case.

The cross-correlation function (Figure 10.5) for housing starts and completions is very revealing. Starts and completions are highly correlated at all displacements, and a clear pattern emerges as well: Although the contemporaneous correlation is high (0.78), completions are maximally correlated with starts lagged by roughly 6 to 12 months (around 0.90). Again, this makes good sense in light of the time it takes to build a house.

Now we proceed to model starts and completions. We need to select the order, p, of our VAR(p); we use *SIC* and *AIC*. We examine VARs of order 1 through 36, and we graph *SIC* and *AIC* as functions of order in Figure 10.6. *SIC* achieves a distinct minimum at $p = 4$. *AIC*, on the other hand, is quite flat

TABLE 10.2   Housing Starts Correlogram

Sample: 1968:01 1991:12
Included observations: 288

	Acorr.	P. Acorr.	Std. Error	Ljung-Box	p-value
1	0.937	0.937	0.059	255.24	0.000
2	0.907	0.244	0.059	495.53	0.000
3	0.877	0.054	0.059	720.95	0.000
4	0.838	-0.077	0.059	927.39	0.000
5	0.795	-0.096	0.059	1113.7	0.000
6	0.751	-0.058	0.059	1280.9	0.000
7	0.704	-0.067	0.059	1428.2	0.000
8	0.650	-0.098	0.059	1554.4	0.000
9	0.604	0.004	0.059	1663.8	0.000
10	0.544	-0.129	0.059	1752.6	0.000
11	0.496	0.029	0.059	1826.7	0.000
12	0.446	-0.008	0.059	1886.8	0.000
13	0.405	0.076	0.059	1936.8	0.000
14	0.346	-0.144	0.059	1973.3	0.000
15	0.292	-0.079	0.059	1999.4	0.000
16	0.233	-0.111	0.059	2016.1	0.000
17	0.175	-0.050	0.059	2025.6	0.000
18	0.122	-0.018	0.059	2030.2	0.000
19	0.070	0.002	0.059	2031.7	0.000
20	0.019	-0.025	0.059	2031.8	0.000
21	-0.034	-0.032	0.059	2032.2	0.000
22	-0.074	0.036	0.059	2033.9	0.000
23	-0.123	-0.028	0.059	2038.7	0.000
24	-0.167	-0.048	0.059	2047.4	0.000

as a function of p, but continues to wander down slightly, and fails to achieve a minimum even by $p = 36$. The parsimony principle suggests adopting the VAR(4).

First consider the starts equation (Table 10.4), residual plot (Figure 10.7), and residual correlogram (Table 10.5 and Figure 10.8). The explanatory power of the model is good, as judged by the R^2 as well as the plots of actual and fitted values, and the residuals appear white, as judged by the residual sample autocorrelations, partial autocorrelations, and Ljung-Box statistics. Note as well that no lag of completions has a significant effect on starts, which makes sense—we obviously expect starts to cause completions, but not conversely. The completions equation (Table 10.6), residual plot (Figure 10.9), and residual correlogram (Table 10.7 and Figure 10.10) ap-

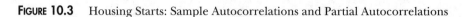

FIGURE 10.3   Housing Starts: Sample Autocorrelations and Partial Autocorrelations

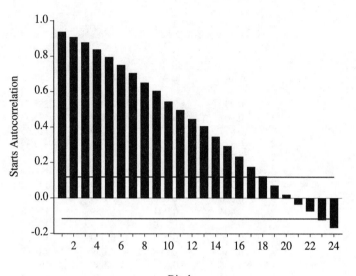

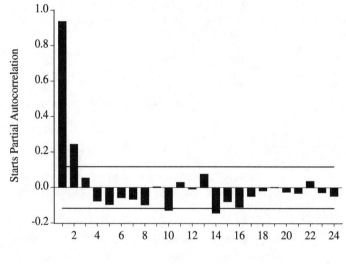

TABLE 10.3   Housing Completions Correlogram

Sample: 1968:01 1991:12
Included observations: 288

	Acorr.	P. Acorr.	Std. Error	Ljung-Box	p-value
1	0.939	0.939	0.059	256.61	0.000
2	0.920	0.328	0.059	504.05	0.000
3	0.896	0.066	0.059	739.19	0.000
4	0.874	0.023	0.059	963.73	0.000
5	0.834	-0.165	0.059	1168.9	0.000
6	0.802	-0.067	0.059	1359.2	0.000
7	0.761	-0.100	0.059	1531.2	0.000
8	0.721	-0.070	0.059	1686.1	0.000
9	0.677	-0.055	0.059	1823.2	0.000
10	0.633	-0.047	0.059	1943.7	0.000
11	0.583	-0.080	0.059	2046.3	0.000
12	0.533	-0.073	0.059	2132.2	0.000
13	0.483	-0.038	0.059	2203.2	0.000
14	0.434	-0.020	0.059	2260.6	0.000
15	0.390	0.041	0.059	2307.0	0.000
16	0.337	-0.057	0.059	2341.9	0.000
17	0.290	-0.008	0.059	2367.9	0.000
18	0.234	-0.109	0.059	2384.8	0.000
19	0.181	-0.082	0.059	2395.0	0.000
20	0.128	-0.047	0.059	2400.1	0.000
21	0.068	-0.133	0.059	2401.6	0.000
22	0.020	0.037	0.059	2401.7	0.000
23	-0.038	-0.092	0.059	2402.2	0.000
24	-0.087	-0.003	0.059	2404.6	0.000

pear similarly good. Lagged starts, moreover, most definitely have a significant effect on completions.

Table 10.8 shows the results of formal causality tests. The hypothesis that starts don't cause completions is simply that the coefficients on the four lags of starts in the completions equation are all 0. The F-statistic is overwhelmingly significant, which is not surprising in light of the previously noticed highly significant t-statistics. Thus we reject noncausality from starts to completions at any reasonable level. Perhaps more surprising is the fact that we also reject noncausality from completions to starts at roughly the 5% level. Thus the causality appears bidirectional, in which case we say there is **feedback.**

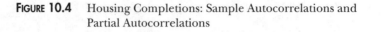

FIGURE 10.4   Housing Completions: Sample Autocorrelations and
Partial Autocorrelations

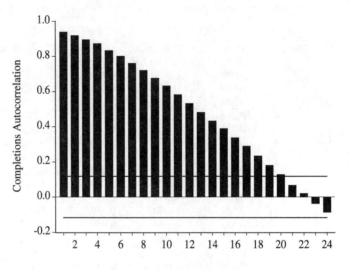

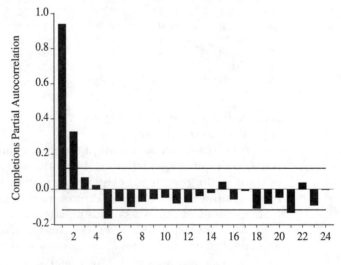

FIGURE 10.5 Housing Starts and Completions: Sample Cross Correlations

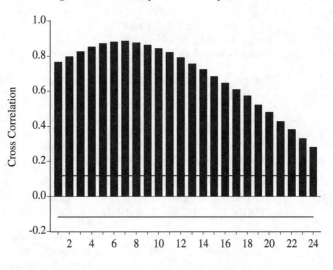

Note: We graph the sample correlation between completions at time t and starts at time $t - i$, $i = 1, 2, \ldots, 24$.

FIGURE 10.6 VAR Order Selection with *AIC* and *SIC*

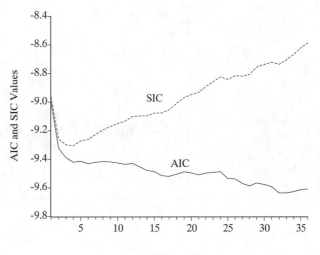

TABLE 10.4   VAR Housing Starts Equations

LS // Dependent Variable is STARTS
Sample(adjusted): 1968:05 1991:12
Included observations: 284 after adjusting endpoints

Variable	Coefficient	Std. Error	t-Statistic	Prob.
C	0.146871	0.044235	3.320264	0.0010
STARTS(-1)	0.659939	0.061242	10.77587	0.0000
STARTS(-2)	0.229632	0.072724	3.157587	0.0018
STARTS(-3)	0.142859	0.072655	1.966281	0.0503
STARTS(-4)	0.007806	0.066032	0.118217	0.9060
COMPS(-1)	0.031611	0.102712	0.307759	0.7585
COMPS(-2)	-0.120781	0.103847	-1.163069	0.2458
COMPS(-3)	-0.020601	0.100946	-0.204078	0.8384
COMPS(-4)	-0.027404	0.094569	-0.289779	0.7722

R-squared	0.895566	Mean dependent var	1.574771
Adjusted R-squared	0.892528	S.D. dependent var	0.382362
S.E. of regression	0.125350	Akaike info criterion	-4.122118
Sum squared resid	4.320952	Schwarz criterion	-4.006482
Log likelihood	191.3622	F-statistic	294.7796
Durbin-Watson stat	1.991908	Prob(F-statistic)	0.000000

FIGURE 10.7   VAR Housing Starts Equation: Residual Plot

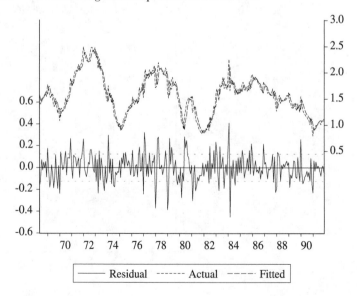

TABLE 10.5   VAR Housing Starts Equation: Residual Correlogram

Sample: 1968:01 1991:12
Included observations: 284

	Acorr.	P. Acorr.	Std. Error	Ljung-Box	p-value
1	0.001	0.001	0.059	0.0004	0.985
2	0.003	0.003	0.059	0.0029	0.999
3	0.006	0.006	0.059	0.0119	1.000
4	0.023	0.023	0.059	0.1650	0.997
5	-0.013	-0.013	0.059	0.2108	0.999
6	0.022	0.021	0.059	0.3463	0.999
7	0.038	0.038	0.059	0.7646	0.998
8	-0.048	-0.048	0.059	1.4362	0.994
9	0.056	0.056	0.059	2.3528	0.985
10	-0.114	-0.116	0.059	6.1868	0.799
11	-0.038	-0.038	0.059	6.6096	0.830
12	-0.030	-0.028	0.059	6.8763	0.866
13	0.192	0.193	0.059	17.947	0.160
14	0.014	0.021	0.059	18.010	0.206
15	0.063	0.067	0.059	19.199	0.205
16	-0.006	-0.015	0.059	19.208	0.258
17	-0.039	-0.035	0.059	19.664	0.292
18	-0.029	-0.043	0.059	19.927	0.337
19	-0.010	-0.009	0.059	19.959	0.397
20	0.010	-0.014	0.059	19.993	0.458
21	-0.057	-0.047	0.059	21.003	0.459
22	0.045	0.018	0.059	21.644	0.481
23	-0.038	0.011	0.059	22.088	0.515
24	-0.149	-0.141	0.059	29.064	0.218

In order to get a feel for the dynamics of the estimated VAR before producing forecasts, we compute impulse-response functions and variance decompositions. We present results for starts first in the ordering, so that a current innovation to starts affects only current starts, but the results are robust
to reversal of the ordering.

In Figure 10.11, we display the impulse-response functions. First we consider the own-variable impulse responses, that is, the effects of a starts innovation on subsequent starts or a completions innovation on subsequent completions; the effects are similar. In each case, the impulse response is large
and decays in a slow, approximately monotonic fashion. In contrast, the
cross-variable impulse responses are very different. An innovation to starts
produces no movement in completions at first, but the effect gradually builds
and becomes large, peaking at about 14 months. (It takes time to build
houses.) An innovation to completions, however, produces little movement
in starts at any time.

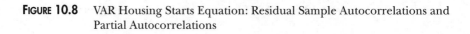

FIGURE 10.8   VAR Housing Starts Equation: Residual Sample Autocorrelations and
Partial Autocorrelations

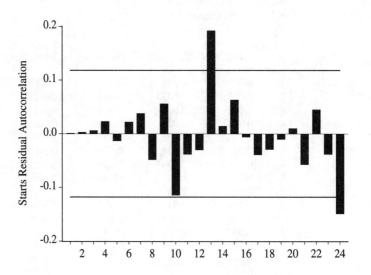

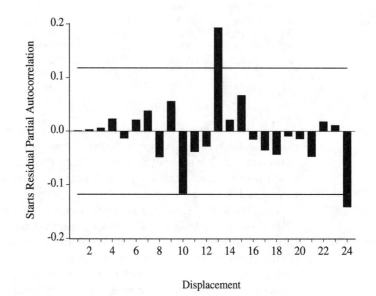

TABLE 10.6   VAR Housing Completions Equation

LS // Dependent Variable is COMPS
Sample(adjusted): 1968:05 1991:12
Included observations: 284 after adjusting endpoints

Variable	Coefficient	Std. Error	t-Statistic	Prob.
C	0.045347	0.025794	1.758045	0.0799
STARTS(-1)	0.074724	0.035711	2.092461	0.0373
STARTS(-2)	0.040047	0.042406	0.944377	0.3458
STARTS(-3)	0.047145	0.042366	1.112805	0.2668
STARTS(-4)	0.082331	0.038504	2.138238	0.0334
COMPS(-1)	0.236774	0.059893	3.953313	0.0001
COMPS(-2)	0.206172	0.060554	3.404742	0.0008
COMPS(-3)	0.120998	0.058863	2.055593	0.0408
COMPS(-4)	0.156729	0.055144	2.842160	0.0048

R-squared	0.936835	Mean dependent var	1.547958
Adjusted R-squared	0.934998	S.D. dependent var	0.286689
S.E. of regression	0.073093	Akaike info criterion	-5.200872
Sum squared resid	1.469205	Schwarz criterion	-5.085236
Log likelihood	344.5453	F-statistic	509.8375
Durbin-Watson stat	2.013370	Prob(F-statistic)	0.000000

FIGURE 10.9   VAR Housing Completions Equation: Residual Plot

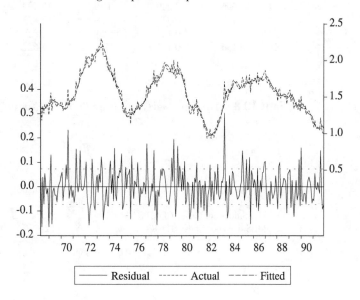

TABLE 10.7   VAR Housing Completions Equation: Residual Correlogram

Sample: 1968:01 1991:12
Included observations: 284

	Acorr.	P. Acorr.	Std. Error	Ljung-Box	p-value
1	-0.009	-0.009	0.059	0.0238	0.877
2	-0.035	-0.035	0.059	0.3744	0.829
3	-0.037	-0.037	0.059	0.7640	0.858
4	-0.088	-0.090	0.059	3.0059	0.557
5	-0.105	-0.111	0.059	6.1873	0.288
6	0.012	0.000	0.059	6.2291	0.398
7	-0.024	-0.041	0.059	6.4047	0.493
8	0.041	0.024	0.059	6.9026	0.547
9	0.048	0.029	0.059	7.5927	0.576
10	0.045	0.037	0.059	8.1918	0.610
11	-0.009	-0.005	0.059	8.2160	0.694
12	-0.050	-0.046	0.059	8.9767	0.705
13	-0.038	-0.024	0.059	9.4057	0.742
14	-0.055	-0.049	0.059	10.318	0.739
15	0.027	0.028	0.059	10.545	0.784
16	-0.005	-0.020	0.059	10.553	0.836
17	0.096	0.082	0.059	13.369	0.711
18	0.011	-0.002	0.059	13.405	0.767
19	0.041	0.040	0.059	13.929	0.788
20	0.046	0.061	0.059	14.569	0.801
21	-0.096	-0.079	0.059	17.402	0.686
22	0.039	0.077	0.059	17.875	0.713
23	-0.113	-0.114	0.059	21.824	0.531
24	-0.136	-0.125	0.059	27.622	0.276

TABLE 10.8   Housing Starts and Completions: Causality Tests

Sample: 1968:01 1991:12
Lags: 4
Obs: 284

Null Hypothesis:	F-Statistic	Probability
STARTS does not Cause COMPS	26.2658	0.00000
COMPS does not Cause STARTS	2.23876	0.06511

FIGURE 10.10 VAR Housing Completions Equation: Residual Sample
Autocorrelations and Partial Autocorrelations

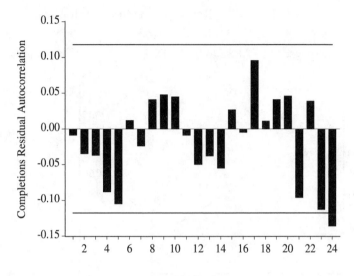

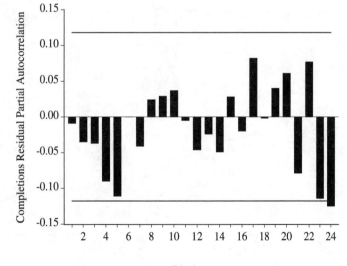

FIGURE 10.11   Housing Starts and Completions: VAR Impulse-Response Functions

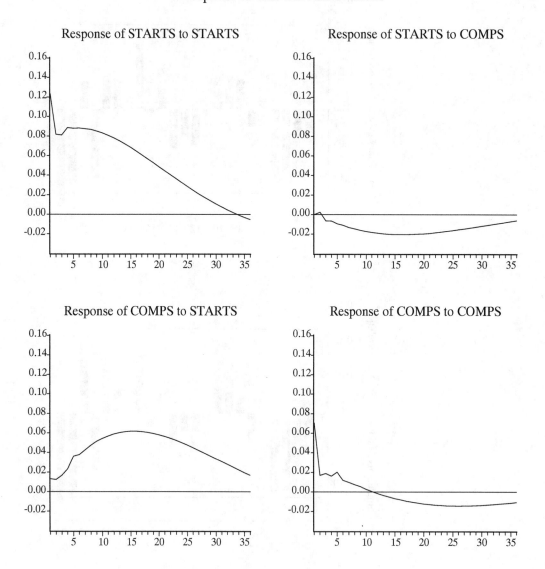

Response to One S.D. Innovations

Figure 10.12 shows the variance decompositions. The fraction of the error variance in forecasting starts due to innovations in starts is close to 100 percent at all horizons. In contrast, the fraction of the error variance in forecasting completions due to innovations in starts is near 0 at short horizons, but it rises steadily and is near 100 percent at long horizons, again reflecting time-to-build effects.

Finally, we construct forecasts for the out-of-sample period, 1992.01–1996.06. The starts forecast appears in Figure 10.13. Starts begin their recovery before 1992.01, and the VAR projects continuation of the recovery. The VAR forecast captures the general pattern quite well, but it forecasts quicker mean reversion than actually occurs, as is clear when comparing the forecast and realization in Figure 10.14. The figure also makes clear that the recovery of housing starts from the recession of 1990 was slower than the previous recoveries in the sample, which naturally makes for difficult forecasting. The

FIGURE 10.12   Housing Starts and Completions: VAR Variance Decompositions

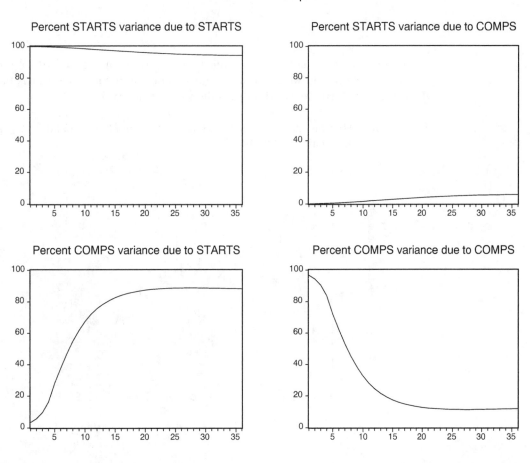

FIGURE **10.13**   Housing Starts: History, 1968.01–1991.12, and Forecast,
1992.01–1996.06

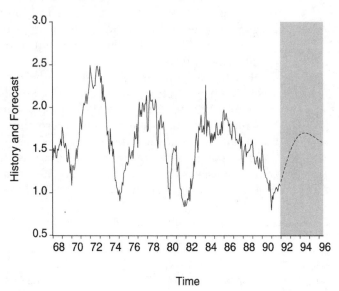

Time

completions forecast suffers the same fate, as shown in Figures 10.15 and
10.16. Interestingly, however, completions had not yet turned by 1991.12, but
the forecast nevertheless correctly predicts the turning point.

FIGURE **10.14**   Housing Starts: History, 1968.01–1991.12, and Forecast and
Realization, 1992.01–1996.06

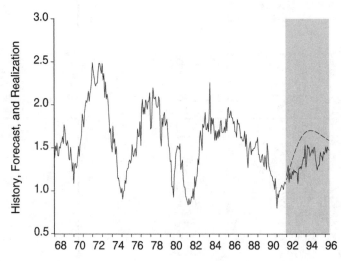

Time

FIGURE 10.15   Housing Completions: History, 1968.01–1991.12, and Forecast, 1992.01–1996.06

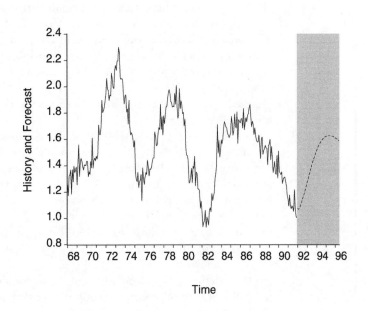

FIGURE 10.16   Housing Completions: History, 1968.01–1991.12, and Forecast and Realization, 1992.01–1996.06

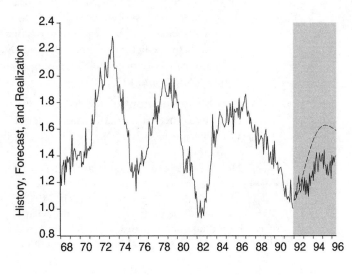

PROBLEMS AND COMPLEMENTS

1. (Econometrics, time series analysis, and forecasting) As recently as the early 1970s, time series analysis was mostly univariate and made little use of economic theory. Econometrics, in contrast, stressed the cross-variable dynamics associated with economic theory, with equations estimated using multiple regression. Econometrics, moreover, made use of simultaneous systems of such equations, requiring complicated estimation methods. Thus, the econometric and time series approaches to forecasting were very different.[11]

    As Klein (1981) notes, however, the complicated econometric system estimation methods had little payoff for practical forecasting and were therefore largely abandoned, whereas the rational distributed lag patterns associated with time series models led to large improvements in practical forecast accuracy.[12] Thus, in more recent times, the distinction between econometrics and time series analysis has largely vanished, with the union incorporating the best of both. In many respects the VAR is a modern embodiment of both traditions. VARs use economic considerations to determine which variables to include in the VAR and which (if any) restrictions should be imposed, allow for rich multivariate dynamics, typically require only simple estimation techniques, and are explicit forecasting models.

2. (Forecasting crop yields) Consider the following dilemma in agricultural crop yield forecasting:

    > The possibility of forecasting crop yields several years in advance would, of course, be of great value in the planning of agricultural production. However, the success of long-range crop forecasts is contingent not only on our knowledge of the weather factors determining yield, but also on our ability to predict the weather. Despite an abundant literature in this field, no firm basis for reliable long-range weather forecasts has yet been found. (Sanderson, 1953, p. 3)

    (a) How is the situation related to our concerns in this chapter, and specifically to the issue of conditional versus unconditional forecasting?
    (b) What variables other than weather might be useful for predicting crop yield?
    (c) How would you suggest that the forecaster proceed?

    ---

    11. Klein and Young (1980) and Klein (1983) provide good discussions of the traditional econometric simultaneous equations paradigm, as well as the link between structural simultaneous equations models and reduced-form time series models. Wallis (1995) provides a good summary of modern large-scale macroeconometric modeling.

    12. For an acerbic assessment circa the mid-1970s, see Jenkins (1979).

3. (Regression forecasting models with expectations, or anticipatory, data) A number of surveys address anticipated market conditions, investment intentions, buying plans, advance commitments, consumer sentiment, and so on.

   (a) Search the World Wide Web for such series and report your results. A good place to start is the Resources for Economists page mentioned in chapter 1.

   (b) How might you use the series you found in an unconditional regression forecasting model of GDP? Are the implicit forecast horizons known for all the anticipatory series you found? If not, how might you decide how to lag them in your regression forecasting model?

   (c) How would you test whether the anticipatory series you found provide incremental forecast enhancement relative to the own past history of GDP?

4. (Business cycle analysis and forecasting: expansions, contractions, turning points, and leading indicators[13]) The use of anticipatory data is linked to business cycle analysis in general, and leading indicators in particular. During the first half of the twentieth century, much research was devoted to obtaining an empirical characterization of the business cycle. The most prominent example of this work was Burns and Mitchell (1946), whose summary empirical definition was:

   > Business cycles are a type of fluctuation found in the aggregate economic activity of nations that organize their work mainly in business enterprises: a cycle consists of expansions occurring at about the same time in many economic activities, followed by similarly general recessions, contractions, and revivals which merge into the expansion phase of the next cycle. (p. 3)

   The comovement among individual economic variables was a key feature of Burns and Mitchell's definition of business cycles. Indeed, the comovement among series, taking into account possible leads and lags in timing, was the centerpiece of Burns and Mitchell's methodology. In their analysis, Burns and Mitchell considered the historical concordance of hundreds of series, including those measuring commodity output, income, prices, interest rates, banking transactions, and transportation services, and they classified series as leading, lagging, or coincident. One way to define a leading indicator is to say that a series x is a leading indicator for a series y if x causes y in the predictive sense. According to that definition, for example, our analysis of housing starts and completions indicates that starts are a leading indicator for completions.

   ---

   13. This complement draws in part upon Diebold and Rudebusch (1996).

Leading indicators have the potential to be used in forecasting equations in the same way as anticipatory variables. Inclusion of a leading indicator, appropriately lagged, can improve forecasts. Zellner and Hong (1989) and Zellner, Hong, and Min (1991), for example, make good use of that idea in their ARLI (autoregressive leading-indicator) models for forecasting aggregate output growth. In those models, Zellner and colleagues build forecasting models by regressing output on lagged output and lagged leading indicators; they also use shrinkage techniques to coax the forecasted growth rates toward the international average, which improves forecast performance.

Burns and Mitchell (1946) used the clusters of turning points in individual series to determine the monthly dates of the turning points in the overall business cycle, and to construct composite indexes of leading, coincident, and lagging indicators. Such indexes have been produced by the National Bureau of Economic Research (a think tank in Cambridge, Massachusetts), the Department of Commerce (a U.S. government agency in Washington, D.C.), and the Conference Board (a business membership organization based in New York). Composite indexes of leading indicators are often used to gauge likely future economic developments, but their usefulness is by no means uncontroversial and remains the subject of ongoing research. For example, leading indexes apparently cause aggregate output in analyses of ex post historical data (Auerbach, 1982), but they appear much less useful in real-time forecasting, which is what is relevant (Diebold and Rudebusch, 1991).

5. (Subjective information, Bayesian VARs, and the Minnesota prior) When building and using forecasting models, we frequently have hard-to-quantify subjective information, such as a reasonable range we expect for a parameter. We can incorporate such subjective information in a number of ways. One way is informal judgmental adjustment of estimates. Based on a variety of factors, for example, we might feel that an estimate of a certain parameter in a forecasting model is too high, so we might reduce it a bit.

Bayesian analysis allows us to incorporate subjective information in a rigorous and replicable way. We summarize subjective information about parameters with a probability distribution called the prior distribution, and as always we summarize the information in the data with the likelihood function. The centerpiece of Bayesian analysis is a mathematical formula called Bayes' rule, which tells us how to combine the information in the prior and the likelihood to form the posterior distribution of model parameters, which then feed their way into forecasts.

The Minnesota prior (introduced and popularized by Robert Litterman and Christopher Sims at the University of Minnesota) is commonly used for Bayesian estimation of VAR forecasting models, called Bayesian VARs, or BVARs. The Minnesota prior is centered on a parameterization called a random walk, in which the current value of each variable is equal to its lagged value plus a white noise error term. Thus the parameter estimates in BVARs are coaxed, but not forced, in the direction of univariate random walks. This sort of stochastic restriction has an immediate shrinkage interpretation, which suggests that it is likely to improve forecast accuracy.[14] This hunch is verified in Doan, Litterman, and Sims (1984), who study forecasting with standard and Bayesian VARs. Ingram and Whiteman (1994) replace the Minnesota prior with a prior derived from macroeconomic theory, and they obtain even better forecasting performance.

6. (Housing starts and completions, continued) Our VAR analysis of housing starts and completions, as always, involved many judgment calls. Using the starts and completions data, assess the adequacy of our models and forecasts. Among other things, you may want to consider the following questions:

   (a) Should we allow for a trend in the forecasting model?
   (b) How do the results change if, in light of the results of the causality tests, we exclude lags of completions from the starts equation, re-estimate by seemingly unrelated regression, and forecast?
   (c) Are the VAR forecasts of starts and completions more accurate than univariate forecasts?

7. (Nonlinear regression models I: **functional form** and Ramsey's test) The idea of using powers of a right-hand-side variable to pick up nonlinearity in a regression can also be used to test for linearity of functional form, following Ramsey (1969). If we were concerned that we had missed some important nonlinearity, an obvious strategy to capture it, based on the idea of a Taylor series expansion of a function, would be to include powers and cross products of the various x variables in the regression. Such a strategy would be wasteful of degrees of freedom, however, particularly if there were more than just one or two right-hand-side variables in the regression and/or if the nonlinearity were severe, so that fairly high powers and interactions would be necessary to capture it. In light of this, Ramsey suggests first fitting a linear regression and obtaining the fitted values, $\hat{y}_t$, $t = 1, \ldots, T$. Then, to test for nonlinearity, we run the regression again with powers of $\hat{y}_t$ included. There is no need to include the first power of $\hat{y}_t$, because that would be redundant with the included x variables. Instead we include powers $\hat{y}_t^2$, $\hat{y}_t^3$, $\ldots$, $\hat{y}_t^m$, where m is a maximum power determined in advance. Note that the powers of $\hat{y}_t$ are linear combinations of powers and cross products of the x variables. Significance of the

---

14. Effectively, the shrinkage allows us to recover a large number of degrees of freedom.

included set of powers of $\hat{y}_t$ can be checked using an F-test or an asymptotic likelihood ratio test.

8. (Nonlinear regression models II: **logarithmic regression models**) We have already seen the use of logarithms in our studies of trend and seasonality. In those setups, however, we had occasion to take logs of only the left-hand-side variable. In more general regression models, such as those that we are studying now, with variables other than trend or seasonals on the right-hand side, it is sometimes useful to take logs of *both* the left- and right-hand-side variables. Doing so allows us to pick up multiplicative nonlinearity. To see this, consider the regression model,

$$y_t = \beta_0 \, x_t^{\beta_1} \, e^{\varepsilon_t}$$

This model is clearly nonlinear due to the multiplicative interactions. Direct estimation of its parameters would require special techniques. Taking natural logs, however, yields the model

$$\ln y_t = \ln \beta_0 + \beta_1 \ln x_t + \varepsilon_t$$

This transformed model can be immediately estimated by ordinary least squares, by regressing ln y on an intercept and ln x. Such "log-log regressions" often capture nonlinearities relevant for forecasting, while maintaining the convenience of ordinary least squares.

9. (Nonlinear regression models III: neural networks) Neural networks amount to a particular nonlinear functional form associated with repeatedly running linear combinations of inputs through nonlinear "squashing" functions. The 0–1 squashing function is useful in classification, and the logistic function is useful for regression.

The neural net literature is full of biological jargon, which serves to obfuscate rather than clarify. We speak, for example, of a "single-output feedforward neural network with n inputs and 1 hidden layer with q neurons." But the idea is simple. If the output is y and the inputs are x's, we write

$$y_t = \Phi \left(\beta_0 + \sum_{i=1}^{q} \beta_i \, h_{it} \right)$$

where

$$h_{it} = \Psi \left(\gamma_{i0} + \sum_{j=1}^{n} \gamma_{ij} \, x_{jt} \right), \, i = 1, \ldots, q$$

are the "neurons" ("hidden units"), and the "activation functions" Ψ and Φ are arbitrary, except that Ψ (the squashing function) is generally restricted to be bounded. (Commonly, $\Phi(x) = x$.) Assembling it all, we write

$$y_t = \Phi\left[\beta_0 + \sum_{i=1}^{q} \beta_i \Psi\left(\gamma_{i0} + \sum_{j=1}^{n} \gamma_{ij} x_{jt}\right)\right] = f(x_t; \theta)$$

which makes clear that a neural net is just a particular nonlinear functional form for a regression model.

To allow for dynamics, we can allow for autoregressive effects in the hidden units. A dynamic ("recurrent") neural network is

$$y_t = \Phi\left(\beta_0 + \sum_{i=1}^{q} \beta_i h_{it}\right)$$

where

$$h_{it} = \Psi\left(\gamma_{i0} + \sum_{j=1}^{n} \gamma_{ij} x_{jt} + \sum_{r=1}^{q} \delta_{ir} h_{r,t-1}\right), \ i = 1, \ldots, q$$

Compactly,

$$y_t = \Phi\left[\beta_0 + \sum_{i=1}^{q} \beta_i \Psi\left(\gamma_{i0} + \sum_{j=1}^{n} \gamma_{ij} x_{jt} + \sum_{r=1}^{q} \delta_{ir} h_{r,t-1}\right)\right]$$

Recursive back substitution reveals that y is a nonlinear function of the history of the x's.

$$y_t = g(x^t; \theta)$$

where $x^t = (x_t, \ldots, x_1)$ and $x_t = (x_{1t}, \ldots, x_{nt})$.

The Matlab Neural Network Toolbox implements a variety of networks. The toolbox manual is itself a useful guide to the literature on the practical aspects of constructing and forecasting with neural nets. Kuan and Liu (1995) use a dynamic neural network to predict foreign exchange rates, and Faraway and Chatfield (1995) provide an insightful case study of the efficacy of neural networks in applied forecasting. Ripley (1996) provides a fine and statistically informed (in contrast to much of the neural net literature) survey of the use of neural nets in a variety of fields.

10. (**Spurious regression**) Consider two variables y and x, both of which are highly serially correlated, as are most series in business, finance, and economics. Suppose in addition that y and x are completely unrelated, but that we don't know they are unrelated, and we regress y on x using ordinary least squares.

   (a) If the usual regression diagnostics (e.g., R^2, t-statistics, F-statistic) were reliable, we would expect to see small values of all of them. Why?

   (b) In fact, the opposite occurs; we tend to see large R^2, t-, and F-statistics, and *a very low Durbin-Watson statistic*. Why the low Durbin-Watson? Why, given the low Durbin-Watson, might you *expect* misleading R^2, t-, and F-statistics?

   (c) This situation, in which highly persistent series that are in fact unrelated nevertheless appear highly related, is called *spurious regression*. Study of the phenomenon dates to the early twentieth century, and a key study by Granger and Newbold (1974) drove home the prevalence and potential severity of the problem. How might you insure yourself against the spurious regression problem? (*Hint:* Consider allowing for lagged dependent variables or dynamics in the regression disturbances, as we have advocated repeatedly.)

BIBLIOGRAPHICAL AND COMPUTATIONAL NOTES

Some software, such as Eviews, automatically accounts for parameter uncertainty when forming conditional regression forecast intervals by using variants of the techniques we introduced in section 2. Similar but advanced techniques are sometimes used to produce unconditional forecast intervals for dynamic models, such as autoregressions (see Lütkepohl, 1991), but bootstrap simulation techniques are becoming increasingly popular (Efron and Tibshirani, 1993).

Chatfield (1993) argues that innovation uncertainty and parameter estimation uncertainty are likely of minor importance compared to specification uncertainty. We rarely acknowledge specification uncertainty because we don't know how. Quantifying it is a major challenge for future research.

The idea that regression models with serially correlated disturbances are more restrictive than other sorts of transfer function models has a long history in econometrics and engineering and is highlighted in a memorably titled paper, "Serial Correlation as a Convenient Simplification, Not a Nuisance," by Hendry and Mizon (1978). Engineers have scolded econometricians for not using more general transfer function models, as, for example, in Jenkins (1979). But the fact is, as we have seen repeatedly, that generality for generality's sake in business and economic forecasting is not necessarily helpful and can be positively harmful. The shrinkage principle asserts that the imposition of restrictions—even false restrictions—can be helpful in forecasting.

Sims (1980) is an influential paper arguing the virtues of VARs. The idea of predictive causality and associated tests in VARs is due to Granger (1969) and Sims (1972), who build on earlier work by the mathematician Norbert Weiner. Lütkepohl (1991) is a good reference on VAR analysis and forecasting, and the RATS software is particularly strong in VARs, including Bayesian VARs.

Gershenfeld and Weigend (1993) provide a perspective on time series forecasting from the computer-science/engineering/nonlinear/neural-net perspective, and Swanson and White (1995) compare and contrast a variety of linear and nonlinear forecasting methods.

CONCEPTS FOR REVIEW

Conditional forecasting model

Cross-correlation function

Cross-variable dynamics

Distributed lag model

Distributed lag regression model
  with ARMA disturbances

Distributed lag regression model
  with lagged dependent variables

Feedback

Forecasting the right-hand-side
  variables problem

Functional form

Impulse-response function

Innovation uncertainty

Logarithmic regression models

Parameter uncertainty

Polynomial distributed lag

Predictive causality

Rational distributed lag

Scenario, or contingency, analysis

Specification uncertainty

Spurious regression

Transfer function model

Unconditional forecasting model

Variance decomposition

Vector autoregression of order p

REFERENCES AND ADDITIONAL READINGS

Auerbach, A. J. (1982), "The Index of Leading Indicators: 'Measurement Without Theory' Thirty-Five Years Later," *Review of Economics and Statistics*, 64, 589–595.

Burns, A. F., and Mitchell, W. C. (1946), *Measuring Business Cycles*. New York: National Bureau of Economic Research.

Chatfield, C. (1993), "Calculating Interval Forecasts," *Journal of Business and Economic Statistics*, 11, 121–135.

Diebold, F. X., and Rudebusch, G. D. (1991), "Forecasting Output with the Composite Leading Index: An Ex Ante Analysis," *Journal of the American Statistical Association*, 86, 603–610. Reprinted in Diebold and Rudebusch (1999).

Diebold, F. X., and Rudebusch, G. D. (1996), "Measuring Business Cycles: A Modern Perspective," *Review of Economics and Statistics*, 78, 67–77. Reprinted in Diebold and Rudebusch (1999).

Diebold, F. X., and Rudebusch, G. D. (1999), *Business Cycles: Durations, Dynamics, and Forecasting*. Princeton, N.J.: Princeton University Press.

Doan, T., Litterman, R., and Sims, C. (1984), "Forecasting and Conditional Prediction Using Realistic Prior Distributions," *Econometric Reviews*, 3, 1–144.

Efron, B., and Tibshirani, R. J. (1993), *An Introduction to the Bootstrap*. New York: Chapman and Hall.

Engle, R. F., and Granger, C. W. J. (1987), "Co-Integration and Error Correction: Representation, Estimation and Testing," *Econometrica*, 55, 251–276.

Engle, R. F., and Yoo, B. S. (1987), "Forecasting and Testing in Cointegrated Systems," *Journal of Econometrics*, 35, 143–159.

Faraway, J., and Chatfield, C. (1995), "Time Series Forecasting with Neural Networks: A Case Study," Research Report 95–06, Statistics Group, University of Bath, UK.

Gershenfeld, N. A., and Weigend, A. S. (1993), "The Future of Time Series," in A. S. Weigend and N. A. Gershenfeld (eds.), *Time Series Prediction: Forecasting the Future and Understanding the Past*, 1–70. Reading, Mass.: Addison-Wesley.

Granger, C. W. J. (1969), "Investigating Causal Relations by Econometric Models and Cross-Spectral Methods," *Econometrica*, 37, 424–438.

Granger, C. W. J., and Newbold, P. (1974), "Spurious Regressions in Econometrics," *Journal of Econometrics*, 2, 111–120.

Hamilton, J. D. (1989), "A New Approach to the Economic Analysis of Nonstationary Time Series and the Business Cycle," *Econometrica*, 57, 357–384.

Hamilton, J. D. (1994), *Time Series Analysis*. Princeton, N.J.: Princeton University Press.

Hendry, D. F., and Mizon, G. E. (1978), "Serial Correlation as a Convenient Simplification, Not a Nuisance: A Comment on a Study of the Demand for Money by the Bank of England," *Economic Journal,* 88, 549–563.

Ingram, B., and Whiteman, C. (1994), "Supplanting the 'Minnesota' Prior: Forecasting Macroeconomic Time Series Using Real Business Cycle Model Priors," *Journal of Monetary Economics,* 34, 497–510.

Jenkins, G. M. (1979), "Practical Experiences with Modelling and Forecasting Time Series," in O. D. Anderson (ed.), *Forecasting.* Amsterdam: North-Holland.

Johansen, S. (1995), *Likelihood Based Inference in Cointegrated Vector Autoregressive Models.* Oxford: Oxford University Press.

Klein, L. R. (1981), *Econometric Models as Guides for Decision Making.* New York: The Free Press.

Klein, L. R. (1983), *Lectures in Econometrics.* Amsterdam: North-Holland.

Klein, L. R., and Young, R. M. (1980), *An Introduction to Econometric Forecasting and Forecasting Models.* Lexington, Mass.: D.C. Heath and Company.

Kuan, C. M., and Liu, Y. (1995), "Forecasting Exchange Rates Using Feedforward and Recurrent Neural Networks," *Journal of Applied Econometrics,* 10, 347–364.

Lütkepohl, H. (1991), *Introduction to Multiple Time Series Analysis.* New York: Springer Verlag.

Pindyck, R. S., and Rubinfeld, D. L. (1991), *Econometric Models and Economic Forecasts,* third edition. New York: McGraw-Hill.

Ramsey, J. (1969), "Tests for Specification Errors in Classical Linear Least Squares Regression Analysis," *Journal of the Royal Statistical Society B,* 31, 350–371.

Ripley, B. D. (1996), *Pattern Recognition and Neural Networks.* Oxford: Oxford University Press.

Sanderson, F. H. (1953), *Methods of Crop Forecasting.* Cambridge, Mass.: Harvard University Press.

Sims, C. A. (1972), "Money, Income and Causality," *American Economic Review,* 62, 540–552.

Sims, C. A. (1980), "Macroeconomics and Reality," *Econometrica,* 48, 1–48.

Stock, J. H., and Watson, M. W. (1988), "Variable Trends in Economic Time Series," *Journal of Economic Perspectives,* 2, 147–174.

Swanson, N. R., and White, H. (1995), "A Model-Selection Approach to Assessing the Information in the Term Structure Using Linear-Models and Artificial Neural Networks," *Journal of Business and Economic Statistics,* 13, 265–275.

Wallis, K. F. (1995), "Large-Scale Macroeconometric Modeling," in M. H. Pesaran and M. R. Wickens (eds.), *Handbook of Applied Econometrics.* Oxford: Blackwell.

Zellner, A., and Hong, C. (1989), "Forecasting International Growth Rates Using Bayesian Shrinkage and Other Procedures," *Journal of Econometrics*, 40, 183–202.

Zellner, A., Hong, C., and Min, C.-K. (1991), "Forecasting Turning Points in International Output Growth Rates Using Bayesian Exponentially Weighted Autoregression, Time-Varying Parameter, and Pooling Techniques," *Journal of Econometrics*, 49, 275–304.

CHAPTER 11

EVALUATING AND COMBINING FORECASTS

As we have stressed repeatedly, good forecasts lead to good decisions. The importance of forecast evaluation and combination techniques follows immediately. Given a track record of forecasts, $y_{t+h,t}$, and corresponding realizations, y_{t+h}, we naturally want to monitor and improve forecast performance. In this chapter we show how to do so. First we discuss evaluation of a single forecast. Second, we discuss the **evaluation and comparison of forecast accuracy.** Third, we discuss whether and how a set of forecasts may be combined to produce a superior composite forecast.

1. EVALUATING A SINGLE FORECAST

Evaluating a single forecast amounts to checking whether it has the properties expected of an optimal forecast. Denote the covariance stationary time series of interest by y_t. The Wold representation is

$$y_t = \mu + \varepsilon_t + b_1 \varepsilon_{t-1} + b_2 \varepsilon_{t-2} + \ldots$$

$$\varepsilon_t \sim WN(0, \sigma^2)$$

Thus, the h-step-ahead linear least squares forecast is

$$y_{t+h,t} = \mu + b_h \varepsilon_t + b_{h+1} \varepsilon_{t-1} + \dots$$

and the corresponding h-step-ahead forecast error is

$$e_{t+h,t} = y_{t+h} - y_{t+h,t} = \varepsilon_{t+h} + b_1 \varepsilon_{t+h-1} + \dots + b_{h-1} \varepsilon_{t+1}$$

with variance

$$\sigma_h^2 = \sigma^2 \left(1 + \sum_{i=1}^{h-1} b_i^2 \right)$$

Four key properties of optimal forecasts, which we can easily check, follow immediately:

1. Optimal forecasts are unbiased.
2. Optimal forecasts have 1-step-ahead errors that are white noise.
3. Optimal forecasts have h-step-ahead errors that are at most $MA(h-1)$.
4. Optimal forecasts have h-step-ahead errors with variances that are non-decreasing in h and that converge to the unconditional variance of the process.

Testing Properties of Optimal Forecasts

(a) Optimal Forecasts Are Unbiased   If the forecast is unbiased, then the forecast error has a mean of 0. A variety of tests of the zero-mean hypothesis can be performed, depending on the assumptions we are willing to maintain. For example, if $e_{t+h,t}$ is Gaussian white noise (as might reasonably be the case for 1-step-ahead errors), then the standard t-test is the obvious choice. We would simply regress the forecast error series on a constant and use the reported t-statistic to test the hypothesis that the population mean is 0. If the errors are non-Gaussian but remain independent and identically distributed (iid), then the t-test is still applicable in large samples.

If the forecast errors are dependent, then more sophisticated procedures are required. Serial correlation in forecast errors can arise for many reasons. Multi-step-ahead forecast errors will be serially correlated, even if the forecasts are optimal, because of the forecast-period overlap associated with multi-step-ahead forecasts. More generally, serial correlation in forecast errors may indicate that the forecasts are suboptimal. The upshot is simply that when regressing forecast errors on an intercept, we need to be sure that any serial correlation in the disturbance is appropriately modeled. A reasonable starting point for a regression involving h-step-ahead forecast errors is $MA(h-1)$ disturbances, which we would expect if the forecast were optimal. The forecast may, of course, *not* be optimal, so we don't adopt $MA(h-1)$ disturbances uncritically; instead, we try a variety of models using *AIC* and *SIC* to guide selection in the usual way.

(b) Optimal Forecasts Have 1-Step-Ahead Errors That Are White Noise

Under various sets of maintained assumptions, we can use standard tests of the white noise hypothesis. For example, the sample autocorrelation and partial autocorrelation functions, together with Bartlett asymptotic standard errors, are often useful in that regard. Tests based on the first autocorrelation (e.g., the Durbin-Watson test), as well as more general tests, such as the Box-Pierce and Ljung-Box statistics, are useful as well. We implement all of these tests by regression on a constant term.

(c) Optimal Forecasts Have h-Step-Ahead Errors That Are at Most MA(h – 1)

The $MA(h-1)$ structure implies a cutoff in the forecast error's autocorrelation function beyond displacement $h-1$. This immediately suggests examining the statistical significance of the sample autocorrelations beyond displacement $h-1$ using the Bartlett standard errors. In addition, we can regress the errors on a constant, allowing for $MA(q)$ disturbances with $q > (h-1)$, and test whether the moving-average parameters beyond lag $h-1$ are 0.

(d) Optimal Forecasts Have h-Step-Ahead Errors with Variances That Are Nondecreasing in h

It is often useful to examine the sample h-step-ahead forecast error variances as a function of h, both to be sure they are nondecreasing in h and to see their *pattern*, which often conveys useful information.

Assessing Optimality with Respect to an Information Set

The key property of optimal forecast errors, from which all others follow (including those cataloged above), is that they should be unforecastable on the basis of information available at the time the forecast was made. This **unforecastability principle** is valid in great generality; it holds, for example, regardless of whether linear-projection optimality or conditional-mean optimality is of interest, regardless of whether the relevant loss function is quadratic, and regardless of whether the series being forecast is stationary.

Many of the tests of properties of optimal forecasts introduced above are based on the unforecastability principle. For example, 1-step-ahead errors had better be white noise because otherwise we could forecast the errors using information readily available when the forecast is made. Those tests, however, make incomplete use of the unforecastability principle, insofar as they assess only the *univariate* properties of the errors.

We can make a more complete assessment by broadening the information set and assessing optimality with respect to various sets of information, by estimating regressions of the form

$$e_{t+h,t} = \alpha_0 + \sum_{i=1}^{k-1} \alpha_i x_{it} + u_t$$

The hypothesis of interest is that all the α's are 0, which is a necessary condition for forecast optimality with respect to the information contained in the x's. The particular case of testing optimality with respect to $y_{t+h,t}$ is very important in practice. The relevant regression is

$$e_{t+h,t} = \alpha_0 + \alpha_1 y_{t+h,t} + u_t$$

and optimality corresponds to $(\alpha_0, \alpha_1) = (0, 0)$. Keep in mind that the disturbances may be serially correlated, especially if the forecast errors are multi-step-ahead, in which case they should be modeled accordingly.

If the above regression seems a little strange to you, consider what may seem like a more natural approach to testing optimality—regression of the realization on the forecast:

$$y_{t+h} = \beta_0 + \beta_1 y_{t+h,t} + u_t$$

This is called a "Mincer-Zarnowitz regression." If the forecast is optimal with respect to the information used to construct it, then we would expect $(\beta_0, \beta_1) = (0, 1)$, in which case

$$y_{t+h} = y_{t+h,t} + u_t$$

Note, however, that if we start with the regression

$$y_{t+h} = \beta_0 + \beta_1 y_{t+h,t} + u_t$$

and then subtract $y_{t+h,t}$ from each side, we obtain

$$e_{t+h,t} = \alpha_0 + \alpha_1 y_{t+h,t} + u_t$$

where $(\alpha_0, \alpha_1) = (0, 0)$ when $(\beta_0, \beta_1) = (0, 1)$. Thus, the two approaches are identical.

2. EVALUATING TWO OR MORE FORECASTS: COMPARING FORECAST ACCURACY

Measures of Forecast Accuracy

In practice, it is unlikely that we will ever stumble upon a fully optimal forecast; instead, situations often arise in which a number of forecasts (all of them suboptimal) are compared and possibly combined. Even for very good forecasts, the actual and forecasted values may be very different. To take an extreme example, note that the linear least squares forecast for a zero-mean white noise process is simply 0—the paths of forecasts and realizations will look very different, yet there does not exist a better linear forecast under quadratic loss. This highlights the inherent limits to forecastability, which depends on the process being forecast; some processes are inherently easy to forecast, whereas others are difficult to forecast. In other words, sometimes the information on which the forecaster conditions is very valuable, and sometimes it isn't.

The crucial object in measuring forecast accuracy is the loss function, $L(y_{t+h}, y_{t+h,t})$, often restricted to $L(e_{t+h,t})$, which charts the "loss," "cost," or "disutility" associated with various pairs of forecasts and realizations.[1] In addition to the shape of the loss function, the forecast horizon h is of crucial importance. Rankings of forecast accuracy may, of course, be very different across different loss functions and different horizons.

Let us discuss a few accuracy measures that are important and popular. Accuracy measures are usually defined on the forecast errors, $e_{t+h,t} = y_{t+h} - y_{t+h,t}$, or percent errors, $p_{t+h,t} = (y_{t+h} - y_{t+h,t})/y_{t+h}$. **Mean error,**

$$ME = \frac{1}{T} \sum_{t=1}^{T} e_{t+h,t}$$

measures **bias,** which is one component of accuracy. Other things being the same, we prefer a forecast with a small bias. **Error variance,**

$$EV = \frac{1}{T} \sum_{t=1}^{T} (e_{t+h,t} - ME)^2$$

measures dispersion of the forecast errors. Other things the same, we prefer a forecast whose errors have small variance. Although the mean error and

1. Because in many applications the loss function will be a direct function of the forecast error, $L(y_t, y_{t+h,t}) = L(e_{t+h,t})$, we write $L(e_{t+h,t})$ from this point on to economize on notation, recognizing, however, that certain loss functions (such as direction-of-change) don't collapse to the $L(e_{t+h,t})$ form.

the error variance are components of accuracy, neither provides an overall accuracy measure.

The most common overall accuracy measures, by far, are **mean squared error,**

$$MSE = \frac{1}{T} \sum_{t=1}^{T} e_{t+h,t}^2$$

and mean squared percent error,

$$MSPE = \frac{1}{T} \sum_{t=1}^{T} p_{t+h,t}^2$$

Often the square roots of these measures are used to preserve units, yielding the **root mean squared error,**

$$RMSE = \sqrt{\frac{1}{T} \sum_{t=1}^{T} e_{t+h,t}^2}$$

and the root mean squared percent error,

$$RMSPE = \sqrt{\frac{1}{T} \sum_{t=1}^{T} p_{t+h,t}^2}$$

To understand the meaning of "preserving units," and why it is sometimes helpful to do so, suppose that the forecast errors are measured in dollars. Then the mean squared error, which is built up from *squared* errors, is measured in dollars *squared.* Taking square roots—that is, moving from *MSE* to *RMSE*—brings the units back to dollars.

Somewhat less popular but nevertheless common accuracy measures are the **mean absolute error,**

$$MAE = \frac{1}{T} \sum_{t=1}^{T} |e_{t+h,t}|$$

and mean absolute percent error,

$$MAPE = \frac{1}{T} \sum_{t=1}^{T} |p_{t+h,t}|$$

Statistical Comparison of Forecast Accuracy

All the accuracy measures we have discussed are actually *sample estimates* of *population* accuracy. Population *MSE*, for example, is defined as the *expected squared error*,

$$MSE_{pop} = E(e^2_{t+k,t})$$

which we estimate by replacing the expectation with a sample average,

$$MSE = \frac{1}{T} \sum_{t=1}^{T} e^2_{t+h,t}$$

yielding the sample *MSE*.

Once we have decided on a loss function, it is often of interest to know whether one forecast is more accurate than another. In hypothesis testing terms, we might want to test the equal accuracy hypothesis,

$$E\,[L(e^a_{t+h,t})] = E\,[L(e^b_{t+h,t})]$$

against the alternative hypothesis that one or the other is better. Equivalently, we might want to test the hypothesis that the expected loss differential is zero,

$$E\,(d_t) = E\,[L(e^a_{t+h,t})] - E\,[L(e^b_{t+h,t})] = 0$$

The hypothesis concerns population expected loss; we test it by using sample average loss.

In fact, we can show that if d_t is a covariance stationary series, then the large-sample distribution of the sample mean loss differential is[2]

$$\sqrt{T}\,(\,\overline{d} - \mu) \sim N(\,0, f\,)$$

where

$$\overline{d} = \frac{1}{T} \sum_{t=1}^{T} \left[L(e^a_{t+h,t}) - L(e^b_{t+h,t}) \right]$$

is the sample mean loss differential, f is the variance of the sample mean loss differential, and μ is the population mean loss differential. This implies that

---

2. We simply assert the result here; its proof is beyond the scope of this book.

in large samples, under the null hypothesis of a zero population mean loss differential, the standardized sample mean loss differential has a standard normal distribution,

$$B = \frac{\bar{d}}{\sqrt{\frac{\hat{f}}{T}}} \sim N(0, 1)$$

where $\hat{f}$ is a consistent estimator of f. In practice, in many cases an adequate estimator is provided by using

$$\hat{f} = \sum_{\tau = -M}^{M} \hat{\gamma}_d(\tau)$$

where $M = T^{1/3}$, and $\hat{\gamma}_d(\tau)$ denotes the sample autocovariance of the loss differential at displacement τ.

Note that the statistic B is just a t-statistic for the hypothesis of a zero population mean loss differential, adjusted to reflect the fact that the loss differential series is not necessarily white noise. We can compute it by regressing the loss differential series on an intercept, taking care to correct the equation for serial correlation. The procedure outlined above amounts to a "nonparametric" way of doing so. It is called nonparametric because instead of assuming a particular model for the serial correlation, we use the sample autocorrelations of the loss differential directly.

The nonparametric serial correlation correction is a bit tedious, however, and it involves the rather arbitrary selection of the truncation lag, M. Alternatively, and perhaps preferably, we can proceed by regressing the loss differential on an intercept, allowing for ARMA(p,q) disturbances, and using information criteria to select p and q. This model-based parametric serial correlation correction is easy to do, economizes on degrees of freedom, and makes use of convenient model selection procedures.

3. FORECAST ENCOMPASSING AND FORECAST COMBINATION

In forecast accuracy comparison, we ask which forecast is best with respect to a particular loss function. Such "horse races" arise constantly in practical work. Regardless of whether one forecast is significantly better than the others, however, the question arises as to whether competing forecasts may be fruitfully combined to produce a composite forecast superior to all the original forecasts. Thus, forecast combination, although obviously related to forecast accuracy comparison, is logically distinct and of independent interest.

Forecast Encompassing

We use **forecast encompassing** tests to determine whether one forecast incorporates (or encompasses) all the relevant information in competing forecasts. If one forecast incorporates all the relevant information, nothing can be gained by combining forecasts. For simplicity, let us focus on the case of two forecasts, $y^a_{t+h,t}$ and $y^b_{t+h,t}$. Consider the regression

$$y_{t+h} = \beta_a y^a_{t+h,t} + \beta_b y^b_{t+h,t} + \varepsilon_{t+h,t}$$

If $(\beta_a, \beta_b) = (1, 0)$, we say that model a forecast-encompasses model b, and if $(\beta_a, \beta_b) = (0, 1)$, we'll say that model b forecast-encompasses model a. For other (β_a, β_b) values, neither model encompasses the other, and both forecasts contain useful information about y_{t+h}. In covariance stationary environments, encompassing hypotheses can be tested using standard methods.[3] If neither forecast encompasses the other, forecast combination is potentially desirable.

Forecast Combination

Failure of each model's forecasts to encompass other model's forecasts indicates that all the models are misspecified, and that there may be gains from **forecast combining.** It should come as no surprise that such situations are typical in practice because forecasting models are *likely* to be misspecified—they are intentional abstractions of a much more complex reality.

Many combining methods have been proposed, and they fall into roughly two groups, "variance-covariance" methods and "regression" methods. As we shall see, the **variance-covariance forecast combination method** is in fact a special case of the **regression-based forecast combination method,** so there is really only one method. However, for historical reasons—and more important, to build valuable intuition—it is important to understand the variance-covariance forecast combination, so we begin with that. Suppose we have two unbiased forecasts from which we form a composite as

$$y^c_{t+h,t} = \omega y^a_{t+h,t} + (1 - \omega) y^b_{t+h,t}$$

Because the weights sum to unity, the composite forecast will necessarily be unbiased. Moreover, the combined forecast error will satisfy the same relation as the combined forecast; that is,

$$e^c_{t+h,t} = \omega e^a_{t+h,t} + (1 - \omega) e^b_{t+h,t}$$

---

3. Note that $\varepsilon_{t+h,t}$ may be serially correlated, particularly if $h > 1$, and any such serial correlation should be taken into account.

with variance

$$\sigma_c^2 = \omega^2 \sigma_{aa}^2 + (1 - \omega)^2 \sigma_{bb}^2 + 2\omega(1 - \omega)\sigma_{ab}^2$$

where σ_{aa}^2 and σ_{bb}^2 are the forecast error variances and σ_{ab}^2 is their covariance. We find the optimal combining weight by minimizing the variance of the combined forecast error with respect to ω, which yields

$$\omega^* = \frac{\sigma_{bb}^2 - \sigma_{ab}^2}{\sigma_{bb}^2 + \sigma_{aa}^2 - 2\sigma_{ab}^2}$$

The optimal combining weight is a simple function of the variances and co-variances of the underlying forecast errors. The forecast error variance associated with the optimally combined forecast is less than or equal to the smaller of σ_{aa}^2 and σ_{bb}^2; thus, in population, we have nothing to lose by combining forecasts, and potentially much to gain. In practical applications, the unknown variances and covariances that underlie the optimal combining weights are unknown, so we replace them with consistent estimates; that is, we estimate ω^* by replacing σ_{ij}^2 with

$$\hat{\sigma}_{ij}^2 = \frac{1}{T} \sum_{t=1}^{T} e_{t+h,t}^i \, e_{t+h,t}^j$$

yielding the combining weight estimates,

$$\hat{\omega}^* = \frac{\hat{\sigma}_{bb}^2 - \hat{\sigma}_{ab}^2}{\hat{\sigma}_{bb}^2 + \hat{\sigma}_{aa}^2 - 2\hat{\sigma}_{ab}^2}$$

To gain intuition for the formula that defines the optimal combining weight, consider the special case in which the forecast errors are uncorrelated, so that $\sigma_{ab}^2 = 0$. Then

$$\omega^* = \frac{\sigma_{bb}^2}{\sigma_{bb}^2 + \sigma_{aa}^2}$$

As σ_{aa}^2 approaches 0, forecast a becomes progressively more accurate. The formula for ω^* indicates that as σ_{aa}^2 approaches 0, ω^* approaches 1, so that all weight is put on forecast a, which is desirable. Similarly, as σ_{bb}^2 approaches 0, forecast b becomes progressively more accurate. The formula for ω^* indicates that as σ_{bb}^2 approaches 0, ω^* approaches 0, so that all weight is put on forecast b, which is also desirable. In general, the forecast with the smaller error variance receives the higher weight, with the precise size of the weight depending on the disparity between variances.

The full formula for the optimal combining weight indicates that not only the variances, but also the covariance, are relevant, but the basic intuition remains valid. Effectively, we are forming a portfolio of forecasts, and as we know from standard results in finance, the optimal shares in a portfolio depend on the variances *and* covariances of the underlying assets.

Now consider the regression method of forecast combination. The form of forecast-encompassing regressions immediately suggests combining forecasts by simply regressing realizations on forecasts. This intuition proves accurate, and in fact the optimal variance-covariance combining weights have a regression interpretation as the coefficients of a linear projection of y_{t+h} onto the forecasts, subject to two constraints: the weights sum to unity and the intercept is excluded.

In practice, of course, population linear projection is impossible, so we simply run the regression on the available data. Moreover, it is usually preferable *not* to force the weights to add to unity, or to exclude an intercept. Inclusion of an intercept, for example, facilitates bias correction and allows biased forecasts to be combined. Typically, then, we simply estimate the regression,

$$y_{t+h} = \beta_0 + \beta_1 y^a_{t+h,t} + \beta_2 y^b_{t+h,t} + \varepsilon_{t+h,t}$$

Extension to the fully general case of more than two forecasts is immediate.

In general, the regression method is simple and flexible. There are many variations and extensions, because any regression tool is potentially applicable. The key is to use generalizations with sound motivation. We give four examples in an attempt to build an intuitive feel for the sorts of extensions that are possible: time-varying combining weights, dynamic combining regressions, shrinkage of combining weights toward equality, and nonlinear combining regressions.

(a) Time-Varying Combining Weights   Relative accuracies of different forecasts may change, and if they do, we naturally want to weight the improving forecasts progressively more heavily and the worsening forecasts less heavily. Relative accuracies can change for a number of reasons. For example, the design of a particular forecasting model may make it likely to perform well in some situations, but poorly in others. Alternatively, people's decision rules and firms' strategies may change over time, and certain forecasting techniques may be relatively more vulnerable to such change.

We allow for time-varying combining weights in the regression framework by using weighted or rolling estimation of combining regressions, or by allowing for explicitly time-varying parameters. If, for example, we suspect that the combining weights are evolving over time in a trend-like fashion, we might use the combining regression

$$y_{t+h} = (\beta_0^0 + \beta_0^1 \ TIME) + (\beta_a^0 + \beta_a^1 \ TIME)y_{t+h,t}^a$$
$$+ (\beta_b^0 + \beta_b^1 \ TIME)y_{t+h,t}^b + \varepsilon_{t+h,t}$$

which we estimate by regressing the realization on an intercept, time, each of the two forecasts, the product of time and the first forecast, and the product of time and the second forecast. We assess the importance of time variation by examining the size and statistical significance of the estimates of β_0^1, β_a^1, and β_b^1.

(b) Serial Correlation   It is a good idea to allow for serial correlation in combining regressions, for two reasons. First, as always, even in the best of conditions we need to allow for the usual serial correlation induced by overlap when forecasts are more than 1-step-ahead. This suggests that instead of treating the disturbance in the combining regression as white noise, we should allow for $MA(h-1)$ serial correlation,

$$y_{t+h} = \beta_0 + \beta_a \ y_{t+h,t}^a + \beta_b \ y_{t+h,t}^b + \varepsilon_{t+h,t}$$
$$\varepsilon_{t+h,t} \sim MA(h-1)$$

Second, and very important, the $MA(h-1)$ error structure is associated with forecasts that are optimal with respect to their information sets, of which there is no guarantee. That is, although the primary forecasts were designed to capture the dynamics in y, there is no guarantee that they do so. Thus, just as in standard regressions, it is important in combining regressions to allow for either serially correlated disturbances or lagged dependent variables, to capture any dynamics in y not captured by the various forecasts. A combining regression with $ARMA(p,q)$ disturbances,

$$y_{t+h} = \beta_0 + \beta_a \ y_{t+h,t}^a + \beta_b \ y_{t+h,t}^b + \varepsilon_{t+h,t}$$
$$\varepsilon_{t+h,t} \sim ARMA(p,q)$$

with p and q selected using information criteria in conjunction with other diagnostics, is usually adequate.

(c) Shrinkage of Combining Weights toward Equality   Simple arithmetic averages of forecasts—that is, combinations in which the weights are constrained to be equal—sometimes perform very well in out-of-sample forecast competitions, even relative to "optimal" combinations. The equal-weights constraint eliminates sampling variation in the combining weights at the cost

of possibly introducing bias. Sometimes the benefits of imposing equal weights exceed the cost, so that the *MSE* of the combined forecast is reduced.

The equal-weights constraint associated with the arithmetic average is an example of extreme shrinkage; regardless of the information contained in the data, the weights are forced into equality. We have seen before that shrinkage can produce forecast improvements, but typically we want to *coax* estimates in a particular direction, rather than to force them. In that way we guide our parameter estimates toward reasonable values when the data are uninformative, but nevertheless pay a great deal of attention to the data when they are *informative*.

Thus, instead of imposing a *deterministic* equal-weights constraint, we might like to impose a *stochastic* constraint. With this in mind, we sometimes coax the combining weights toward equality without forcing equality. A simple way to do so is to take a weighted average of the simple average combination and the least-squares combination. Let the shrinkage parameter γ be the weight put on the simple average combination, and let $(1 - \gamma)$ be the weight put on the least-squares combination, where γ is chosen by the user. The larger γ is, the more the combining weights shrink toward equality. Thus the combining weights are coaxed toward the arithmetic mean, but the data are still allowed to "speak" when they have something important to say.

(d) Nonlinear Combining Regressions   There is no reason to force linearity of combining regressions, and various of the nonlinear techniques that we have already introduced may be used. We might, for example, regress realizations not only on forecasts, but also on squares and cross products of the various forecasts, in order to capture quadratic deviations from linearity,

$$y_{t+h} = \beta_0 + \beta_a y^a_{t+h,t} + \beta_b y^b_{t+h,t} + \beta_{aa} (y^a_{t+h,t})^2 + \beta_{bb} (y^b_{t+h,t})^2$$
$$+ \beta_{ab} y^a_{t+h,t} y^b_{t+h,t} + \varepsilon_{t+h,t}$$

We assess the importance of nonlinearity by examining the size and statistical significance of estimates of β_{aa}, β_{bb}, and β_{ab}; if the linear combining regression is adequate, those estimates should be insignificantly different from 0. If, on the other hand, the nonlinear terms are found to be important, then the full nonlinear combining regression should be used.

4. APPLICATION: OVERSEA SHIPPING VOLUME ON THE ATLANTIC EAST TRADE LANE

OverSea Services, Inc., is a major international cargo shipper. To help guide fleet allocation decisions, each week OverSea makes forecasts of volume shipped over each of its major trade lanes, at horizons ranging from 1-week ahead through 16-weeks ahead. In fact, OverSea produces two sets of fore-casts—a quantitative forecast is produced using modern quantitative tech-niques, and a judgmental forecast is produced by soliciting the opinion of the sales representatives, many of whom have years of valuable experience.

Here we examine the realizations and 2-week-ahead forecasts of volume on the Atlantic East trade lane (North America to Europe). We have almost 10 years of data on weekly realized volume (VOL) and weekly 2-week-ahead forecasts (the quantitative forecast VOLQ, and the judgmental forecast VOLJ), from January 1988 through mid-July 1997, for a total of 499 weeks.

In Figure 11.1, we plot realized volume versus the quantitative forecast, and in Figure 11.2 we show realized volume versus the judgmental forecast. The two plots look similar, and both forecasts appear quite accurate; it is not too difficult to forecast shipping volume just two weeks ahead.

In Figures 11.3 and 11.4, we plot the errors from the quantitative and judgmental forecasts, respectively, which are more revealing. The quantita-tive error, in particular, appears roughly centered on 0, whereas the judg-mental error seems to be a bit higher than 0 on average. That is, the judg-mental forecast appears biased in a pessimistic way—on average, actual realized volume is a bit higher than forecast volume.

In Figures 11.5 and 11.6, we show histograms and related statistics for the quantitative and judgmental forecast errors, respectively. The histograms confirm our earlier suspicions based on the error plots; the histogram for the quantitative error is centered on a mean of -0.03, whereas that for the judg-mental error is centered on 1.02. The error standard deviations, however, re-veal that the judgmental forecast errors vary a bit less around their mean than do the quantitative errors. Finally, the Jarque-Bera test cannot reject the hypothesis that the errors are normally distributed.

In Tables 11.1 and 11.2 and Figures 11.7 and 11.8, we show the correlo-grams of the quantitative and judgmental forecast errors. In each case, the errors appear to have MA(1) structure; the sample autocorrelations cut off at displacement 1, whereas the sample partial autocorrelations display damped oscillation, which is reasonable for 2-step-ahead forecast errors.

To test for the statistical significance of bias, we need to account for the MA(1) serial correlation. To do so, we regress the forecast errors on a con-stant, allowing for MA(1) disturbances. We show the results for the quantita-tive forecast errors in Table 11.3, and those for the judgmental forecast er-rors in Table 11.4. The t-statistic indicates no bias in the quantitative forecasts, but sizable and highly statistically significant bias in the judgmental forecasts.

In Tables 11.5 and 11.6, we show the results of Mincer-Zarnowitz regres-sions; both forecasts fail miserably. We expected the judgmental forecast to fail, because it is biased, but until now no defects were found in the quantita-tive forecast.

FIGURE 11.1   Shipping Volume: Quantitative Forecast and Realization

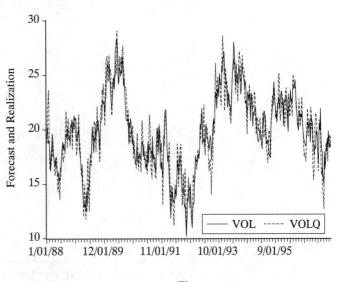

FIGURE 11.2   Shipping Volume: Judgmental Forecast and Realization

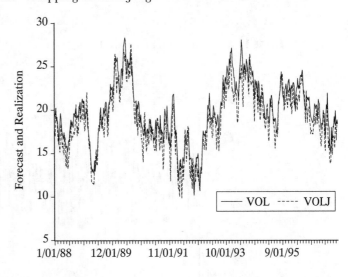

FIGURE 11.3   Quantitative Forecast Error

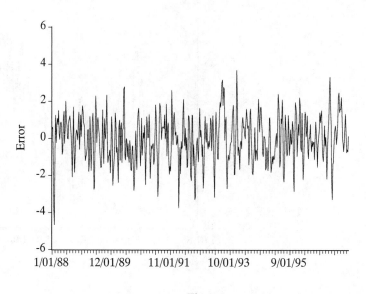

Time

FIGURE 11.4   Judgmental Forecast Error

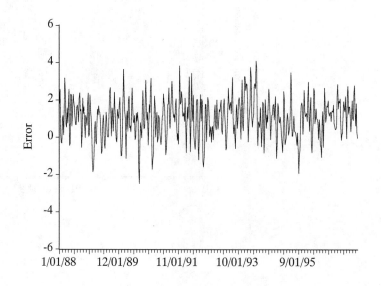

Time

FIGURE 11.5   Quantitative Forecast Error: Histogram and Related Statistics

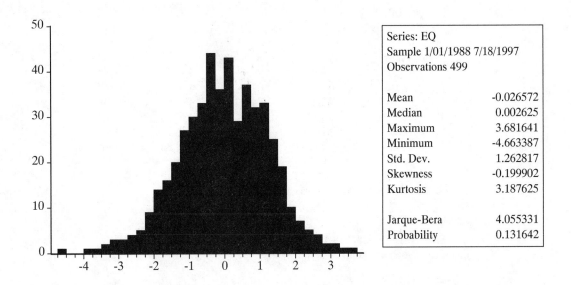

FIGURE 11.6   Judgmental Forecast Error: Histogram and Related Statistics

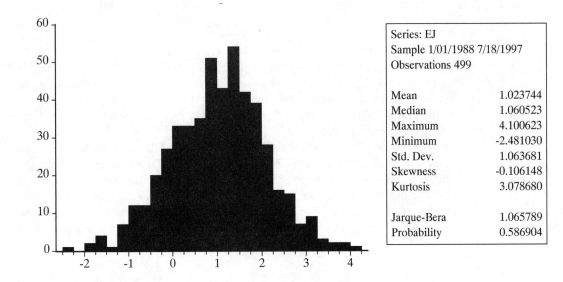

TABLE 11.1   Quantitative Forecast Error Correlogram

Sample: 1/01/1988 7/18/1997
Included observations: 499

	Acorr.	P. Acorr.	Std. Error	Ljung-Box	p-value
1	0.518	0.518	.045	134.62	0.000
2	0.010	-0.353	.045	134.67	0.000
3	-0.044	0.205	.045	135.65	0.000
4	-0.039	-0.172	.045	136.40	0.000
5	0.025	0.195	.045	136.73	0.000
6	0.057	-0.117	.045	138.36	0.000

TABLE 11.2   Judgmental Forecast Error Correlogram

Sample: 1/01/1988 7/18/1997
Included observations: 499

	Acorr.	P. Acorr.	Std. Error	Ljung-Box	p-value
1	0.495	0.495	.045	122.90	0.000
2	-0.027	-0.360	.045	123.26	0.000
3	-0.045	0.229	.045	124.30	0.000
4	-0.056	-0.238	.045	125.87	0.000
5	-0.033	0.191	.045	126.41	0.000
6	0.087	-0.011	.045	130.22	0.000

Now let us compare forecast accuracy. We show the histogram and descriptive statistics for the squared quantitative and judgmental errors in Figures 11.9 and 11.10, respectively. The histogram for the squared judgmental error is pushed rightward relative to that of the quantitative error, due to bias. The RMSE of the quantitative forecast is 1.26, whereas that of the judgmental forecast is 1.48.

In Figure 11.11 we show the (quadratic) loss differential; it is fairly small and looks a little negative. In Figure 11.12 we show the histogram of the loss differential; the mean is −0.58, which is small relative to the standard deviation of the loss differential, but remember that we have not yet corrected for serial correlation. In Table 11.7 we show the correlogram of the loss differential, which strongly suggests MA(1) structure. The sample autocorrelations

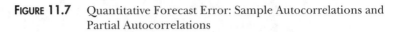

FIGURE 11.7 Quantitative Forecast Error: Sample Autocorrelations and Partial Autocorrelations

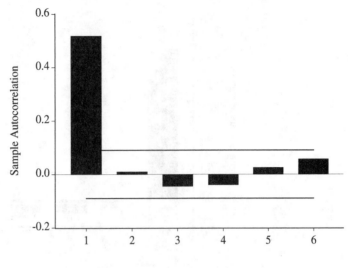

Displacement

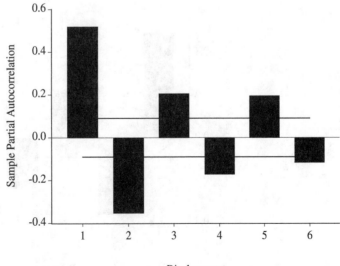

Displacement

FIGURE 11.8   Judgmental Forecast Error: Sample Autocorrelations
and Partial Autocorrelations

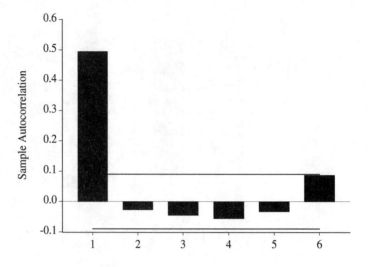

Displacement

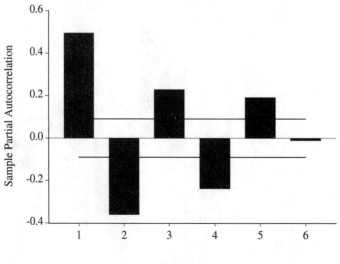

Displacement

TABLE 11.3 Quantitative Forecast Error: Regression on Intercept, MA(1) Disturbances

LS // Dependent Variable is EQ
Sample: 1/01/1988 7/18/1997
Included observations: 499
Convergence achieved after 6 iterations

Variable	Coefficient	Std. Error	t-Statistic	Prob.
C	-0.024770	0.079851	-0.310200	0.7565
MA(1)	0.935393	0.015850	59.01554	0.0000

R-squared	0.468347	Mean dependent var	-0.026572
Adjusted R-squared	0.467277	S.D. dependent var	1.262817
S.E. of regression	0.921703	Akaike info criterion	-0.159064
Sum squared resid	422.2198	Schwarz criterion	-0.142180
Log likelihood	-666.3639	F-statistic	437.8201
Durbin-Watson stat	1.988237	Prob(F-statistic)	0.000000

Inverted MA Roots   -.94

TABLE 11.4 Judgmental Forecast Error: Regression on Intercept, MA(1) Disturbances

LS // Dependent Variable is EJ
Sample: 1/01/1988 7/18/1997
Included observations: 499
Convergence achieved after 7 iterations

Variable	Coefficient	Std. Error	t-Statistic	Prob.
C	1.026372	0.067191	15.27535	0.0000
MA(1)	0.961524	0.012470	77.10450	0.0000

R-squared	0.483514	Mean dependent var	1.023744
Adjusted R-squared	0.482475	S.D. dependent var	1.063681
S.E. of regression	0.765204	Akaike info criterion	-0.531226
Sum squared resid	291.0118	Schwarz criterion	-0.514342
Log likelihood	-573.5094	F-statistic	465.2721
Durbin-Watson stat	1.968750	Prob(F-statistic)	0.000000

Inverted MA Roots   -.96

TABLE 11.5   Quantitative Forecast Error: Mincer-Zarnowitz Regression

LS // Dependent Variable is VOL
Sample: 1/01/1988 7/18/1997
Included observations: 499
Convergence achieved after 10 iterations

Variable	Coefficient	Std. Error	t-Statistic	Prob.
C	2.958191	0.341841	8.653696	0.0000
VOLQ	0.849559	0.016839	50.45317	0.0000
MA(1)	0.912559	0.018638	48.96181	0.0000

R-squared	0.936972	Mean dependent var	19.80609
Adjusted R-squared	0.936718	S.D. dependent var	3.403283
S.E. of regression	0.856125	Akaike info criterion	-0.304685
Sum squared resid	363.5429	Schwarz criterion	-0.279358
Log likelihood	-629.0315	F-statistic	3686.790
Durbin-Watson stat	1.815577	Prob(F-statistic)	0.000000

Inverted MA Roots   -.91

Wald Test:
Null Hypothesis:	C(1)=0	C(2)=1	
F-statistic	39.96862	Probability	0.000000
Chi-square	79.93723	Probability	0.000000

TABLE 11.6   Judgmental Forecast Error: Mincer-Zarnowitz Regression

LS // Dependent Variable is VOL
Sample: 1/01/1988 7/18/1997
Included observations: 499
Convergence achieved after 11 iterations

Variable	Coefficient	Std. Error	t-Statistic	Prob.
C	2.592648	0.271740	9.540928	0.0000
VOLJ	0.916576	0.014058	65.20021	0.0000
MA(1)	0.949690	0.014621	64.95242	0.0000

R-squared	0.952896	Mean dependent var	19.80609
Adjusted R-squared	0.952706	S.D. dependent var	3.403283
S.E. of regression	0.740114	Akaike info criterion	-0.595907
Sum squared resid	271.6936	Schwarz criterion	-0.570581
Log likelihood	-556.3715	F-statistic	5016.993
Durbin-Watson stat	1.917179	Prob(F-statistic)	0.000000

Inverted MA Roots   -.95

Wald Test:
Null Hypothesis:	C(1)=0	C(2)=1	
F-statistic	143.8323	Probability	0.000000
Chi-square	287.6647	Probability	0.000000

FIGURE 11.9   Squared Quantitative Forecast Error: Histogram and Related Statistics

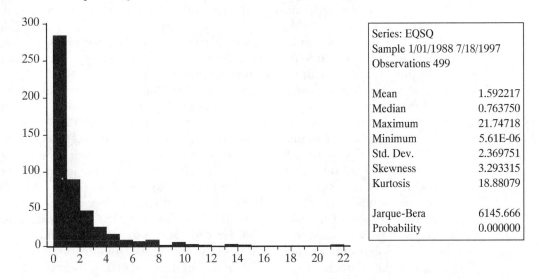

FIGURE 11.10   Squared Judgmental Forecast Error: Histogram and Related Statistics

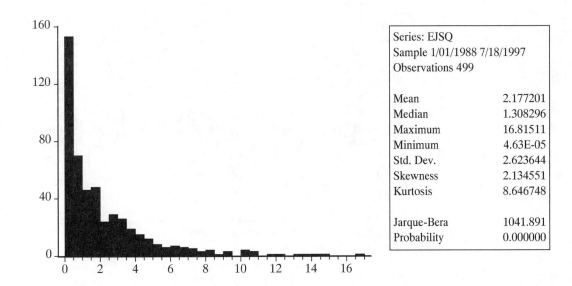

and partial autocorrelations, shown in Figure 11.13, confirm that impression. Thus, to test for significance of the loss differential, we regress it on a constant and allow for MA(1) disturbances; we show the results in Table 11.8. The mean loss differential is highly statistically significant, with a *p*-value less than 0.01; we conclude that the quantitative forecast is more accurate than the judgmental forecast under quadratic loss.

Now we combine the forecasts. Both failed Mincer-Zarnowitz tests, which suggests that there may be scope for combining. The correlation between the two forecast errors is 0.54, positive but not too high. In Table 11.9 we show the results of estimating the unrestricted combining regression with MA(1) errors (equivalently, a forecast encompassing test). Neither forecast encompasses the other; both combining weights, as well as the intercept, are highly statistically significantly different from 0. Interestingly, the judgmental forecast actually gets *more* weight than the quantitative forecast in the combination, in spite of the fact that its RMSE was higher. That is because, after correcting for bias, the judgmental forecast appears a bit more accurate.

It is interesting to track the RMSEs as we progress from the original forecasts to the combined forecast. The RMSE of the quantitative forecast is 1.26, and that of the judgmental forecast is 1.48. The RMSE associated with using the modified quantitative forecast that we obtain using the weights estimated

FIGURE 11.11   Loss Differential

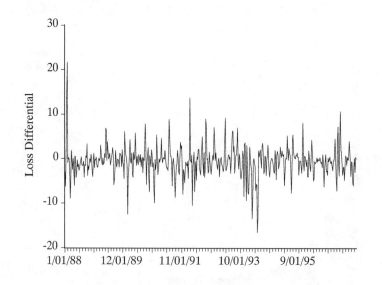

Figure 11.12   Loss Differential: Histogram and Related Statistics

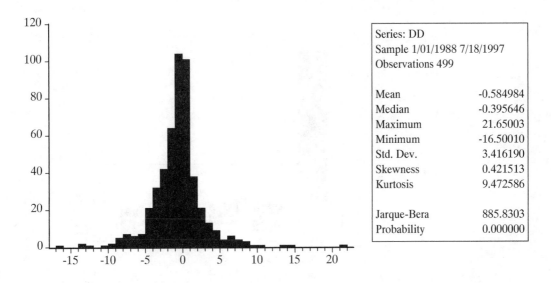

Series: DD	
Sample 1/01/1988 7/18/1997	
Observations 499	
Mean	-0.584984
Median	-0.395646
Maximum	21.65003
Minimum	-16.50010
Std. Dev.	3.416190
Skewness	0.421513
Kurtosis	9.472586
Jarque-Bera	885.8303
Probability	0.000000

Table 11.7   Loss Differential Correlogram

Sample: 1/01/1988 7/18/1997
Included observations: 499

	Acorr.	P. Acorr.	Std. Error	Ljung-Box	p-value
1	0.357	0.357	.045	64.113	0.000
2	-0.069	-0.226	.045	66.519	0.000
3	-0.050	0.074	.045	67.761	0.000
4	-0.044	-0.080	.045	68.746	0.000
5	-0.078	-0.043	.045	71.840	0.000
6	0.017	0.070	.045	71.989	0.000

in the Mincer-Zarnowitz regression is 0.85, and that of the modified judgmental forecast is 0.74. Finally, the RMSE of the combined forecast is 0.70. In this case, we get a big improvement in forecast accuracy from using the modifications associated with the Mincer-Zarnowitz regressions, and a smaller, but not negligible, additional improvement from using the full combining regression.[4]

---

4. The RMSEs associated with forecasts from the partial optimality regressions as well as from the full combining regression are, of course, in-sample RMSEs. It remains to be seen how they will perform out-of-sample, but all indications look good.

FIGURE 11.13   Loss Differential: Sample Autocorrelations
and Partial Autocorrelations

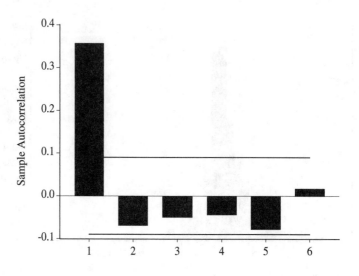

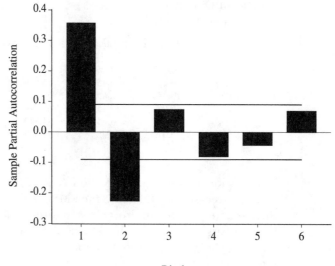

TABLE 11.8 Loss Differential: Regression on Intercept with MA(1) Disturbances

LS // Dependent Variable is DD
Sample: 1/01/1988 7/18/1997
Included observations: 499
Convergence achieved after 4 iterations

Variable	Coefficient	Std. Error	t-Statistic	Prob.
C	-0.585333	0.204737	-2.858945	0.0044
MA(1)	0.472901	0.039526	11.96433	0.0000

R-squared	0.174750	Mean dependent var	-0.584984
Adjusted R-squared	0.173089	S.D. dependent var	3.416190
S.E. of regression	3.106500	Akaike info criterion	2.270994
Sum squared resid	4796.222	Schwarz criterion	2.287878
Log likelihood	-1272.663	F-statistic	105.2414
Durbin-Watson stat	2.023606	Prob(F-statistic)	0.000000

Inverted MA Roots   -.47

TABLE 11.9 Shipping Volume Combining Regression

LS // Dependent Variable is VOL
Sample: 1/01/1988 7/18/1997
Included observations: 499
Convergence achieved after 11 iterations

Variable	Coefficient	Std. Error	t-Statistic	Prob.
C	2.181977	0.259774	8.399524	0.0000
VOLQ	0.291577	0.038346	7.603919	0.0000
VOLJ	0.630551	0.039935	15.78944	0.0000
MA(1)	0.951107	0.014174	67.10327	0.0000

R-squared	0.957823	Mean dependent var	19.80609
Adjusted R-squared	0.957567	S.D. dependent var	3.403283
S.E. of regression	0.701049	Akaike info criterion	-0.702371
Sum squared resid	243.2776	Schwarz criterion	-0.668603
Log likelihood	-528.8088	F-statistic	3747.077
Durbin-Watson stat	1.925091	Prob(F-statistic)	0.000000

Inverted MA Roots   -.95

PROBLEMS AND COMPLEMENTS

1. (Forecast evaluation in action) Discuss in detail how you would use forecast evaluation techniques to address each of the following questions.

    (a) Are asset returns (e.g., stocks, bonds, exchange rates) forecastable over long horizons?

    (b) Do forward exchange rates provide unbiased forecasts of future spot exchange rates at all horizons?

    (c) Are government budget projections systematically too optimistic, perhaps for strategic reasons?

    (d) Can interest rates be used to provide good forecasts of future inflation?

2. (What are we forecasting? Preliminary series, revised series, and the limits to forecast accuracy) Many economic series are revised as underlying source data increase in quantity and quality. For example, a typical quarterly series might be issued as follows. First, shortly after the end of the relevant quarter, a "preliminary" value for the current quarter is issued. A few months later, a "revised" value is issued, and a year or so later the "final revised" value is issued.

    (a) If you are evaluating the accuracy of a forecast or forecasting technique, you have to decide on what to use for the "actual" values, or realizations, to which the forecasts will be compared. Should you use the preliminary value? The final revised value? Something else? Be sure to weigh as many relevant issues as possible in defending your answer.

    (b) Morgenstern (1963) assesses the accuracy of economic data and reports that the great mathematician Norbert Wiener, after reading an early version of Morgenstern's book, remarked that "economics is a one or two digit science." What might Wiener have meant?

    (c) Theil (1966) is well aware of the measurement error in economic data; he speaks of "predicting the future and *estimating* the past." Klein (1981) notes that, in addition to the usual innovation uncertainty, measurement error in economic data—even "final revised" data—provides additional limits to measured forecast accuracy. That is, even if a forecast were perfect, so that forecast errors were consistently zero, *measured* forecast errors would be nonzero due to measurement error. The larger the measurement error, the more severe the inflation of measured forecast error. Evaluate.

3. (Ex post versus real-time forecast evaluation) If you are evaluating a forecasting model, you also have to take a stand on precisely what information is available to the forecaster, and when it is available. Suppose, for

example, that you are evaluating the forecasting accuracy of a particular regression model.

(a) Do you prefer to estimate and forecast recursively, or simply estimate once using the full sample of data?

(b) Do you prefer to estimate using final-revised values of the left- and right-hand-side variables, or do you prefer to use the preliminary, revised, and final-revised data as they became available in real time?

(c) If the model is explanatory rather than causal, do you prefer to substitute the true realized values of right-hand-side variables, or to substitute forecasts of the right-hand-side variables that could actually be constructed in real time?

These sorts of timing issues can make large differences in conclusions. For an application to using the composite index of leading indicators to forecast industrial production, see Diebold and Rudebusch (1991).

4. (What do we know about the accuracy of macroeconomic forecasts?) Zarnowitz and Braun (1993) provide a fine assessment of the track record of economic forecasts since the late 1960s. Read their paper and try to assess just what we really know about:

(a) comparative forecast accuracy at business cycle turning points versus other times

(b) comparative accuracy of judgmental versus model-based forecasts

(c) improvements in forecast accuracy over time

(d) the comparative forecastability of various series.

Other well-known and useful comparative assessments of U.S. macroeconomic forecasts have been published over the years by Stephen K. McNees, a private consultant formerly with the Federal Reserve Bank of Boston. McNees (1988) is a good example. Similarly useful studies for the United Kingdom, with particular attention to decomposing forecast error into its various possible sources, have recently been produced by Kenneth F. Wallis and his coworkers at the ESRC Macroeconomic Modelling Bureau at the University of Warwick. Wallis and Whitley (1991) is a good example. Finally, the Model Comparison Seminar, founded by Lawrence R. Klein of the University of Pennsylvania and now led by Michael Donihue of Colby College, is dedicated to the ongoing comparative assessment of macroeconomic forecasting models. Klein (1991) provides a good survey of some of the group's recent work, and more recent information can be found on the web at http://www.colby.edu/economics/mcs/

5. (Forecast evaluation when realizations are unobserved) Sometimes we never see the realization of the variable being forecast. Pesaran and Samiei (1995), for example, develop models for forecasting ultimate re-

source recovery, such as the total amount of oil in an underground reserve. The actual value, however, won't be known until the reserve is depleted, which may be decades away. Such situations obviously make for difficult accuracy evaluation! How would you evaluate such forecasting models?

6. (Forecast error variances in models with estimated parameters) As we have seen, computing forecast error variances that acknowledge parameter estimation uncertainty is very difficult; that is one reason why we have ignored it. We have learned a number of lessons about optimal forecasts while ignoring parameter estimation uncertainty, such as:

    (a) Forecast error variance grows as the forecast horizon lengthens.
    (b) In covariance stationary environments, the forecast error variance approaches the (finite) unconditional variance as the horizon grows.

    Such lessons provide valuable insight and intuition regarding the workings of forecasting models and provide a useful benchmark for assessing actual forecasts. They sometimes need modification, however, when parameter estimation uncertainty is acknowledged. For example, in models with estimated parameters:

    (c) Forecast error variance need not grow monotonically with horizon. Typically we *expect* forecast error variance to increase monotonically with horizon, but it doesn't *have* to.
    (d) Even in covariance stationary environments, the forecast error variance need not converge to the unconditional variance as the forecast horizon lengthens; instead, it may grow without bound. Consider, for example, forecasting a series that is just a stationary AR(1) process around a linear trend. With known parameters, the point forecast will converge to the trend as the horizon grows, and the forecast error variance will converge to the unconditional variance of the AR(1) process. With estimated parameters, however, if the estimated trend parameters are even the slightest bit different from the true values (as they almost surely will be, due to sampling variation), that error will be magnified as the horizon grows, so the forecast error variance will grow.

    Thus, results derived under the assumption of known parameters should be viewed as a benchmark to guide our intuition, rather than as precise rules.

7. (Decomposing *MSE* into variance and bias components)

    (a) Verify that population *MSE* can be decomposed into the sum of population variance and squared bias,

$$E(e^2_{t+k,t}) = \text{var}\,(e_{t+k,t}) + (E(e_{t+k,t}))^2$$

(b) Verify that sample *MSE* can be decomposed into the sum of sample variance and squared bias,

$$\frac{1}{T}\sum_{t=1}^{T}e_{t+h,t}^{2}=\frac{1}{T}\sum_{t=1}^{T}\left(e_{t+h,t}-\frac{1}{T}\sum_{t=1}^{T}e_{t+h,t}\right)^{2}+\left(\frac{1}{T}\sum_{t=1}^{T}e_{t+h,t}\right)^{2}$$

(c) The decomposition of *MSE* into bias and variance components makes clear the trade-off between bias and variance that is implicit in *MSE*. This, again, provides motivation for the potential forecasting gains from shrinkage. If our accuracy measure is *MSE*, we would be willing to accept a small increase in bias in exchange for a large reduction in variance.

8. (The empirical success of forecast combination) In the text we mentioned that we have nothing to lose by forecast combination, and potentially much to gain. That is certainly true in population, with optimal combining weights. However, in finite samples of the size typically available, sampling error contaminates the combining weight estimates, and the problem of sampling error may be exacerbated by the collinearity that typically exists between $y_{t+h,t}^{a}$ and $y_{t+h,t}^{b}$. Thus, although we hope to reduce out-of-sample forecast *MSE* by combining, there is no guarantee that we can. Fortunately, however, in practice, forecast combination often leads to very good results. The efficacy of forecast combination is well documented in Clemen's (1989) review of the vast literature, and it emerges clearly in Stock and Watson (1999).

9. (Forecast combination and the Box-Jenkins paradigm) In an influential book, Box and Jenkins (latest edition, Box, Jenkins, and Reinsel, 1994) envision an ongoing, iterative process of model selection and estimation, forecasting, and forecast evaluation. What is the role of forecast combination in that paradigm? In a world in which information sets can be instantaneously and costlessly combined, there is no role; it is always optimal to combine information sets rather than forecasts. That is, if no model forecast-encompasses the others, we might hope to eventually figure out what has gone wrong, learn from our mistakes, and come up with a model based on a combined information set that *does* forecast-encompass the others. But in the short run—particularly when deadlines must be met and timely forecasts produced—pooling of information sets is typically either impossible or prohibitively costly. This simple insight motivates the pragmatic idea of forecast combination, in which forecasts rather than models are the basic object of analysis, due to an assumed inability to combine information sets. Thus, forecast combination can be viewed as a key link between the short-run, real-time forecast production process and the longer-run, ongoing process of model development.

10. (Theil's *U*-statistic) Sometimes it is informative to compare the accuracy of a forecast to that of a "naive" competitor. A simple and popular such comparison is achieved by the *U*-statistic, which is the ratio of the 1-step-ahead *MSE* for a given forecast relative to that of a random walk forecast $y_{t+1,t} = y_t$; that is,

$$
U = \frac{\displaystyle\sum_{t=1}^{T} \left(y_{t+1} - y_{t+1,t} \right)^2}{\displaystyle\sum_{t=1}^{T} \left(y_{t+1} - y_t \right)^2}
$$

One must remember, of course, that the random walk is not necessarily a naive competitor, particularly for many economic and financial variables, so that values of *U* near 1 are not necessarily "bad."

The *U*-statistic is due to Theil (1966, p. 28), and is often called "Theil's *U*-statistic." Several authors, including Armstrong and Fildes (1995), have advocated using the *U*-statistic and close relatives for comparing the accuracy of various forecasting methods across series.

11. (Consensus forecasts) A number of services, some commercial and some nonprofit, regularly survey economic and financial forecasters and publish "consensus" forecasts, typically the mean or median of the forecasters surveyed. The consensus forecasts often perform very well relative to the individual forecasts. The Survey of Professional Forecasters is a leading consensus forecast that has been produced each quarter since the late 1960s; currently it is produced by the Federal Reserve Bank of Philadelphia. See Zarnowitz and Braun (1993) and Croushore (1993).

12. (Quantitative forecasting, judgmental forecasting, forecast combination, and shrinkage) Interpretation of the modern quantitative approach to forecasting as eschewing judgment is most definitely misguided. How is judgment used routinely and informally to modify quantitative forecasts? How can judgment be formally used to modify quantitative forecasts via forecast combination? How can judgment be formally used to modify quantitative forecasts via shrinkage? Discuss the comparative merits of each approach. Klein (1981) provides an insightful discussion of the interaction between judgment and models, as well as the comparative track record of judgmental versus model-based forecasts.

13. (The Delphi method for combining experts' forecasts) The "Delphi method" is a structured judgmental forecasting technique that some-

times proves useful in very difficult forecasting situations not amenable to quantification, such as new-technology forecasting. The basic idea is to survey a panel of experts anonymously, reveal the distribution of opinions to the experts so they can revise their opinions, repeat the survey, and so on. Typically the diversity of opinion is reduced as the iterations proceed.

(a) Delphi and related techniques are fraught with difficulties and pitfalls. Discuss them.

(b) At the same time, it is not at all clear that we should dispense with such techniques; they may be of real value. Why?

14. (The algebra of forecast combination) Consider the combined forecast,

$$y_{t+h,t}^c = \omega y_{t+h,t}^a + (1 - \omega) y_{t+h,t}^b$$

Verify the following claims made in the text:

(a) The combined forecast error will satisfy the same relation as the combined forecast; that is,

$$e_{t+h,t}^c = \omega e_{t+h,t}^a + (1 - \omega) e_{t+h,t}^b$$

(b) Because the weights sum to unity, if the primary forecasts are unbiased, then so is the combined forecast.

(c) The variance of the combined forecast error is

$$\sigma_c^2 = \omega^2 \sigma_{aa}^2 + (1 - \omega)^2 \sigma_{bb}^2 + 2\,\omega\,(1 - \omega)\sigma_{ab}^2$$

where σ_{11}^2 and σ_{22}^2 are unconditional forecast error variances, and σ_{12}^2 is their covariance.

(d) The combining weight that minimizes the combined forecast error variance (and hence the combined forecast error *MSE*, by unbiasedness) is

$$\omega^* = \frac{\sigma_{bb}^2 - \sigma_{ab}^2}{\sigma_{bb}^2 + \sigma_{aa}^2 - 2\sigma_{ab}^2}$$

(e) If neither forecast encompasses the other, then

$$\sigma_c^2 < \min(\sigma_{aa}^2, \sigma_{bb}^2)$$

(f) If one forecast encompasses the other, then

$$\sigma_c^2 = \min(\sigma_{aa}^2, \sigma_{bb}^2)$$

BIBLIOGRAPHICAL AND COMPUTATIONAL NOTES

This chapter draws on Diebold and Lopez (1996) and Diebold (1989).

Mincer-Zarnowitz regressions are due to Mincer and Zarnowitz (1969).

The test for a zero expected loss differential, due to Diebold and Mariano (1995), builds on earlier work by Granger and Newbold (1986) and has been improved and extended by Harvey, Leyborne, and Newbold (1996), West (1996), and White (1997).

The idea of forecast encompassing dates at least to Nelson (1972), and was formalized and extended by Chong and Hendry (1986) and Fair and Shiller (1990).

The variance-covariance method of forecast combination is due to Bates and Granger (1969), and the regression interpretation is due to Granger and Ramanathan (1984).

Winkler and Makridakis (1983) document the frequent good performance of simple averages. In large part motivated by that finding, Clemen and Winkler (1986) and Diebold and Pauly (1990) develop forecast combination techniques that feature shrinkage toward the mean, and Stock and Watson (1998) arrive at a similar end via a very different route.

CONCEPTS FOR REVIEW

Bias

Error variance

Evaluation and comparison of
   forecast accuracy

Forecast combination

Forecast encompassing

Mean absolute error

Mean error

Mean squared error

Regression-based forecast
   combination method

Root mean squared error

Unforecastability principle

Variance-covariance forecast
   combination method

REFERENCES AND ADDITIONAL READINGS

Bates, J. M., and Granger, C. W. J. (1969), "The Combination of Forecasts," *Operations Research Quarterly*, 20, 451–468.

Box, G. E. P., Jenkins, G. W., and Reinsel, G. (1994), *Time Series Analysis, Forecasting and Control*, third edition. Englewood Cliffs, N.J.: Prentice Hall.

Chong, Y. Y., and Hendry, D. F. (1986), "Econometric Evaluation of Linear Macroeconomic Models," *Review of Economic Studies*, 53, 671–690.

Clemen, R. T. (1989), "Combining Forecasts: A Review and Annotated Bibliography," *International Journal of Forecasting*, 5, 559–581.

Clemen, R. T., and Winkler, R. L. (1986), "Combining Economic Forecasts," *Journal of Business and Economic Statistics,* 4, 39–46.

Croushore, D. (1993), "The Survey of Professional Forecasters," *Business Review,* Federal Reserve Bank of Philadelphia, November–December.

Diebold, F. X. (1989), "Forecast Combination and Encompassing: Reconciling Two Divergent Literatures," *International Journal of Forecasting,* 5, 589–592.

Diebold, F. X., and Lopez, J. (1996), "Forecast Evaluation and Combination," in G. S. Maddala and C. R. Rao (eds.), *Handbook of Statistics.* Amsterdam: North-Holland, 241–268.

Diebold, F. X., and Mariano, R. (1995), "Comparing Predictive Accuracy," *Journal of Business and Economic Statistics,* 13, 253–265. Reprinted in Diebold and Rudebusch (1999).

Diebold, F. X., and Pauly, P. (1990), "The Use of Prior Information in Forecast Combination," *International Journal of Forecasting,* 6, 503–508.

Diebold, F. X., and Rudebusch, G. D. (1989), "Scoring the Leading Indicators," *Journal of Business,* 62, 369–391. Reprinted in Diebold and Rudebusch (1999).

Diebold, F. X., and Rudebusch, G. D. (1991), "Forecasting Output with the Composite Leading Index: An Ex Ante Analysis," *Journal of the American Statistical Association,* 86, 603–610. Reprinted in Diebold and Rudebusch (1999).

Diebold, F. X., and Rudebusch, G. D. (1999), *Business Cycles: Durations, Dynamics, and Forecasting.* Princeton, N.J.: Princeton University Press.

Fair, R. C., and Shiller, R. J. (1990), "Comparing Information in Forecasts from Econometric Models," *American Economic Review,* 80, 375–389.

Granger, C. W. J., and Newbold, P. (1986), *Forecasting Economic Time Series,* second edition. San Diego: Academic Press.

Granger, C. W. J., and Ramanathan, R. (1984), "Improved Methods of Forecasting," *Journal of Forecasting,* 3, 197–204.

Harvey, D. I., Leyborne, S. J., and Newbold, P. (1997), "Testing the Equality of Prediction Mean Squared Errors," *International Journal of Forecasting,* 13, 281–291.

Klein, L. R. (1981), *Econometric Models as Guides for Decision Making.* New York: The Free Press.

Klein, L. R., ed. (1991), *Comparative Performance of U.S. Econometric Models.* Oxford: Oxford University Press.

McNees, S. K. (1988), "How Accurate Are Macroeconomic Forecasts?" *New England Economic Review,* July/August, 15–36.

Mincer, J., and Zarnowitz, V. (1969), "The Evaluation of Economic Forecasts," in J. Mincer (ed.), *Economic Forecasts and Expectations.* New York: National Bureau of Economic Research.

Morgenstern, O. (1963), *On the Accuracy of Economic Observations.* Princeton, N.J.: Princeton University Press.

Nelson, C. R. (1972), "The Prediction Performance of the F.R.B.-M.I.T.-Penn Model of the U.S. Economy," *American Economic Review,* 62, 902–917.

Pesaran, M. H., and Samiei, H. (1995), "Forecasting Ultimate Resource Recovery," *International Journal of Forecasting,* 11, 543–555.

Stock, J. H., and Watson, M. W. (1998), "A Dynamic Factor Model Framework for Forecast Combination," Manuscript, Kennedy School, Harvard University, and Woodrow Wilson School, Princeton University.

Stock, J. H., and Watson, M.W. (1999), "A Comparison of Linear and Nonlinear Univariate Models for Forecasting Macroeconomic Time Series," in R. Engle and H. White (eds.), *Cointegration, Causality, and Forecasting: A Festschrift in Honor of Clive W.J. Granger,* 1–44. Oxford: Oxford University Press.

Theil, H. (1966), *Applied Economic Forecasting.* Amsterdam: North-Holland.

Wallis, K. F., and Whitley, J. D. (1991), "Sources of Error in Forecasts and Expectations: UK Economic Models, 1984–88," *Journal of Forecasting,* 10, 231–253.

West, K. D. (1996), "Asymptotic Inference about Predictive Ability," *Econometrica,* 64, 1067–1084.

White, H. (1997), "A Reality Check for Data Snooping," Manuscript, Department of Economics, University of California, San Diego.

Winkler, R. L., and Makridakis, S. (1983), "The Combination of Forecasts," *Journal of the Royal Statistical Society A,* 146, 150–157.

Zarnowitz, V., and Braun, P. (1993), "Twenty-Two Years of the N.B.E.R.-A.S.A. Quarterly Economic Outlook Surveys: Aspects and Comparisons of Forecasting Performance," in J. H. Stock and M. W. Watson (eds.), *Business Cycles, Indicators and Forecasting.* Chicago: University of Chicago Press for National Bureau of Economic Research.

UNIT ROOTS, STOCHASTIC TRENDS, ARIMA FORECASTING MODELS, AND SMOOTHING

Thus far we have handled nonstationarities, such as trend, using deterministic components. Now we consider an alternative, stochastic approach. Stochastic trend is important insofar as it sometimes provides a good description of certain business, economic, and financial time series, and it has a number of special properties and implications. As we will see, for example, if we knew for sure that a series had a stochastic trend, then we would want to difference the series and then fit a stationary model to the difference.[1] The strategy of differencing to achieve stationarity contrasts with the approach of earlier chapters, in which we worked in levels and included deterministic trends. In practice, it is sometimes very difficult to decide whether trend is best modeled as deterministic or stochastic, and the decision is an important part of the science—and art—of building forecasting models.

1. STOCHASTIC TRENDS AND FORECASTING

Consider an ARMA(p,q) process,

$$\Phi(L)y_t = \Theta(L)\varepsilon_t$$

---

1. We speak of modeling in "differences," as opposed to "levels." We also use "differences" and "changes" interchangeably.

with all the autoregressive roots on or outside the unit circle, at most one autoregressive root on the unit circle, and all moving average roots outside the unit circle. We say that y has a unit **autoregressive root,** or simply a **unit root,** if one of the p roots of its autoregressive lag-operator polynomial is 1, in which case we can factor the autoregressive lag-operator polynomial as

$$\Phi(L) = \Phi'(L)\,(1 - L)$$

where $\Phi'(L)$ is of degree $p - 1$. Thus y is really an ARMA$(p - 1, q)$ process in differences, because

$$\Phi'(L)\,(1 - L)y_t = \Theta(L)\varepsilon_t$$

is simply

$$\Phi'(L)\,\Delta y_t = \Theta(L)\varepsilon_t$$

Note that y is not covariance stationary because one of the roots of its autoregressive lag-operator polynomial is on the unit circle, whereas covariance stationarity requires all roots to be outside the unit circle. However, Δy is a covariance stationary and invertible ARMA$(p - 1, q)$ process.

You may recall from calculus that we can "undo" an integral by taking a derivative. By analogy, we say that a nonstationary series is **integrated** if its nonstationarity is appropriately "undone" by differencing. If only one difference is required (as with the series y above), we say that the series is integrated of order 1, or $I(1)$ (pronounced "eye-one") for short. More generally, if d differences are required, the series is $I(d)$. The order of integration equals the number of autoregressive unit roots. In practice $I(0)$ and $I(1)$ processes are by far the most important cases, which is why we restricted the discussion above to allow for at most one unit root.[2]

To get a feel for the behavior of $I(1)$ processes, let us take a simple and very important example, the **random walk,** which is nothing more than an AR(1) process with a unit coefficient,

$$y_t = y_{t-1} + \varepsilon_t$$

$$\varepsilon_t \sim WN(0, \sigma^2)$$

The random walk is not covariance stationary, because the AR(1) coefficient is not less than 1. In particular, it doesn't display **mean reversion;** in contrast to a stationary AR(1), it wanders up and down randomly, as its name suggests, with no tendency to return to any particular point. Although the ran-

---

2. $I(2)$ series sometimes, but rarely, arise, and orders of integration higher than 2 are almost unheard of.

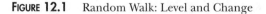

FIGURE 12.1   Random Walk: Level and Change

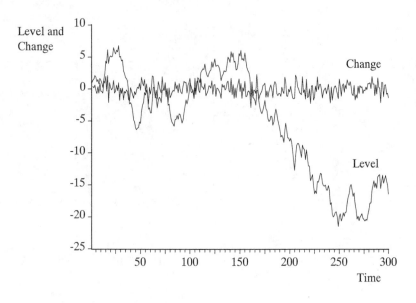

dom walk is somewhat ill-behaved, its first difference is the ultimate well-behaved series: zero-mean white noise.

As an illustration, we show a random walk realization of length 300, as well as its first difference, in Figure 12.1.[3] The difference of the random walk is white noise, which vibrates randomly. In contrast, the level of the random walk, which is the cumulative sum of the white noise changes, wanders aimlessly and persistently.

Now let us consider a **random walk with drift,**

$$y_t = \delta + y_{t-1} + \varepsilon_t$$

$$\varepsilon_t \sim WN(0, \sigma^2)$$

Note that the random walk with drift is effectively a model of trend, because on average it grows each period by the drift, δ. Thus the drift parameter plays the same role as the slope parameter in our earlier model of linear deterministic trend. We call the random walk with drift a model of **stochastic trend,** because the trend is driven by stochastic shocks, in contrast to the **deterministic trends** considered in chapter 4.

---

3. The random walk was simulated on a computer with $y_1 = 1$ and $N(0,1)$ innovations.

FIGURE 12.2   Random Walk with Drift: Level and Change

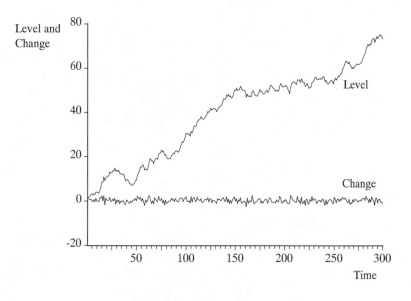

Just as the random walk has no particular level to which it returns, so too the random walk with drift has no particular trend to which it returns. If a shock lowers the value of a random walk, for example, there is no tendency for it to necessarily rise again—we expect it to stay permanently lower. Similarly, if a shock moves the value of a random walk with drift below the currently projected trend, there is no tendency for it to return—the trend simply begins anew from the new location of the series. Thus shocks to random walks have completely permanent effects; a unit shock forever moves the expected future path of the series by one unit, regardless of the presence of drift.

For illustration, we show in Figure 12.2 a realization of a random walk with drift, in levels and differences. As before, the sample size is 300 and $y_1 = 1$. The innovations are $N(0,1)$ white noise and the drift is $\delta = 0.3$ per period, so the differences are white noise with a mean of 0.3. It is difficult to notice the nonzero mean in the difference because the stochastic trend in the level, which is the cumulative sum of $N(0.3,1)$ white noise, dominates the scale.

Let us study the properties of random walks in greater detail. The random walk is

$$y_t = y_{t-1} + \varepsilon_t$$

$$\varepsilon_t \sim WN(0, \sigma^2)$$

Assuming the process started at some time 0 with value y_0, we can write it as

$$y_t = y_0 + \sum_{i=1}^{t} \varepsilon_i$$

Immediately,

$$E(y_t) = y_0$$

and

$$\text{var}(y_t) = t\sigma^2$$

In particular, note that

$$\lim_{t \to \infty} \text{var}(y_t) = \infty$$

so that the variance grows continuously rather than converging to some finite unconditional variance.

Now consider the random walk with drift. The process is

$$y_t = \delta + y_{t-1} + \varepsilon_t$$

$$\varepsilon_t \sim WN(0, \sigma^2)$$

Assuming the process started at some time 0 with value y_0, we have

$$y_t = t\delta + y_0 + \sum_{i=1}^{t} \varepsilon_i$$

Immediately,

$$E(y_t) = y_0 + t\delta$$

and

$$\text{var}(y_t) = t\sigma^2$$

As with the simple random walk, then, the random walk with drift also has the property that

$$\lim_{t \to \infty} \text{var}(y_t) = \infty$$

Just as white noise is the simplest $I(0)$ process, the random walk is the simplest $I(1)$ process. And just as $I(0)$ processes with richer dynamics than white noise can be constructed by transforming white noise, so too can $I(1)$

processes with richer dynamics than the random walk be obtained by transforming the random walk. We are led immediately to the **ARIMA($p,1,q$) model,**

$$\Phi(L)\,(1-L)y_t = c + \Theta(L)\varepsilon_t$$

or

$$(1-L)y_t = c\,\Phi^{-1}(1) + \Phi^{-1}(L)\Theta(L)\varepsilon_t$$

where

$$\Phi(L) = 1 - \Phi_1 L - \ldots - \Phi_p\,L^p$$

$$\Theta(L) = 1 - \Theta_1 L - \ldots - \Theta_q\,L^q$$

and all the roots of both lag operator polynomials are outside the unit circle. ARIMA stands for autoregressive *integrated* moving average. The ARIMA ($p,1,q$) process is just a stationary and invertible ARMA(p,q) process in first differences.

More generally, we can work with the **ARIMA(p,d,q) model,**

$$\Phi(L)\,(1-L)^d y_t = c + \Theta(L)\varepsilon_t$$

or

$$(1-L)^d y_t = c\,\Phi^{-1}(1) + \Phi^{-1}(L)\Theta(L)\varepsilon_t$$

where

$$\Phi(L) = 1 - \Phi_1 L - \ldots - \Phi_p\,L^p$$

$$\Theta(L) = 1 - \Theta_1 L - \ldots - \Theta_q\,L^q$$

and all the roots of both lag operator polynomials are outside the unit circle. The ARIMA(p,d,q) process is a stationary and invertible ARMA(p,q) after differencing d times. In practice, $d = 0$ and $d = 1$ are by far the most important cases. When $d = 0$, y is covariance stationary, or $I(0)$, with mean $c\,\Phi^{-1}(1)$. When $d = 1$, y is $I(1)$ with drift, or stochastic linear trend, of $c\,\Phi^{-1}(1)$ per period.

It turns out that more complicated ARIMA($p,1,q$) processes behave like random walks in certain key respects. First, ARIMA($p,1,q$) processes are appropriately made stationary by differencing. Second, shocks to ARIMA($p,1,q$) processes have permanent effects.[4] Third, the variance of an ARIMA($p,1,q$) process grows without bound as time progresses. The special properties of

---

4. In contrast to random walks, however, the long-run effect of a unit shock to an ARIMA($p,1,q$) process may be greater or less than unity, depending on the parameters of the process.

$I(1)$ series, associated with the fact that innovations have permanent effects, have important implications for forecasting. In regard to point forecasting, the permanence of shocks means that optimal forecasts, even at very long horizons, don't completely revert to a mean or a trend. In regard to interval and density forecasting, the fact that the variance of an $I(1)$ process approaches infinity as time progresses means that the uncertainty associated with our forecasts, which translates into the width of interval forecasts and the spread of density forecasts, increases without bound as the forecast horizon grows.[5]

Let us see how all this works in the context of a simple random walk, which is an AR(1) process with a unit coefficient. Recall that for the AR(1) process,

$$y_t = \varphi y_{t-1} + \varepsilon_t$$

$$\varepsilon_t \sim WN(0, \sigma^2)$$

the optimal forecast is

$$y_{T+h,T} = \varphi^h y_T$$

Thus in the random walk case of $\varphi = 1$, the optimal forecast is simply the current value, regardless of horizon. This makes clear the way that the permanence of shocks to random walk processes affects forecasts: any shock that moves the series up or down today also moves the optimal forecast up or down at all horizons. In particular, the effects of shocks don't wash out as the forecast horizon lengthens, because there is no mean to which we expect the series to revert.

In Figure 12.3, we illustrate the important differences in forecasts from deterministic-trend and stochastic-trend models for U.S. GDP per capita. We show GDP per capita for 1869–1933, followed by the forecasts for 1934–1993 from the best-fitting deterministic-trend and stochastic-trend models made in 1933. The best-fitting deterministic-trend model is an AR(2) in levels with linear trend, and the best-fitting stochastic-trend model is an AR(1) in differences (that is, an ARIMA(1,1,0)) with a drift.[6] Because 1932 and 1933 were years of severe recession, the forecasts are made from a position well below trend. The forecast from the deterministic-trend model reverts to trend quickly, in sharp contrast to that from the stochastic-trend model, which remains permanently lower. As it happens, the forecast from the deterministic-trend model turns out to be distinctly better in this case, as shown in Figure 12.4, which includes the realization.

---

5. This is true even if we ignore parameter estimation uncertainty.

6. Note well that the two dashed lines in Figures 12.3 and 12.4 are two different point extrapolation forecasts, not an interval forecast.

FIGURE 12.3   U.S. Per Capita GDP: History and Two Forecasts

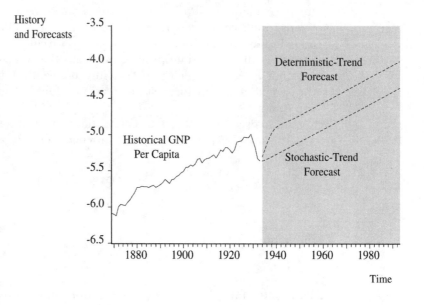

FIGURE 12.4   U.S. Per Capita GDP: History, Two Forecasts, and Realization

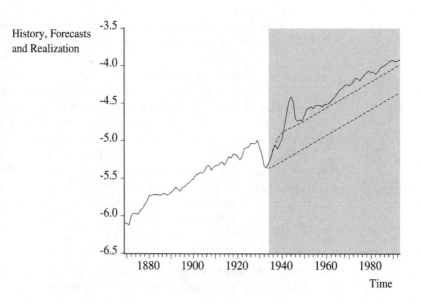

Now let us consider interval and density forecasts from $I(1)$ models. Again, it is instructive to consider a simple random walk. Recall that the error associated with the optimal forecast of an AR(1) process is

$$e_{T+h,T} = (y_{T+h} - y_{T+h,T}) = \varepsilon_{T+h} + \varphi \varepsilon_{T+h-1} + \ldots + \varphi^{h-1} \varepsilon_{T+1}$$

with variance

$$\sigma_h^2 = \sigma^2 \sum_{i=0}^{h-1} \varphi^{2i}$$

Thus in the random walk case the error is the sum of h white-noise innovations,

$$e_{T+h,T} = \sum_{i=0}^{h-1} \varepsilon_{T+h-i}$$

with variance $h\sigma^2$. The forecast error variance is proportional to h and therefore grows without bound as h grows. An h-step-ahead 95% interval forecast for any future horizon is then $y_T \pm 1.96\sigma\sqrt{h}$, and an h-step-ahead density forecast is $N(y_T, h\sigma^2)$.

Thus far we have explicitly illustrated the construction of point, interval, and density forecasts for a simple random walk. Forecasts from more complicated $I(1)$ models are constructed similarly. Point forecasts of levels of ARIMA$(p,1,q)$ processes, for example, are obtained by recognizing that ARIMA processes are ARMA processes in differences, and we know how to forecast ARMA processes. Thus we forecast the changes, cumulate the forecasts of changes, and add them to the current level, yielding

$$y_{T+h,T} = y_T + (\Delta y)_{T+1,T} + \ldots + (\Delta y)_{T+h,T}$$

2. UNIT ROOTS: ESTIMATION AND TESTING

Least Squares Regression with Unit Roots

The properties of least squares estimators in models with unit roots are of interest to us because they have implications for forecasting. We will use a random walk for illustration, but the results carry over to general ARIMA$(p,1,q)$ processes. Suppose that y is a random walk, so that

$$y_t = y_{t-1} + \varepsilon_t$$

but we don't know that the autoregressive coefficient is 1, so we estimate the AR(1) model,

$$y_t = \varphi y_{t-1} + \varepsilon_t$$

Two key and offsetting properties of the least squares estimator emerge: superconsistency and bias.

First we consider superconsistency. In the unit root case of $\varphi = 1$, the difference between $\hat{\phi}_{LS}$ and 1 vanishes quickly as the sample size grows; in fact, it shrinks like $1/T$. Thus, $T(\hat{\phi}_{LS} - 1)$ converges to a nondegenerate random variable. In contrast, in the covariance stationary case of $|\varphi| < 1$, the difference between $\hat{\phi}_{LS}$ and φ shrinks more slowly, like $1/\sqrt{T}$, so that $\sqrt{T}(\hat{\phi}_{LS} - \varphi)$ converges to a nondegenerate random variable. The extra-fast convergence in the unit root case is called **superconsistency;** we say that the least squares estimator of a unit root is superconsistent.

Now we consider bias. It can be shown that the least squares estimator, $\hat{\phi}_{LS}$, is biased downward, so that if the true value of φ is φ^*, the expected value of $\hat{\phi}_{LS}$ is less than φ^*.[7] Other things being the same, the larger the true value of φ, the larger the bias, so the bias is worst in the unit root case. The bias is also larger if an intercept is included in the regression, and larger still if a trend is included. The bias vanishes as the sample size grows, as the estimate converges to the true population value, but in samples of the size that concern us, the bias can be sizable.

Superconsistency and bias have offsetting effects as regards forecasting. Superconsistency is helpful; it means that the sampling uncertainty in our parameter estimates vanishes unusually quickly as sample size grows. Bias, in contrast, is harmful because badly biased parameter estimates can translate into poor forecasts. The superconsistency associated with unit roots guarantees that bias vanishes quickly as sample size grows, but it may nevertheless be highly relevant in small samples.

Effects of Unit Roots on the Sample Autocorrelation and Partial Autocorrelation Functions

If a series has a unit root, its autocorrelation function isn't well defined in the population, because its variance is infinite. But the *sample* autocorrelation function can, of course, be mechanically computed in the usual way because the computer software doesn't know or care whether the data being fed into it have a unit root. The sample autocorrelation function will tend to damp extremely slowly; loosely speaking, we say that it fails to damp. The reason is that, because a random walk fails to revert to any population mean, any given sample path will tend to wander above and below its sample mean for long periods of time, leading to very large positive sample autocorrela-

---

7. The bias in the least squares estimator in the unit-root and near-unit-root cases was studied by Dickey (1976) and Fuller (1976), and is sometimes called the Dickey-Fuller bias.

tions, even at long displacements. The sample partial autocorrelation function of a unit root process, in contrast, will tend to be very large and close to 1 at displacement 1, but will tend to be smaller and decay quickly thereafter.

If the properties of the sample autocorrelations and partial autocorrelations of unit root processes appear rather exotic, the properties of the sample autocorrelations and partial autocorrelations of *differences* of unit root processes are much more familiar. That is because the first difference of a process with a unit root, by definition, is covariance stationary and invertible.

We illustrate the properties of sample autocorrelations and partial autocorrelations of levels and differences of unit root processes in Figures 12.5 and 12.6. In Figure 12.5 we show the correlogram of our simulated random walk. The sample autocorrelations fail to damp, and the sample partial autocorrelation is huge at displacement 1 but tiny thereafter. In Figure 12.6 we show the correlogram of the first differences of the random walk. All the sample autocorrelations and partial autocorrelations are insignificantly different from zero, as expected, because the first difference of a random walk is white noise.

Unit Root Tests

In light of the special properties of series with unit roots, it is sometimes of interest to test for their presence, with an eye toward the desirability of imposing them, by differencing the data, if they seem to be present. Let us start with the simple AR(1) process,

$$y_t = \varphi y_{t-1} + \varepsilon_t$$

$$\varepsilon_t \overset{iid}{\sim} N(0, \sigma^2)$$

We can regress y_t on y_{t-1}, and then use the standard t-test for testing $\varphi = 1$,

$$\hat{\tau} = \frac{\hat{\varphi} - 1}{s\sqrt{\dfrac{1}{\displaystyle\sum_{t=2}^{T} y_{t-1}^2}}}$$

where s is the standard error of the regression. Note that the $\hat{\tau}$ statistic is *not* the t-statistic computed automatically by regression packages; the standard t-statistic is for the null of a zero coefficient, whereas $\hat{\tau}$ is the t-statistic for a *unit* coefficient. A simple trick, however, coaxes standard software into printing $\hat{\tau}$ automatically. Simply rewrite the first-order autoregression as

$$y_t - y_{t-1} = (\varphi - 1) y_{t-1} + \varepsilon_t$$

FIGURE 12.5   Random Walk, Levels: Sample Autocorrelation Function (Top Panel);
Sample Partial Autocorrelation Function (Bottom Panel)

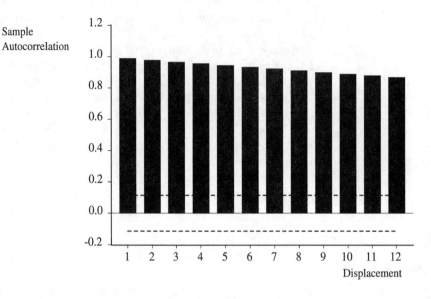

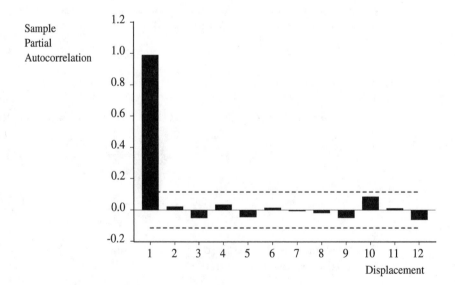

FIGURE 12.6 Random Walk, First Differences: Sample Autocorrelation Function (Top Panel); Sample Partial Autocorrelation Function (Bottom Panel)

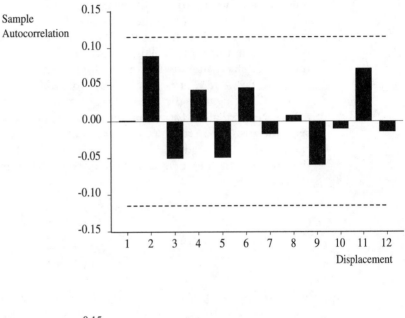

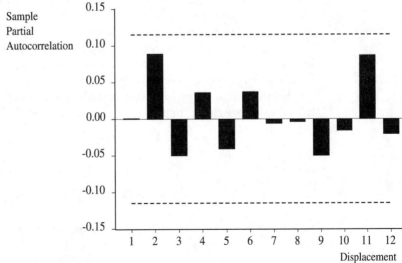

Thus, $\hat{\tau}$ is the usual t-statistic in a regression of the first *difference* of y on the first *lag* of y.

A key result is that, in the unit root case, $\hat{\tau}$ does *not* have the t-distribution. Instead, it has a special distribution now called the **Dickey-Fuller distribution,** named for two statisticians who studied it extensively in the 1970s and 1980s. Fuller (1976) presents tables of the percentage points of the distribution of $\hat{\tau}$, which we call the Dickey-Fuller statistic, under the null hypothesis of a unit root. Because we are allowing only for roots on or outside the unit circle, a one-sided test is appropriate.

Thus far we have shown how to test the null hypothesis of a random walk with no drift against the alternative of a zero-mean, covariance-stationary AR(1). Now we allow for a **nonzero mean, μ, under the alternative hypothesis,** which is of potential importance because business and economic data can rarely be assumed to have zero mean. Under the alternative hypothesis, the process becomes a covariance stationary AR(1) process *in deviations from the mean,*

$$(y_t - \mu) = \varphi(y_{t-1} - \mu) + \varepsilon_t$$

which we can rewrite as

$$y_t = \alpha + \varphi y_{t-1} + \varepsilon_t$$

where $\alpha = \mu(1 - \varphi)$. If we knew μ, we could simply center the data and proceed as before. In practice, of course, μ must be estimated along with the other parameters. Although α vanishes under the unit root null hypothesis of $\varphi = 1$, it is nevertheless present under the alternative hypothesis, and so we include an intercept in the regression. The distribution of the corresponding Dickey-Fuller statistic, $\hat{\tau}_\mu$, has been tabulated under the null hypothesis of $(\alpha, \varphi) = (0,1)$; tables appear in Fuller (1976).

Finally, let us **allow for deterministic linear trend under the alternative hypothesis,** by writing the AR(1) in deviations from a linear trend,

$$(y_t - a - b\ TIME_t) = \varphi(y_{t-1} - a - b\ TIME_{t-1}) + \varepsilon_t$$

or

$$y_t = \alpha + \beta TIME_t + \varphi y_{t-1} + \varepsilon_t$$

where $\alpha = a(1 - \varphi) + b\varphi$ and $\beta = b(1 - \varphi)$. Under the unit root hypothesis that $\varphi = 1$, we have a random walk with drift,

$$y_t = b + y_{t-1} + \varepsilon_t$$

which is a stochastic trend, but under the deterministic-trend alternative hypothesis both the intercept and the trend enter and so they must be included in the regression. The random walk with drift is a null hypothesis that frequently arises in economic applications; stationary deviations from linear trend are a natural alternative. The distribution of the Dickey-Fuller statistic $\hat{\tau}_\tau$, which allows for linear trend under the alternative hypothesis, has been tabulated under the unit root null hypothesis by Fuller (1976).

Now we generalize the test to allow for higher-order autoregressive dynamics. Consider the $AR(p)$ process

$$y_t + \sum_{j=1}^{p} \varphi_j\, y_{t-j} = \varepsilon_t$$

which we rewrite as

$$y_t = \rho_1\, y_{t-1} + \sum_{j=2}^{p} \rho_j\, (y_{t-j+1} - y_{t-j}) + \varepsilon_t$$

where $p \geq 2$, $\rho_1 = -\Sigma_{j=1}^{p}\, \varphi_j$, and $\rho_i = \Sigma_{j=i}^{p}\, \varphi_j$, $i = 2, \ldots, p$. If there is a unit root, then $\rho_1 = 1$, and y is simply an $AR(p-1)$ in first differences. The Dickey-Fuller statistic for the null hypothesis of $\rho_1 = 1$ has the same asymptotic distribution as $\hat{\tau}$. Thus, the results for the $AR(1)$ process generalize (asymptotically) in a straightforward manner to higher-order processes.

To allow for a nonzero mean in the $AR(p)$ case, we write

$$(y_t - \mu) + \sum_{j=1}^{p} \varphi_j\, (y_{t-j} - \mu) = \varepsilon_t$$

or

$$y_t = \alpha + \rho_1\, y_{t-1} + \sum_{j=2}^{p} \rho_j\, (y_{t-j+1} - y_{t-j}) + \varepsilon_t$$

where $\alpha = \mu(1 + \Sigma_{j=1}^{p}\, \varphi_j)$, and the other parameters are as above. Under the null hypothesis of a unit root, the intercept vanishes, because in that case $\Sigma_{j=1}^{p}\, \varphi_j = -1$. The distribution of the Dickey-Fuller statistic for testing $\rho_1 = 1$ in this regression is asymptotically identical to that of $\hat{\tau}_\mu$.

Finally, to allow for linear trend under the alternative hypothesis, we write

$$(y_t - a - bTIME_t) + \sum_{j=1}^{p} \varphi_j\, (y_{t-j} - a - b\, TIME_{t-j}) = \varepsilon_t$$

which we rewrite as

$$y_t = k_1 + k_2 \, TIME_t + \rho_1 y_{t-1} + \sum_{j=2}^{p} \rho_j \, (y_{t-j+1} - y_{t-j}) + \varepsilon_t$$

where

$$k_1 = a \left(1 + \sum_{i=1}^{p} \varphi_i \right) - b \sum_{i=1}^{p} i\varphi_i$$

and

$$k_2 = b \, TIME_t \left(1 + \sum_{i=1}^{p} \varphi_i \right)$$

Under the null hypothesis,

$$k_1 = -b \sum_{i=1}^{p} i \, \varphi_i \text{ and } k_2 = 0$$

The Dickey-Fuller statistic for the hypothesis that $\rho_1 = 1$ has the $\hat{\tau}_\tau$ distribution asymptotically.

Now we consider general ARMA representations. We have seen that the original Dickey-Fuller test for a unit root in AR(1) models is easily generalized to test for a unit root in the AR(p) case, $p < \infty$; we simply augment the test regression with lagged first differences, which is called an **augmented Dickey-Fuller test,** or augmented Dickey-Fuller regression. Matters are more complex in the ARMA(p,q) case, however, because the corresponding autoregression is of infinite order. A number of tests have been suggested, and the most popular of which is to approximate the infinite autoregression with a finite-order augmented Dickey-Fuller regression. We let the number of augmentation lags increase with sample size, but at a slower rate. Hall (1994) shows that, under certain conditions, the asymptotic null distribution of the Dickey-Fuller statistic with augmentation lag order selected by *SIC* is the same as if the true order were known, so that *SIC* provides a useful guide to augmentation lag order selection in Dickey-Fuller regressions. Ng and Perron (1995), however, argue that standard *t*-testing provides more reliable inference. Further research is needed, but it does appear that, unlike when selecting lag orders for forecasting models, it may be better to use less harsh degrees-of-freedom penalties, such as those associated with *t*-testing or *AIC*, when selecting augmentation lag orders in Dickey-Fuller regressions.

Depending on whether a zero mean, a nonzero mean, or a linear trend is allowed under the alternative hypothesis, we write either

$$y_t = \rho_1 y_{t-1} + \sum_{j=2}^{k-1} \rho_j (y_{t-j+1} - y_{t-j}) + \varepsilon_t$$

$$y_t = \alpha + \rho_1 y_{t-1} + \sum_{j=2}^{k-1} \rho_j (y_{t-j+1} - y_{t-j}) + \varepsilon_t$$

or

$$y_t = k_1 + k_2 TIME_t + \rho_1 y_{t-1} + \sum_{j=2}^{k-1} \rho_j (y_{t-j+1} - y_{t-j}) + \varepsilon_t$$

where $k-1$ augmentation lags have been included. The Dickey-Fuller statistics on y_{t-1} continue to have the $\hat{t}$, $\hat{t}_\mu$, and $\hat{t}_\tau$ asymptotic distributions under the null hypothesis of a unit root. For selecting the number of augmentation lags, $k-1$, we can use *SIC* or *AIC*, as well as the *t*-statistics on the various lags of Δy, which have the standard normal distribution in large samples regardless of whether the unit root hypothesis is true or false.

New tests, with better power than the Dickey-Fuller tests in certain situations, have been proposed recently.[8] But power and size problems will always plague unit root tests; power problems because the relevant alternative hypotheses are typically very close to the null hypothesis, and size problems because we should include infinitely many augmentation lags in principle, but we cannot in practice.

Thus, although unit root tests are sometimes useful, don't be fooled into thinking they are the end of the story in regard to the decision of whether to specify models in levels or differences. For example, the fact that we cannot reject a unit root doesn't necessarily mean that we should impose it—the power of unit root tests against alternative hypotheses near the null hypothesis, which are the relevant alternatives, is likely to be low. On the other hand, it may sometimes be desirable to impose a unit root even when the true root is less than 1, if the true root is nevertheless very close to 1, because the Dickey-Fuller bias plagues estimation in levels. We need to use introspection and theory, in addition to formal tests, to guide the difficult decision of whether to impose unit roots, and we need to compare the forecasting performance of different models with and without unit roots imposed.

---

8. See Elliott, Rothenberg, and Stock (1996), Dickey and Gonzalez-Farias (1992), and the comparisons in Pantula, Gonzalez-Farias, and Fuller (1994).

In certain respects, the most important part of unit root theory for forecasting concerns estimation, not testing. It is important for forecasters to understand the effects of unit roots on consistency and small-sample bias. Such understanding, for example, leads to the insight that at least *asymptotically* we are probably better off estimating forecasting models in levels with trends included, because then we will get an accurate approximation to the dynamics in the data regardless of the true state of the world, unit root or no unit root. If there is no unit root, then, of course, it is desirable to work in levels, and if there is a unit root, the estimated largest root will converge appropriately to unity, and at a fast rate. On the other hand, differencing is appropriate only in the unit root case, and inappropriate differencing can be harmful, even asymptotically.

3. APPLICATION: MODELING AND FORECASTING THE YEN/DOLLAR EXCHANGE RATE

Here we apply and illustrate what we have learned by modeling and forecasting the yen/dollar exchange rate. For convenience, we call the yen/dollar series y, the log level $\ln y$, and the change in the log level $\Delta \ln y$. We have end-of-month data from 1973.01 through 1996.07; we plot $\ln y$ in the top panel of Figure 12.7, and $\Delta \ln y$ in the bottom panel.[9] The plot of $\ln y$ looks very highly persistent; perhaps it has a unit root. Conversely, $\Delta \ln y$ looks thoroughly stationary, and in fact rather close to white noise. Figure 12.8, which shows the correlogram for $\ln y$, and Figure 12.9, which shows the correlogram for the $\Delta \ln y$, confirm the impression we gleaned from the plots. The sample autocorrelations of $\ln y$ are all very large and fail to damp, and the first sample partial autocorrelation is huge, whereas all the others are insignificantly different from 0. The correlogram of $\Delta \ln y$, however, looks very different. Both the sample autocorrelation and partial autocorrelation functions damp quickly; in fact, beyond displacement 1 they are all insignificantly different from 0. All of this suggests that $\ln y$ is $I(1)$.

Now we fit forecasting models. We base all analysis and modeling on $\ln y$, 1973.01–1994.12, and we reserve 1995.01–1996.07 for out-of-sample forecasting. We begin by fitting deterministic-trend models to $\ln y$; we regress $\ln y$ on an intercept and a time trend, allowing for up to ARMA(3,3) dynamics in the disturbances. In Tables 12.1 and 12.2 we show the *AIC* and *SIC* values for all the ARMA(p,q) combinations. *AIC* selects an ARMA(3,1) model, whereas *SIC*

---

9. Throughout, we work with the log of the exchange rate because the change in the log has the convenient interpretation of approximate percentage change. Thus, when we refer to the level of the exchange rate, we mean the log of the level ($\ln y$), and when we refer to the change, we mean the change of the log exchange rate ($\Delta \ln y$).

Figure 12.7   Log Yen/Dollar Exchange Rate (Top Panel); Change in Log Yen/Dollar Exchange Rate (Bottom Panel)

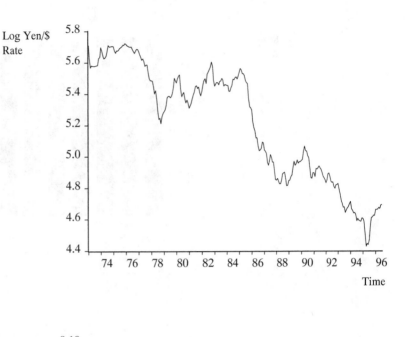

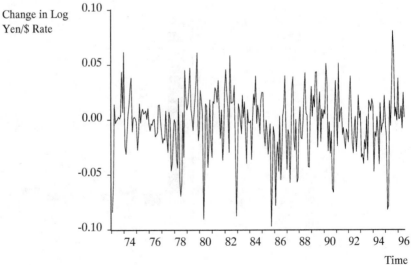

FIGURE 12.8   Log Yen/Dollar Exchange Rate: Sample Autocorrelations (Top
Panel); Sample Partial Autocorrelations (Bottom Panel)

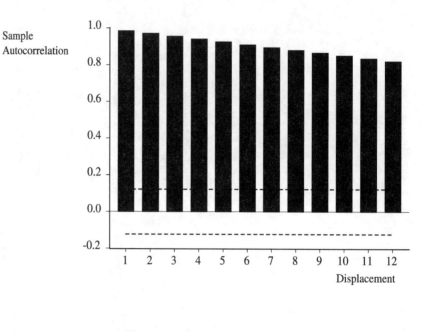

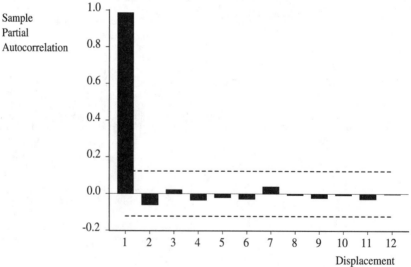

FIGURE 12.9   Log Yen/Dollar Exchange Rate, First Differences: Sample Autocorrelations (Top Panel); Sample Partial Autocorrelations (Bottom Panel)

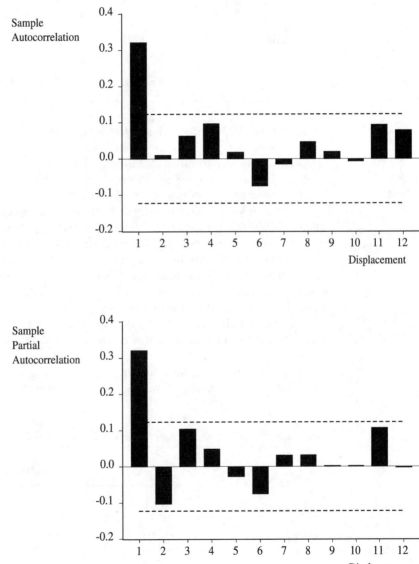

TABLE 12.1   Log Yen/Dollar Rate, Levels: AIC Values for Various ARMA Models

		MA Order			
		0	1	2	3
	0		−5.171	−5.953	−6.428
AR Order	1	−7.171	−7.300	−7.293	−7.287
	2	−7.319	−7.314	−7.320	−7.317
	3	−7.322	−7.323	−7.316	−7.308

selects an AR(2). We proceed with the more parsimonious model selected by *SIC.* The estimation results appear in Table 12.3 and the residual plot in Figure 12.10; note in particular that the dominant inverse root is very close to 1 (0.96), whereas the second inverse root is positive but much smaller (0.35).

Out-of-sample forecasts appear in Figures 12.11 to 12.13. Figure 12.11 shows the history, 1990.01–1994.12, and point and interval forecasts, 1995.01–1996.07. Although the estimated highly persistent dynamics imply very slow reversion to trend, it happens that the end-of-sample values of ln y in 1994 are very close to the estimated trend. Thus, to a good approximation, the forecast simply extrapolates the fitted trend. In Figure 12.12, we show the history together with a very long horizon forecast (through 2020.12), to illustrate the fact that the confidence intervals eventually flatten at ±2 standard errors. Finally, Figure 12.13 displays the history and forecast together with the realization. Most of the realization is inside the 95% confidence intervals.

In light of the suggestive nature of the correlograms, we now perform a formal unit root test, with trend allowed under the alternative hypothesis. In

TABLE 12.2   Log Yen/Dollar Rate, Levels: SIC Values for Various ARMA Models

		MA Order			
		0	1	2	3
	0		−5.130	−5.899	−6.360
AR Order	1	−7.131	−7.211	−7.225	−7.205
	2	−7.265	−7.246	−7.238	−7.221
	3	−7.253	−7.241	−7.220	−7.199

TABLE 12.3   Log Yen/Dollar Exchange Rate:
Best-Fitting Deterministic-Trend Model

LS // Dependent Variable is LYEN
Sample(adjusted): 1973:03 1994:12
Included observations: 262 after adjusting endpoints
Convergence achieved after 3 iterations

Variable	Coefficient	Std. Error	t-Statistic	Prob.
C	5.904705	0.136665	43.20570	0.0000
TIME	-0.004732	0.000781	-6.057722	0.0000
AR(1)	1.305829	0.057587	22.67561	0.0000
AR(2)	-0.334210	0.057656	-5.796676	0.0000

R-squared	0.994468	Mean dependent var	5.253984
Adjusted R-squared	0.994404	S.D. dependent var	0.341563
S.E. of regression	0.025551	Akaike info criterion	-7.319015
Sum squared resid	0.168435	Schwarz criterion	-7.264536
Log likelihood	591.0291	F-statistic	15461.07
Durbin-Watson stat	1.964687	Prob(F-statistic)	0.000000

Inverted AR Roots	.96	.35

FIGURE 12.10   Log Yen/Dollar Exchange Rate: Best-Fitting Deterministic-Trend
Model, Residual Plot

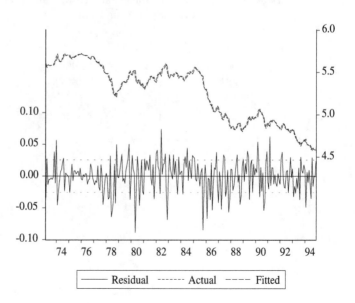

FIGURE 12.11   Log Yen/Dollar Rate: History and Forecast, AR(2) in Levels with
Linear Trend

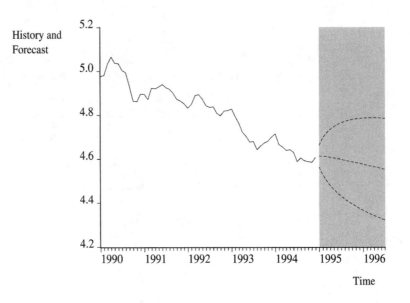

FIGURE 12.12   Log Yen/Dollar Rate: History and Long-Horizon Forecast, AR(2) in
Levels with Linear Trend

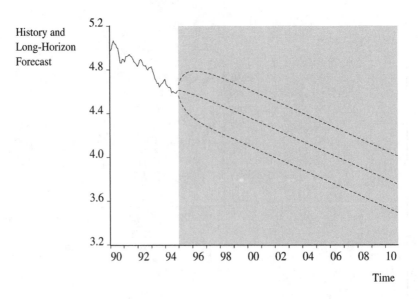

FIGURE 12.13 Log Yen/Dollar Rate: History, Forecast, and Realization, AR(2) in Levels with Linear Trend

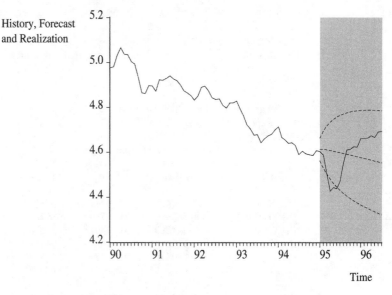

Table 12.4 we show the results with three augmentation lags.[10] There is no evidence whatsoever against the unit root; thus, we consider modeling $\Delta \ln y$. We regress $\Delta \ln y$ on an intercept and allow for up to ARMA(3,3) dynamics in the disturbance. The *AIC* values appear in Table 12.5, and the *SIC* values in Table 12.6. *AIC* selects an ARMA(3,2), and *SIC* selects an AR(1). Note that the models for $\ln y$ and $\Delta \ln y$ selected by *SIC* are consistent with each other under the unit root hypothesis—an AR(2) with a unit root in levels is equivalent to an AR(1) in differences—in contrast to the models selected by *AIC*. For this reason and, of course, for the usual parsimony considerations, we proceed with the AR(1) selected by *SIC*. We show the regression results in Table 12.7 and Figure 12.14; note the small but nevertheless significant coefficient of 0.32.[11]

Out-of-sample forecasting results appear in Figures 12.15 to 12.17. In Figure 12.15 we show the history and forecast. The forecast looks very similar—in fact, almost identical—to the forecast from the deterministic-trend model

10. We considered a variety of augmentation lag orders, and the results were robust—the unit root hypothesis cannot be rejected. For the record, *SIC* selected one augmentation lag, whereas *AIC* and *t*-testing selected three augmentation lags.

11. The ARMA(3,2) selected by *AIC* is, in fact, very close to an AR(1) because the two estimated MA roots nearly cancel with two of the estimated AR roots, which would leave an AR(1).

TABLE 12.4   Log Yen/Dollar Exchange Rate: Augmented Dickey-Fuller
Unit Root Test

Augmented Dickey-Fuller Test Statistic	-2.498863	1% Critical Value	-3.9966
		5% Critical Value	-3.4284
		10% Critical Value	-3.1373

Augmented Dickey-Fuller Test Equation
LS // Dependent Variable is D(LYEN)
Sample(adjusted): 1973:05 1994:12
Included observations: 260 after adjusting endpoints

Variable	Coefficient	Std. Error	t-Statistic	Prob.
LYEN(-1)	-0.029423	0.011775	-2.498863	0.0131
D(LYEN(-1))	0.362319	0.061785	5.864226	0.0000
D(LYEN(-2))	-0.114269	0.064897	-1.760781	0.0795
D(LYEN(-3))	0.118386	0.061020	1.940116	0.0535
C	0.170875	0.068474	2.495486	0.0132
@TREND(1973:01)	-0.000139	5.27E-05	-2.639758	0.0088

R-squared	0.142362	Mean dependent var	-0.003749
Adjusted R-squared	0.125479	S.D. dependent var	0.027103
S.E. of regression	0.025345	Akaike info criterion	-7.327517
Sum squared resid	0.163166	Schwarz criterion	-7.245348
Log likelihood	589.6532	F-statistic	8.432417
Durbin-Watson stat	2.010829	Prob(F-statistic)	0.000000

TABLE 12.5   Log Yen/Dollar Rate, Changes: AIC Values for Various ARMA Models

		MA Order			
		0	1	2	3
	0		−7.298	−7.290	−7.283
AR Order	1	−7.308	−7.307	−7.307	−7.302
	2	−7.312	−7.314	−7.307	−7.299
	3	−7.316	−7.309	−7.340	−7.336

TABLE 12.6   Log Yen/Dollar Rate, Changes: SIC Values for Various ARMA Models

		MA Order			
		0	1	2	3
	0		−7.270	−7.249	−7.228
AR Order	1	−7.281	−7.266	−7.252	−7.234
	2	−7.271	−7.259	−7.238	−7.217
	3	−7.261	−7.241	−7.258	−7.240

examined earlier. That is because the stochastic-trend and deterministic-trend models are, in fact, extremely close to one another in this case; even when we don't impose a unit root, we get an estimated dominant root that is very close to unity. In Figure 12.16 we show the history and a very long horizon forecast. The long horizon forecast reveals one minor and one major difference between the forecasts from the deterministic-trend and stochastic-trend models. The minor difference is that, by the time we are out to 2010, the point forecast from the deterministic-trend model is a little lower, reflecting the fact that the estimated trend slope is a bit more negative for the deterministic-trend model than for the stochastic-trend model. Statistically speaking, however, the point forecasts are indistinguishable. The major difference concerns the interval forecasts: The interval forecasts from the

TABLE 12.7   Log Yen/Dollar Exchange Rate: Best-Fitting Stochastic-Trend Model

LS // Dependent Variable is DLYEN
Sample(adjusted): 1973:03 1994:12
Included observations: 262 after adjusting endpoints
Convergence achieved after 3 iterations

Variable	Coefficient	Std. Error	t-Statistic	Prob.
C	-0.003697	0.002350	-1.573440	0.1168
AR(1)	0.321870	0.057767	5.571863	0.0000

R-squared	0.106669	Mean dependent var	-0.003888
Adjusted R-squared	0.103233	S.D. dependent var	0.027227
S.E. of regression	0.025784	Akaike info criterion	-7.308418
Sum squared resid	0.172848	Schwarz criterion	-7.281179
Log likelihood	587.6409	F-statistic	31.04566
Durbin-Watson stat	1.948933	Prob(F-statistic)	0.000000

Inverted AR Roots   .32

FIGURE 12.14   Log Yen/Dollar Exchange Rate: Best-Fitting Stochastic-Trend Model, Residual Plot

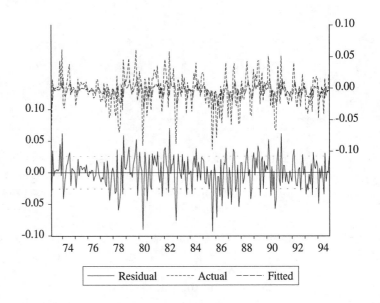

FIGURE 12.15   Log Yen/Dollar Rate: History and Forecast, AR(1) in Differences with Intercept

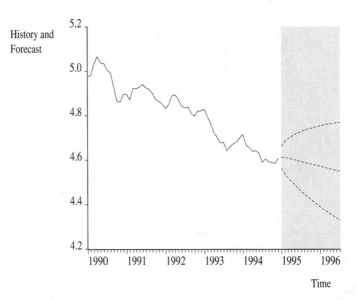

FIGURE 12.16 Log Yen/Dollar Rate: History and Long Horizon Forecast, AR(1) in Differences with Intercept

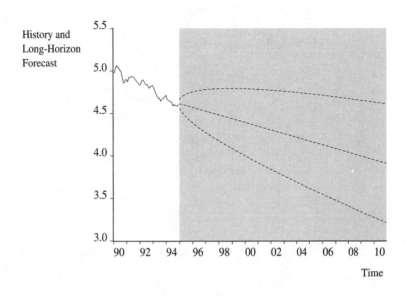

stochastic trend model widen continuously as the horizon lengthens, whereas the interval forecasts from the deterministic trend model do not. Finally, in Figure 12.17 we show the history and forecast together with the realization 1995.01–1996.07.

Comparing the AR(2) with trend in levels (the levels model selected by *SIC*) and the AR(1) in differences (the differences model selected by *SIC*), it appears that the differences model is favored in that it has a lower *SIC* value. The AR(1) in differences fits only slightly worse than the AR(2) in levels—recall that the AR(2) in levels had a near unit root—and saves one degree of freedom.[12] Moreover, economic and financial considerations suggest that exchange rates should be close to random walks because, if the change were predictable, one could make a lot of money with very little effort, and the very act of doing so would eliminate the opportunity.[13]

Ironically enough, in spite of the arguments in favor of the stochastic-trend model for ln *y*, the deterministic-trend model does slightly better in

---

12. *Caution:* In a sense, the AR(1) model in differences may not save the degree of freedom, insofar as the decision to impose a unit root was itself based on an earlier estimation (the augmented Dickey-Fuller test), which is not acknowledged when computing *SIC* for the AR(1) in differences.

13. As for the trend (drift), it may help as a local approximation, but be wary of too long an extrapolation. See the Problems and Complements at the end of this chapter.

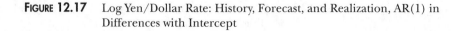

FIGURE 12.17   Log Yen/Dollar Rate: History, Forecast, and Realization, AR(1) in Differences with Intercept

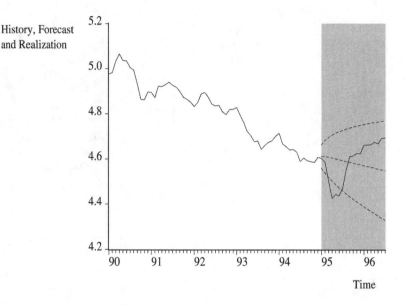

out-of-sample forecasting on this particular dataset. The mean-squared forecast error from the deterministic-trend model is 0.0107, whereas that from the stochastic-trend model is 0.0109. The difference, however, is likely statistically insignificant.

4. SMOOTHING

We encountered the idea of time series smoothing early on, when we introduced simple moving-average smoothers as ways of estimating trend.[14] Now we introduce additional smoothing techniques and show how they can be used to produce forecasts.

Smoothing techniques, as traditionally implemented, have a different flavor than the modern model-based methods that we have used in this book. Smoothing techniques, for example, don't require "best-fitting models," and they don't generally produce "optimal forecasts." Rather, they are simply a way to tell a computer to draw a smooth line through data, just as we would do with a pencil, and to extrapolate the smooth line in a reasonable and replicable way.

---

14. See the Problems and Complements of chapter 4.

When using smoothing techniques, we make no attempt to find the model that best fits the data; rather, we force a prespecified model on the data. Some academics don't like smoothing techniques for that reason, but such bias reflects a shallow understanding of key aspects of applied forecasting—smoothing techniques have been used productively for many years, and for good reason. They are most useful in situations when model-based methods cannot, or should not, be used. First, available samples of data are sometimes very small. Suppose, for example, that we must produce a forecast based on a sample of historical data containing only four observations. This scenario sounds extreme, and it is, but such scenarios arise occasionally in certain important applications, as when forecasting the sales of a newly introduced product. In such cases, available degrees of freedom are so limited as to render any estimated model of dubious value. Smoothing techniques, in contrast, require no, or minimal, estimation.

Second, the forecasting task is sometimes immense. Suppose, for example, that each week we must forecast the prices of 10,000 inputs to a manufacturing process. Again, such situations are extreme, but they do occur in practice—think of how many parts there are in a large airplane. In such situations, even if historical data are plentiful (and, of course, they might not be), there is simply no way to provide the tender loving care required for estimation and maintenance of 10,000 different forecasting models. Smoothing techniques, in contrast, require little attention. They are one example of what are sometimes called "automatic" forecasting methods, and they are often useful for forecasting voluminous, high-frequency data.

Finally, smoothing techniques *do* produce optimal forecasts under certain conditions, which turn out to be intimately related to the presence of unit roots in the series being forecast. That is why we waited until now to introduce them. Moreover, fancier approaches produce optimal forecasts only under certain conditions as well, such as correct specification of the forecasting model. As we have stressed throughout, all our models are approximations, and all are surely false. Any procedure with a successful track record in practice is worthy of serious consideration, and smoothing techniques do have successful track records in the situations sketched above.

Moving-Average Smoothing, Revisited

As a precursor to the more sophisticated smoothing techniques that we will soon introduce, recall the workings of simple moving-average smoothers. Denote the original data by $\{y_t\}_{t=1}^{T}$ and the smoothed data by $\{\bar{y}_t\}$. Then the two-sided moving average is

$$\bar{y}_t = (2m+1)^{-1} \sum_{i=-m}^{m} y_{t-i}$$

the one-sided moving average is

$$\bar{y}_t = (m+1)^{-1} \sum_{i=0}^{m} y_{t-i}$$

and the one-sided weighted moving average is

$$\bar{y}_t = \sum_{i=0}^{m} w_i y_{t-i}$$

The standard one-sided moving average corresponds to a one-sided weighted moving average with all weights equal to $(m+1)^{-1}$. The user must choose the smoothing parameter, m; the larger m is, the more smoothing is done.

One-sided weighted moving averages turn out to be very useful in practice. The one-sided structure means that at any time t, we need only current and past data for computation of the time-t smoothed value, which means that it can be implemented in real time. The weighting, moreover, enables flexibility in the way that we discount the past. Often, for example, we want to discount the distant past more heavily than the recent past. Exponential smoothing, to which we now turn, is a particularly useful and convenient way of implementing such a moving average.

Exponential Smoothing

Exponential smoothing, also called **simple exponential smoothing,** or **single exponential smoothing,** is what is called an **exponentially weighted moving average,** for reasons that will be apparent soon. The basic framework is simple. Imagine that a series c_0 is a random walk,

$$c_{0t} = c_{0,t-1} + \eta_t$$

$$\eta_t \sim WN(0, \sigma_\eta^2)$$

in which case the level of c_0 wanders randomly up and down, and the best forecast of any future value is simply the current value. Suppose, however, that we don't see c_0; instead, we see y, which is c_0 plus white noise,[15]

$$y_t = c_{0t} + \varepsilon_t$$

where ε is uncorrelated with η at all leads and lags. Then our optimal forecast of any future y is just our optimal forecast of future c_0, which is current

---

15. We can think of the added white noise as measurement error.

c_0 plus our optimal forecast of future ε, which is 0. The problem, of course, is that we don't know current c_0, the current "local level." We do know current and past y, however, which should contain information about current c_0. When the data-generating process is as written above, exponential smoothing constructs the optimal estimate of c_0—and hence the optimal forecast of any future value of y—on the basis of current and past y. When the data-generating process is not as written above, the exponential smoothing forecast will not be optimal, but hopefully it won't be too far off.

As is common, we state the exponential smoothing procedure as an algorithm for converting the observed series, $\{y_t\}_{t=1}^T$, into a smoothed series, $\{\bar{y}_t\}_{t=1}^T$, and forecasts, $\hat{y}_{T+h,T}$:

1. Initialize at $t = 1$: $\bar{y}_1 = y_1$.
2. Update: $\bar{y}_t = \alpha\, y_t + (1-\alpha)\, \bar{y}_{t-1}$, $t = 2, \ldots, T$.
3. Forecast: $\hat{y}_{T+h,T} = \bar{y}_T$.

Referring to the level of c_0, we call $\bar{y}_t$ the estimate of the *level* at time t. The smoothing parameter α is in the unit interval, $\alpha \in [0,1]$. The smaller α is, the smoother the estimated level. As α approaches 0, the smoothed series approaches constancy, and as α approaches 1, the smoothed series approaches point-by-point interpolation. Typically, the more observations we have per unit of calendar time, the more smoothing we need; thus we would smooth weekly data (52 observations per year) more than quarterly data (4 observations per year). There is no substitute, however, for a trial-and-error approach involving a variety of values of the smoothing parameter.

It is not obvious at first that the algorithm we just described delivers a one-sided moving average with exponentially declining weights. To convince yourself, start with the basic recursion,

$$\bar{y}_t = \alpha\, y_t + (1-\alpha)\, \bar{y}_{t-1}$$

and substitute backward for $\bar{y}$, which yields

$$\bar{y}_t = \sum_{j=0}^{t-1} w_j\, y_{t-j}$$

where

$$w_j = \alpha\, (1-\alpha)^j$$

Suppose, for example, that $\alpha = 0.5$. Then

$$w_0 = 0.5(1-0.5)^0 = 0.5$$

$$w_1 = 0.5(1-0.5) = 0.25$$

$$w_2 = 0.5(1-0.5)^2 = 0.125$$

and so forth. Thus moving average weights decline exponentially, as claimed.

Notice that exponential smoothing has a recursive structure, which can be very convenient when data are voluminous. At any time t, the new time t estimate of the level, $\bar{y}_t$, is a function only of the previously computed estimate, $\bar{y}_{t-1}$, and the new observation, y_t. Thus there is no need to re-smooth the entire dataset as new data arrive.

Holt-Winters Smoothing

Now imagine that we have not only a slowly evolving local level, but also a trend with a slowly evolving local slope,

$$y_t = c_{0t} + c_{1t} TIME_t + \varepsilon_t$$

$$c_{0t} = c_{0,t-1} + \eta_t$$

$$c_{1t} = c_{1,t-1} + v_t$$

where all the disturbances are orthogonal at all leads and lags. Then the optimal smoothing algorithm, named **Holt-Winters smoothing** after the researchers who worked it out in the 1950s and 1960s, is

1. Initialize at $t = 2$:

$$\bar{y}_2 = y_2$$

$$F_2 = y_2 - y_1$$

2. Update:

$$\bar{y}_t = \alpha \, y_t + (1 - \alpha) \, (\bar{y}_{t-1} + F_{t-1}), \qquad 0 < \alpha < 1$$

$$F_t = \beta(\bar{y}_t - \bar{y}_{t-1}) + (1 - \beta)F_{t-1}, \qquad 0 < \beta < 1$$

$$t = 3, 4, \ldots, T$$

3. Forecast:

$$\hat{y}_{T+h,T} = \bar{y}_T + h \, F_T$$

$\bar{y}_t$ is the estimated, or smoothed, level at time t, and F_t is the estimated slope at time t. The parameter α controls smoothing of the level, and β controls smoothing of the slope. The h-step-ahead forecast simply takes the estimated level at time T and augments it with h times the estimated slope at time T.

Again, note that although we have displayed the data-generating process for which Holt-Winters smoothing produces optimal forecasts, when we apply Holt-Winters we don't assume that the data are actually generated by that process. We hope, however, that the actual data-generating process is close to the one for which Holt-Winters is optimal, in which case the Holt-Winters forecasts may be close to optimal.

Holt-Winters Smoothing with Seasonality

We can augment the **Holt-Winters smoothing algorithm to allow for seasonality** with period s. The algorithm becomes:

1. Initialize at $t = s$:

$$\bar{y}_s = \frac{1}{s} \sum_{t=1}^{s} y_t$$

$$F_s = 0$$

$$G_j = \frac{y_j}{\left(\dfrac{1}{s} \sum_{t=1}^{s} y_t \right)}, \, j = 1, 2, \ldots, s$$

2. Update:

$$\bar{y}_t = \alpha \, (y_t - G_{t-s}) + (1 - \alpha) \, (\bar{y}_{t-1} + F_{t-1}), \qquad 0 < \alpha < 1$$
$$F_t = \beta \, (\bar{y}_t - \bar{y}_{t-1}) + (1 - \beta) \, F_{t-1}, \qquad 0 < \beta < 1$$
$$G_t = \gamma \, (y_t - \bar{y}_t) + (1 - \gamma) \, G_{t-s}, \qquad 0 < \gamma < 1$$
$$t = s + 1, \ldots, T$$

3. Forecast:

$$\hat{y}_{T+h, T} = \bar{y}_T + hF_T + G_{T+h-s}, \qquad h = 1, 2, \ldots, s$$
$$\hat{y}_{T+h, T} = \bar{y}_T + hF_T + G_{T+h-2s}, \qquad h = s + 1, s + 2, \ldots, 2s$$
etc.

The only new thing is the recursion for the seasonal, with smoothing parameter γ.

Forecasting with Smoothing Techniques

Regardless of which smoothing technique we use, the basic paradigm is the same. We plug data into an algorithm that smooths the data and lets us generate point forecasts. The resulting point forecasts are optimal for certain data-generating processes, as we indicated for simple exponential smoothing and Holt-Winters smoothing without seasonality. In practice, of course, we don't know if the actual data-generating process is close to the one for which the adopted smoothing technique is optimal; instead, we just forge ahead. That is the main contrast with the model-based approach, in which we typically spend a lot of time trying to find a "good" specification.

The "one-size-fits-all" flavor of the smoothing approach has its costs, because surely one size does *not* fit all, but it also has benefits in that no, or just a few, parameters need be estimated. Sometimes we simply set the smoothing parameter values based upon our knowledge of the properties of the series being considered, and sometimes we select parameter values that provide the best *h*-step-ahead forecasts under the relevant loss function. For example, under 1-step-ahead squared-error loss, if the sample size is large enough so that we are willing to entertain estimation of the smoothing parameters, we can estimate them as,

$$\hat{\theta} = \underset{\theta}{\operatorname{argmin}} \sum_{t=m+1}^{T} (y_t - \hat{y}_{t-1,t})^2$$

where *m* is an integer large enough such that the start-up values of the smoothing algorithm have little effect.

In closing this section, we note that smoothing techniques, as typically implemented, produce point forecasts only. They may produce optimal point forecasts for certain special data-generating processes, but typically we don't assume that those special data-generating processes are the truth. Instead, the smoothing techniques are used as *black boxes* to produce point forecasts, with no attempt to exploit the stochastic structure of the data to find a best-fitting model, which could be used to produce interval or density forecasts in addition to point forecasts.

5. EXCHANGE RATES, CONTINUED

Now we forecast the yen/dollar exchange rate using a smoothing procedure. In the ARIMA(p,d,q) models considered earlier, we always allowed for a trend (whether deterministic or stochastic). To maintain comparability, we use a Holt-Winters smoother, which allows for locally linear trend. We present the estimation results in Table 12.8. The estimate of α is large, so the estimated local level moves closely with the series. The estimate of β, on the other hand, is small, so the local slope of the trend is much less adaptive.

The Holt-Winters forecast is simply the trend line beginning at the estimated end-of-period level, with the estimated end-of-period slope. Because the estimated slope of the trend at the end of the sample is larger in absolute

TABLE 12.8   Log Yen/Dollar Exchange Rate: Holt-Winters Smoothing

Sample: 1973:01 1994:12
Included observations: 264
Method: Holt-Winters, No Seasonal
Original Series: LYEN
Forecast Series: LYENSM

Parameters:	Alpha		1.000000
	Beta		0.090000
Sum of Squared Residuals			0.202421
Root Mean Squared Error			0.027690
End of Period Levels:		Mean	4.606969
		Trend	-0.005193

value than the corresponding trend slopes in the deterministic-trend and stochastic-trend models studied earlier, we expect the Holt-Winters point forecasts to decrease a bit more quickly than those from the ARIMA models. In
Figure 12.18, we show the history and out-of-sample forecast. No confidence
intervals appear with the forecast because the smoothing techniques don't
produce them. The forecast looks similar to those of the ARIMA models, except that it drops a bit more quickly, as is made clear by the very long horizon
forecast that we show in Figure 12.19. Finally, in Figure 12.20, we show the re-

FIGURE 12.18   Log Yen/Dollar Rate: History and Forecast, Holt-Winters Smoothing

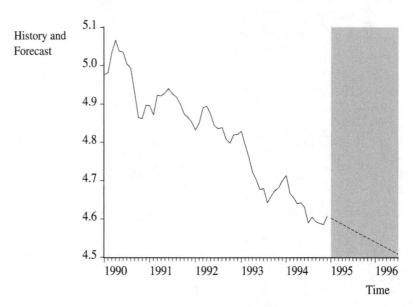

FIGURE 12.19   Log Yen/Dollar Rate: History and Long Horizon Forecast, Holt-Winters Smoothing

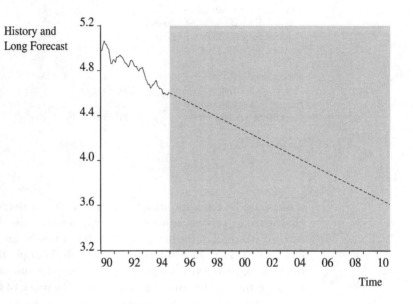

FIGURE 12.20   Log Yen/Dollar Rate: History, Forecast, and Realization, Holt-Winters Smoothing

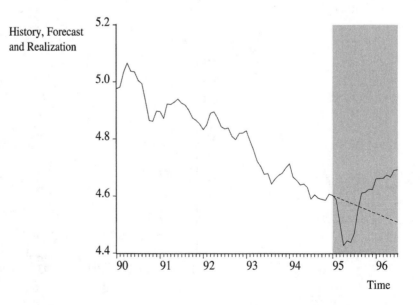

alization as well. For out-of-sample forecasting, Holt-Winters fares the worst of all the forecasting methods tried in this chapter; the mean squared forecast error is 0.0135.

PROBLEMS AND COMPLEMENTS

1. (Modeling and forecasting the deutsche mark/dollar exchange rate) On the data disk you will find monthly data on the deutsche mark/dollar exchange rate for the same sample period as the yen/dollar data studied in the text.

    (a) Model and forecast the deutsche mark/dollar rate in parallel with the analysis in the text, and discuss your results in detail.
    (b) Redo your analysis using forecasting approaches without trends—a levels model without trend, a first-differenced model without drift, and simple exponential smoothing.
    (c) Compare the forecasting ability of the approaches with and without trend.
    (d) Do you feel comfortable with the inclusion of trend in an exchange rate forecasting model? Why or why not?

2. (Automatic ARIMA modeling) *Automatic* forecasting software exists for implementing the ARIMA and exponential smoothing techniques of this and previous chapters without any human intervention.

    (a) What do you think are the benefits of such software?
    (b) What do you think are the costs?
    (c) When do you think it would be most useful?
    (d) Read Ord and Lowe (1996), who review most of the automatic forecasting software, and report what you learned. After reading Ord and Lowe, how, if at all, would you revise your answers to parts (a), (b), and (c) above?

3. (The multiplicative seasonal ARIMA$(p,d,q) \times (P,D,Q)$ model) Consider the forecasting model,

$$\Phi_s(L^s)\, \Phi(L)\, (1 - L)^d\, (1 - L^s)^D\, y_t = \Theta_s(L^s)\, \Theta(L)\, \varepsilon_t$$

$$\Phi_s(L^s) = 1 - \varphi_1^s\, L^s - \ldots - \varphi_P^s\, L^{Ps}$$

$$\Phi(L) = 1 - \varphi_1\, L - \ldots - \varphi_p\, L^p$$

$$\Theta_s(L^s) = 1 - \theta_1^s\, L^s - \ldots - \theta_Q^s\, L^{Qs}$$

$$\Theta(L) = 1 - \theta_1\, L - \ldots - \theta_q\, L^q$$

(a) The standard ARIMA(p,d,q) model is a special case of this more general model. In what situation does it emerge? What is the meaning of the ARIMA$(p,d,q) \times (P,D,Q)$ notation?

(b) The operator $(1 - L^s)$ is called the seasonal difference operator. What does it do when it operates on y_t? Why might it routinely appear in models for seasonal data?

(c) The appearance of $(1 - L^s)$ in the autoregressive lag operator polynomial moves us into the realm of **stochastic seasonality,** in contrast to the deterministic seasonality of chapter 5, just as the appearance of $(1 - L)$ produces stochastic as opposed to deterministic trend. Comment.

(d) Can you provide some intuitive motivation for the model? (*Hint:* Consider a purely seasonal ARIMA(P,D,Q) model, shocked by serially correlated disturbances.) Why might the disturbances be serially correlated? What, in particular, happens if an ARIMA(P,D,Q) model has ARIMA(p,d,q) disturbances?

(e) The multiplicative structure implies restrictions. What, for example, do you get when you multiply $\Phi_s(L)$ and $\Phi(L)$?

(f) What do you think are the costs and benefits of forecasting with the multiplicative ARIMA model versus the "standard" ARIMA model?

(g) Recall that in chapter 9 we analyzed and forecast liquor sales using an ARMA model with deterministic trend. Instead, analyze and forecast liquor sales using an ARIMA$(p,d,q) \times (P,D,Q)$ model, and compare the results.

4. (The Dickey-Fuller regression in the AR(2) case) Consider the AR(2) process,

$$y_t + \varphi_1\, y_{t-1} + \varphi_2\, y_{t-2} = \varepsilon_t$$

(a) Show that it can be written as

$$y_t = \rho_1\, y_{t-1} + \rho_2(y_{t-1} - y_{t-2}) + \varepsilon_t$$

where

$$\rho_1 = -(\varphi_1 + \varphi_2)$$

$$\rho_2 = \varphi_2$$

(b) Show that it can also be written as a regression of Δy_t on y_{t-1} and Δy_{t-1}.

(c) Show that if $\rho_1 = 1$, the AR(2) process is really an AR(1) process in first differences; that is, the AR(2) process has a unit root.

5. (ARIMA models, smoothers, and shrinkage) From the vantage point of the shrinkage principle, discuss the trade-offs associated with *optimal* forecasts from fitted ARIMA models versus "ad hoc" forecasts from smoothers.

6. (Holt-Winters smoothing with multiplicative seasonality) Consider a seasonal Holt-Winters smoother, written as

(1) Initialize at $t = s$:

$$\bar{y}_s = \frac{1}{s} \sum_{t=1}^{s} y_t$$

$$T_s = 0$$

$$F_j = \frac{y_j}{\left(\dfrac{1}{s} \displaystyle\sum_{t=1}^{s} y_t \right)}, \quad j = 1, 2, \ldots, s$$

(2) Update:

$$\bar{y}_t = \alpha \left(\frac{y_t}{F_{t-s}} \right) + (1 - \alpha)\,(\bar{y}_{t-1} + T_{t-1}), \qquad 0 < \alpha < 1$$

$$T_t = \beta\,(\bar{y}_t - \bar{y}_{t-1}) + (1 - \beta)\,T_{t-1}, \qquad 0 < \beta < 1$$

$$F_t = \gamma \left(\frac{y_t}{\bar{y}_t} \right) + (1 - \gamma)\,F_{t-s}, \qquad 0 < \gamma < 1$$

$$t = s + 1, \ldots, T$$

(3) Forecast:

$$\hat{y}_{T+h,T} = (\bar{y}_T + h T_T)\,F_{T+h-s}, \qquad h = 1, 2, \ldots, s$$

$$\hat{y}_{T+h,T} = (\bar{y}_T + h T_T)\,F_{T+h-2s}, \qquad h = s+1, s+2, \ldots, 2s$$

etc.

(a) The Holt-Winters seasonal smoothing algorithm given in the text is more precisely called Holt-Winters seasonal smoothing with additive seasonality. The algorithm given above, in contrast, is called Holt-Winters seasonal smoothing with multiplicative seasonality. How does this algorithm differ from the one given in the text, and what, if anything, is the significance of the difference?

(b) Assess the claim that Holt-Winters with multiplicative seasonality is appropriate when the seasonal pattern exhibits increasing variation.

(c) How does Holt-Winters with multiplicative seasonality compare with the use of Holt-Winters with additive seasonality applied to logarithms of the original data?

7. (Using stochastic-trend unobserved-components models to implement smoothing techniques in a probabilistic framework) In the text we noted that smoothing techniques, as typically implemented, are used as *black boxes* to produce point forecasts. There is no attempt to exploit stochastic structure to produce interval or density forecasts in addition to point forecasts. Recall, however, that the various smoothers produce optimal forecasts for specific data-generating processes specified as unobserved-components models.

(a) For what data-generating process is exponential smoothing optimal?

(b) For what data-generating process is Holt-Winters smoothing optimal?

(c) Under the assumption that the data-generating process for which exponential smoothing produces optimal forecasts is in fact the true data-generating process, how might you estimate the unobserved-components model and use it to produce optimal interval and density forecasts? (*Hint:* Browse through Harvey (1989).)

(d) How would you interpret the interval and density forecasts produced by the method of part (c), if we no longer assume a particular model for the true data-generating process?

8. (Volatility dynamics and exponential smoothing of squares) Consider exponential smoothing of the *square*, rather than the level, of a series. The exponential smoothing recursion is

$$\bar{y}_t^2 = \gamma \, y_t^2 + (1 - \gamma) \, \bar{y}_{t-1}^2$$

Back substitution yields,

$$\bar{y}_t^2 = \sum_{j=0}^{t-1} w_j \, y_{t-j}^2$$

where

$$w_j = \gamma \, (1 - \gamma)^j$$

which makes clear that the smoothed squared series is an exponentially weighted moving average of the past values of the squared series. Now consider, for example, a GARCH(1,1) process,

$$h_t = \omega + \alpha\, y_{t-1}^2 + \beta h_{t-1}$$

Back substitution yields

$$h_t = \frac{\omega}{1-\beta} + \alpha \sum_{j=1}^{\infty} \beta^{j-1} y_{t-j}^2$$

which is also an exponentially weighted moving average of the past values of the squared series! Discuss.

9. (Housing starts and completions, continued) As always, our VAR analysis of housing starts and completions involved many judgment calls. Using the starts and completions data, assess the adequacy of our models and forecasts. Among other things, you may want to consider the following questions:

(a) How would you choose the number of augmentation lags? How sensitive are the results of the augmented Dickey-Fuller tests to the number of augmentation lags?

(b) When performing augmented Dickey-Fuller tests, is it adequate to allow only for an intercept under the alternative hypothesis, or should we allow for both intercept and trend?

(c) Should we allow for a trend in the forecasting model?

(d) Does it make sense to allow a large number of lags in the augmented Dickey-Fuller tests, but not in the actual forecasting model?

(e) How do the results change if, in light of the results of the causality tests, we exclude lags of completions from the starts equation, re-estimate by seemingly unrelated regression, and forecast?

(f) Are the VAR forecasts of starts and completions more accurate than univariate forecasts?

10. (Cointegration) Consider two series, x and y, both of which are $I(1)$. In general, there is no way to form a weighted average of x and y to produce an $I(0)$ series, but in the very special case where such a weighting does exist, we say that x and y are cointegrated. **Cointegration** corresponds to situations in which variables tend to cling to one another, in the sense that the cointegrating combination is stationary, even though each variable is nonstationary. Such situations arise frequently in business, economics, and finance. To take a business example, it is often the case that both inventories and sales of a product appear $I(1)$, yet their ratio (or, when working in logs, their difference) appears $I(0)$, a natural byproduct of various schemes that adjust inventories to sales. Engle and

Granger (1987) is the key early research paper on cointegration; Johansen (1995) surveys most of the more recent developments, with emphasis on maximum likelihood estimation.

(a) Consider the bivariate system,

$$x_t = x_{t-1} + v_t, \qquad v_t \sim WN(0, \sigma^2)$$

$$y_t = x_t + \varepsilon_t, \qquad \varepsilon_t \sim WN(0, \sigma^2)$$

Both x and y are $I(1)$. Why? Show, in addition, that x and y are cointegrated. What is the cointegrating combination?

(b) Engle and Yoo (1987) show that optimal long-run forecasts of cointegrated variables obey the cointegrating relationship exactly. Verify their result for the system at hand.

11. (Error correction) In an **error-correction model,** we take a long-run model relating $I(1)$ variables, and we augment it with short-run dynamics. Suppose, for example, that in long-run equilibrium, y and x are related by $y = bx$. Then the deviation from equilibrium is $z = y - bx$, and the deviation from equilibrium at any time may influence the future evolution of the variables, which we acknowledge by modeling Δx as a function of lagged values of itself, lagged values of Δy, *and the lagged value of* z, *the error-correction term.* For example, allowing for one lag of Δx and one lag of Δy on the right-hand side, we write the equation for x as

$$\Delta x_t = \alpha_x \Delta x_{t-1} + \beta_x \Delta y_{t-1} + \gamma_x z_{t-1} + \varepsilon_{xt}$$

Similarly, the y equation is

$$\Delta y_t = \alpha_y \Delta x_{t-1} + \beta_y \Delta y_{t-1} + \gamma_y z_{t-1} + \varepsilon_{yt}$$

As long as one or both of γ_1 and γ_2 are nonzero, the system is very different from a VAR in first differences; the key feature that distinguishes the error-correction system from a simple VAR in first differences is the inclusion of the error-correction term, so that the deviation from equilibrium affects the evolution of the system.

(a) Engle and Granger (1987) establish the key result that existence of cointegration in a VAR and existence of error correction are equivalent—a VAR is cointegrated if and only if it has an error-correction representation. Try to sketch some intuition as to why the two should be linked. Why, in particular, might cointegration imply error correction?

(b) Why are cointegration and error correction of interest to forecasters in business, finance, economics, and government?

(c) Evaluation of forecasts of cointegrated series poses special challenges, insofar as traditional accuracy measures don't value the preservation of cointegrating relationships, although presumably they *should*. For details and constructive suggestions, see Christoffersen and Diebold (1998).

12. (Forecast encompassing tests for $I(1)$ series) An alternative approach to testing for forecast encompassing, which complements the one presented in chapter 11, is particularly useful in $I(1)$ environments. It is based on forecasted *h*-step *changes*. We run the regression

$$(y_{t+h} - y_t) = \beta_a (y^a_{t+h,t} - y_t) + \beta_b (y^b_{t+h,t} - y_t) + \varepsilon_{t+h,t}$$

As before, forecast encompassing corresponds to coefficient values of $(1,0)$ or $(0,1)$. Under the null hypothesis of forecast encompassing, the regression based on levels and the regression based on changes are identical.

13. (Evaluating forecasts of integrated series) The unforecastability principle remains intact regardless of whether the series being forecast is stationary or integrated: the errors from optimal forecasts are not predictable on the basis of information available at the time the forecast was made. However, some additional implications of the unforecastability principle emerge in the case of forecasting $I(1)$ series, including:

(a) If the series being forecast is $I(1)$, then so too is the optimal forecast.

(b) An $I(1)$ series is always cointegrated with its optimal forecast, which means that there exists an $I(0)$ linear combination of the series and its optimal forecast, in spite of the fact that both the series and the forecast are $I(1)$.

(c) The cointegrating combination is simply the difference of the actual and forecasted values—the forecast error. Thus the error corresponding to an optimal forecast of an $I(1)$ series is $I(0)$, in spite of the fact that the series is not. Cheung and Chinn (1996) make good use of these results in a study of the information content of U.S. macroeconomic forecasts; try to sketch their intuition. (*Hint:* Suppose the error in forecasting an $I(1)$ series were *not* $I(0)$. What would that imply?)

BIBLIOGRAPHICAL AND COMPUTATIONAL NOTES

We expect random walks, or near random walks, to be good models for financial asset prices, and they are (see Malkiel, 1981). More general ARIMA($p,1,q$) models have found wide application in business, finance, economics, and government. Beveridge and Nelson (1981) show that $I(1)$ processes can always be decomposed into the sum of a random walk component and a covariance stationary component. Tsay (1984) shows that information criteria such as *SIC* remain valid for selecting ARMA model orders regardless of whether a unit autoregressive root is present.

In parallel to the 1979 Nerlove, Grether, and Carvalho (see 1996, second edition) treatment of unobserved-components models with deterministic trend, Harvey (1989) treats specification, estimation, and forecasting with unobserved-components models with stochastic trend, estimated by using state-space representations in conjunction with the Kalman filter.

The forecasts of U.S. GDP per capita that we examine in the text, and the related discussion, draw heavily on Diebold and Senhadji (1996).

Development of methods for removing the Dickey-Fuller bias from the parameters of estimated forecasting models, which might lead to improved forecasts, is currently an active research area. See, among others, Andrews (1993), Rudebusch (1993), and Fair (1996).

In an influential book, Box and Jenkins propose an iterative modeling process that consists of repeated cycles of model specification, estimation, diagnostic checking, and forecasting. (The latest edition is Box, Jenkins, and Reinsel, 1994.) One key element of the Box-Jenkins modeling strategy is the assumption that the data follow an ARIMA model (sometimes called a Box-Jenkins model),

$$\Phi(L)\,(1 - L)^{d}y_{t} = \Theta(L)\varepsilon_{t}$$

Thus, although y_t is nonstationary, it is assumed that its dth difference follows a stationary and invertible ARMA process. The appropriateness of the Box-Jenkins tactic of differencing to achieve stationarity depends on the existence of one or more unit roots in the autoregressive lag-operator polynomial, which is partly responsible for the large amount of subsequent research on unit root tests.

Dickey-Fuller tests trace to Dickey (1976) and Fuller (1976). Using simulation techniques, MacKinnon (1991) obtains highly accurate estimates of the percentage points of the various Dickey-Fuller distributions.

Alternatives to Dickey-Fuller unit root tests, called Phillips-Perron tests, are proposed in Phillips and Perron (1988). The basic idea of Phillips-Perron tests is to estimate a Dickey-Fuller regression without augmentation,

$$x_{t} = \varphi x_{t-1} + e_{t}$$

and then to correct the Dickey-Fuller statistic for general forms of serial correlation and/or heteroskedasticity that might be present in e_t. See Hamilton (1994) for a detailed discussion of the Phillips-Perron tests and a comparison to augmented Dickey-Fuller tests.

A key concern for forecasters is the determination of comparative costs of misspecifying forecasting models in levels versus differences, as a function of sample size, forecast horizon, true value of the dominant root, and so forth. As a related matter, we need to learn more about the efficacy for forecasting of rules such as "impose a unit root unless a Dickey-Fuller test rejects at the 5 percent level."[16] Campbell and Perron (1991) make some initial progress in that direction, Diebold and Kilian (2000) explore the issue in detail and argue that such strategies are likely to be successful, and in an extensive forecasting competition, Stock and Watson (1999) show that such strategies are in fact successful.

Smoothing techniques were originally proposed as reasonable, if ad hoc, forecasting strategies; only later were they formalized in terms of optimal forecasts for underlying stochastic-trend unobserved-components models. This idea—implementing smoothing techniques in stochastic environments via stochastic-trend unobserved-components models—is a key theme of Harvey (1989), which also contains references to important earlier contributions to the smoothing literature, including Holt (1957) and Winters (1960). The impressive Stamp[17] software of Koopman et al. (1995) can be used to estimate and diagnose stochastic-trend unobserved-components models, and to use these models to produce forecasts. For a review, see Diebold, Giorgianni, and Inoue (1996).

CONCEPTS FOR REVIEW

ARIMA(p,d,q) model

Augmented Dickey-Fuller test

Cointegration

Deterministic trend

Dickey-Fuller distribution

Error correction model

Exponentially weighted moving average

Exponential smoothing

Holt-Winters smoothing

Random walk, with and without drift

Simple exponential smoothing

Single exponential smoothing

Stochastic seasonality

Stochastic trend

Superconsistency

Unit autoregressive root

Unit root

Unit root test with deterministic

---

16. Notice that, once again, the shrinkage principle appears. Such rules, which impose the unit root unless there is strong evidence against it, may lead to forecasting models that perform better than unrestricted models, even if the unit root restriction is false. And, of course, if the restriction is true, it is helpful to impose it—all the more so in light of the Dickey-Fuller bias that plagues estimation in levels.

17. Stamp stands for "structural time series analyzer, modeller, and predictor"; unobserved-components models are sometimes called structural time series models.

Holt-Winters smoothing with seasonality

Integrated series

Mean reversion

Nonzero mean, μ, under the alternative hypothesis

linear trend allowed under the alternative hypothesis

Unit root test with nonzero mean allowed under the alternative hypothesis

REFERENCES AND ADDITIONAL READINGS

Andrews, D. W. K. (1993), "Exactly Median-Unbiased Estimation of First Order Autoregressive/Unit Root Models," *Econometrica,* 61, 139–165.

Armstrong, J. S., and Fildes, R. (1995), "On the Selection of Error Measures for Comparisons Among Forecasting Methods," *Journal of Forecasting,* 14, 67–71.

Beveridge, S., and Nelson, C. R. (1981), "A New Approach to the Decomposition of Economic Time Series into Permanent and Transient Components with Particular Attention to Measurement of the Business Cycle," *Journal of Monetary Economics,* 7, 151–174.

Box, G. E. P., Jenkins, G. W., and Reinsel, G. (1994), *Time Series Analysis, Forecasting and Control,* third edition. Englewood Cliffs, N.J.: Prentice Hall.

Campbell, J. Y., and Perron, P. (1991), "Pitfalls and Opportunities: What Macroeconomists Should Know About Unit Roots," in O. J. Blanchard and S. S. Fischer (eds.), *NBER Macroeconomics Annual, 1991.* Cambridge, Mass.: MIT Press.

Cheung, Y.-W., and Chinn, M. D. (1996), "Are Macroeconomic Forecasts Informative? Cointegration Evidence from the ASA/NBER Surveys," Working Paper #350, University of California, Santa Cruz.

Christoffersen, P. F., and Diebold, F. X. (1998), "Cointegration and Long-Horizon Forecasting," *Journal of Business and Economic Statistics,* 16, 450–458.

Dickey, D. A. (1976), *Estimation and Hypothesis Testing in Nonstationary Time Series.* Ph.D. dissertation, Iowa State University.

Dickey, D. A., and Gonzalez-Farias, G. (1992), "A New Maximum-Likelihood Approach to Testing for Unit Roots," Manuscript, Department of Statistics, North Carolina State University.

Diebold, F. X., Giorgianni, L., and Inoue, A. (1996), "STAMP 5.0: A Review," *International Journal of Forecasting,* 12, 309–315.

Diebold, F. X., and Kilian, L. (2000), "Unit Root Tests Are Useful for Selecting Forecasting Models," *Journal of Business and Economic Statistics,* 18.

Diebold, F. X., and Rudebusch, G. D. (1999), *Business Cycles: Durations, Dynamics, and Forecasting.* Princeton, N.J.: Princeton University Press.

Diebold, F. X., and Senhadji, A. (1996), "Deterministic vs. Stochastic Trend in U.S. GNP, Yet Again," *American Economic Review,* 86, 1291–1298. Reprinted in Diebold and Rudebusch (1999).

Elliott, G., Rothenberg, T. J., and Stock, J. H. (1996), "Efficient Tests for an Autoregressive Unit Root," *Econometrica*, 64, 813–836.

Engle, R. F., and Granger, C. W. J. (1987), "Co-Integration and Error Correction: Representation, Estimation and Testing," *Econometrica*, 55, 251–276.

Engle, R. F., and Yoo, B. S. (1987), "Forecasting and Testing in Cointegrated Systems," *Journal of Econometrics*, 35, 143–159.

Fair, R. C. (1996), "Computing Median Unbiased Estimates in Macroeconometric Models," *Journal of Applied Econometrics*, 11, 431–435.

Fuller, W. A. (1976), *Introduction to Statistical Time Series*. New York: Wiley.

Hall, A. (1994), "Testing for a Unit Root in Time Series with Pretest Data-Based Model Selection," *Journal of Business and Economic Statistics*, 12, 461–470.

Hamilton, J. D. (1994), *Time Series Analysis*. Princeton, N.J.: Princeton University Press.

Harvey, A. C. (1989), *Forecasting, Structural Time Series Models and the Kalman Filter*. Cambridge: Cambridge University Press.

Holt, C. C. (1957), "Forecasting Seasonals and Trends by Exponentially Weighted Moving Averages," ONR Research Memorandum No. 52, Carnegie Institute of Technology.

Johansen, S. (1995), *Likelihood Based Inference in Cointegrated Vector Autoregressive Models*. Oxford: Oxford University Press.

Koopman, S. J., Harvey, A. C., Doornik, J. A., and Shephard, N. (1995), *Stamp 5.0: Structural Time Series Analyzer, Modeller and Predictor*. London: Chapman and Hall.

MacKinnon, J. G. (1991), "Critical Values for Cointegration Tests," in R. F. Engle and C. W. J. Granger (eds.), *Long-Run Economic Relationships*. Oxford: Oxford University Press.

Malkiel, B. G. (1981), *A Random Walk Down Wall Street*. New York: Norton.

Nerlove, M., Grether, D. M., and Carvalho, J. L. (1996), *Analysis of Economic Time Series: A Synthesis*, second edition. New York: Academic Press.

Ng, S., and Perron, P. (1995), "Unit Root Tests in ARMA Models with Data-Dependent Methods for the Selection of the Truncation Lag," *Journal of the American Statistical Association*, 90, 268–281.

Ord, K., and Lowe, S. (1996), "Automatic Forecasting," *American Statistician*, 50, 88–94.

Pantula, S. G., Gonzalez-Farias, G., and Fuller, W. A. (1994), "A Comparison of Unit Root Test Criteria," *Journal of Business and Economic Statistics*, 12, 449–459.

Phillips, P. C. B., and Perron, P. (1988), "Testing for a Unit Root in Time Series Regression," *Biometrika*, 75, 335–346.

Rudebusch, G. D. (1993), "The Uncertain Unit Root in Real GNP," *American Economic Review*, 83, 264–272. Reprinted in Diebold and Rudebusch (1999).

Stock, J. H., and Watson, M. W. (1999), "A Comparison of Linear and Non-linear Univariate Models for Forecasting Macroeconomic Time Series," in R. Engle and H. White (eds.), *Cointegration, Causality, and Forecasting: A Festschrift in Honor of Clive W.J. Granger,* 1–44. Oxford: Oxford University Press.

Theil, H. (1966), *Applied Economic Forecasting.* Amsterdam: North-Holland.

Tsay, R. (1984), "Order Selection in Nonstationary Autoregressive Models," *Annals of Statistics,* 12, 1425–1433.

Winters, P. R. (1960), "Forecasting Sales by Exponentially Weighted Moving Averages," Management Science, 6, 324–342.

BIBLIOGRAPHY

Akaike, H. (1974), "A New Look at the Statistical Model Identification," *IEEE Transactions on Automatic Control*, AC-19, 716–723.

Andrews, D. W. K. (1993), "Exactly Median-Unbiased Estimation of First Order Autoregressive/Unit Root Models," *Econometrica*, 61, 139–65.

Anscombe, F. J. (1973), "Graphs in Statistical Analysis," *American Statistician*, 27, 17–21.

Armstrong, J. S. (1978), *Long Run Forecasting: From Crystal Ball to Computer*. New York: Wiley.

Armstrong, J. S., and Fildes, R. (1995), "On the Selection of Error Measures for Comparisons Among Forecasting Methods," *Journal of Forecasting*, 14, 67–71.

Auerbach, A. J. (1982), "The Index of Leading Indicators: 'Measurement Without Theory' Thirty-Five Years Later," *Review of Economics and Statistics*, 64, 589–595.

Bails, D. G., and Peppers, L. C. (1997), *Business Fluctuations*, second edition. Englewood Cliffs, N.J.: Prentice Hall.

Bartlett, M. (1946), "On the Theoretical Specification of Sampling Properties of Autocorrelated Time Series," *Journal of the Royal Statistical Society B*, 8, 27–41.

Bates, J. M., and Granger, C. W. J. (1969), "The Combination of Forecasts," *Operations Research Quarterly,* 20, 451–468.

Beveridge, S., and Nelson, C. R. (1981), "A New Approach to the Decomposition of Economic Time Series into Permanent and Transient Components with Particular Attention to Measurement of the Business Cycle," *Journal of Monetary Economics,* 7, 151–174.

Bollerslev, T. (1986), "Generalized Autoregressive Conditional Heteroskedasticity," *Journal of Econometrics,* 31, 307–327.

Bollerslev, T., Chou, R. Y., and Kroner, K. F. (1992), "ARCH Modeling in Finance: A Selective Review of the Theory and Empirical Evidence," *Journal of Econometrics,* 52, 5–59.

Box, G. E. P., Jenkins, G. W., and Reinsel, G. (1994), *Time Series Analysis, Forecasting and Control,* third edition. Englewood Cliffs, N.J.: Prentice Hall.

Box, G. E. P., and Pierce, D. A. (1970), "Distribution of Residual Autocorrelations in ARIMA Time-Series Models," *Journal of the American Statistical Association,* 65, 1509–1526.

Breidt, F. J., Davis, R. A., and Dunsmuir, W. T. M. (1995), "Improved Bootstrap Prediction Intervals for Autoregressions," *Journal of Time Series Analysis,* 16, 177–200.

Brown, R. L., Durbin, J., and Evans, J.M. (1975), "Techniques for Testing the Constance of Regression Relationships Over Time," *Journal of the Royal Statistical Society B,* 37, 149–163.

Burns, A. F. and Mitchell, W. C. (1946), *Measuring Business Cycles.* New York: National Bureau of Economic Research.

Campbell, J. Y., and Perron, P. (1991), "Pitfalls and Opportunities: What Macroeconomists Should Know about Unit Roots," in O. J. Blanchard and S. S. Fischer (eds.), *NBER Macroeconomics Annual,* 1991. Cambridge, Mass.: MIT Press.

Chatfield, C. (1993), "Calculating Interval Forecasts (with Discussion)," *Journal of Business and Economic Statistics,* 11, 121–144.

Chatfield, C. (1995), "Model Uncertainty, Data Mining and Statistical Inference (with Discussion)," *Journal of the Royal Statistical Society A,* 158, Part 3, 419–466.

Chatfield, C. (1996), *The Analysis of Time Series: An Introduction,* fifth edition. London: Chapman and Hall.

Cheung, Y.-W., and Chinn, M. D. (1996), "Are Macroeconomic Forecasts Informative? Cointegration Evidence from the ASA/NBER Surveys," Working Paper #350, University of California, Santa Cruz.

Chong, Y. Y., and Hendry, D. F. (1986), "Econometric Evaluation of Linear Macroeconomic Models," *Review of Economic Studies,* 53, 671–690.

Christoffersen, P. F., and Diebold, F. X. (1998), "Cointegration and Long-Horizon Forecasting," *Journal of Business and Economic Statistics,* 16, 450–458.

Clemen, R. T. (1989), "Combining Forecasts: A Review and Annotated Bibliography," *International Journal of Forecasting*, 5, 559–581.

Clemen, R. T., and Winkler, R. L. (1986), "Combining Economic Forecasts," *Journal of Business and Economic Statistics*, 4, 39–46.

Clements, M. P., and Hendry, D. F. (1994), "Towards a Theory of Economic Forecasting," in C. P. Hargreaves (ed.), *Nonstationary Times Series Analysis and Cointegration*. Oxford: Oxford University Press.

Clements, M. P., and Hendry, D. F. (1997), *The Marshall Lectures in Economic Forecasting*. Cambridge: Cambridge University Press.

Cleveland, W. S. (1993), *Visualizing Data*. Summit, N.J.: Hobart Press.

Cleveland, W. S. (1994), *The Elements of Graphing Data*, second edition. Monterey Park, Calif.: Wadsworth.

Cook, R. D., and Weisberg, S. (1994), *An Introduction to Regression Graphics*. New York: Wiley.

Croushore, D. (1993), "The Survey of Professional Forecasters," *Business Review*, Federal Reserve Bank of Philadelphia, November-December.

Dickey, D. A. (1976), *Estimation and Hypothesis Testing in Nonstationary Time Series*. Ph.D. dissertation, Iowa State University.

Dickey, D. A., and Gonzalez-Farias, G. (1992), "A New Maximum-Likelihood Approach to Testing for Unit Roots," Manuscript, Department of Statistics, North Carolina State University.

Diebold, F. X. (1989), "Forecast Combination and Encompassing: Reconciling Two Divergent Literatures," *International Journal of Forecasting*, 5, 589–592.

Diebold, F. X., Giorgianni, L., and Inoue, A. (1996), "STAMP 5.0: A Review," *International Journal of Forecasting*, 12, 309–315.

Diebold, F. X., and Kilian, L. (2000), "Unit Root Tests Are Useful for Selecting Forecasting Models," *Journal of Business and Economic Statistics*, 18, in press.

Diebold, F. X., Lee, J.-H., and Weinbach, G. (1994), "Regime Switching with Time-Varying Transition Probabilities," in C. Hargreaves (ed.), *Nonstationary Time Series Analysis and Cointegration*, 283–302. Oxford: Oxford University Press. Reprinted in Diebold and Rudebusch (1999).

Diebold, F. X., and Lopez, J. (1995), "Modeling Volatility Dynamics," in Kevin Hoover (ed.), *Macroeconometrics: Developments, Tensions and Prospects*, 427–472. Boston: Kluwer Academic Press.

Diebold, F. X., and Lopez, J. (1996), "Forecast Evaluation and Combination," in G. S. Maddala and C. R. Rao (eds.), *Handbook of Statistics*, 241–268. Amsterdam: North-Holland.

Diebold, F. X., and Mariano, R. (1995), "Comparing Predictive Accuracy," *Journal of Business and Economic Statistics*, 13, 253–265. Reprinted in Diebold and Rudebusch (1999).

Diebold, F. X., and Pauly, P. (1990), "The Use of Prior Information in Forecast Combination," *International Journal of Forecasting,* 6, 503–508.

Diebold, F. X., and Rudebusch, G. D. (1989), "Scoring the Leading Indicators," *Journal of Business,* 62, 369–391. Reprinted in Diebold and Rudebusch (1999).

Diebold, F. X., and Rudebusch, G. D. (1991), "Forecasting Output with the Composite Leading Index: An Ex Ante Analysis," *Journal of the American Statistical Association,* 86, 603–610. Reprinted in Diebold and Rudebusch (1999).

Diebold, F. X., and Rudebusch, G. D. (1996), "Measuring Business Cycles: A Modern Perspective," *Review of Economics and Statistics,* 78, 67–77. Reprinted in Diebold and Rudebusch (1999).

Diebold, F. X., and Rudebusch, G.D. (1999), *Business Cycles: Durations, Dynamics, and Forecasting.* Princeton, N.J.: Princeton University Press.

Diebold, F. X., and Senhadji, A. (1996), "Deterministic vs. Stochastic Trend in U.S. GNP, Yet Again," *American Economic Review,* 86, 1291–1298. Reprinted in Diebold and Rudebusch (1999).

Diebold, F. X., Stock, J. H., and West, K. D., eds. (1999), *Forecasting and Empirical Methods in Macroeconomics and Finance, II,* special issue of *Review of Economics and Statistics,* 81.

Diebold, F. X., and Watson, M. W., eds. (1996), *New Developments in Economic Forecasting,* special issue of *Journal of Applied Econometrics,* 11, 453–594.

Diebold, F. X., and West, K. D., eds. (1998), *Forecasting and Empirical Methods in Macroeconomics and Finance,* special issue of *International Economic Review,* 39, 811–1144.

Doan, T., Litterman, R., and Sims, C. (1984), "Forecasting and Conditional Prediction Using Realistic Prior Distributions," *Econometric Reviews,* 3, 1–144.

Efron, B., and Tibshirani, R. J. (1993), *An Introduction to the Bootstrap.* New York: Chapman and Hall.

Elliott, G., Rothenberg, T. J., and Stock, J. H. (1996), "Efficient Tests for an Autoregressive Unit Root," *Econometrica,* 64, 813–836.

Engle, R. F. (1982), "Autoregressive Conditional Heteroskedasticity with Estimates of the Variance of U.K. Inflation," *Econometrica,* 50, 987–1008.

Engle, R. F., and Brown, S. J. (1986), "Model Selection for Forecasting," *Applied Mathematics and Computation,* 20, 313–327.

Engle, R. F., and Granger, C. W. J. (1987), "Co-Integration and Error Correction: Representation, Estimation and Testing," *Econometrica,* 55, 251–276.

Engle, R. F., and Yoo, B. S. (1987), "Forecasting and Testing in Cointegrated Systems," *Journal of Econometrics,* 35, 143–159.

Fair, R. C. (1996), "Computing Median Unbiased Estimates in Macroeconometric Models," *Journal of Applied Econometrics,* 11, 431–435.

Fair, R. C., and Shiller, R. J. (1990), "Comparing Information in Forecasts from Econometric Models," *American Economic Review,* 80, 375–389.

Faraway, J., and Chatfield, C. (1995), "Time Series Forecasting with Neural Networks: A Case Study," Research Report 95–06, Statistics Group, University of Bath, UK.

Ferrall, C. (1994), "A Review of Stata 3.1," *Journal of Applied Econometrics,* 9, 469–478.

Findley, D. F. (1983), "On the Use of Multiple Models for Multi-Period Forecasting," *Proceedings of the American Statistical Association, Business and Economic Statistics Section,* 1983, 528–531.

Findley, D. F. (1985), "Model Selection for Multi-Step-Ahead Forecasting," in *Identification and System Parameter Estimation,* 7th IFAC/FORS Symposium, 1039–1044.

Frumkin, N. (1994), *Guide to Economic Indicators,* second edition. Armonk, N.Y.: M.E. Sharpe.

Fuller, W. A. (1976), *Introduction to Statistical Time Series.* New York: Wiley.

Gershenfeld, N. A., and Weigend, A. S. (1993), "The Future of Time Series," in A.S. Weigend and N.A. Gershenfeld (eds.), *Time Series Prediction: Forecasting the Future and Understanding the Past,* 1–70. Reading, Mass.: Addison-Wesley.

Granger, C. W. J. (1969), "Investigating Causal Relations by Econometric Models and Cross-Spectral Methods," *Econometrica,* 37, 424–438.

Granger, C. W. J. (1990), "Aggreagtion of Time Series Variables: A Survey," in T. Barker and M. H. Pesaran (eds.), *Disaggregation in Econometric Modelling.* London and New York: Routledge.

Granger, C. W. J., King, M. L., and White, H. (1995), "Comments on the Testing of Economic Theories and the Use of Model Selection Criteria," *Journal of Econometrics,* 67, 173–187.

Granger, C. W. J., and Newbold, P. (1974), "Spurious Regressions in Econometrics," *Journal of Econometrics,* 2, 111–120.

Granger, C. W. J., and Newbold, P. (1986), *Forecasting Economic Time Series,* second edition. Orlando, Fla.: Academic Press.

Granger, C. W. J., and Ramanathan, R. (1984), "Improved Methods of Forecasting," *Journal of Forecasting,* 3, 197–204.

Granger, C. W. J., and Teräsvirta, Y. (1993), *Modelling Nonlinear Economic Relationships.* Oxford: Oxford University Press.

Hall, A. (1994), "Testing for a Unit Root in Time Series with Pretest Data-Based Model Selection," *Journal of Business and Economic Statistics,* 12, 461–470.

Hallman, J. (1993), "Review of S+ ," *Journal of Applied Econometrics,* 8, 213–220.

Hamilton, J. D. (1989), "A New Approach to the Economic Analysis of Nonstationary Time Series and the Business Cycle," *Econometrica,* 57, 357–384.

Hamilton, J. D. (1994), *Time Series Analysis.* Princeton, N.J.: Princeton University Press.

Harvey, A. C. (1989), *Forecasting, Structural Time Series Models and the Kalman Filter.* Cambridge: Cambridge University Press.

Harvey, A. C. (1990), *The Econometric Analysis of Time Series,* second edition. Cambridge, Mass.: MIT Press.

Harvey, A. C. (1993), *Time Series Models,* second edition. Cambridge, Mass.: MIT Press.

Harvey, D. I., Leyborne, S. J., and Newbold, P. (1997), "Testing the Equality of Prediction Mean Squared Errors," *International Journal of Forecasting,* 13, 281–291.

Hendry, D. F., and Mizon, G. E. (1978), "Serial Correlation as a Convenient Simplification, Not a Nuisance: A Comment on a Study of the Demand for Money by the Bank of England," *Economic Journal,* 88, 549–563.

Holt, C. C. (1957), "Forecasting Seasonals and Trends by Exponentially Weighted Moving Averages," *ONR Research Memorandum No. 52,* Carnegie Institute of Technology.

Ingram, B., and Whiteman, C. (1994), "Supplanting the 'Minnesota' Prior: Forecasting Macroeconomic Time Series Using Real Business Cycle Model Priors," *Journal of Monetary Economics,* 34, 497–510.

Jarque, C. M., and Bera, A. K. (1987), "A Test for Normality of Observations and Regression Residuals," *International Statistical Review,* 55, 163–172.

Jenkins, G. M. (1979), "Practical Experiences with Modelling and Forecasting Time Series," in O. D. Anderson (ed.), *Forecasting.* Amsterdam: North-Holland.

Johansen, S. (1995), *Likelihood Based Inference in Cointegrated Vector Autoregressive Models.* Oxford: Oxford University Press.

Jorgenson, D. (1966), "Rational Distributed Lag Functions," *Econometrica,* 34, 135–149.

Kennedy, P. (1998), *A Guide to Econometrics,* fourth edition. Cambridge, Mass.: MIT Press.

Kim, J., and Trivedi, P. (1995), "Econometric Time Series Analysis Software: A Review," *American Statistician,* 48, 336–346.

Klein, L. R. (1971), *An Essay on the Theory of Economic Prediction.* Chicago: Markham Publishing Company.

Klein, L. R. (1981), *Econometric Models as Guides for Decision Making.* New York: The Free Press.

Klein, L. R. (1983), *Lectures in Econometrics.* Amsterdam: North-Holland.

Klein, L. R., ed. (1991), *Comparative Performance of U.S. Econometric Models.* Oxford: Oxford University Press.

Klein, L. R., and Young, R. M. (1980), *An Introduction to Econometric Forecasting and Forecasting Models.* Lexington, Mass.: D.C. Heath.

Koopman, S. J., Harvey, A. C., Doornik, J. A., and Shephard, N. (1995), *Stamp 5.0: Structural Time Series Analyzer, Modeller and Predictor.* London: Chapman and Hall.

Krämer, W., Ploberger, W., and Alt, R. (1988), "Testing for Structural Change in Dynamic Models," *Econometrica,* 56, 1355–1369.

Kuan, C. M., and Liu, Y. (1995), "Forecasting Exchange Rates Using Feedforward and Recurrent Neural Networks," *Journal of Applied Econometrics,* 10, 347–364.

Levenbach, H., and Cleary, J. P. (1984), *The Modern Forecaster.* Belmont, Calif.: Lifetime Learning Publications.

Ljung, G. M., and Box, G. E. P. (1978), "On a Measure of Lack of Fit in Time-Series Models," *Biometrika,* 65, 297–303.

Lütkepohl, H. (1991), *Introduction to Multiple Time Series Analysis.* New York: Springer Verlag.

MacKinnon, J. G. (1991), "Critical Values for Cointegration Tests," in R. F. Engle and C. W. J. Granger (eds.), *Long-Run Economic Relationships.* Oxford: Oxford University Press.

Maddala, G. S. (in press), *Introduction to Econometrics,* third edition. New York: Macmillan.

Makridakis, S., and Wheelwright, S. (1987), *The Handbook of Forecasting: A Manager's Guide,* second edition. New York: Wiley.

Makridakis, S., and Wheelwright, S. (1997), *Forecasting: Methods and Applications,* third edition. New York: Wiley.

Malkiel, B. G. (1981), *A Random Walk Down Wall Street.* New York: W.W. Norton.

McCullough, B. D., and Vinod, H. D. (1999), "The Numerical Reliability of Econometric Software," *Journal of Economic Literature,* 37, 633–665.

McNees, S. K. (1988), "How Accurate Are Macroeconomic Forecasts?" *New England Economic Review,* July/August, 15–36.

Mincer, J., and Zarnowitz, V. (1969), "The Evaluation of Economic Forecasts," in J. Mincer (ed.), *Economic Forecasts and Expectations.* New York: National Bureau of Economic Research.

Morgenstern, O. (1963), *On the Accuracy of Economic Observations.* Princeton, N.J.: Princeton University Press.

Nelson, C. R. (1972), "The Prediction Performance of the F.R.B.-M.I.T.-Penn Model of the U.S. Economy," *American Economic Review,* 62, 902–917.

Nerlove, M., Grether, D. M., and Carvalho, J. L. (1996), *Analysis of Economic Time Series: A Synthesis,* second edition. New York: Academic Press.

Newbold, P., Agiakloglou, C., and Miller, J. P. (1994), "Adventures with ARIMA Software," *International Journal of Forecasting,* 10, 573–581.

Ng, S., and Perron, P. (1995), "Unit Root Tests in ARMA Models with Data-Dependent Methods for the Selection of the Truncation Lag," *Journal of the American Statistical Association,* 90, 268–281.

Ord, K., and Lowe, S. (1996), "Automatic Forecasting," *American Statistician,* 50, 88–94.

Pantula, S. G., Gonzalez-Farias, G., and Fuller, W. A. (1994), "A Comparison of Unit Root Test Criteria," *Journal of Business and Economic Statistics,* 12, 449–459.

Pesaran, M. H., Pierse, R. G., and Kumar, M.S. (1989), "Econometric Analysis of Aggregation in the Context of Linear Prediction Models," *Econometrica,* 57, 861–888.

Pesaran, M. H., and Samiei, H. (1995), "Forecasting Ultimate Resource Recovery," *International Journal of Forecasting,* 11, 543–555.

Phillips, P. C. B., and Perron, P. (1988), "Testing for a Unit Root in Time Series Regression," *Biometrika,* 75, 335–346.

Pindyck, R. S., and Rubinfeld, D. L. (1997), *Econometric Models and Economic Forecasts,* fourth edition. New York: McGraw-Hill.

Press, W. H., et al. (1992), *Numerical Recipes: The Art of Scientific Computing.* Cambridge: Cambridge University Press.

Ramsey, J. (1969), "Tests for Specification Errors in Classical Linear Least Squares Regression Analysis," *Journal of the Royal Statistical Society B,* 31, 350–371.

Ripley, B. D. (1996), *Pattern Recognition and Neural Networks.* Oxford: Oxford University Press.

Rudebusch, G. D. (1993), "The Uncertain Unit Root in Real GNP," *American Economic Review,* 83, 264–272. Reprinted in Diebold and Rudebusch (1999).

Rust, J. (1993), "Gauss and Matlab: A Comparison," *Journal of Applied Econometrics,* 8, 307–324.

Rycroft, R. S. (1993), "Microcomputer Software of Interest to Forecasters in Comparative Review: An Update," *International Journal of Forecasting,* 9, 531–575.

Sanderson, F. H. (1953), *Methods of Crop Forecasting.* Cambridge, Mass.: Harvard University Press.

Schwarz, G. (1978), "Estimating the Dimension of a Model," *Annals of Statistics,* 6, 461–464.

Shibata, R. (1980), "Asymptotically Efficient Selection of the Order of the Model for Estimating the Parameters of a Linear Process," *Annals of Statistics,* 8, 147–164.

Sims, C. A. (1972), "Money, Income and Causality," *American Economic Review,* 62, 540–552.

Sims, C. A. (1980), "Macroeconomics and Reality," *Econometrica,* 48, 1–48.

Slutsky, E. (1927), "The Summation of Random Causes as the Source of Cyclic Processes," *Econometrica,* 5, 105–146.

Stine, R. A. (1987), "Estimating Properties of Autoregressive Forecasts," *Journal of the American Statistical Association,* 82, 1072–1078.

Stock, J. H., and Watson, M.W. (1988), "Variable Trends in Economic Time Series," *Journal of Economic Perspectives,* 2, 147–174.

Stock, J. H., and Watson, M. W. (1999), "A Comparison of Linear and Nonlinear Univariate Models for Forecasting Macroeconomic Time Series," in R. Engle and H. White (eds.), *Cointegration, Causality, and Forecasting: A Festschrift in Honor of Clive W. J. Granger,* 1–44. Oxford: Oxford University Press.

Stock, J. H., and Watson, M. W. (1998), "A Dynamic Factor Model Framework for Forecast Combination," Manuscript, Kennedy School, Harvard University, and Woodrow Wilson School, Princeton University.

Swanson, N. R., and White, H. (1995), "A Model-Selection Approach to Assessing the Information in the Term Structure Using Linear-Models and Artificial Neural Networks," *Journal of Business and Economic Statistics,* 13, 265–275.

Taylor, S. (1996), *Modeling Financial Time Series,* second edition. New York: Wiley.

Theil, H. (1966), *Applied Economic Forecasting.* Amsterdam: North-Holland.

Tiao, G. C., and Tsay, R. S. (1994), "Some Advances in Non-Linear and Adaptive Modeling in Time Series," *Journal of Forecasting,* 13, 109–131.

Tong, H. (1990), *Non-Linear Time Series.* Oxford: Clarendon Press.

Tsay, R. (1984), "Order Selection in Nonstationary Autoregressive Models," *Annals of Statistics,* 12, 1425–1433.

Tufte, E. R. (1983), *The Visual Display of Quantitative Information.* Cheshire, Conn.: Graphics Press.

Tukey, J. W. (1977), *Exploratory Data Analysis.* Reading, Mass.: Addison-Wesley.

Varian, H. (1974), "A Bayesian Approach to Real Estate Assessment," in S. E. Feinberg and A. Zellner (eds.), *Studies in Bayesian Econometrics and Statistics in Honor of L. J. Savage.* Amsterdam: North-Holland.

Wallis, K. F. (1995), "Large-Scale Macroeconometric Modeling," in M. H. Pesaran and M. R. Wickens (eds.), *Handbook of Applied Econometrics.* Oxford: Blackwell.

Wallis, K. F., and Whitley, J. D. (1991), "Sources of Error in Forecasts and Expectations: UK Economic Models, 1984–88," *Journal of Forecasting,* 10, 231–253.

West, K. D. (1996), "Asymptotic Inference about Predictive Ability," *Econometrica,* 64, 1067–1084.

White, H. (1997), "A Reality Check for Data Snooping," Manuscript, Department of Economics, University of California, San Diego.

Winkler, R. L., and Makridakis, S. (1983), "The Combination of Forecasts," *Journal of the Royal Statistical Society A,* 146, 150–157.

Winters, P. R. (1960), "Forecasting Sales by Exponentially Weighted Moving Averages," *Management Science,* 6, 324–342.

Wold, H. O. (1954), *A Study in the Analysis of Stationary Time Series,* second edition. Uppsala, Sweden: Almquist and Wicksell.

Wonnacott, T. H., and Wonnacott, R. J. (1990), *Introductory Statistics,* fifth edition. New York: Wiley.

Zarnowitz, V., and Braun, P. (1993), "Twenty-Two Years of the N.B.E.R.-A.S.A. Quarterly Economic Outlook Surveys: Aspects and Comparisons of Forecasting Performance," in J. H. Stock and M. W. Watson (eds.), *Business Cycles, Indicators and Forecasting*. Chicago: University of Chicago Press for National Bureau of Economic Research.

Zellner, A. (1986), "Bayesian Estimation and Prediction Using Asymmetric Loss Functions," *Journal of the American Statistical Association*, 81, 446–451.

Zellner, A., and Hong, C. (1989), "Forecasting International Growth Rates Using Bayesian Shrinkage and Other Procedures," *Journal of Econometrics*, 40, 183–202.

Zellner, A., Hong, C., and Min, C.-K. (1991), "Forecasting Turning Points in International Output Growth Rates Using Bayesian Exponentially Weighted Autoregression, Time-Varying Parameter, and Pooling Techniques," *Journal of Econometrics*, 49, 275–304.

Zellner, A. (1992), "Statistics, Science and Public Policy," *Journal of the American Statistical Association*, 87, 1–6.

NAME INDEX

SUBJECT INDEX

1-step-ahead forecast errors, 127, 130, 187

Note: Entries in italics indicate figures or tables; entries including the letter "n" indicate information will be found in the footnotes.